Russian Research Center Studies

36

PAN-TURKISM AND ISLAM IN RUSSIA

Pan-Turkism and Islam
in Russia

Serge A. Zenkovsky

HARVARD UNIVERSITY PRESS   1967

Cambridge, Massachusetts

The Russian Research Center of Harvard University is supported by a grant from the Carnegie Corporation. The Center carries out inter-disciplinary study of Russian institutions and behavior and related subjects.

This volume was prepared under a grant from the Carnegie Corporation of New York. That Corporation is not, however, the author, owner, publisher, or proprietor of this publication and is not to be understood as approving by virtue of its grant any of the statements made or views expressed therein.

Library of Congress Catalog Card Number 60–5399

Printed in the United States of America

TO THE MEMORY OF MY MOTHER,

who took under her roof Haji and Gulam,
two Tatar boys who became my closest childhood friends.

PREFACE

During the years 1905 to 1920, the era of the liberalization and subsequent fall of the tsarist regime, the various peoples of Russia had an opportunity to voice their national aspirations more openly than at any other time in their recent history. Among these peoples, the Turkic national groups—the tremendous majority being Moslem—were the least exposed to the process of Westernization, and in their cultural and social life differed considerably from the national groups of European stock in Russia. Forming, after the Slavs, the largest family of nationalities of imperial and Soviet Russia, these groups represent a very substantial part of the Islamic world. While their economic and cultural activities as well as their numerical strength have often influenced Russia's attitude toward the East, their geographical location on the eastern borders of Russia have frequently made them the show window of Russia's policies in Asia. At the present time, interest in the history of these peoples is stimulated by the effervescent situation in which most of the Islamic world finds itself. From Indonesia to Morocco Moslem peoples are in a state of flux, and perhaps better knowledge of one section of them which has been the first to experience the process and effects of modern revolution may contribute some clues to an understanding of the whole.

The initial title of this research was "Pan-Turkism in Russia, 1905–1920," a title which reflected the author's earlier opinion of the nature of the Turkic movement in Russia. Turkic nationalism or "Pan-Turkism" seemed to be the main force animating the minds and political efforts of Russian Turks in these memorable years of their history. As work on the book progressed, however, it became evident that the efforts of Russia's Turkic peoples to maintain their own identity were in many instances conditioned less by national ideals than by their common attachment to the religion and culture of Islam. Even in the revolutionary period 1917–1920, Islam—not as a purely religious force, but as a cultural and social system—continued to determine the mentality of Russian Turks at least as much as, and frequently more than, conscious nationalism or Pan-Turkism. Therefore, upon completion, the research's original title no longer seemed to reflect the true nature of those forces which inspired the Turks of Russia in this particular period, and the word "Islam" was added to it. This book does not deal, however, with either the dogma or the philosophy of Islam. Only the political and social implications of that religion which served to unite the Turkic peoples of Russia are considered in this study. Subsequently the dates 1905–1920 were deleted from the title, since considerable additional material was added to explain the evolution of Islam in Russia in earlier periods. The research ends with 1920–1921 because in that year a new, Soviet, era began in the history of Russia's Moslems to which the author hopes to devote another work.

Some technical obstacles to the publication of a study on Russia require comment. The change from the Old Style calendar to the Gregorian was made by the Soviet government on February 1, 1918. Many authors, however, both Soviet and Western, begin the New Style with the day of the Soviet upheaval; others, with January 1, 1918. Russian documents of 1917–1921 written in areas not occupied by the Soviets were still dated in the Old Style. These discrepancies inevitably contribute to some confusion, and occasional errors in dating are difficult to avoid. For the sake of simplicity, I have used the Old Style through December 31, 1917, and the New Style beginning with January 14, 1918, the first thirteen days of that month being cancelled by the calendar's shift.

Statistics present still greater difficulty. For population figures, students of Russian affairs of the period involved use the data of the censuses of 1897 and 1926. These seem reliable enough in determining the linguistic and national distribution of the population at those particular times, and are used in this work. Migrations, the casualties of World War I, famine, and the Civil War, however, affected the composition and size of population statistics for the years 1905–1920. The estimates of various imperial Russian and Soviet agencies are understandably only indicative, and their use generally calls for caution. For illustrative purposes, however, they must be used.

One of the most complicated problems in the publication of any research based on Russian materials is transliteration. In the bibliography and notes, I have used the transliteration system of the Library of Congress, omitting the diacritical signs. Throughout the text personal names have been used in their Russian forms in preference to the Turkic or Persian, which requires the inclusion of -oglu, -zadeh, or -beyli, and are not always readily identifiable in this form in source material. Moreover, in most of the official Turkic sources, as, for instance, the proceedings of the Moslem Congress in 1906 and 1917, the Turks themselves used the standard Russian forms of their names. In transliterating, the simplest English spelling has been used, and I have standardized the spelling of geographic and some personal names to correspond to Webster's dictionary. Indeed, it must be kept in mind that difficulties of transliteration are increased by the fact that Arabic names were first modified by Persian spelling, then by Turkic pronunciation, which varies in the different parts of Russia. The letter corresponding to "j," for instance, is pronounced in the English way among the Tatars, in the French manner among the Kazakhs, and in the German among the Uzbeks. "Jemal," then, is "Dzhemal" for Tatars or Bashkirs, "Zhemal" for Kazakhs, and "Yemal" for Uzbeks.

It should be added that this research was completed and submitted for publication in the summer of 1957, and for that reason the books, articles, and documents connected with this subject published since that time could not be utilized by the author. However, for the reader's information, the most important of them which appeared in 1957–58 have been included in the bibliography of this volume.

The completion of this book was made possible by the support and assistance of several organizations and persons to whom the author is happy to express his gratitude. First, the Indiana University Graduate School, the Research Program on the CPSU, New York, and the Institute for the Study of the USSR are gratefully remembered for their initial financial assistance in the conducting of this research. The final version of this work was prepared while I was a Research Fellow of the Russian Research Center at Harvard University. This organization and the Committee on the Promotion of Graduate Slavic Studies have assisted in the final preparation and publication. Second, I thank with appreciation for their annotations those persons who read my manuscript in whole or in part: Professors Michael Karpovich, Richard Pipes, and Richard Frye, of Harvard University, and Professor Nicholas Poppe of the University of Washington. The translation of some Tatar texts was greatly facilitated by the help of Mr. Hamid Rashid of Columbia University. It is understood that I alone am responsible for any errors which may be contained in this publication.

Of capital importance for treating and analysing the events described on the following pages were discussions and talks with participants in and eyewitnesses to the various phases of the Turkic national movement in Russia, whom I had the privilege of meeting either in the 1930's and 1940's in Europe or in the 1950's in this country. I feel especially obligated to express my thanks to the following persons, many of whom, regretfully, are no longer living: Ahmed Tsalikov, president of the Moslem Congress and Moslem Central Bureau in Russia in 1917, who shared many of his books and materials with me; Mustafa Chokaev, chairman of the Turkestan Autonomous Administration, 1917–1918; Ayaz Iskhakov, Tatar political leader and novelist; Ahmed Zeki Validov (Velidi Togan), head of the Bashkir national movement; his opponent, General I. G. Akulinin of the Orenburg Cossacks; Colonel F. Gnezin, organizer of the Tashkent anti-Soviet resistance in September 1917; and Messrs. A. Baikov and Yu. Semenov, who led Russian national groups in Transcaucasia during the years of the Civil War.

Finally, I express my most grateful appreciation to my wife, Betty Jean, for her patient help in editing the manuscript. Without her assistance and encouragement this work might never have been carried to completion.

June 1959   Serge A. Zenkovsky

Note to the Second Printing

In this second printing I have corrected some errors and misprints in the original printing and have introduced in the first chapter of the book the data of the Soviet census of 1959 concerning the changes in the Turkic population of the Soviet Union.

May 1967   S. A. Z.

CONTENTS

	Preface	vii
I	The Turks of Russia	1
II	Tatar Rebirth	12
III	Pan-Islamism and Ismail bey Gasprinsky	24
IV	The National Movement: Parties and Programs in 1905	37
V	The Kazakh Problem	55
VI	Uzbek Liberals and the Young Bukhariotes	72
VII	Azerbaijani Awakening	92
VIII	Pan-Turkists and the Tatarists	105
IX	World War I and the Central Asian Revolt of 1916	123
X	Russia's Moslems in the Revolution of 1917	139
XI	Idel-Ural Dreams	165
XII	The Road to Red Tatary	179
XIII	Validov's Little Bashkiria	195
XIV	The Civil War and the Kazakhs	209
XV	The Revolution in the Central Asian Oases	225
XVI	The Jadids and the Communist Party	238
XVII	Two Years of National Azerbaijan	254
XVIII	Conclusion	268
	Notes	285
	Bibliography	321
	Index	337

MAPS

Turkic Population of Russia 4-5

Kazakh Steppes and Central Asia before the Revolution of 1917 70

Tatar-Bashkir Regions in 1918-1920 156

Pan-Turkism and Islam in Russia

CHAPTER I

The Turks of Russia

The word "Turk," in the minds of most American and West European readers, is usually associated with the inhabitants of the Republic of Turkey, heir to the once glorious and much feared Ottoman Empire. It is sometimes disregarded or simply forgotten that in addition to these Turks—or Ottoman Turks, as they were called until the 1920's—there are several other groups of peoples living in other countries who also speak languages or dialects closely related to the national tongue of the Turkish republic and who are also called "Turks," or "Turkic" peoples. English-speaking linguists as well as American and British reference books customarily refer to the national tongue of the Republic of Turkey as "Turkish," while the term "Turkic" is applied to all of the tongues of that entire linguistic family as a group. Thus, "Turkish" corresponds to the word "German," and "Turkic" to "Germanic."

The total number of Turkic peoples at the present time is about forty six to fifty million.[1] Of these, some twenty million live in Turkey, another twenty million in the Soviet Union, and the remainder in Sinkiang (the westernmost province of China), northern Afghanistan, Persia, and the countries of the Balkan peninsula, which has preserved sizable Turkish minority groups ever since the time of its inclusion in the Ottoman Empire.

The languages which these Turkic peoples speak are closely related to the Mongolic and Tungusic languages and form with them the Altaic family of languages—the Altai Mountains being considered the most ancient home of Turks and Mongols.[2] The Altaic family seems to show some linguistic kinship to the Finno-Ugric, or Uralic, group, to which the Finns, Hungarians, and some others belong. The once popular theory of the existence of a broader Uralo-Altaic linguistic family—or, as some writers in the late nineteenth and early twentieth centuries called it, the "Turanian"—has been rejected, however, by most modern linguists.

In the fifth and sixth centuries after Christ the Turks moved west from the Altai Mountains and Mongolia and conquered vast regions of present Kazakhstan and western Central Asia, absorbing and Turkizing the Indo-European, Iranian-speaking nomads and agriculturalists whom they encountered. Subsequent migrations and military campaigns, which were especially successful in the eleventh century, brought into the Turkic nomads' possession most of Iran, the Caucasus, Asia Minor, and southern Russia. In that same century the Turkic Seljukid dynasty founded a powerful empire in Iran, Iraq, and Asia Minor which, under its successor, the dynasty of the Ottomans, engulfed Byzantium in 1453 and became for some centuries the mightiest state of southeastern Europe and western Asia.

Migration, geographic dispersion, and the influence of the languages of conquered alien peoples and their neighbors—mainly Iranian, Arab, Finnish, and Mongolian—led to linguistic differentiation among the Turks. As early as 1072–1074 a medieval Central Asian scholar, Mahmud of Kashgar, distinguished two distinct branches of Turkic: the eastern and the western. A similar evolution led to the formation of two literary languages, which were the only written languages of the Turks until the middle of the last century. One, the western, was the Ottoman, which absorbed many Iranian and Arabic grammatical forms and words and was used by the Ottoman Turks, and at times by the Azerbaijani and the Crimean Tatars.[3] The other, in the east, was Chagatai, the literary language of Central Asia and the Golden Horde. With further linguistic differentiation, however, by the nineteenth century, Chagatai became a dead language no longer understandable to the majority of eastern and northern Turks, and new literary languages based on the popular dialects grew up among the East European and Central Asian Turkic populations.[4] The first of these was the Tatar tongue used by the Turkic people of the Volga region; then, literary Kazakh, developed by the Kazakh intelligentsia in the course of the nineteenth and twentieth centuries; finally, medieval Chagatai gave way in literature even in Central Asia to the living languages of the Uzbeks, Turkmenians, and Kirghiz. Most recently, in accord with the old maxim, *divide et impera,* and faced with the need to combat illiteracy, the Soviet government has sponsored the development of new Turkic literary languages based on local dialects, and new Turkic alphabets, grammars, primers, and literatures have mushroomed since the 1920's.

In the Soviet Union, as well as in former imperial Russia, Turkic peoples populate the vast areas in the east and southeast of this tremendous territory. The steppes of Kazakhstan, the plains and mountains of Central Asia, eastern Transcaucasia, much of the middle-Volga Region and Ural Mountains, and the huge semiarctic Lena River Basin in eastern Siberia are the principal areas of Turkic population. In addition, quite compact groups of Turks are to be found in Viatka, Perm, Gorki (formerly Nizhni Novgorod), Penza, and other eastern provinces of European Russia and western Siberia. Even the environs of the city of Kasimov, only a hundred miles southeast of Moscow, and the neighborhood of the Lithuanian capital, Vilno, are still inhabited by active Tatar groups whose ancestors moved there in the late Middle Ages to serve the Muscovite and Lithuanian princes. In most Russian cities there are significant colonies of Tatars and other Turkic peoples, and it would not be an exaggeration to say that Turks can be encountered throughout almost all of the Soviet Union, either as natives or as newly arrived inhabitants.

TURKIC LANGUAGES AND NATIONAL GROUPS

The Turkic languages are usually divided by linguists into four main groups, corresponding to their geographic distribution: northwestern, southwestern, southeastern, and northeastern.[5] Apart from these four basic groups stands the language of the Turkic Chuvash, who live in a compact body on the southern banks of the upper Volga, to the west of the city of Kazan. In 1937 there were 1,397,000 Chuvash.[6] Their language is different from the other Turkic tongues because of considerable morphological, phonetic, and structural peculiarities, as well as differences in vocabulary. The forebears of the Chuvash, the Bulgars—who appeared on the plains of eastern Europe in the company of the Huns—were the avant-garde of subsequent Turkic invaders and probably became isolated very early from the main body of Turkic peoples, hence undergoing a separate linguistic evolution. The Chuvash have never embraced Islam, the religion of most Turkic peoples, which fact has contributed to the difference in their cultural evolution. Some of them are Orthodox Christians; others preserved their ancient pagan religion up to the revolution of 1917.

THE NORTHWESTERN LINGUISTIC GROUP

All the Turkic people of the northwestern group, with minor exceptions, are located within the confines of the Soviet Union and form a slightly interrupted belt stretching from the Kazan region of

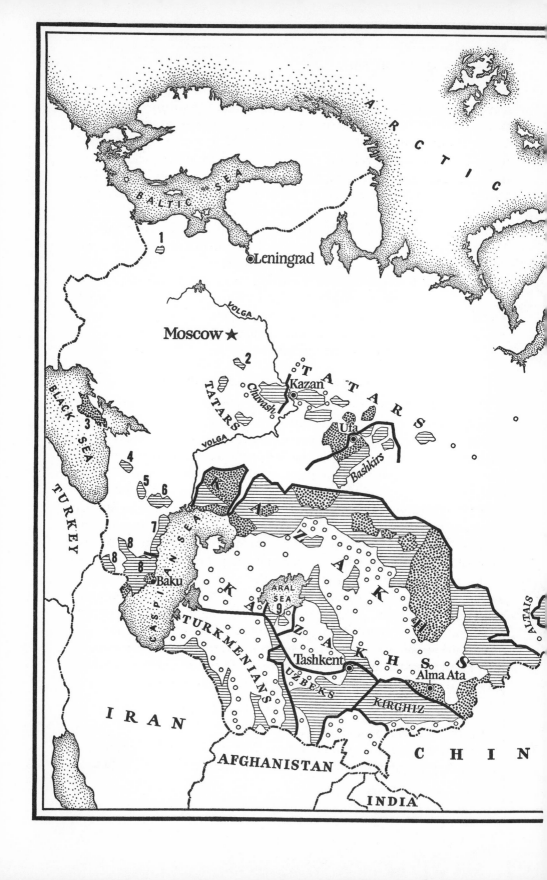

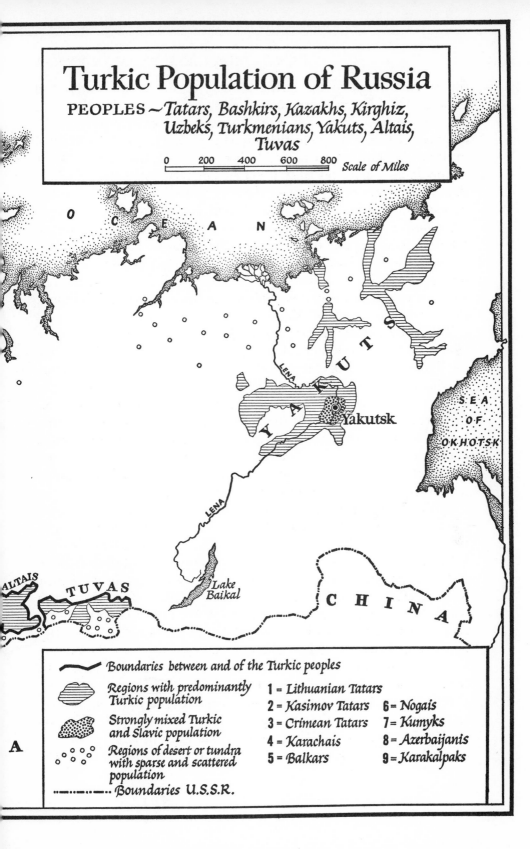

Turkic Population of Russia

PEOPLES ~ *Tatars, Bashkirs, Kazakhs, Kirghiz, Uzbeks, Turkmenians, Yakuts, Altais, Tuvas*

0   200   400   600   800   *Scale of Miles*

O C E A N

LENA

Y A K U T S

LENA

Yakutsk

SEA OF OKHOTSK

ALTAIS

T U V A S

Lake Baikal

C H I N A

Boundaries between and of the Turkic peoples

Regions with predominantly Turkic population

Strongly mixed Turkic and Slavic population

Regions of desert or tundra with sparse and scattered population

Boundaries U.S.S.R.

1 = Lithuanian Tatars
2 = Kasimov Tatars
3 = Crimean Tatars
4 = Karachais
5 = Balkars
6 = Nogais
7 = Kumyks
8 = Azerbaijanis
9 = Karakalpaks

A

the middle Volga to the Soviet-Chinese border in the Altais and Central Asia. The westernmost of these peoples are the Tatars of the Volga and Urals, as well as of some scattered settlements throughout eastern Russia. In 1926 they numbered 2,913,000 and 4,968,000 in 1959. A third of them (1,393,000 in 1959) live in the Tatar Autonomous Soviet Socialist Republic on the Volga River, where they form about 49 per cent of the local population. The Tatar Republic, whose capital is the city of Kazan, is the most distant western extension of intensive Turkic settlement and is surrounded on all sides by Russians and other non-Turkic peoples. There are nearly 800,000 Tatars in Bashkiria and slightly less than 1,000,000 in neighboring regions of the eastern part of European Russia, while the rest are widely dispersed over the whole of the Soviet Union. For instance, there were about 840,000 Tatars in Central Asia in 1959.[7]

To the east of the Tatars are the Bashkirs of the southern Urals, who speak a language only slightly different from Tatar. Now, like the Tatars, the Bashkirs have their own Autonomous Soviet Republic, in which they are no more numerous than the Tatars, forming only 23 per cent of the total population in 1926. In 1926 there were altogether 713,000 Bashkirs in the Soviet Union. In 1959 their number rose to 989,000. After World War II rich deposits of oil were found in their territories, so that Bashkiria has now grown into an important industrial region which, together with neighboring areas, supplies more than half of the Soviet Union's oil.

In the second part of the last century the Kazakhs, who now number 3,622,000, still occupied nearly the entire prairie of present Kazakhstan, and all were nomads who had preserved their ancient tribal and clan social structure based on family ties and the authority of the elders. In the last fifty or sixty years the settlement of their lands by Russians, Ukrainians, and other migrants from European Russia has progressed rapidly, and in 1959 a little less than 30 per cent of the total population of 9,300,000 in the Kazakh Soviet Republic were Kazakhs. Industrialization and the growth of agriculture in Kazakhstan in the past half-century have completely changed the entire economic life of the Kazakhs.

A similar evolution was undergone by the Kirghiz, who also belong to the northwestern Turkic linguistic group. The Kirghiz occupy the Russian and Chinese slopes of the Tien Shan Mountains and the adjacent valleys. In Russia alone there were 768,000 Kirghiz in 1926, and in their republic they represented some 60 per cent of the total population.[8] Because of heavy immigration from European Russia, they formed in 1959 41 per cent of the population of their own republic, their total number being 968,000. The rich valleys of the Tien Shan attract a large number of settlers from European Russia, and there were over 640,000 Russians there in 1959.

Three smaller groups of Turks belonging to the northwestern group should be added to this list: the Karakalpaks of the mouth of the Amu River in northern Uzbekistan (173,000), and the Balkars and Karachai (42,000 and 81,000, respectively), who lived in the northern Caucasus until the end of World War II. Accused of collaborating with the Germans in 1942–1943, the latter two national groups were displaced to Kazakhstan and Central Asia. Soviet agencies reported at the beginning of 1957 that both peoples were to be returned to their original homes, but at the time of this writing no definite information regarding their repatriation has been made available.

THE SOUTHEASTERN GROUP

The southeastern group is represented in the Soviet Union by its most numerous people, the Uzbeks, who now number slightly over 6,015,000 (3,904,000 in 1926). The Uzbeks occupy the Central Asian mesopotamia: lands between the Amu Daria and Syr Daria rivers, the neighboring oases, and the rich Ferghana Valley. They are heavily mixed with Iranian-speaking Tajiks, the original inhabitants of Central Asia, who still live in its mountainous southeastern corner and some Central Asian cities.

In 1959 the population of Uzbekistan consisted of Uzbeks (62 per cent), other Turks (11.5 per cent), Tajiks (4 per cent), and Russians (13.5 per cent).[9] In Tajikistan in 1959 there were 53 per cent Tajiks, 23 per cent Uzbeks, and 11 per cent Russians.[10] After 1939, particularly during the war years and the German offensive, when part of the urban population of European Russia was evacuated to Central Asia, the proportion of Russian and other Slavic settlers in the Central Asian republics grew very substantially, and there are now 7,410,000 Russians and 12,110,000 native Turkic inhabitants.

THE SOUTHWESTERN GROUP

The southwestern group is represented in the Soviet Union by the

Azerbaijanis (2,940,000) in eastern Transcaucasia, and the Turkomens (1,002,000) in the southwestern corner of Central Asia, both of
whom face each other across the Caspian Sea. In the northern provinces of Iran, Azerbaijanis and Turkomens are still numerous, despite
the steady efforts of the Iranian government to Iranize these remnants of the land's former Turkic conquerors. To the southwestern
group also belong some Turkomen tribes to be found in northern
Afghanistan, as well as the Turks of Turkey, or the Ottoman Turks,
of whom there are about twenty million. They are not only the most
numerous Turkic nation of this group, but of all the various Turkic
peoples as well, and unquestionably the most important politically
and the best known in history.

THE NORTHEASTERN GROUP

Finally, to the last and smallest linguistic groups of Turks, the northeastern, belong the Yakuts (237,000) of eastern Siberia, who, like the
Chuvash, have not undergone the impact of Islam and who broke
their geographical contact with the other Turkic people several centuries ago. Their isolation in the northern tundra and forest and considerable changes in their linguistic, spiritual, and social patterns have
made them a typical people of the arctic lands.

In the Altai and Tuva regions on the Chinese-Siberian border can
still be found some remnants of their original Turkic population—
the Tuvas (or Uriankhais), amounting to some 100,000, and the Al-
taians (or Oirats), with a population of 50,000.[11]

NATIONAL CONSCIOUSNESS AND ISLAM

A national awakening among these Turkic peoples of Russia started
only in the middle and last part of the nineteenth century. This late
development was largely due to the fact that the Moslem peoples of
Asia and eastern Europe have more often identified themselves with
the religion and culture of Islam than with any national or racial
group. To a dweller of the Central Asian oases before the revolution
of 1917, a Moslem and Iranian-speaking Tajik was a member of the
same social and cultural community as a Moslem Turk, while a
Turkic-speaking but Christian Tatar, Yakut, or Chuvash would
have been considered a representative of an alien and perhaps inimical
culture. Such an identification was long preserved in the Moslem lands
of Persia and Turkey as well as in the Russian Empire. The Russian

government itself granted or restricted the rights and privileges of its subjects according to their denominational affiliations. The strongly traditional Great Russian Old Believers, for instance, were more restricted in their rights, up to 1905, than were either Moslems or Jews, while anyone's conversion to Orthodoxy or Lutheranism immediately opened the door for him to any type of career. In the eyes of the tsarist government, then, all the Moslems of Russia—whether the Turkic Tatars and Kazakhs, the Finnic-speaking Votiaks or Cheremiss, the Iranian-speaking Ossets and Tajiks, or the Caucasian Kabardinians or Cherkess—belonged alike simply to the group called "Mohammedans." Only in the late nineteenth century did the Russian government begin to distinguish various ethnic groups among the Moslems, but insufficient knowledge of dialects and of the Arabic alphabet often led to confusion and to the application of the term "Tatar" to every Moslem, no matter to what national group he belonged. And, as a matter of fact, the Tatar tongue was the *lingua franca* of Russia's Moslems and of official documents concerning them. Such an approach to identification actually helped the Turkic peoples to preserve a religious rather than a national self-awareness. Even the Moslemized Caucasians, who often did not speak any Turkic tongue at all, mingled more willingly with Tatars or Azerbaijanis than with Russians, and in the eyes of both the converts and the Russian administration, conversion to Islam was usually an act of tatarization. Since the revolution these religious and cultural ties grew weaker and now it is much more difficult to assume the existence of any solidarity among the national groups with Moslem background in contemporary Soviet Russia. Summarizing these facts, it may be concluded that 85 percent of Russia's Moslems spoke Turkic dialects and that 90 percent of Turkic-speaking people were Moslems. Only Chuvash, Yakuts, some 120,000 Tatars and some other minor groups were Christian or preserved their ancestral beliefs. Besides these 21,000,000 Russian "Turks," there are also 1,400,000 Tajiks and nearly 2,000,000 Caucasian mountaineers who historically were affiliated with Islam. In the 1920's, however, the total number of Moslems in Russia was below 18 million.

This primacy of religious identification in Russia resulted in a specific phenomenon in the nineteenth century: the Turkic national awakening was preceded by a Moslem cultural revival. A linguistic, national, or racial consciousness among Russian Turks did not overcome the feeling of Moslem cultural unity until the 1920's, when even Turkic Communists still spoke of a "Moslem revolution" and "Moslem" educational problems.

Besides the dominance of a religious over a national orientation, a great hindrance to the birth of national ideas among the Turkic peoples of Russia was presented by the problem of a written language for literature, trade, and education. Moslems, generally, have always used Arabic as their language for worship. The first attempt in Russia to introduce a Turkic language for prayer was not made until the late nineteenth century, and was regarded as a real heresy by pious mullahs.[12] In 1908 a group of Tatar mullahs from Kazan complained to the Russian government that their "revolutionary" colleagues were attempting to read the holiday prayers in mosques in the Tatar language, which was strictly forbidden by the Moslem religion.[13] A somewhat progressive Tatar mullah, Sadyk Imankulov, wrote in a liberal Tatar newspaper in 1912 that it was impossible and almost blasphemy to translate the Koran into such a vulgar language as Tatar.[14] The teaching of the Koran and Moslem law, which regulates all aspects of Moslem life, has continued to be conducted in Arabic even in the most advanced Moslem educational institutions and has never been replaced by Turkic. Moreover, the study of Arabic itself was done by means of textbooks written in Persian. Thus, young Tatar or Uzbek pupils in the nineteenth century began their study of prayers and the Koran in a foreign language, with the help of manuals written in another completely alien language.

IRANIAN INFLUENCE

Persian (Iranian) influence was particularly strong in the southern provinces of Russia, among the Turkic peoples living in Central Asia and Transcaucasia, on the northern fringe of Iranian culture. Here most of the literature was written in Iranian (or Tajik) rather than in the native Turkic tongue, which was usually considered profane or vulgar. The competition or coexistence of Iranian and Turkic lasted till the Bolshevik revolution, and most Azerbaijani and Uzbek intellectuals around 1900–1920 were bilingual. Until 1920 Persian was the court language in the khanate of Bukhara, and panegyrics, chronicles, and official documents were written more often in Persian than in Uzbek, the language of most of the population of Bukhara.[15] Most Central Asian and Transcaucasian cities were equally bilingual. Educated Turks of Central Asia not infrequently declared, even in the early twentieth century, that "for them, pure Persian was easier than the Tatar language." [16] Persian cultural domination was not limited to the Turks of Russia: in Turkey, Persian literary forms dominated Ottoman letters for centuries, although the grammar of Ottoman poets was almost purely Turkic. Persian influence gave way to Western influence in Ottoman literature only after the reforms of the 1840's–1880's, the so-called Tanzimat era, when a new Western—mainly French—cultural orientation was initiated.

Another obstacle to the rise of nationalism among the Russian Turkic peoples—particularly the Kazakhs and Turkomens of the steppe, the Kirghiz and Uzbeks of the mountains and oases, and the Yakuts of the polar forest and tundra—was the fact that many of them were still nomads, lacking any written language whatsoever. These people, in fact, often did not even know to which nation they belonged. Tribal or clan membership precluded any national feeling.

A national renaissance was further forestalled by alien migration to centuries-long Turkic or nomadic lands. At about the same time that the first English colonists settled the American continent, Russian Cossacks penetrated Siberia. In the years of mass Slavic emigration to the United States, between 1895 and 1914, other Slavic peasants were moving from their homes in eastern Europe to Kazakhstan, very comparable in its resources to the American West.

IMPORTANCE OF THE TURKIC PROBLEM

Despite all these obstacles, the Turks of Russia in the last century —particularly in the decades preceding the October Revolution— achieved substantial successes in the economic and political life of the empire. Three main factors, among others, were responsible for the progress of the Turks of Russia and their role in Russian history:

(1) *The numerical importance of Turks in the former tsarist Russian Empire and in the present Soviet Union.* Turks comprise about 10–11 per cent of the total population of the Soviet Union, and the Turkic-speaking inhabitants of the USSR are second numerically only to the eastern Slavs.

(2) *The geographic distribution of Turks throughout most of the important areas and cities of Russia.* From Vilno to Yakutsk, from Baku to Stalinabad, they are scattered throughout the Eurasian plain.

(3) *Their long coexistence with Russians.* For fifteen hundred years Turks and Slavs have mingled, and each group has had a lasting influence on the other.

CHAPTER II

Tatar Rebirth

Slavs and Turks first met on the plains of eastern Europe at the very dawn of the Middle Ages. Annals indicate the presence of the Slavic Antes in what is now southern Russia in the middle of the fourth century A.D., and at approximately the same time the Hunnic hordes, composed of Turkic and Mongol tribes, appeared on the banks of the Volga River and began their conquest of the Pontic steppes.[1] The struggle between the Slavs and the newcomers from Asia for the vast Eurasian expanses began in these dark centuries of European history. Slowly but persistently the Slavs moved ever eastward, through and around the forests of today's Russia, while Asia ejected ever-increasing waves of nomads into the steppes to meet them. Avars, Hungarians, Pechenegs, Cumans (Polovtsians), and Mongols presented a centuries-long nomadic threat to the agricultural civilization of the Slavs. In the mid-thirteenth century Slavic resistance was overcome by the armies of the heirs of Genghis Khan, and for the next two hundred years the eastern Slavs were subjects of the Golden Horde. During their conquest these nomads decimated a large part of the Slavic population, taking others into slavery, while Russia became isolated from the European Christian world into which it had previously been drawn. Turkic raids continued long after Russia's liberation from the Golden Horde. In the seventeenth century alone, over 200,000 Russian slaves were sold in Crimean and Anatolian markets by the Tatars. As late as the latter part of the eighteenth century, Crimean Tatar raiders continued to rove the Ukraine, and when Russian troops took Bukhara in 1868, they freed scores of Russian slaves held by the Uzbek nobles and traders.[2]

In the fifteenth century, however, the wheel of fate had started to turn in the opposite direction. The human wellsprings of nomadic Asia seemed to have dried up, for the hordes of Genghis Khan were the last significant migration from Asia to Europe. Some two centuries after the death of this great conqueror, the empires of his successors began to decline. Armed with gunpowder, Christian Europe took the offensive. On the westernmost borders of Europe the Spaniards defeated the Moslem princes of Granada, erasing the last trace of nomadic Africa in the Iberian peninsula, while the Slavic plowmen in the east threw off their fetters of dependence upon the Asiatic Golden Horde, which soon after disintegrated and disappeared from the pages of history.

The descendants of these nomadic conquerors, however, remained in the Eastern European steppes and gradually became integrated into Muscovite tsardom. Before the final collapse of the Golden Horde, in 1439, a Tatar prince named Kasim offered his services to the Great Prince of Moscow. In return, he was awarded a small territory about one hundred miles southeast of Moscow, along the Oka River.[3] This little Tatar princedom became the first Turkic minority group in the Russian state. A hundred years later, in 1552, the khanate of Kazan, won by Ivan the Terrible, became a part of Russia, and in 1555 the Bashkirs of the Ural region recognized the sovereignty of Moscow. In 1556, almost unopposed, Russian troops took Astrakhan, at the mouth of the Volga, gaining access to the shores of the Caspian Sea. The entire Volga River was now in Russian hands and the gates to Asia were opened for Russian expansion. At about the same time the Russians won the river Terek and Ivan the Terrible married a Kabardinian princess, marking symbolically the beginning of Russian ties with the northern Caucasus.

The annexation of Kazan in 1552 and the inclusion of large bodies of Tatar peoples into the Russian state was significant both for Russia and for the Turkic peoples of the Russian sphere. The Tatars were not only the first but also the most numerous[4] and influential Turkic minority of Russia up to the end of the tsarist regime, and the entire Turkic and Moslem problem of the Russian Empire hinged upon and developed in the light of Russian-Tatar relations.

Due to their outstanding economic capabilities and their knowledge of the Russians, the Tatars occupied the leading position among Russia's Turkic peoples up to 1917. Many Tatars served in the Russian army or administration and assisted in the formation of the new Russian state. Under Ivan the Terrible a Tatar, Simeon Bekbulatovich, was regent, and Boris Godunov prided himself on his Tatar ancestry. Saburovs, Yusupovs, Aksakovs, Kugushevs, Meshcherskies, Nebolsins, Karamzins, and many other noble or aristocratic families of Tatar ancestry were prominent representatives of Russian political and cultural life.

ETHNIC BACKGROUND OF THE TATARS

The Volga and Ural Tatars present a complicated amalgamation of various ethnic elements, among which three are the most important. The oldest population of the Volga region was the Finno-Ugric tribes, which had settled there in prehistoric times and which are partially preserved to this day in the Mordvinians and Maris. During the great migration of the peoples in the fourth century A.D., when the Huns swept over the Pontic steppes—now southern Russia—they brought with them the Turkic tribe of Bulgars, some of whom settled in the Balkans, giving their name to the present Bulgarians. In the seventh century another group of these Bulgars appeared on the upper Volga at its junction with the Kama River and formed there the kingdom of the Volga Bulgars. In 922 a Bulgar prince accepted the religion of Mohammed, and thus arose the northernmost nidus of Islamic culture.[5] Another part of these Volga Bulgars escaped Islamization, remaining pagan, and their descendants continue to live along the Volga, under the name of "Chuvash."

The Moslem Bulgar state was independent at first, then existed as a part of the Golden Horde until the end of the fourteenth century. During this last Mongol invasion, the Horde brought with it new Turkic and Mongol tribes which reinforced the nomadic population of the Volga region. One of these Mongol tribes, that of the Tatars, gave its name to the Turkic population inhabiting this region, and as such it continues to be known. [6]

In 1438, led by Ulug Mehmed, a prince of the Golden Horde, these Turko-Tatars founded a principality—the Kazan khanate—at the junction of the Volga and Kama rivers, on the former territory of the Moslem Volga Bulgars. Gradually all these various ethnic strains —the Moslem Volga Bulgars, some Finno-Ugric tribes, and the Turkic nomads (Tatars)—merged to form one ethnic whole bearing the name of Tatars.

RUSSIAN COLONIZATION AMONG THE TATARS

After Ivan the Terrible's conquest of Kazan in 1552, Russia began to colonize the middle-Volga plains and made some attempts to Russify the Turkic peoples of the area. The migration of sizable contingents of Russian agriculturalists to the expanses of the sparsely settled Volga and Ural regions resulted in successful colonization, for in the seventeenth century these areas had assumed the aspect of largely Russian lands. Today Russians form the majority of the population in the lands along the Volga and in the Ural Mountains. Russification of the Turkic natives, however, was much less successful. Most Tatars were Moslem. And since the Russian government met in Islam an obstacle to the Tatars' cultural conversion or Russification, it set about to Christianize them. In 1555, only three years after the conquest of Kazan, a Russian bishop, Gurius, began missionary work there. Meeting the Tatars' resistance, missionary activity was reinforced by administrative measures against them. After their rebellion of 1556, unconverted Tatars were prohibited from living in the city of Kazan, and the city's mosques were closed or destroyed.

The Tatars remained faithful to Islam, however, and perhaps only one tenth of them—probably those who had never become Moslem and held to Shamanism—converted to Orthodoxy. The government attempted to combat the spread of Islam and to preserve Finno-Ugric tribes, as well as some other pagan tribes, from Moslem influence. Since the mosques were the center of resistance to Russification and missionary activity, an edict of 1592 proclaimed that all Tatar mosques be torn down and no more built without the Russian government's permission.[7]

In the course of the seventeenth century Russia relaxed its struggle against Islam, but continued energetic colonization of the free lands along the Volga and Kama. Unconverted Tatar nobles and aristocrats were prohibited from owning Christian serfs, and according to a decree of 1681 the lands of many Moslem Tatar nobles were confiscated. Although the latter measure was not carried out consistently, nevertheless such enactments strongly undermined the influence of the Tatar aristocracy, which was further weakened in the following century by intermixing with the merchants. The position of Tatar peasants was much better. While over half of Russian peasants at that time were serfs, Tatar peasants and those of other non-Russian groups of the Volga and Ural regions remained free. No more than 1–2 per cent among them were serfs, while among Great Russians about 50 per cent of the peasantry were the serfs of noble landowners.[8]

Under Peter the Great and his immediate successors, the pressure upon the Tatars for conversion was renewed. After the violent schism in the Russian Orthodox Church, Kievan monks gained primacy in church affairs, and many of them—such as Alexis Raifsky, Hilarion Rogalevsky, Sylvester Golovatsky, Benjamin Puchek-Grigorovich, and Luke Konashevich—were sent to Russia's frontiers to conduct missionary activity there. Sometimes, in their ardor, these missionaries practiced forceful conversion and the purchase of souls. Tatars could relax once again only in 1735–1738, when a conservative Muscovite, Gabriel, became the metropolitan of Kazan. Gabriel was not so much concerned with the conversion of Tatars as he was with the struggle between Westernizers, the supporters of innovations introduced by Peter the Great, and conservative Russians, and he was eager "to eradicate everything which had not existed in Russia before the time of Peter the First." [9]

Missionary zeal reached its apogee in 1740, after the establishment of the Missionary Office of Affairs of New Converts. Tatar children were required to be sent to Russian missionary schools, new converts were granted privileges, and the building of new mosques was again prohibited. Even army chaplains were required to convert pagan and Moslem soldiers to Orthodoxy.[10]

In the year 1743 alone, nearly five hundred mosques, both old and new, were razed, under the pretext that they had been built without the government's permission. Actual results in terms of conversions in the first half of the eighteenth century, however, did not correspond to the efforts exerted by Russia. Many Tatars who had converted to Christianity remained secret Moslems. In general, the number of conversions was not great: in 1828 the number of newly converted Tatars was only twelve thousand. (Tatars converted under Gurius in the sixteenth century were called "old converts," those in the eighteenth century, "new converts.") While the old Tatar converts adhered to Orthodoxy, the new ones easily relapsed to Islam. Bishop Alexis Raifsky, an ardent missionary of 1720–1740, admitted that "Mohammedans are die-hards in their customs, and none of them seek conversion on their own initiative." [11] Later, in 1778, Prince Shcherbatov expressed doubt as to the usefulness of missionary activity and wrote that "the schools formerly established to convert young Moslems did not contribute to a spread of the faith, but sooner to a hatred of it." [12]

In 1755 the native population's bitterness threatened to burst into general disorder. During the Pugachev rebellion, which was not only a peasant movement but also an uprising of religious minorities—Old Believers as well as Moslems—the Russian clergy paid a heavy toll for the activities of its missionaries. In the Kazan province alone one hundred thirty two clerics were killed.

CATHERINE THE SECOND'S POLICIES OF RELIGIOUS TOLERANCE

In 1766 Catherine II summoned a legislative commission to convene in Petersburg for the purpose of revising the Russian Code of Laws. Among the deputies representing the various provinces of the empire were delegates sent by the Moslem Tatar population of the Volga and Ural regions. In the memoranda which these delegates presented to the commission and in the instructions which they had received from their electors were embodied the main grievances of the Tatar people. Their complaints concerned their difficult religious and economic situation, for since the conquest of the Kazan khanate by Ivan the Terrible, Tatars had not only been subjected to permanent persecution for their faith but had also become severely restricted in their rights.[13] The Tatar delegates asked for recognition of their faith, for the removal of limitations on their trade activity, and for restitution of the rights of the Tatar nobility.

Catherine undertook the first step toward improvement of the situation of her Moslem subjects in 1767, one year after the commission had assembled, when she visited the Volga region and the city of Kazan. The industrious population favorably impressed her, and she gave audience to representatives of its various social and national groups. The Tatars presented her their petitions personally and received her verbal permission to build two mosques in the city.[14] At the same time, Catherine nullified the regulation prohibiting unconverted Tatars from living in Kazan.[15] These steps toward reform were soon followed by laws and decrees which completely changed the legal status of Tatar economic and religious life, opening the way for Tatar revival in the next century.

In 1773 Catherine's verbal permission to build mosques was confirmed by an imperial edict which not only authorized construction of temples but also promulgated tolerance of the Moslem religion.[16] The need to pacify Russia's eastern lands after Pugachev's rebellion in 1773–1774 served as impetus for Catherine's further reforms. A law of 1776 revoked rules restricting the trade activity of Tatar merchants, and in 1784 Catherine re-established the rights of the Tatar gentry, which had demonstrated its loyalty to her by opposing the rebellion of Pugachev.[17] Finally, in 1788, the empress created a special ecclesiastic administration for the followers of Islam. This new law, which became the Act of Tolerance for Moslems in Russia, organized the Moslem church administration and laid the foundation for Moslem religious education, making possible the subsequent development of Tatar-Islamic culture in Russia.[18] The entire Moslem administration in eastern Russia was put in the hands of the Mufti, head of the newly created Moslem Ecclesiastic Administration, with residence in Orenburg (later in Ufa). Mohammed Jan Hussein, a leading Moslem cleric, was named the first Mufti. This legislation and the Russian government's new policy toward Moslems led to their social and religious emancipation and further facilitated the Tatar people's economic and cultural revival in the nineteenth century. In effect, it was of such significance that it determined the direction taken by Tatar society in its development up to the Bolshevik revolution of 1917.

TATAR ECONOMIC EXPANSION

Appeasement and conquest of the steppes created conditions favorable for the economic development of this area. After their emancipation by Catherine II, the Tatars became partners in, and often the leading element of, Russian expansion in the southeast. Russian penetration into Central Asia in the nineteenth century opened up new markets for Tatar tradesmen in regions populated primarily by a people related to them both in language and in culture, a kinship which put the Tatars in an advantageous position vis-à-vis rival Russian tradesmen. By the end of the eighteenth century the merchant class had become the strongest segment of Tatar society, while the Tatar nobility, despite Catherine's reformative legislation, was on its way to disappearing as a class, owing to the irremediable losses it had suffered at the height of Russia's anti-Moslem policies. Its most dynamic members joined the Tatar bourgeoisie, and toward the turn of the century the names of Tatar princes and *murzas* (gentry) were often to be found among the lists of tradesmen and industrialists.[19] At the same time, the Tatar merchant class was augmented by people of peasant origin, and a decree of 1821 enabled Tatar peasants to engage in trade.[20]

Owing to the traditional trade relations which had existed since the early Middle Ages between eastern Europe and Asia, and to the geographic location of Tatars, Tatar merchants had long played an important role in commerce. In the tenth century, when the Bulgars were converted to Islam, their main city—Bulgar—was a lively outpost connecting the Near and Middle East with countries of eastern and northern Europe. The Tatars continued the mercantile activities of their ancestors, and by the seventeenth century Tatar traders from the Volga, together with the Uzbeks and Tajiks of Bukhara and Khiva, maintained control of commercial activity in Central Asia and the Siberian frontier, where the local population was even "Tatarized" and converted to Islam.[21]

By the first part of the eighteenth century the most important sector of Russian trade in the East, that with Central Asia, had become dominated by Central Asian Moslems,[22] since Tatar merchants had become restricted by the Russian government in their economic activities. After these restrictions were lifted by Catherine II, however, the Tatars gained the dominant position in Eastern trade. Further pacification of the steppes permitted a large part of Central Asian trade to pass along routes through Tatar lands, and two new routes— one from Orenburg to Bukhara, the other from Semipalatinsk to Tashkent—were added to the ancient one from the Volga to Central Asia via Astrakhan, the Caspian Sea, and Khiva. Orenburg and its suburb, Seitovsky Posad, became the Tatar gates for trade from Central Asia by the end of the eighteenth century. In 1792, of the 2,674 Tatar male inhabitants of the Posad, 1,820 were engaged in commerce.[23]

CENTRAL ASIAN TRADE

By the beginning of the nineteenth century the Tatars, favored by Russian expansion in Asia, had nearly gained a monopoly in Russia's trade with the Kazakh steppes and Uzbek khanates.[24] The Russian government supported the commercial activity of its subjects in Central Asia and assisted them in eliminating their foreign competition by forbidding the latter access to the Russian hinterland. The Uzbek and Persian dealers became restricted to markets organized in the main Russian fortresses along the Kazakh steppes, which later became the main points of concentration of Tatar capital. While Russian protective regulations, of course, aided the Tatars in overcoming their foreign rivals, the Tatars' linguistic and religious affinity to the peoples of Central Asia further contributed to their commercial success there. Not only was it an easy matter for the Tatars to communicate and trade with the Central Asians, but due to their community of faith, the Uzbek markets of Bukhara, Khiva, and Kokand —which were closed to Christian or Jewish merchants because of the local Moslem population's fanaticism—were open to Tatars. For this reason Russian businessmen preferred not to travel to the Central Asian khanates, and traded there only through their Tatar partners or agents. Even as late as 1872 Petrovsky, a Russian observer in Bukhara, found only one Russian merchant there.[25]

With the growth of Central Asian trade and the development of Tatar monopolies with both Kazakhstan and Turkestan, from the end of the eighteenth century on Tatar prosperity also grew. Trade was on a barter basis in the Kazakh steppes, making great gains possible to the Tatar merchants. Around the end of the eighteenth century, for example, an iron kettle bought for 2.50 rubles on the Siberian market could be exchanged in the Kazakh steppes for furs valued at 50 rubles.[26] The main products imported from the steppes to Russia were livestock and the by-products of cattle breeding, and from the Uzbek khanates cotton, Persian lamb, carpets, and dried fruits. Tatars supplied the markets of Central Asia with Russian textiles, iron goods, sugar, and, later, kerosene. The combined yearly averages of imports and exports between Russia and Central Asia between the years 1773 and 1832 were as follows:

1773–1777	83,000 rubles
1793–1797	624,000 rubles
1832	11,336,000 rubles [27]

With increased turnover and improved transportation during the latter part of the nineteenth century, the rate of profit decreased, but in Central Asia, and particularly in the Kazakh steppes, trade continued to be advantageous. The account books of the large Tatar firm of the Husseinov brothers reveal that merchandise bought in Orenburg toward the turn of the century was sold in Kazalinsk (in the Kazakh steppe) for prices three to six times higher than in Orenburg.[28]

RISE OF THE TATAR BOURGEOISIE

Such profits enabled the Tatars to accumulate considerable wealth, which in turn strengthened their economic influence in other parts of Russia. At the end of the nineteenth century not only Central Asia but also the Volga region, the Urals, western and eastern Siberia, the Russian Far East, and many cities of central Russia were included in the network of Tatar firms and agencies. As Tatar trade and economic activity moved eastward, the importance of Kazan as an economic center began to decrease, although Kazan did remain the cultural and political center of Tatar life up to the revolution of 1917. Toward the turn of the century, commercial activity increased in Orenburg, Troitsk, Semipalatinsk, and Perm,[29] cities which came to rival Uralsk, Astrakhan, Orsk, and Kizlar in their accumulation of capital. The rapid development of large enterprises, some of which gained extensive monopolies in their regions, was a characteristic feature of the Tatar merchant class. Such a firm was, for example, that of the Husseinovs, illiterate but brilliant tradesmen and the founders of a vast commercial empire in the Kazakh steppes and Urals. Their main offices were in Orenburg and Kazan, but they had agents in the leading cities of Russia as well as in Berlin, London, and New York, and the capital of this enterprise was many tens of millions of rubles. A similar firm was that of the Tatar, Yanyshev, which occupied a monopolistic position in Troitsk; in Alma-Ata (Verny) the market was dominated by another wealthy Tatar, Valeev. The magnates in Kazan, along with the Husseinovs, were Selimjanov and Karimov, and in Moscow the Tatar millionaire, Karamyshev, led all firms which dealt in Russian trade with the East.[30]

Tatar commercial penetration into new regions of Central and Eastern Asia very often preceded Russian political expansion. Tatars appeared in Manchuria, the Far East, and Tuva (called the Urjankhai region before the revolution of 1917) even before the appearance of Russian administration there. Tatar merchants were involved in trade with China, especially Sinkiang, and gained a foothold in the border market of Chuguchak as early as the beginning of the nineteenth century.[31]

Industry, as well as trade, also attracted the interest and capital of Tatar businessmen. After the construction of a road connecting Kazan and the Volga with new industrial regions of the Urals in the time of Peter the Great, Kazan also became an important center for industry.[32] By 1812 Tatars owned nine out of ten large industrial enterprises in Kazan, and by the 1890's they owned one third of all the industry there.[33] Akchurin, Agichev, Apanaev, Burnabaev, Yunusov, and Rakhmatulin were all Tatars who became leaders in east Russian textile production and the soap and leather industries.[34] In the Urals, Tatars were engaged in goldmining and lumbering. Still, however, trade and moneylending, in the East, remained the favored fields of Tatar economic activity, and the merchant bourgeoisie developed into the strongest and most influential segment of Tatar society.

EMERGENCE OF RUSSIAN COMPETITION

The Tatar trade empire in the eastern reaches of Russia continued to expand and flourish until the Bolshevik revolution, but in the last quarter of the nineteenth century the Tatars' monopoly in Central Asian trade was coming to an end, undermined by increasing Russian competition. Conquest of Turkestan in the 1870's incorporated Turkestan's economy into that of the Russian Empire, and neither Moslem fanaticism nor restrictive measures undertaken by the local khans could seriously hamper the penetration of Russian capital in Central Asia. In the mid-nineteenth century only such Russian businessmen as P. V. Golubkov of Moscow and F. R. Pegulin of Rostov had ventured to trade with the Usbek khanates, but after the annexation of Turkestan the number of Russian tradesmen there grew very rapidly.[35] Russia's chief import from Central Asia was, of course, cotton, since the Central Asian oases were the only cotton-producing regions in the empire at that time. The growth of cotton production demanded, in turn, capital investment in the related branches of trade, industry, and transport, and in the years 1914–1916 over 313,-000,000 rubles were invested in Central Asia by Russian industrialists and financiers.[36] The Tatar economic monopoly in Turkestan was doomed by the increasing importance of cotton and the tremendous amounts of Russian capital being invested in it, with which the Tatars could not compete. Construction of the Transcaspian and Orenburg-Tashkent railways further accelerated the elimination of Tatar intermediaries between the Moscow industrial area and Turkestan.[37]

Tatar trade in Kazakhstan also became imperiled by Russian competition, which grew with Russia's colonization of the Kazakh steppe and the Russians' increasing knowledge of the Kazakh language and customs. The Russian firms of Ivanov, Lakhtin, and Pervushin extended the network of their trading posts and stores,[38] and it became evident that despite the Tatars' economic toe hold in Kazakhstan and Turkestan, they were losing their monopoly and were being reduced, at least in the cotton trade, to the role of minor partner and broker of Russian capital.

However, because of the advantages enjoyed by Tatar merchants in Central Asia through their linguistic and cultural affinity with the native population and their ability in commercial transactions, Russian businessmen found competition severe in Central Asia, and pressed the local authorities to restrict Tatar activity by administrative regulations and by limitation of governmental credit to Tatars. They succeeded in obtaining governmental restrictions against the Tatars' purchase of real estate in Turkestan and against the formation of large trading companies by Tatars,[39] but they failed—both during the office of Prime Minister P. A. Stolypin (1907–1911) and in 1914 after Bark's nomination to the Ministry of Finance—in their attempt to limit the financing of Tatar enterprises by state and private banks.[40] Both Stolypin and Bark categorically refused to introduce any economic restrictions which would discriminate against the Tatar minority, and Tatar firms continued to enjoy credit with government banks on the same terms as their Russian competitors.

Although growing Russian competition in the Kazakh steppe and Central Asia succeeded in partially dislodging Tatar trade from its leading position, the ever-developing Russian economy steadily created new outlets for Tatar skill and energy. The Tatars strengthened their interests in Volga industry and Ural mining, increased their exchange with China and Mongolia, and were quick to invest in the Siberian market. Economic prospects in the Russian territories were sufficiently broad to absorb the energies of an active people.

CHAPTER III

Pan-Islamism and Ismail bey Gasprinsky

The Tatar revival of the nineteenth century was not restricted to economic life but extended to the spheres of religion and culture as well. The decree of 1788 had greatly facilitated the development of religious education, necessary for the training of the *imam*, or priest, and for the creation of a Moslem ecclesiastic administration. Since such schools as Tatars had at the end of the eighteenth century were on a very low scholastic level, Tatars turned their eyes toward the Islamic educational institutions of Central Asia. Bukhara's *madrasas*, or theological schools, had been famous through the eastern Moslem world since the tenth century, and it was to these madrasas that young Tatars were sent for the completion of their education.[1] Soon, however, Tatar students became dissatisfied with the formal, medieval scholastic method employed in Central Asian schools, and early in the nineteenth century a prominent Volga Tatar theologian, Abdul Nazir Kursavi (1775–1813), protested against the abstract system of Bukhara's theologians.[2] But it was Shihabeddin Merjani (1815–1889), the first modern Tatar historian and reformer, who initiated the new period of genuine Tatar cultural revival. Returning in 1849 from a twelve-year stay in Bukhara, Merjani took up the struggle for the improvement of Moslem schools in the Volga region. He sought to replace the formal, scholastic study of the Koran and Islam by a less theoretical, more practical approach, and insisted that every true believer could interpret the Koran himself. He considered that the old textbooks did not clarify, but rather beclouded, the original content of the Koran and the meaning of Mohammed's teachings. Further, he believed that a contemporary education and knowledge of the Russian language would not harm Moslem religious feeling but, on the contrary, would help Moslems better to understand Islam and raise their cultural level.

Merjani was not merely a theoretician of enlightenment, but a practical pedagogue as well. He put his ideas into practice and fought persistently for the creation of better madrasas. After a twenty-year struggle he succeeded in convincing a wealthy Kazan merchant, Ibragim Yunusov, to finance the creation of a new school. Merjani wrote several fundamental works on the history of the Volga Bulgars and Tatars, and closely cooperated with Russian scholars of the universities of Kazan and Petersburg. His historical work was instrumental both in awakening the Tatars' interest in their past and in the formation of their national consciousness. In 1876, at the age of sixty-one, Merjani became a teacher in a school for Tatars founded by Russian authorities in Kazan for the purpose of training teachers.

Owing largely to Merjani's efforts, many Tatars succeeded in overcoming their prejudice against the Russian language and Western, "Christian" culture, and as a result of his endeavors the enlightenment began to take hold among the Tatars.[3] Merjani's leading student was Hussein Feitskhani (1826–1866), a lecturer in Kazan and, later, in the Petersburg university. Feitskani elaborated a plan for modernizing the madrasas which was later utilized in reformed Tatar schools. A still greater role in the Tatar enlightenment was played by the energetic Tatar writer and printer, Abdul Kaium Nasyri (1824–1907). His numerous textbooks, dictionaries, and calendars were not written in Chagatai, the traditional eastern Turkic literary language, which was becoming incomprehensible to the masses,[4] but in the spoken Tatar tongue. For the first time, Tatars were furnished with geographical, historical, and contemporary scientific information in their own language. In his book, "Fruits of Conversation," Nasyri wrote of the colloquial Volga Tatar language that "the Tatar tongue is second to none in eloquence and adaptability at expressing ideas, and in some respects it possesses even greater potentialities."[5] Later, in the twentieth century, this very tongue became the language of Tatar literature.

Nasyri was not only the first to introduce spoken Tatar in literature, but he also compiled a Tatar grammar, as well as Russian-Tatar and Tatar-Russian dictionaries. Owing to his activity, contemporary science and literature for the first time became available to the average Tatar, and it is possible to compare Nasyri's work in its practical effect with that of Russia's Lomonosov and Novikov.[6]

PUBLISHING ACTIVITIES AND SCHOOLS

By mid-nineteenth century, education and printing had made considerable progress among the Tatars of the Volga and Ural lands. It was largely the Tatar bourgeoisie which was responsible for the growth of Tatar cultural life, for it financed the building of schools and mosques and the printing of books. The Tatars had obtained their first license to print Moslem religious books in Russia after the enactment of liberal legislation by Catherine II, and by 1802 some 14,300 copies of such books, including the Koran, had been printed. Fifty years later, during the period 1853–1859, Kazan University alone published 326,700 copies of the Koran and other books in Tatar, and in the decade 1854–1864 the number of books published by Tatars exceeded one million.[7] The network of Tatar schools under the supervision of the Moslem Ecclesiastic Administration expanded no less rapidly. By 1844 there were four madrasas (Moslem theological seminaries) in Kazan, and by 1860 there were 1,859 Tatar *maktabs* (elementary schools conducted by the mullahs at the mosques) throughout the mid-Volga region and southern Urals. Of these, 408 were located in the Kazan province alone.[8]

INCEPTION OF TATAR NATIONALISM

Any ally which grows in strength and independence begins to embarrass its partner. Thus, it is not surprising that the rapid cultural and economic successes of the Tatars in the middle of the nineteenth century occasioned apprehension in Russian government circles. In addition, during the reign of Alexander II the size of the Moslem and Turkic populations of Russia sharply increased, reaching some ten million by 1865, and it was the Tatars—whom the Russians themselves supported as the guardians of their kinsmen—who won the position of cultural and political leadership of Russia's Turkic minority. With the incorporation of the Kazakh steppe into the empire, together with conquest of the Uzbek khanates of Central Asia and pacification of the Caucasus, the thousand-year struggle between Slavs and Turks—between agriculturalists and nomads—was ended. The Turks ceased to be an external enemy, but there arose the problem of their integration into the empire.

The evolution of Russian-Tatar relations was further complicated by the growing Slavophil mood of governing circles. Russia's role as defender of Orthodoxy and the Slavs' part in the wars of 1854–1855 and 1877–1878 against Turkey could not but have an adverse effect upon the state's attitude toward its Moslem subjects. The slogan

"Orthodoxy and Nationality" (*Pravoslavie i narodnost'*), which became a byword for the tsarist government's program in the 1830's,
reflected the empire's new Russian-Slavophil national ideology. But
simultaneously with the growth of nationalism in Europe and Russia,
a national consciousness was also beginning to develop among the
Tatars. The construction of railroads and improved maritime communications facilitated contact both among the various Turkic peoples of Russia and between them and Ottoman Turkey. The latter,
headed by a sultan-caliph and possessing the holy places of Mecca
and Medina, understandably enjoyed great prestige among the Moslem peoples of Russia.

PRO-ISLAMIC AGITATION

The Crimean war furnished the first incentive for a serious sharpening of relations between the Tatars and the tsarist government. At
the beginning of hostilities in 1854, K. K. Grot, governor of the
province of Samara, wrote that "Tatars, having heard of the rising
disagreement between Russia and the Ottoman Empire and that
Christians are suffering persecution in Turkey, have taken it into
their heads that the Russian government behaves likewise toward the
followers of Islam." Rumors of the success of the Turkish army began
to circulate in the Volga region and talk arose to the effect that mullahs should pray in the mosques for the triumph of Turkish Moslems.[9]
Under such influence, Tatars began to protest against serving in the
Russian army and hundreds of Tatar recruits deserted.[10] At the close
of the Crimean War, in 1856, about 140,000 Crimean Tatars—over
half the entire number living in the peninsula—left for Turkey, and
the fever of emigration to the Ottoman Empire began to spread to
the Volga Tatars.[11] This growth of attraction toward Constantinople
was the first germ of Pan-Islamism and Pan-Turkism among the
Tatars of Russia.

Another manifestation of a growing feeling of religious and ethnic
unity among the Tatars was the mass defection of newly converted
Tatars back to Islam, as well as the success of Moslem propaganda
among other non-Russian peoples of the Volga region. The conversion to Islam of many Chuvash and Finno-Ugric groups of the Volga
and Urals, and Tatar defections, were regarded by Russian authorities
as a Tatar cultural victory. It would not be proper, however, to over-
emphasize the growth of Tatar–Moslem cultural influence in the

Volga region in the nineteenth century, because Orthodoxy later proved to have sent out deep roots among the old Tatar converts and other tribes of the Volga. (This is witnessed by the fact that after the proclamation of religious freedom in 1905, less than one-quarter of the converted Tatars returned to Islam, and after the turn of the century there was no further conversion to Islam among the Chuvash. Even in 1926, during the period when the Orthodox Church endured persecution by the Soviet regime, more than 100,000 Tatars described themselves as converts to Orthodoxy.) Nevertheless, the government always feared Turkization and Islamization of the non-Moslem minority groups of the Volga region, and when the Tatars' intense cultural activity and propaganda for Islam led to new cases of defection in 1860–1866, the tsarist administration took counteractive measures. Defections to Islam frightened Russian authorities, but counteraction, in turn, angered the Tatars. After the war of 1877-1878 it was rumored that all Tatars were to be forcefully converted to Orthodoxy, and this resulted in a number of riots and demonstrations in Kazan, Samara, and Viatka. Several Tatars were convicted for their participation in these disturbances and were deported to Siberia, and the Russian authorities accused the Tatar intelligentsia of not having taken measures to stop the spread of unfounded rumor or to check the agitators.[12]

Despite the fact that the administration began to have misgivings about the Tatars and the desirability of Moslem schools, it undertook no measures to strengthen Russian cultural influence among the non-Russian peoples of eastern Russia. Missionary activity had been suspended after the reign of Catherine II, and attempts to draw Turkic and Finno-Ugric children into Russian schools were unsuccessful. Hostile to Russian culture and ignorant of the Russian language, they did not enroll in Russian schools, and without schools they did not learn the language.

ILMINSKY'S EDUCATIONAL PROGRAM

In the 1860's, a Russian educator, N. I. Ilminsky, a professor in the Kazan Orthodox theological seminary, began to develop a new type of educational institution for non-Russian natives. Ilminsky logically considered that the Russian government should attempt to combat the exclusive impact of the Moslem schools and Islamic culture on the Tatars—an influence which led directly to their isolation and estrangement from the Russian state. Since the purely Russian school was unpopular with the Tatar population because of the latter's ignorance of the Russian language, Ilminsky elaborated a new curriculum for a "Russian-Tatar" school which would be partially conducted in the native language. In the lower classes Tatar students would study their own language and "elements of Russian civilization in translation." In the upper classes Russian language would be introduced.[13] Ilminsky firmly believed that "primary education [in Russian schools] of the non-Russian populations in their native tongues is the most promising path to the future spread of the Russian language and Russian ways." Ilminsky even invented a special Tatar alphabet, based not on Arabic but on Russian letters. Considerably easier than Arabic, "Ilminsky's alphabet" met with success among his pupils. The first such Russian-Tatar school was opened, with Tatar teachers, in 1863 in Kazan.

The Russian administration was very skeptical toward Ilminsky's experiment at the beginning. Conservatives accused him of supporting the nationalistic aspirations of non-Russian peoples, of creating a separatist movement and undermining Russian culture. But K. Pobedonostsev, the supervisor of the Holy Synod, lent Ilminsky his support and, with the help of the Orthodox Church, by the end of the nineteenth century more than a hundred such schools were created for Tatars, as well as for other Volga minority peoples—especially the Chuvash, Maris, and Votiaks.[14] Ilminsky's schools proved to be very successful, and were highly instrumental in the formation of the first intellectuals among the Chuvash, Christianized Tatars, Maris, and other non-Russian populations of the eastern provinces. Pedagogically, they were considerably superior to the Moslem schools, in which education was conducted either in Persian or Arabic and where nothing beyond the Koran was learned.[15]

The practicability of Ilminsky's Russian-native schools in facilitating the spread of Russian language and culture among the non-Russian populations of the empire was later proved by the Soviet government's adoption of the very principles of his system. The Soviets introduced in their schools for non-Russians both the basic subjects of Ilminsky's curriculum and his alphabet.

The Tatar clergy and intelligentsia, however, met Ilminsky's project with unconcealed hostility, seeing in it a powerful tool for Russification. To their minds, the spread of such schools would endanger

the Moslem clergy's ascendancy over the Tatar population. Fortu-
nately for the Tatar clergy, the Russian government did not open
enough new Russian-Tatar schools of this type to compete with the
Moslem madrasas which were in every Tatar village.

GASPRINSKY AND THE OTTOMAN REVIVAL

Tatar educational progress and the growth of national feeling became especially significant when a Russian-educated Crimean Tatar,
Ismail bey Gasprinsky, became their main espouser. The most outstanding figure in the history of Russian Turks in the nineteenth
century, Gasprinsky (1851–1914) received his education in Bakhchisarai (the Crimea) and Moscow, where he met the well-known Russian journalist and publisher of *Moskovskie Vedomosti*, M. N. Katkov. Apparently it was through Katkov that Gasprinsky was introduced to the teachings of the Slavophils and Pan-Slavists, which were
reflected in his own national ideology.[16] After his return to Bakhchisarai, Gasprinsky became familiar with the writings of Chernyshevsky, Pisarev, Belinsky, Herzen, and other liberal Russian thinkers,
whose works he found, paradoxically enough, in the library of the
local chief of police.[17] In 1870, during the Greek uprising against
Turkish authority in Crete, Gasprinsky was quick to demonstrate his
pro-Turkish sympathies by volunteering to join the Ottoman army
to assist in suppressing the rebellion (he was not accepted, however).
A later stay in Constantinople and then in Paris left a lasting mark on
Gasprinsky's future activity, which was filled with the spirit of liberal
nationalism.

Besides Pan-Slavism and impressions gained in France, two intellectual currents in contemporary Turkey had deep influence on
Gasprinsky. The first was the Young Ottoman movement, initiated by the writers and journalists Kemal Pasha (Namik Kemal),
Shinasi Efendi, and Ziia Pasha. This movement arose during the
period of administrative and educational reform in the Ottoman Empire, the so-called Tanzimat (1840–1880). These young Ottoman
intellectuals were the guiding lights of Turkey's revolutionary cultural and literary Europeanization which started after 1859. As
E. J. W. Gibb, the distinguished historian of Turkish literature, has
pointed out, Ottoman culture "was, so to speak, born and reared in
Persia." After 1859 Turkish writers broke with the Persian tradition,
switching in literature from the poetic heritage of Firdousi, Jami, and
Fuzuli to the prose of Hugo, Balzac, Flaubert, and Dumas. Gibb has

written, "In science the new learning transported Turkey from the Middle Ages to the present day; in politics it created the Young Turkey party." [18]

The second ideological current which influenced young intellectuals in Constantinople in the period 1860-1870, and which became a source of inspiration for Ismail bey Gasprinsky, was Pan-Islamism, a product of the Afghan religious thinker and reformer, Jemal al Din Afghani (1839–1897). Jemal al Din preached the need to purify the Moslem faith and its religious practices from superstition and vulgar popular beliefs, and to raise intellectual and educational standards. On the political level, he sought to liberate Islamic lands from Christian European domination, to remove interdenominational barriers in Islamic society, and to unify all Moslems politically in one strong state or federation.[19] Such unification—or Pan-Islamism—became very popular among Moslem youths in the latter part of the nineteenth century and was part of the political philosophy of the dread sultan, Abdul Hamid (1876–1907). As sultan-caliph, Abdul Hamid sponsored Pan-Islamic propaganda in the Ottoman Empire in the hope that Moslem unification would raise him to the position of leader of all Moslems.

TARJUMAN

Returning to the Crimea, Gasprinsky took up pedagogical activity and, after 1881, initiated propaganda for the unification of Russian Moslems, following the recommendations of Jemal al Din. On April 10, 1883, there appeared the first issue of his newspaper, *Tarjuman* (The Interpreter), named after Shenasi Efendi's organ, *Tarjuman Ahval*. Gasprinsky's journal helped shape the minds of Russian Turks for almost a quarter of a century. But pedagogical and journalistic activity did not exhaust Gasprinsky's energies and interests. He was first and foremost a national and social leader, and he continually visited the various Moslem provinces of Russia, trying, through personal contacts as well as the printed word, to inspire his coreligionists to unite. In the period 1880–1890 Gasprinsky was the most popular and influential Turkic leader in Russia, and his words were listened to with attention even abroad.

MOSLEM UNITY

Gasprinsky placed three principles of "unity" at the basis of his work and thought: unity of language, unity of mind, and unity of action.[20] By unity he meant the unity of all Russian Moslems, but since the majority of Russia's Moslems were Turkic peoples, Gasprinsky's appeal for their religious unification amounted to an appeal for the national rallying of Russian Turks. Thus, though perhaps unconsciously at the beginning, Gasprinsky and his followers laid the foundation for Turkic nationalism in Russia. Gasprinsky's second principle, that of unity of language, further strengthened this national appeal because, quite understandably, the common language for Russian Moslems could only be a Turkic tongue. Theoretically, however, Gasprinsky was envisioning the unity of the Moslem world in general, regardless of national borders and Moslem dispersion. He urged a departure from the psychology of the Middle Ages which prevailed among them and resulted in their cultural segregation, and sought to include them in modern European culture.[21] He was no less categorical on the points of liberating Moslem women and introducing certain reforms in the Moslem way of life. At the same time, however, his platform was not without provisions supporting Moslem culture. While he insisted on the need to study the Turkish language in Moslem schools, he continued to recognize the need to study Arabic as the language of Mohammed and of Islamic culture. But he would replace the old Persian textbooks of Arabic grammar by modern Turkish ones imported from Constantinople.

In his struggle for Moslem cultural unity, Gasprinsky recommended introducing Ottoman Turkish as a common literary language in the Moslem schools and press of Russia. In his newspaper, *Tarjuman*, Gasprinsky himself used neither medieval Chagatai, which Russian Turks had used for centuries as their written language, nor the spoken Volga Tatar tongue first used in literature by Nasyri. He used, rather, the modernized literary language of Ottoman Turkey, which had been purged of Persian and Arabic words by the Young Ottomans.[22] To enforce the spread of this language by introducing it in all Russia's Turkic schools was not an easy task, because the Ottoman Turkish language was just as incomprehensible to the majority of Russia's Turkic peoples as was Chagatai. The Crimean Tatars understood it, in view of their nearness to Turkey, while the Tatars of the Crimea's southern shores spoke a tongue very similar to it; and the Azerbaijanis, belonging to the same linguistic group as the Ottoman Turks, could understand the language of Gasprinsky's *Tarjuman* with no great difficulty. But to the ordinary reader in the

Volga region, the Kazakh steppe or Central Asia, Ottoman Turkish could not be understood without study. Therefore, despite all of Gasprinsky's efforts and those of the Tatar intelligentsia, the attempt to create one common Turkic literary language understandable to all Turks was unsuccessful. Linguistic differentiation had progressed too far among the Turkic peoples to permit them to find a common language suitable for literature a thousand years after their territorial and linguistic unity had been disrupted.

GASPRINSKY AND RUSSIA

It seems incredible that, preoccupied with the idea of Turkic religious, cultural, and linguistic unity, Gasprinsky refrained from any clearly national-political agitation. In urging Russian Turks to unite on the basis of culture and religion, he apparently had in mind the strengthening of the entire Moslem world. He understood, however, that neither the regime of imperial Russia nor that of Ottoman Turkey in the nineteenth century was inclined to tolerate any open political activity directed at weakening these supranational states. In serving the cause of Moslem cultural unity, Gasprinsky was very careful in his attitude toward the Russian state. He regarded the Russian and Ottoman empires as states which had evolved as the result of unavoidable historical processes, and he even came forward as an apologist for their continued existence. In his pamphlet, "Russian-Eastern Agreement," published in 1896, he wrote, "Moslems and Russians can plow, sow, raise cattle, trade and make their livings together, or side-by-side." In 1905 he. added, "Russians and Turks are bound together in a huge common plain extending from the foothills of the Altais and Pamirs to the swamps of the Baltic Sea. . . . Such it was in the past, and in the future these peoples will understand that they must walk hand in hand in order to find the way of life they both need." [23] He even thought that history would lead all Turkic peoples to coexistence with Russia in one state organism: "In moments of historical necessity, the principalities of Riazan [sic], Kazan, Astrakhan, Siberia, Crimea and even the khanates of the Transcaucasus became a part of Russia, and in recent times the Russian Empire has incorporated some khanates of Central Asia, where we believe that Russia has not yet attained its natural historical boundaries; but we think that sooner or later Russian borders will include within them all Tatar peoples. . . . In the future, perhaps, Russia will become one of the most important Moslem states, which, I suppose, will in no way diminish her importance as a great Christian power." [24]

Gasprinsky considered Russia's most urgent political task to be the creation of friendly relations between herself and her Moslem neighbors, Persia and Turkey, and even suggested an alliance with them. "Let us imagine that Russia entered into friendly relations with Turkey and Persia. . . . The securing of Russia's southern border . . . by means of a lasting agreement with the adjacent Moslem kingdoms would certainly bolster Russian power in the West and Far East. . . . Backed by Turkey and Persia, Russia would become kindred to the entire Moslem East and would certainly stand at the head of Moslem nations and their civilization, which England is attempting so persistently to do." [25]

While allowing for historical reality and the situation of Turks in Russia, Gasprinsky sought to preserve both Moslem faith and Turkic identity there. He pointed out that the rapprochement of Turks and Russians—or, as he expressed it, the Turks' "moral Russification"— could best be accomplished through the heightening of the Tatars' intellectual level, which itself could be realized only through the Russian government's recognition of the Tatar language in education.

THE NEW METHOD—"USUL JADID"

In Gasprinsky's eyes, education was the main weapon for the preservation of Moslem society, particularly in the case of the Tatars, and for national rebirth and Turkic-Moslem unification. Consequently, his main efforts were directed toward education and the creation of new reformed schools. In his native Bakhchisarai, former capital of the Crimean khanate—which, thanks to the publication there of *Tarjuman*, had once again become an important Tatar cultural center —Gasprinsky founded a reformed school which subsequently served as an example for other "new-method" schools.[26] "New method" (*Usul jadid*) became the slogan of progressive Tatar reformers, and they themselves began to be called "Jadids," that is, "innovators." In the new type of school, students were taught Arabic phonetically rather than by the alphabetical names of the letters, and this method of instruction quickly spread not only among the Turks of Russia, but beyond the borders to China, Persia, and India. Gasprinsky left the study of the Koran and fundamentals of Moslem law in the curriculum of these Moslem schools, but he introduced also such "worldly" subjects as mathematics, history, and geography.

Unnoticed by even Gasprinsky himself, however, the new-method school also bore with it, besides a new principle of education, secularization—the school's partial alienation from Islamic tradition, the substitution of Turkic for Arabic, and a departure from the old conservative culture. This became a bone of contention between the Jadids and their opponents, the traditionalist "Kadimists," supporters of *Usul kadim* (the old method). But the new method spread very quickly, and by 1914 some 5,000 Tatar and other Moslem schools had adopted it. The Moslem schools of Central Asia, some in the Caucasus, and those supported by conservatives in the Volga-Ural region, however, rejected the Jadids' pedagogical system, regarding the reformers as heretics and apostates. Nevertheless, as a result of the development of the Tatar schools, there were 25,000 of them by 1912, and the rate of literacy among the Tatars before the revolution was only slightly less than among the Russians.[27] Conditions in Tatar higher schools, however, were worse. Elements of contemporary higher education were introduced into the programs of only a few madrasas, such as the Alieh madrasa founded in Ufa in 1906, the Husseinieh madrasa in Orenburg, and the Muhammedieh madrasa in Kazan.[28]

While the Tatar bourgeoisie, which had long been the leading group in Tatar society, initially regarded Gasprinsky's activity with some distrust, it later gave him its full support. The sharpening of relations with the Russian authorities lent impetus to the growth of national consciousness in the Tatar bourgeoisie, and the Tatar merchants saw advantages in the new school programs and contributed to the financing of new maktabs and madrasas as well as to the education of teachers and the printing of textbooks.

TATAR CULTURAL EVOLUTION

Despite the rapid success of these Tatar schools during the last half-century of the tsarist Russian regime, however, the Moslem educational system was not yet fully developed, and the level of education available in the madrasas was no higher than that of the middle classes of the gymnasium (the Russian high school). It is significant that the majority of progressive Tatar nationalists in the twentieth century did not come from Tatar schools, but from Russian-Tatar teachers' colleges in Kazan, from Russian gymnasiums and universities, or from schools in Constantinople or France.[29]

Toward the beginning of the twentieth century quite a sizable

Tatar intelligentsia was beginning to form, differing little from its Russian counterpart in composition. The Tatar city of Kazan, because of its numerous educational institutions, publishing houses, and intensive intellectual life, became one of the four cultural capitals of the Moslem world.[30] The majority of Tatars had been and continued to be quite devout, but in their political and social thinking they now came under the influence of Moscow, Petersburg, Constantinople, and, to some extent, Paris, rather than of Bukhara and traditional Moslem thought. Tatar political groupings also reflected to a significant degree their correspondents in Russian society.

Changes in Tatar daily life were to be found as well. The Tatar woman, in educated society, was relatively emancipated; the home of a Tatar nobleman, landlord, intellectual, or businessman differed little from a Russian's; and a Tatar's external appearance, his clothes, manners, and way of life were in no way Asian. It was symptomatic that *Fiuzat*, the leading Azerbaijani review of 1905–1907, chose as its motto: "Islamic faith, French thought, European appearance." [31] In 1906 when Yusuf Akchurin explained the program of the Moslem Constitutional Democrats (Kadets) to the Russian Kadet congress, he did so in brilliant French.[32] Thus, in less than half a century, the Tatar upper class experienced a rapid cultural evolution and became Europeanized to a significant extent.

The situation of the lower Tatar social classes, however, was very different, especially in the case of the rural population, which, in the Kazan province in 1897, for example, still accounted for 95 per cent of all the Tatars.[33] Concentrated in their villages, most of the Tatar peasantry maintained very little contact with Russians and lived in a world still strictly regulated by the laws and rules of the Koran and the spiritual guidance of the Moslem clergy. While the Tatar merchants had prospered in trade with the eastern regions and foreign lands, Tatar peasants remained in the state of isolation which Ilminsky had sought to break through.[34] Only in the last decades before the revolution, under the impact of the developing Russian economy, did the situation begin to change, and many Tatars from the Kazan, Ufa, and Orenburg regions began to migrate toward the larger cities and industrial regions, especially Moscow and the Donets Basin. In the remote countryside, however, the way of life in the Tatar village did not begin to change until after the abortive revolution of 1905, which opened a new chapter in the situation of Russia's Turkic peoples.

CHAPTER IV

The National Movement: Parties and Programs in 1905

The first clear note of a national movement among Russia's Turks was not sounded until 1905. The efforts of Tatar liberal innovators until then had been mainly of a cultural and religious nature and had aimed merely at establishing contact among the various Moslem groups in Russia, reforming education, and modernizing Tatar life. Neither Ismail bey Gasprinsky nor his supporters had displayed any political motives in the 1880's and 1890's, and no clearly nationalistic goals were discernible in their activity. They were realistic enough not to endanger their initial success for the sake of the doubtful benefits resulting from agitation, a move which would have led them into conflict with the Russian administration. Once, in 1905, in response to an enthusiastic young Tatar liberal who, under the influence of socialist pamphlets, dreamed of class struggle and internal conflicts within Tatar society, Gasprinsky philosophically remarked, "You are not experienced, my son, and therefore you display too much enthusiasm for words. . . . A people without culture cannot have any industry. And without industry there are not any internal conflicts. Our task of today consists in building up our culture." [1]

The young Tatar and Azerbaijani generation which entered the realm of social action in the mid-1890's, however, was less patient, and from its ranks emerged the new leaders of a clearly Turkic national movement. The political views of the majority of them had taken final form in Constantinople or Paris, where they had gone to complete their education. One of the first of them to initiate political agitation among the Turks of Russia was Reshid Ibragimov, a former *kazi* (judge) in the Moslem Ecclesiastic Administration in Ufa. Ibragimov emigrated to Turkey and in 1895 published there *Chulpan Ildizi* (Northern Star), the first anti-Russian pamphlet ever to issue from the pen of a Tatar journalist. In his brochure Ibragimov reiterated the old, unfounded rumor that the Russian government planned to force the Tatars to convert to Christianity, and he called upon Tatars and the Moslem world to resist this attempt. This brochure was circulated clandestinely among the Moslem population of the Volga and Ural regions and even created some disturbances. In 1904 the Constantinople police deported Ibragimov back to Russia, and in Petersburg he began publishing a Tatar periodical, "The Mirror," in which he preached the union of all the Moslems of Russia.[2]

BIRTH OF TURKISM

In that same year in the newspaper *Türk*, published in Cairo by a well-known Turkish journalist, Ali Kemal, an article appeared which had significant repercussions on the further development of both Turkic and Turkish nationalism. The article was entitled "Uç tarzi siiaset" (Three Political Ways), and its author was a young Tatar journalist, Yusuf Akchurin, the son of a wealthy industrialist. Akchurin had studied humanities and law at the University of Paris and had been strongly impressed by the French national ideologists Maurice Barrés and Ernest Renan as well as by German racial theories. In his article Akchurin presented an original doctrine of Turkic nationalism. He analyzed the possible paths of Turkic political ideology in the light of the previous evolution of the Ottoman Empire, and categorically rejected the political theories upon which both Turkish liberals and conservatives based their programs. Akchurin considered that the Pan-Islamic ideas of Jamal al Din and Gasprinsky had become outlived in this era of secularization of Moslem lands. He regarded as equally unsound the theory of Ottomanism proclaimed by the Young Turks, which aimed not at reconstructing the Ottoman Empire on a religious or national basis but rather at transforming it into a multinational state patterned after Austro-Hungary. According to the Young Turks' theories, all Ottoman subjects were to be equal citizens of the Turkish empire, which they promised to reconstruct on a liberal basis after their seizure of power, abolishing all religious or racial discrimination.[3] Akchurin believed that the growth of nationalistic forces among the various Moslem and Christian groups of Ottoman Turkey, however, would jeopardize, if not actually negate, any attempt at reorganizing the empire. Condemning these theories, Akchurin suggested a "third way"—the idea of the political unification of the Turkic peoples of both the Ottoman and the Russian empires, as well as of the Turkic minority groups in other countries. This new doctrine, which came to be called "Turkism," or "Pan-Turkism," after the popular German theories of Pan-Germanism, appeared dangerous or unrealistic to many. Akchurin himself was aware that attempts to carry it out would meet the most decisive opposition of Russia, since its realization would mean Russia's actual dismemberment and loss of vast territories in the Volga, Urals, and Caucasus, as well as the entire Kazakh steppe and Central Asia. He hoped, however, that Russia's resistance could be overcome by a coalition of powers hostile to the tsarist empire.[4] This first statement of the aims of a common Turkic national movement soon became the gospel of Pan-Turkism, and it was to have a deep and lasting influence on the evolution of Turkic thought.

Other Turkic émigré journalists from Russia also collaborated at this time with French and Turkish publications expounding the unification of all Turkic and Moslem peoples, and in their articles they accused the Russian government of limiting the rights of its Moslem subjects. Among these should be mentioned two Azerbaijani politicians, Ahmed bey Agaev (Ahmed bey Aga-Oglu) and Hussein Zadeh (see Chapter VII). Hussein Zadeh was particularly active in Young Turk political circles, and at the third congress of their party, "Union and Progress," became a member of its central committee.[5]

EARLY POLITICAL ACTION

The era of "political spring" proclaimed by the Russian Minister of the Interior, Prince D. P. Sviatopolk-Mirsky, and the revolutionary activities of 1905 caused Turkic émigrés abroad to return to Russia and initiate political agitation among their Tatar and Azerbaijani compatriots. Reshid Ibragimov, who had been deported to Russia in 1904 and was well acquainted with Russian political life, formed in Petersburg a Moslem political organization with a Tatar group at the core. He had already established contacts with various Russian political groups, and on September 20, 1904, he conferred with the head of the zemstvo liberal movement, M. A. Stakhovich, who responded sympathetically to Ibragimov's offer to collaborate.[6] This was only an exploratory effort, but it determined the later orientation of the Tatar Jadids, who became closely associated with the Russian liberal movement subsequently organized by P. N. Miliukov into the

Constitutional Democratic Party, or the Kadets. After deciding to co-ordinate the future political endeavors of Tatar and Russian bourgeois liberals, Ibragimov and Akchurin, who had now also returned to Russia, began to visit Russia's Moslem centers, where they formed germinal groups of the future all-Russian Moslem movement. Ahmed bey Husseinov, the wealthiest of Tatar millionaires and a well-known Maecenas, lent his financial support to the Tatar cause. In Azerbaijan the movement was led by a prominent lawyer, Ali Mardan bey Top-chibashev, a Baku oil industrialist, Tagiev, and the journalists Agaev and Hussein Zadeh, who also returned from Constantinople and Paris to Russia. Among the Bashkirs, the landowner, K. M. B. Tevkelev, and the former Imperial Guard officer, Sh. Syrtlanov, presided over the local branch of the future Moslem Union, and in Crimea the leaders were Gasprinsky and Mustafa Davidovich. The industrialists Veli bey Yavushev and Abdulla Rakhmankulov organized a group in Troitsk, while the Tatars in Orenburg were rallied by the lawyer, Seid Girey Alkin, the writer, Fatyh Karimov, and Professor A. Apanaev. Two outstanding Tatar educators, the brothers Abdulla and Gainulla Bobinsky, lent their support to the movement in the Viatka province.

In early March 1905, more than eighty Tatar industrialists, lawyers, religious and social leaders, educators, and tradesmen met at a pre-liminary meeting in Kazan.[7] (Conservative members of the Moslem Ecclesiastic Administration preferred to refrain from participating in this initial manifestation of Tatar liberal and national forces.) The group decided to continue its efforts to unite Russian Moslems and sent a delegation to Petersburg to petition Count S. Y. Witte, Russian Prime Minister, for the removal of all legal limitations to which Rus-sian Moslems were still subjected and for permission to convene an official congress. In the capital, however, the delegation encountered the opposition of two sworn enemies of the liberal movement, Mufti Yar Sultanov, head of the Ecclesiastic Administration in Ufa, and S. Bayazidov, head mullah in Petersburg. These two did their best to defeat the delegation's purpose, and under their influence the Min-ister of the Interior refused permission to convene the Moslem con-gress. On April 8, 1905, after deliberation with other Moslems in the capital, however, it was decided to hold an All-Russian Moslem Con-gress in Nizhni Novgorod in August, during its fair, despite the government's refusal.[8]

THE FIRST MOSLEM CONGRESS

During this first congress, the Tatars' caution was evident from the very beginning. The fair at Nizhni Novgorod had been selected as the least noticeable occasion for Moslems to gather. At first the participants met in the Hotel Germania, but when the local governor, who was well informed as to this "unofficial" congress, prohibited the use of the hotel premises for such a purpose, they transferred to the pleasure ship *G. Struve*, where the congress took place under the guise of a picnic. The congress' leaders, wishing to avoid compromise by the presence of the socialists, had not informed the latter of the meeting's new location. Led by Ayaz Iskhakov, Fuad Tuktarov, and A. Davletchin, however, the socialists illustrated their political dynamism by catching up with the ship by motorboat.[9] Altogether, more than one hundred and fifty Tatar and Azerbaijani leaders participated in the congress, which was presided over by representatives of the younger generation. Ali Mardan bey Topchibashev, Ibragimov, and Yusuf Akchurin were elected president and vice-presidents of the meetings.

The congress confirmed its participants' decision to organize an all-Russian Moslem union and made the following resolutions:

(1) Unification of Moslem citizens of Russia for the purpose of carrying out certain political, economic, and social reforms.

(2) Legal equality of the Moslem and Russian populations.

(3) Establishment of a constitutional monarchy based on pro-portionate representation of nationalities.

(4) Freedom of press, convention, religion, etc.

(5) Inviolability of personal property. Peasants with little or no landholdings should be given land from the state's and crown's holdings. Expropriation of landed proprietors' holdings would be permissible only if due recompense were paid.[10]

THE SECOND CONGRESS AND COLLABORATION WITH THE KADETS

A second, still not officially authorized, congress was held in Petersburg January 13–23, 1906, and it created the official Union of Russian Moslems (*Russiia musulmanlarin ittifaki*, or *Ittifak*, as it came to be called). Despite its "all-Russian" name, Ittifak was rather an association of the Turkic national leaders of Russia than a real union of various Turkic national groups or societies. The founders and mem-

bers of Ittifak were not acting in the capacity of representatives from
any organizations or regions, but merely as influential personalities.
Furthermore, while the Volga and Ural Tatars, Azerbaijanis, and
Crimeans were widely represented in Ittifak, forming the majority,
there were only a few representatives from the Kazakh steppe, Siberia,
and the northern Caucasus, and none from Central Asia. The Second
Congress' decision to organize sixteen regional centers was never
carried out, especially in Asiatic Russia. Only the Volga Tatars,
Azerbaijanis, and Crimeans maintained close ties with Ittifak subsequently. Conservative Tatars took no part in it, while socialist
groups soon broke off all contact with Ittifak's bourgeois liberals. In
its social and economic program Ittifak was close to the Russian
Kadets, which is not surprising in view of the similar social composition of these two parties. Nearly all of Ittifak's leaders belonged to
the Tatar or Bashkir bourgeoisie, intelligentsia, nobility, or landowner class.

The Second Congress also resolved to cooperate with the Russian
Kadets in elections to the first Russian parliament (Duma) and to
present with them common lists of candidates.[11] On the upper level,
Ittifak's leaders even joined the central executive organ of the Kadet
Party. At the Kadet convention, which took place in Petersburg on
the eve of the Second Moslem Congress, Yusuf Akchurin led a
Moslem delegation and addressed the Kadets at length in French.
Since Ittifak did not claim to be a Turkic national party, but merely
a union for the defense of the cultural rights of Russian Moslems, its
program, as well as Akchurin's speech, stressed primarily Moslem
educational and religious problems. "Just as the agrarian question is
of basic importance for the peasant, so for Moslems the most important is their religion," Akchurin proclaimed.[12] Despite their previous
Pan-Turkic and anti-Russian activities, both Akchurin and Ibragimov
were elected to the central committee of the Kadet Party, in which
they represented Moslem minority interests. Furthermore, in order to
cement the new alliance and meet the Tatars' most essential aspirations,
the Kadets agreed to amend some of the articles of their party's program. The most important of these changes were (1) concession to
the Tatars' demand for full autonomy for the Moslem Ecclesiastic
Administration; (2) recognition that the provisions of the Moslem
canonic and common law (Shariat and Adat) should be taken into
consideration in all subsequent revisions of Russian civil or penal
codes; and (3) the use in education of the language of the local pop-

ulation in those regions populated by non-Russian national groups.[13]

The leaders of Ittifak, eager to follow up their initial success and to avoid compromising future possibilities for legal political action, now renounced in their official declarations all extremist and nationalistic ideas. Ibragimov, who had so sharply attacked the Russian government in his pamphlet in the 1890's, now stated in his request for permission to convene a third Moslem congress, "We, the Moslems of Russia, being loyal to the Russian autocracy and fearing the spread of ideas of Pan-Islamism, socialism, and anarchism—ideologies disruptive to the life of the people and repugnant to the doctrine of Islam—have decided to combat these ideological trends in a legal way. We will serve the White tsar* and his throne just as faithfully as did our fathers and forefathers." [14] In this request Ibragimov also attacked clerical fanaticism, and he stressed that Ittifak's aim was "to free the maktabs and madrasas from the hands of the mullahs and transfer these schools into the hands of the people"—in other words, to emancipate the communities from the influence of the conservative Moslem clergy and its Mufti in Ufa.

Ittifak's union with the Russian Kadets, skillful but moderate propaganda, Tatar solidarity, and the support of the more liberal clergy[15] resulted in a significant victory during the elections to the First Duma, where twenty-five Moslem deputies sat with the Kadet caucus.[16] Unfortunately, the First Duma was so short-lived that the Moslem deputies did not have sufficient opportunity to demonstrate their presence. Only Sh. Syrtlanov, representing the Ufa province, addressed the Duma and insisted on complete legal equality for Moslems.[17] Later, when deputies met in the Finnish city of Vyborg to protest the dissolution of the First Duma, Moslems again manifested their caution. Only six of them participated in the Vyborg consultations, and they were summoned by Syrtlanov to return to Petersburg and to stop urging the population not to pay taxes in protest against the limitation of constitutional liberties.[18]

RUSSIAN TURKS IN THE REVOLUTION OF 1905–1907

The revolution of 1905–1907 did not result in any significant outburst among the Turkic population of the Russian Empire. In Central

---

* The term "White tsar," widely used by the Moslems of the Middle East to designate the emperor of Russia, originated not from a racial characteristic but from the white uniforms of Russian troops in Central Asia and the Caucasus in the second part of the nineteenth century.

Asia, Kazakhstan, and most of the Ural-Volga region, Moslems remained calm and participated only in occasional demonstrations against abuses by the local administration. The voluminous documents and materials published by the Soviet Academy of Sciences on the occasion of the fiftieth anniversary of the revolution of 1905 (*Revoliutsiia 1905–1907 godov*) prove participation in revolutionary events by nearly all the national groups of the empire except the Turks. Only in Azerbaijan were local Moslems involved with Armenians and Russians in strikes and riots, but even in Transcaucasia Moslems displayed far less revolutionary ardor than Russians, Armenians, or Georgians. In European Russia some Tatar workers in the city of Kazan and in the iron- and gold-mining regions of the Urals took part in strikes and demonstrations. In the long lists of agitators, terrorists, and arrested revolutionaries published in the above-mentioned series, however, only two or three Tatar names are to be found.[19] The Tatar, Azerbaijani, Kazakh, and Uzbek press during these years appealed to Moslems to preserve calm, support the authorities, and abstain from participation in revolutionary activities. The Uzbek liberal, Behbudi, writing in the newspaper *Tujor* (The Merchant), recommended, instead of revolting, sending delegates from the "10,000,000 Central Asian Moslems to the benevolent tsar; we can be sure that he will not send them back with empty hands." The Tashkent paper *Khurshid* (The Sun) pointed out that "the ideas of the Social Democrats are harmful illusions and cooperation with them is inadmissible to Moslems." *Hurshid* further urged cooperation with the Kadets. The Azerbaijani newspaper *Haiat*, in which notable nationalists participated, considered that "the constitution is less beneficial for Moslems than autocracy, and it is in the interest of Moslems not to combat the monarchy since the probable new order would be inimical to the [Moslem] religion."[20]

THE TATAR PRESS

Among the many Tatar newspapers which were established after 1905, liberal bourgeois and conservative publications were the most popular. The liberals published *Vakyt* (The Time) in Orenburg, which soon became the largest and most influential Tatar paper, *Kazan Muhbiré* (Messenger of the Truth), and several provincial newspapers. Conservatives were represented by *Din ve Megyishet* (Religion and Life), *Nur* (The Ray), a monarchist organ of the

Petersburg Moslem aristocracy, clergy, and military circles, and *Din ve Edel* (Religion and Morals).

In the socialist sector the most important, although short-lived, papers were the organ of the Moslem labor caucus in the Second Duma, *Duma; Ural*, published by Tatar Social Democrats in the Urals; and *Tan* (Dawn), the official publication of Tatar Socialist Revolutionaries.

THE THIRD CONGRESS

Between the convening of the First and Second Duma—August 16–21, 1906—the third and most significant Moslem congress was held, again in Nizhni Novgorod. This congress played an important role in the development and clarification of Turkic national consciousness and was, in effect, the first gathering at which national slogans, badly disguised by the terms "Moslem" and "Islam," were voiced.

The first session of the congress convened on August 16, visibly fraught with tension. Many of the deputies were indignant at Reshid Ibragimov, whom they accused of opportunism for denouncing Pan-Islamism and attacking the Moslem clergy in his letter to the Minister of the Interior. Such Russian Moslem leaders as the father of the Moslem movement in Russia, Ismail Gasprinsky, the well-known Baku lawyer and editor of *Kaspii*, Ali Mardan bey Topchibashev, and the Duma deputy and editor of *Kazan Muhbiré*, Seid Girey Alkin, even considered abstaining from the work of the congress, or withdrawing from it if Ibragimov did not offer a satisfactory explanation and apology.[21]

Under fire from various quarters, Ibragimov decided to explain himself in his inaugural speech. He proclaimed that Moslem unity should not be limited only to the adherents of Islam in Russia, but that his and the congress' goal should be the unification of all the followers of Mohammed throughout the world. "The fraternity of the peoples of Islam," said Ibragimov, "is not just an abstract theory, but a reality." [22] With a certain pride he pointed out that his initial aim—a meeting of delegates of all the Moslem peoples of Russia—had been successful, since the Third Congress had been authorized by the Russian government and could now proceed with its deliberations officially. After these preliminary remarks, Ibragimov declared the defense of the Moslem faith to be the main duty of believers, and that the congress should do its best to protect the faith and the clergy from encroachment by Christian missionaries, who, he alleged, with the support of the government, promoted Christianity among the Moslems and disturbed the peaceful life of Moslem communities. This was Ibragimov's favorite topic, which he had already expounded in his pamphlet published in 1895. In his address Ibragimov also pointed to the plight of the Moslem clergy, which was responsible not only for the education of its pupils but also for their existence and well-being (in the Moslem schools, the students were usually provided with board and quarters). Completely reversing the attitude toward the clergy that he presented in his letter to the Minister of the Interior, Ibragimov appealed for the communities' wider support of the clergy and pedagogues. He stressed, however, that the communities themselves were often in a precarious financial situation, and that one of the main duties of the congress was to find new means for strengthening and extending the Moslem parochial school system.

Election of the presidium of the congress followed the inaugural address. Topchibashev became chairman. The other members were Gasprinsky, Ibragimov, Duma member Syrtlanov, Galimjan Barudi (Galiev), Abdulla Apanaev, Sh. Koshchegulov (a Kazakh intellectual), Eminjam Ilgamjanov, and Ali Iskander Ashurov. Yusuf Akchurin was appointed first secretary.[23] Then, in the name of the opposition, Gasprinsky expressed his satisfaction with Ibragimov's speech and explanations. The question of Ibragimov's letter was raised once more toward the end of the congress, but he was officially absolved by a regular vote for his tactless and untimely declaration to the Russian Minister.[24] Commissions were set up to organize a new political party (still to be called Ittifak) and to study religious affairs and the school problem. An intensive debate arose around the question of the party's organization and its political plank, since many were opposed to the formation of a united Moslem party. The old hands of the Moslem movement, such as Gasprinsky, considered that the congress should limit its activity to cultural and religious affairs and not be concerned with politics. Ayaz Iskhakov, who was close to the Russian Socialist Revolutionaries, doubted the possibility of building a political party on religious rather than social bases, and expressed apprehension at the difficulties which would be encountered in setting up the framework of a political party heterogeneously composed of elements from such varied groups as the bourgeoisie, the peasantry, and the working class.

The young generation, whose main speaker was Akchurin, as well as many Moslem members of the Duma, particularly Syrtlanov, gave their strongest support to the formation of the party. "Our aim," explained Akchurin, "is to unite the great majority of Russia's Moslems, to create a political party, and to strengthen its action, influence, and authority among the other political parties of the Russian Empire. If we do not do this, the same fate which befell the Moslems of Bulgaria—who, because of internal rivalries, lost their unity and political rights—can befall us likewise. . . . The present political situation of Bulgarian Moslems should be an edifying example for the Moslems of Russia . . . lest we find ourselves in a similar position, we should follow the example of the Poles and the Czechs of Austria, who organized their own national political parties." He categorically rejected the objections of the Tatar Socialist Revolutionaries and their leader, Iskhakov, who regarded the cooperation of various classes in the same political party as something inconceivable. Akchurin considered it both feasible and necessary "to unite Russia's Moslems and to create an effective and influential political party, based on national and religious principles."

The resistance of the older generation crumbled under Akchurin's argumentation, and the party of Moslem Union (Ittifak) finally came into being. Its program consisted of ten parts, subdivided into seventy two articles, and leaned very closely to the Kadets' plank.

Part I (articles 1–2) announced the congress' decision to create a Moslem party with the aim of improving the religious, cultural, social, economic, and political conditions of Russia's Moslems.[25]

Part II (articles 3–16) demanded legal equality for all peoples of Russia, particularly for the Moslems. All legal, social, and cultural discrimination and limitation should be abolished. The Moslems demanded the same access to professional careers and to civil and military service which the Christian subjects of the Russian Empire enjoyed (article 10). The necessity of extending and protecting the liberties granted by the manifestoes of 1905 and 1906 was announced.

Part III (articles 17–24) dealt with constitutional laws and the structure of the imperial administration, already determined by the Kadets' program.

Part IV (articles 25–27) insisted on the complete equality with the Orthodox faith of all other faiths and organized religions.

Part V (articles 28–34) elaborated the details of local self-government. Of particular interest was article 30, which demanded that all local matters, including police and internal security, be turned over entirely to the local, democratically elected organs of the administration. No national territorial autonomy was asked, however, and, as did the Kadets, Ittifak declared the zemstvos—whose rights should be considerably extended—a suitable instrument for satisfying the needs of the local populations.[26]

Part VI (articles 35–45) reiterated the Kadets' demands for the reorganization of justice, abolition of the extraordinary courts and tribunals created by the government in the years 1905–1906, and the strictest separation of the judiciary and executive powers.

Part VII (articles 46–53) was devoted entirely to the reorganization of education. Article 46 pointed out the need for introducing compulsory primary education in the native languages. The following article 47 elaborated the conditions for transferring responsibility for primary education to the local self-government, for setting up education in the communities' main language, and for the use of the "national alphabet" in the schools.[27]

Parts VIII, IX, and X (articles 54–72) dealt with agrarian, economic, and labor problems, attempting to solve them along the general line of the Kadets' political theories. Regarding the agrarian question, the program supported the compulsory sale of landlords' lands to the peasantry. An eight-hour work day, the right to organize labor unions, the introduction of labor inspection and worker-employer courts of conciliation, were the most outstanding features of this part of the program.[28]

The other commissions also prepared their own resolutions and programs on the most vital questions of Moslem life. One of them was dedicated to the general principles of Ittifak policies and to defense of the Moslem faith from encroachment by the Orthodox Russian missionaries and imperial administration. The congress asked the presidium to communicate this resolution by wire to the president of the Imperial Council of Ministers. Only full freedom of conscience and press could protect Moslems and Islam from the attempts to Christianize them and from limitation of their communities' activity. The freedoms of conscience and of the press were proclaimed by an imperial manifesto on October 7, 1905, and were to be enforced. No less important, according to the resolution, was restoration of the activity of the Duma, which had been dissolved shortly before by the government. "Only the convening of the State Duma could furnish a solution of the difficult situation which had resulted." [29]

In purely political questions the congress and the leadership of the new party adhered strongly to the plank and tactics of the Kadets. Of particularly great interest were the resolutions on the school problems, all of which supported the organization of Moslem schools and education of the young generation in the national spirit. The resolution prepared by the commission on education, headed by A. Apanaev, first of all reaffirmed the corresponding articles of the political program, in which the Moslems demanded the introduction of general education for Mohammedans at the expense of the state and local self-government. Then the resolution asked guaranty for the protection of Islamic education from the intervention and influence of the imperial administration. The same resolution recommended the introduction in all Moslem schools of a *single literary Moslem language* (apparently even in the non-Turkic Moslem schools). In the congress' opinion, such a single Moslem literary language could only be Ottoman Turkish. Article 30 of this resolution provided that "particular attention should be paid to the study of the Turkish literary language, in which training is imperative for Moslems in the second and third grades of the secondary schools." It further stated that "study of the Russian language in the primary schools is not necessary, but in the secondary schools it is to be included in the curriculum as a subject of study." [30]

The same resolution appealed to the government for suspension of the regulations on primary schools for the non-Russian population of eastern and southeastern Russia introduced on March 31, 1906, by the Minister of Education, Count Ivan Tolstoy. These would hamper the development of the Moslem educational network and required the teaching of Russian in the parochial grade schools.[31]

Galimjan Barudi, head of Muhammedieh, the most famous Kazan madrasa, and the most respected Moslem theologian and religious leader in Russia (to become Mufti in 1917), presided over the commission for religious affairs. This commission likewise elaborated an extensive resolution which called for the full autonomy of the Moslem Ecclesiastic Administration from the Russian government's supervision and control. All four Muftis—the Tatar Mufti of Orenburg, the Crimean Mufti of Bakhchisarai, and the Sunnite and the Shiite Muftis of Transcaucasia—should no longer be appointed by the government but should be elected by delegates from the Moslem religious communities. Also, a central administration for all Moslems of Russia should be created, headed by Ramsul Ulama, the spiritual head of the all-Russian Islamic community—who would have the right of audience with the tsar (equivalent to the rank of state minister).[32]

Despite the moderateness of the program and resolutions in the political sphere, all of them bore witness to the fact that the Moslems of Russia, led by the Tatars, strove for full cultural and religious autonomy from the imperial administration and sought to escape Russian cultural influence. Furthermore, since the main literary language of this planned autonomous Moslem community was to be Ottoman Turkish, it seemed evident that this autonomy would inevitably gravitate toward a strong cultural, and eventually political, rapprochement with Turkey, and completely avert the Tatars' and other Moslems' intellectual and psychological integration with Russians.

One declaration by the congress concerned the Armenian-Azerbaijani carnage in the Caucasus, demanding that measures be taken to avoid its repetition; and another hailed the promulgation of a constitution in Persia.[33]

The congress also created a Moslem Peoples' Party and elected a central committee for it consisting of the following: (1) Reshid Ibragimov, (2) Yusuf Akchurin, (3) Seid Girey Alkin, (4) Abdulla Apanaev (Orenburg), (5) Galimjan Barudi (Kazan), (6) Sadri Maksudov (Volga Tatar, lawyer), (7) Shahaidar Syrtlanov (Ufa Tatar, landowner, Duma member), (8) Musa Bigeev (student and journalist from Kazan), (9) Bobinski (Tatar, Viatka), (10) Hadi Maksudov (editor of *Yulduz*, Tatar, Kazan), (11) Selim Girey Jantorin (zemstvo leader and Duma member), (12) Ismail bey Gasprinsky (the Crimea), (13) Mustafa Davidovich (mayor of Bakchisarai, in the Crimea), (14) Shah Mardan Koshchegulov (Kazakh, Astrakhan province), and (15) Ali Mardan bey Topchibashev (Azerbaijani).[34] The first eleven were all Tatars from the Ural and Volga regions, forming a solid majority in the central committee.

The decision to create not only a Moslem union but also a people's political party—which was never actually realized—and the provision to introduce the language of Ottoman Turkey as a "common Moslem" language in Russian Moslem schools clearly indicated a stronger national policy on the part of Russia's Turkic leaders. Tatars and their

Turkic allies from Azerbaijan and the Crimea, however, continued to collaborate in the Duma with the Kadets, as they had in the second parliamentary elections. The apparent contradiction in the failure of Tatar leaders to change tactics at this point reflected the complicated cultural and political situation in which Russian Turks—particularly the Tatars—found themselves. It should not be forgotten that in 1905 Russian Turks did not have any literary language of their own with an established tradition, equipped to express all the intricate problems of contemporary science and philosophy. The language which Nasyri had introduced in literature was merely the first step toward creation of a Tatar literary tongue, and although a number of writers followed in Nasyri's path, their language was suitable only for light narrative stories or journalism and not for the transmission of political, artistic, and scientific concepts. Consequently, the Tatars and other Turks of Russia turned to the language of the Ottoman Turks as the tongue most accessible to them linguistically, with its already developed fund of vocabulary and terminology. The introduction of Ottoman Turkish in Russian Moslem schools would have brought Russian Turks closer together culturally and oriented them politically toward Turkey. This would have been a clever political maneuver on the part of the Tatars, who furnished the majority of Russia's Moslem leaders, for it would have enabled them to maintain their dominant position among Russia's Turkic peoples. A common Moslem political party would also have served Tatar ambitions for cultural and political leadership.

Realizing that Russia had to be reckoned with, however, and that in the Volga-Ural region Moslems constituted only a third or a fourth of the total population, the declarations of the Third Moslem Congress were a compromise between the Tatars' political ambitions and Russian reality. The Tatars consciously entered into collaboration with that Russian group which accepted their cultural and religious program.

TATARS IN THE SECOND DUMA AND THEIR PARTIES

Collaboration with the Kadets in the elections to the Second Duma was successful, for Moslems sent thirty-nine deputies to the parliament. Their activity was hindered in the beginning by the absence of an experienced leader, but when A. M. Topchibashev replaced S. G. Alkin as head of Ittifak, he succeeded in coordinating Moslem

action in the Duma. Of the thirty-nine deputies, only eighteen formally joined the Kadet faction, fifteen cooperated with the Kadets,
and six formed a leftist labor group under the chairmanship of K.
Hasanov, called *Musulman Hezret Taifasé* and not connected with
Ittifak.[35] The divergence between "laborites" and Ittifakists stemmed
from a basically different approach to parliamentary and political
action. Ittifak stood firmly on a bourgeois platform and was interested
primarily in national and religious questions. The laborites stressed
the social program and reproached Ittifak for its collaboration with
the "bourgeois" Kadets, preferring to cooperate with the loose, un-
affiliated left-of-center Russian labor caucus, which united both peasant and worker deputies of the Duma. Moslem laborites, who published the newspaper *Duma*, received the nickname *Dumachelar*
(those of the Duma), by which they became known. This group
rapidly disintegrated after dissolution of the Second Duma, and its
supporters joined either the Social Democrats or Socialist Revolutionaries.[36]

In 1905–1907 Tatar Socialist Revolutionaries—who, like their Russian counterparts, were agrarian populists—cooperated both with their
bourgeois compatriots from Ittifak and with their Russian socialist
colleagues. Among their leaders were the energetic and strongly nationalistic Ayaz Iskhakov, Fuad Tuktarov, and A. Davletchin. A distinguished writer and journalist, Iskhakov enjoyed great popularity
among young Tatars, and after the revolution of 1917 he became a
dynamic leader in the Tatar leftist-national wing.[37] Since their main
organ was the newspaper *Tan* (Dawn), they came to be called
Tanchelar (Tan'ists—those of the Dawn).

Social Democrats were not powerful among the Tatars, who were
engaged predominantly in agriculture or trade. The growth of a
Tatar working class at the beginning of the twentieth century and
intensive Social Democratic propaganda, however, won them some
support. The Tatar Social Democrats Sadyk Sageev, Zarif Sadykov,
Hussein Yamashev, Ibrahim Akhtiamov, and Galimjan Seifu carried
on propaganda activities among Tatar workers in Kazan, but the
maximum circulation of their leaflets was only thirteen hundred.
After 1907, Hussein Yamashev began publishing a Social Democratic
paper, *Ural*, in Orenburg, but it closed after some thirty issues had
appeared. From the title of this publication, Social Democrats were
occasionally also called *Uralchelar* (those of the *Ural*).[38] Out of this

little Social Democratic organization was formed the embryo for the Tatar Bolshevik group of the next decade, and its members—particularly Ibrahim Ahtiamov—became the leaders of the Tatar Red Guardists.

Forming the Moslem right wing were conservative clerics of the Ecclesiastic Administration and aristocratic Petersburg Moslems, led by Ahunda S. Bayazidov in Petersburg and Mufti Yar Sultanov in Ufa, who organized the party *Syraté Mustakom*, which collaborated closely with Russian rightists. The spiritual leader of the Kadimists was M. Velihazret, editor of the review *Din ve Megyishet*, which carried on permanent warfare with the liberals.[39] Velihazret's enmity toward the Jadids and the leaders of Ittifak, whom he regarded as heretics and traitors to the cause of Allah and the Prophet, was so great that he did not hesitate to denounce the latter to the police for conducting Pan-Turkic propaganda in the new-method madrasa (for which reason the school of the Bobinski brothers was closed). Denunciations made to the Russian secret police by conservative mullahs were preserved and published after the Bolshevik revolution, and they are interesting for their narrow fanaticism. They considered revolutionary even those mullahs who read the prayers in Tatar instead of Arabic, and accused every teacher who used modern textbooks of spreading Pan-Turkic propaganda. Needless to say, they informed the police of all the actions of their fellow clergymen.[40]

Of these parties and groupings—which reproduced rather closely the picture of Russian political life before the revolution—only Ittifak and the laborites were represented in the Second Duma. They restricted their activities for Moslem action to three main points: emancipation of Moslem schools from Russian governmental supervision, complete equality of Russian Moslems and the Christian population, and reorganization of the Moslem Ecclesiastic Administration. They wanted to replace appointed muftis by elected ones and to free the Administration from any interference by the Russian government.[41] But the appointment of muftis continued up to the revolution, the government not wanting to relinquish such an important means of controlling the Moslems. With the help of the Kadet faction, however, they succeeded in maintaining the independence of their schools.[42]

Another important question which disturbed Moslems in the Second Duma was Russia's colonization policy. The Kazakhs and the

Bashkirs sought to limit Russian settlement in the southeastern regions and prohibit confiscation of nomadic lands for the purpose of agricultural colonization. Karataev, a Kazakh deputy from the Uralsk region, called upon the Duma and the Russian government to recognize the nomads' right to their lands and advised solving the agrarian question through the transfer of landowners' holdings to the peasants, which was in accord with the Kadets' program.[43] These speeches, however, were Ittifak's swan song. Conflict between the Second Duma and the Russian government led to the Duma's dissolution on June 3, 1907, and the changed political situation brought the activities of the Moslem political movement in Russia to nought.

CHAPTER V

The Kazakh Problem

While Tatars and Kazakhs were still bound by religious and linguistic kinship, they had little in common by 1905 as far as their social and economic conditions were concerned. The last nomadic Tatars had become sedentary peasants or urban dwellers many centuries before, while the Kazakhs, as well as their eastern neighbors, the Kirghiz, preserved the customs and culture of Turkic nomadic life until the end of the nineteenth century.* Roaming the steppes far from Iranian, Russian, or Chinese cultural centers, they preserved their language from foreign influence and remained less affected by the impact of Islam than the Tatars, Bashkirs, or Uzbeks.

The Kazakhs' transition from nomadic to sedentary life began in the last few decades of the nineteenth century, along the periphery of their territories, in regions already colonized by Russians in the north and by Uzbeks in the south. Most of their steppe remained an area of nomadic economy. According to statistics of 1897, some four million nomads inhabited the vast expanses of present-day Kazakhstan and Kirghizia. Kazakhs roamed throughout the steppe region from the Volga to the Chinese border in the Altai Mountains, while Kirghiz inhabited the slopes of the Tien Shan Mountains and the valley of southern Semirechie. One of the characteristic peculiarities of the human geography of Kazakhstan was the concentration of population along its northern and eastern borders. The central, southern, and western parts were so dry that the deserts of Ust-Yurt, Kyzyl-Kum, and the Balkhash regions isolated the main body of Kazakh nomads from the oases of Uzbekistan and Turkmenia, and even from the few Kazakh plowmen who had settled along the Syr Daria River.

Before their annexation by Russia, the Kazakh steppes were di-

* Up to 1925 the Kazakhs were called Kirghiz by Russian administrators and by both Russian and Western scholars, while the Kirghiz were designated as Kara Kirghiz. For the reader's convenience and in order to avoid misunderstanding, modern terminology—Kazakh—is used in the present study.

vided politically into three parts (*zhuz*, or hordes), which had been formed toward the end of the era of the Golden Horde—that is, in the late fifteenth or early sixteenth centuries. A zhuz was a separate geographic and political region comprising the territory of a tribal union. The easternmost, "senior" zhuz, or the Great Horde as the Russians called it, roamed the Semirechie region between the Tien Shans, Lake Balkhash, the present Chinese border, and the Altai Mountains. In the middle of the Kazakh steppe, between the rivers Syr Daria, Tobol, and Ishim, were located the tribes of the middle zhuz (Middle Horde), while the Syr Daria and Ural rivers and the Siberian forests comprised the territory of the "junior" zhuz, or Little Horde. In 1771, after the Volga Kalmyks migrated to Sinkiang, the Russian government settled part of the Little Horde on the empty lands between the Volga and the Urals. This part of the Little Horde became known as the Horde of Bukei.[1]

ANNEXATION OF KAZAKHS TO RUSSIA

The gradual inclusion of the Kazakhs in the Russian Empire was the process of two centuries, from the early seventeenth, when Russians conquered Siberia and first entered the Kazakh steppe, until the middle of the nineteenth century, when the Uzbek khanates of Khiva and Bukhara were conquered by Russia. In 1726 the Kazakh Khan Abulhair, nominally khan of all the Kazakhs but whose actual power was restricted mainly to the Little Horde, sought Russian protection from new Mongol inroads and requested the Russian government to include the Kazakhs in its empire. At that time the Kazakh Great Horde was subjugated by the Jungars, a Mongolian tribe which had conquered large parts of present Chinese Central Asia and Kazakhstan almost up to the Ural River, but the western Kazakhs proceeded to acknowledge Russian suzerainty.

During these years the complex dynastic situation in Petersburg drew Russia's attention away from the Kazakh problem, but in 1731 after the accession of Empress Anna the Russian government sent a special mission to Kazakhstan under the leadership of a Tatar, A. Tevkelev.[2] The entire mission, in fact, was composed of Tatars and Bashkirs, and even its convoy was selected from Bashkir troops. Through Tevkelev's diplomacy, the opposition of the Kazakh aristocracy and military leaders was overcome, and in October 1731,

Khan Abulhair and the Kazakhs of the Little Horde swore allegiance to Russia.[3]

Toward the end of the eighteenth century the Middle and Great Hordes were still oscillating between the Chinese, who had displaced the Jungars from eastern Turkestan, and the Russians,[4] and it was not unusual for Kazakh khans to swear allegiance simultaneously to both the Russian and the Chinese governments. Russian authority was acknowledged by the Middle Horde in the early nineteenth century, and in 1822 the Russian government introduced a regulatory system, worked out by M. M. Speransky, into both of the westernmost Hordes. Russian advance into the territory of the Great Horde began after construction of the so-called Siberian military line, which divided Russian possessions from China and constituted Russia's main outposts of expansion toward the Central Asian khanates of Bukhara and Kokand. In 1844 the tribes of the Great Horde acknowledged Russian suzerainty, and final inclusion of all the Kazakhs into the Russian Empire came about in 1864, when Russian troops occupied the cities of Aulie-Ata, Turkestan, Merké, and Chikment. With this, Russian fortresses east of the Urals (the so-called Orenburg military line) joined with those of the Siberian military line, separating the Kazakhs from the Central Asian khanates. Russia's annexation of the vast expanses of Kazakhstan, equivalent in size to the American Midwest, was a comparatively mild process which did not demand large military operations. While the Kazakhs were more numerous than the Indians of the American Midwest, they were not unified as a nation and were only weakly organized by tribes or clans, since the zhuz was more a division of nomadic territory than a state organization. Since the early eighteenth century the khans of the zhuz had had little actual power and had played no political role, while the Kazakh aristocracy was often inclined to see in Russian power a defense against the continual encroachments of Mongols, Chinese, or Uzbeks from Bukhara and Kokand.

ISLAM IN THE STEPPE

Islam penetrated into present Kazakhstan as early as the tenth century, when tribes in the Semirechie region accepted the Moslem faith. Uzbek, khan of the Golden Horde (1313–1341), whose empire included the Kazakh steppe, was particularly instrumental in the spread of the Islamic religion.[5] In view of the nomadic way of life and the absence of permanent temples and religious schools, however, Islam did not have a great influence on the Kazakhs. "Until their annexation to Russia, Kazakhs were only nominal Moslems," wrote the Kazakh geographer, Chokan Valikhanov, in 1860.[6] Literacy was a rare phenomenon even among the few settled Kazakhs along the Syr Daria and in the region of Tashkent. Accustomed to the freedom of the steppe, Kazakhs were little inclined to enter the close cells of the madrasa, and those who actually gained ecclesiastic training were very few. Shariat, the written law of Islam, was unknown in the steppes and mountains, and Kazakh nomads—like the Kirghiz and Turkomens—based their relationships upon Adat, the customary law, until the early twentieth century.[7] Islam did put out some deep roots among the Kazakhs of the south, near the Central Asian oases settled by Uzbek and Tajik peoples, before the Kazakhs' inclusion in the Russian Empire. But in the north and west, where the majority of the Kazakh nomads were scattered, Islam gained a real foothold only after that area's annexation to Russia. Valikhanov wrote that "Moslem law was never definitely accepted by the Kazakhs and was introduced in the steppe only at the government's instigation."[8] Radloff, who was a Russian inspector of Tatar schools in the 1870's, also stated that the Kazakhs had "not yet attained the basic feature of Moslem civilization—that is, acquisition of a clerical and learned body and the consequent tendency toward devoutness, as well as the unavoidable result of this: fanaticism and hatred of non-believers." Furthermore, he continued, the Kazakhs' faith "consists mainly of external forms . . . prayers in the Arabic language, which are usually incomprehensible to them, and if they learn them by heart, they pronounce them dumbly and not the slightest impression is made upon them.[9]

The position of Islam in the Kazakh steppe was strengthened by Empress Catherine II, who sympathized with the Russian Moslems' desire for religious freedom, although she herself was not distinguished by religiosity, being a typical representative of the freethinkers of the eighteenth century. She saw in Islam the most appropriate civilization for the Kazakhs and considered that the spread of literacy and religious schools among them would lead to a "softening of the manners" of the nomads. Catherine selected Tatar mullahs to work among the Kazakhs, and at her order the Russian administration of southern

Siberia and the Urals began to construct mosques in the Kazakh steppe. In a decree to the governor of Ufa, to whose province belonged the territory of the Kazakhs of the Little Horde, she wrote, "The appointment of mullahs [to the mosques and schools] fully corresponds to the realization of our orders. . . . Consider them a necessary expense." [10] The government financed not only the construction among the Kazakhs of mosques and schools, in which the teachers were Tatars, but also dissemination of the Koran and missionary activity conducted by the Tatar clergy. With the establishment of the Moslem Ecclesiastic Administration, whose center was located close to the Kazakh steppe—at first in Orenburg (now Chkalov), then in Ufa—the Kazakhs were submitted to its authority in questions of faith and religious education.[11] The Russian government did not curtail its support of Islam even in 1787–1791, when it became clear that Turkey was exploiting the Moslem clergy of the Little Horde for propagandistic purposes. During these years Turkish agents penetrated Bukhara and Khiva, which were hostile to Russia, for the purpose of rousing these khanates against Russia.[12]

Until the mid-nineteenth century the Kazakh steppe remained a Tatar cultural and economic dominion. The administration, particularly clerks and translators, was entirely Tatar, and the Tatar language (a version of Chagatai) became the official language for relations between the Kazakhs and the Russian government, as well as the language of the native Kazakh schools. Thus, with the help of Catherine II and her patronage of Islam, the Tatars gained an upper hand in the Kazakh steppe and the eastern reaches of the empire (see Chapter II). Ismail bey Gasprinsky referred eulogistically to Catherine II and her "wise and exceptionally useful policies in the east, which did more for Russia in ten years than all the efforts of clerics and statesmen during a whole century." [13]

The Kazakhs, however, responded unenthusiastically to their penetration by Islam and Tatar missionaries, who upset their social order and way of life. In 1830 a Kazakh delegation petitioned Nicholas I "to cease introducing mosques and schools, and to appoint no more clerics." [14] They were no less hostile toward Tatar merchants, whom they accused of exploiting the nomads, and toward Tatar officials for being unduly harsh. Understandably enough, the Tatar economic hegemony was regarded by Kazakhs, Kirghiz, and Bashkirs as indicative of the Tatar people's aspiration for cultural and political leadership as well as economic monopoly. A Kazakh saying even warned, "Avoid the Tatar." [15]

INFLUENCE OF THE RUSSIAN INTELLIGENTSIA

In view of the fact that Russia was for so long represented by Tatars in the Kazakh steppe, Russian cultural influence there did not begin to be felt until the mid-nineteenth century. In 1841 in the city of Khanskaia Stavka (The Khan's Residence), in the far west of the Kazakh steppe between the Volga and the Ural rivers, the first Russian-language school for Kazakhs was opened with the help of the local khan. In 1866 there were eight such schools, but their further growth was prevented by lack of sufficient funds and experienced teachers.[16] Not a few Kazakh students from the families of Kazakh aristocrats and elders were enrolled in the Nepliuev cadet academy in Orenburg and in the academy in Omsk, which played a role in the central steppes similar to that of Orenburg. The outstanding Kazakh scholar of the 1860's, Chokan Valikhanov (quoted above), for example, was a product of Omsk's educational institutions, as were his father and many of his relatives and friends.[17] The easternmost nidus of Russian culture in the Kazakh steppe was the city of Semipalatinsk, where Feodor Dostoevsky, attached to a disciplinary battalion there from 1854 to 1859, became acquainted with Valikhanov and the Kazakhs. During the 1850's and 1860's several other Russian political exiles were stationed in various cities throughout the Kazakh steppe, including such members of the socialistic Petrashevsky circle as the poets S. F. Durov and A. N. Pleshcheev. The presence in Kazakhstan of representatives of the Russian intelligentsia, who were assigned posts in the administration there—among whom should be mentioned the geographers P. P. Semenov, G. N. Potanin, and A. I. Maksheev, as well as the philologist V. I. Dal—also influenced the newly born Kazakh intelligentsia.[18] G. N. Potanin remarked in the second half of the last century that "the Decembrists and Petrashevskyists without a doubt prepared a new generation in Siberia [to which the northern part of Kazakhstan belonged] to which she [Siberia] is indebted for her social awakening." [19] The Russian intellectual's indifference to religion and his frequent atheism served to deepen still more the already apathetic attitude of young Kazakhs toward Islam, and the Russian liberal tradition, with its tendency toward populism and self-dedication, left deep traces in the Kazakh intelligentsia. This is particularly reflected in the writings of the first Kazakh "Westernizers," Valikhanov and Altynsaryn, as well as in the verses of the first and foremost Kazakh poet, Abai.

VALIKHANOV

Valikhanov (Chokan Genghis-Oglu Valikhanov, 1835–1865) came from an aristocratic Kazakh family which prided itself on its direct descent from Genghis Khan. He studied in the cadet academy in Omsk, served in the Russian army in Siberia and Central Asia, and emerged very early as a geographer and oriental anthropologist. His works remain to the present time an important source for the study of Russian and Chinese Central Asia, and his observations on the life of his countrymen are still of great value for the social and cultural anthropology of Kazakhstan. During his military service he became acquainted with a number of Russian scholars and intellectuals, and was particularly close to Dostoevsky, Durov, Potanin, and Semenov. Thanks to these friends, during his two-year stay (1859–1860) in Petersburg, he came into contact immediately with the leading representatives of contemporary Russian intellectual circles, such as Nekrasov, Chernyshevsky, Maikov, Grigoriev, the historian Kostomarov, and so on. Unfortunately, owing to the radical change in climate which he underwent, as well as to long hours devoted to reading and literary work, Valikhanov destroyed his health and contracted tuberculosis. He died at the age of thirty.[20]

Valikhanov's correspondence, particularly that with Dostoevsky, is indicative of his relations with his Russian friends and his attitude toward Russia. Dostoevsky wrote to Valikhanov that he had never felt such an attraction toward anyone as toward him.[21] In another letter, the Russian novelist wrote, "Is it not a great and sacred mission to be the first of your people to explain to Russia the significance of its steppe and your people, and at the same time to serve your people and intercede for it with the Russians?"[22] Valikhanov was, in fact, dedicated "to the useful work of serving his compatriots and defending them from Russian officials and wealthy Kazakhs."[23] In awakening his backward, nomadic people, Valikhanov sought, first of all, to lift their intellectual and economic level through education and their introduction to Russian and European culture. He struggled against the wealthy Kazakh aristocracy and sought to improve the well-being of the ordinary Kazakh. He considered that the tribal order and petrified Islamic culture presented a great obstacle to further Kazakh development. "Ignorance and poverty now rule in Maveranahr [a province in Central Asia between the Amu and Syr Daria]. . . . The libraries of Samarkand, Tashkent, Ferghana, Khiva, and Bukhara, and the observatory in Samarkand, have been irremediably destroyed by Tatar vandalism and the Bukhariote inquisition, which has damned everything except religion. Even great monuments . . . have been reviled as the symbols of man's sinful struggle against the creativeness of Allah." [24] Valikhanov wanted to see the Kazakh steppe freed from the tutelage of the Moslem Ecclesiastic Administration and insisted that the Russian government cease permitting Tatars to appoint the mullahs in Kazakhstan. He considered not only that Kazakhs should be appointed mullahs in the steppes in place of Tatars, but that the number of them should be strictly limited.[25] "The farther away from Tatars, the less fanatic a Kazakh." [26] The government hearkened to the voice of Valikhanov, and in 1868 it enacted measures to free Kazakh religious life from the supervision of the Ufa Moslem Administration.[27]

In the place of the Moslem schools, Valikhanov demanded the organization of Russian-Kazakh schools for the enlightenment of the nomads. He was confident that the Kazakhs could eventually overtake the West in their cultural development and hoped that the experience of Russia and of the West would help the Kazakhs in making up for lost centuries. "Self-development, self-defense, self-government, and self-justice" were the goals which, in his opinion, would best achieve improvement in Kazakh life. He advised changing the legal norms of Russian courts in the steppe, which he regarded as inappropriate to local conditions, introducing self-government by the Kazakh commune instead of by governmental officials and the Kazakh aristocracy; and he sought to defend the simple Kazakh from the arbitrariness of Russian and Kazakh aristocratic power.

It is not difficult to discern that the radical Russian intelligentsia—Chernyshevsky, Pisarev, Belinsky—inspired Valikhanov's liberal and areligious *Weltanschauung*. "What a remarkable man, this Chernyshevsky, and how well he knows life—not only Russian life. After talking with him I was definitely convinced that we Kazakhs would be lost without Russia. Without Russians we would be unenlightened, in despotism and in darkness. Without Russia we are only Asia and can be nothing else without her. Chernyshevsky is our friend." [28]

Despite Valikhanov's early death, his work and philosophy lay very much at the basis of the views of the Kazakh intelligentsia. His belief in the need for enlightenment, equality, and justice was shared by other young Kazakhs, and it lay to a large extent the foundation for the Kazakh intelligentsia's later "Russophilism." Of course, there were other attitudes, particularly in southern Kazakhstan, which were traditionally oriented not toward the north and west but toward the Moslem south. "The steppe was then divided into two parties," wrote G. N. Potanin in the 1860's, "the pro-Russian and the pro-national. . . . The most convinced supporters of the latter roamed the south [were nomads], close to the Golodnaia steppe [the "Hungry" steppe]. The antagonism between these two parties manifested itself in everything, even in the songs of Kazakh bards." [29] Pro-Moslem Kazakh leaders, however, became few and less influential toward the end of the nineteenth century.

ABAI

Two other Kazakh enlighteners also shared the views of Valikhanov: the steppe poet, Abai, and the educator, Altynsaryn. The patriarch of Kazakh literature, Abai Kunanbaev (1845–1904) also became acquainted with the Russian intelligentsia and Russian literature in Semipalatinsk. While still in school he became particularly interested in Russian poetry and introduced it to Kazakhs in the form of folk songs at the so-called *aitysu*, a competitive song-fest. In the 1880's he appeared in the role of a writer and poet, hitherto unknown among the Kazakhs, and he translated into Kazakh Russian folk songs and poems, among them *Eugene Onegin* (including the famous letter of Tatiana). Through Abai's translations, Kazakhs became acquainted not only with Pushkin, Lermontov, Krylov, and Tolstoy, but also with a number of West European writers, such as Byron and Goethe.[30] Like Valikhanov, Abai urged his people into the schools. "Study Russian culture and literature. This is the key to life. If you learn it, your life will be easier. . . . However, at the present time people giving their children a Russian education are training them, with the help of the Russian language, to exist at the expense of other Kazakhs. Don't take this view." [31] Abai considered that the basis of a Kazakh's education should be his native language: "Train children well, but in the beginning they should study their own language, grammar, and elementary subjects." [32] Then, only after Kazakh grammar was learned, he recommended the Russian school, for in Abai's eyes the training to be had in the Tatar madrasas was of little value. "Only the wealthy can study Arabic and Persian," [33] he wrote, meaning that these languages are important only for studying the Moslem culture of the East. Following Valikhanov's example, Abai struggled with the tribal aristocracy for improvement of the peoples' living conditions. The local Kazakh nobility's opposition, and suspicions entertained toward him by the Russian government—which, on the basis of his opponents' denunciations, saw in him a dangerous revolutionary—early undermined the poet's strength. [34]

ALTYNSARYN

The third of the early Kazakh enlighteners, Ibrai Altynsaryn (1841–1889) was an educator and the author of a number of Kazakh textbooks. In 1859 he met the Russian pedagogue, N. I. Ilminsky (see Chapter III), who was at that time living in Orenburg and compiling a Kazakh grammar. Ilminsky, who had long sought to diminish Tatar and Moslem influence, was eager to see the Tatar language replaced by Kazakh in Kazakh schools, and he produced a strong impression on Altynsaryn. They remained close friends till the latter's death. [35] Under Ilminsky's influence, Altynsaryn began working on the theoretical and practical development of the colloquial Kazakh language for literary purposes. He created the first written Kazakh prose, and translated Russian classics into Kazakh. After his appointment in 1874 to the post of inspector of schools in the Turgai region, Altynsaryn introduced in them the native Kazakh language for purposes of instruction, and achieved substantial success in Kazakh education. By 1905 there were 128 Russian–Kazakh schools, conducted in Kazakh, as against only 135 Moslem maktabs. A considerable number of Kazakhs also studied in the 2,011 purely Russian schools in Kazakhstan, in which the language of instruction was Russian. Hence, in Kazakhstan the number of Turkic students in Russian educational institutions was by far higher than in the Moslem institutions, and Kazakhstan became the only Moslem or Turkic region of Russia in which the impact of Islamic culture was drastically overshadowed by Russian. [36]

FORMATION OF THE KAZAKH INTELLIGENTSIA

In order to free the Kazakhs from Tatar influence and to facilitate the growth of Russian–Kazakh schools, two new decrees were enacted by the Russian government. The first, "The Provisional Status of Administration in the Steppe Region," made in 1868, although itself published in the Tatar language for distribution among Kazakhs, forbade the further use of the Tatar tongue in administrative organs in the steppe region (as Kazakhstan was referred to at that time), and it limited the role of Tatar translators in the governmental apparatus. The second decree, "Regulations for the Education of Non-Russian Nationalities," proclaimed in 1870, required that classes in Russian be introduced into Moslem schools in order to facilitate Kazakh students' subsequent education in Russian schools.[37] These measures were further strengthened by a decree of October 14, 1906, which demanded that Moslem schools henceforth be conducted in the native tongue rather than in Tatar, and that the teachers be of the same nationality as their students.[38]

As a result of these measures and of the activity of Kazakh and Russian educators, toward the end of the nineteenth century a Kazakh literary language began to emerge, together with a Kazakh national awareness. During the time of Valikhanov it had been said that Kazakhs were losing their identity under the influence of Tatar culture, but this became impossible by the early twentieth century. Russian–Kazakh schools, which supported a Kazakh cultural evolution independent from that of the Tatars, did not proceed to Russify the natives, however, as the administration may have hoped, but instead created a Kazakh nation with its own unique psychological and cultural features. Although Kazakh intellectuals at the turn of the century were undoubtedly dominated by Russian cultural influence, they nevertheless remained genuine nationalists, desirous of becoming neither Russian, nor Tatar—nor Turkish. All of them—Baitursunov, Dulatov, Karataev, Bukeikhanov, Tanyshbaev, and others who were rallied around the newspaper, *Kazakh*—remained defenders of the Kazakhs' independent path, despite their friendships with Russians or Tatars. Social-mindedness, self-sacrifice, idealism, and thirst for knowledge were their particular characteristics. For instance, the Kazakh writer, M. S. Kashatov, in his "Instructions to Kazakhs" (1908), advised, "Let us study sciences, religion and trade, and lead our people out into the world." "Awaken, Kazakh!" echoed Dulatov in 1910.[39]

The Kazakh press was born in 1899 when *Dala Valaiaty*, a Kazakh literary journal edited by B. Ablaihairov, began to appear in Omsk.

It did not follow any political line, but its fundamental tendency was national-liberal. Its role in the formation of the Kazakh literary language and creation of Kazakh social-mindedness was very great. Later, at the very end of the century, *Turgaiskaia gazeta* began to come out in Orenburg, and after 1905 newspapers in the Kazakh tongue appeared one by one, although they were at times short-lived. *Sharki* was published in Tashkent; *Kazakhstan* and *Ush zhuz* in Urda; *Zatan Tili* and *Alash* in Tashkent; *Aikap* in Troitsk; and *Abai* in Semipalatinsk. A few Kazakhs also participated in Tatar publications, such as *Shura* (published by the Tatar Rameev brothers in Orenburg) and *Akmola*, in Troitsk. In 1913 the newspaper *Kazakh*, edited by A. B. Baitursunov, began to appear in Orenburg and soon became the leading organ of the Kazakh intelligentsia and national movement. Within one year the number of subscribers to *Kazakh* reached three thousand, then eight thousand, while the next largest papers, *Kazakhstan* and *Aikap*, never printed more than a few hundred copies.[40] Of these publications, only *Ush zhuz*, in the south, voiced a particularly sharp anti-Russian and proclerical position, in accord with the more conservative and nationalistic tradition of the southern Kazakhs.[41]

In the first issue of *Kazakh*, Baitursunov declared that "for the preservation of our national identity we must proceed toward enlightenment and develop our own literary language. It should never be forgotten that only that people which creates a literature in its own native language has a right to independent existence." [42] Baitursunov further pointed out that if Kazakhs did not raise their cultural level, they would be absorbed by Russian civilization. He urged Kazakhs to attend Russian schools but demanded that they preserve their Kazakh spirit, language, and traditions from Russian or Tatar domination. He was highly critical of his compatriots who disdained the Kazakh tongue for the sake of some other.[43]

KAZAKHSTAN IN 1905

The period of the 1905 Revolution was stormy in Kazakhstan, but disorders and revolutionary excesses were rife only in those regions settled by Russian and Ukrainian colonizers. Of the four deputies elected to the Second Duma by the European settlers of northern Kazakhstan, three were Social Democrats (Bolsheviks). Among the nomads, however, the proletarian party was not successful; moreover, there were very few propagandists among the Social Democrats who actually knew the Kazakh language. Only a few journalists of the Kazakh paper, *Aikap*, in Troitsk, edited by I. Muhamejin, endeavored to carry on revolutionary work among the natives. Kazakh participation in the revolutionary events of 1905–1907 consisted of a few local demonstrations against the excesses of revolutionary settlers, occasional attendance at meetings organized by Social Democrats or other revolutionaries, and the submission of petitions to open new schools.[44] In 1905 a group of Kazakh intellectuals and tribal elders went to Petersburg to solicit Nicholas II for limitation of colonization in the Kazakh steppe and permission to use the Kazakh language, along with Russian, in the courts and administration. This request was not granted, but during their stay in Petersburg the Kazakhs mended their ties with the Kadet Party. In December 1905, A. Bukeikhanov called a conference of western Kazakhstan's intelligentsia, elders, and aristocracy, who resolved to work closely with the Kadets and even to join that party. A similar resolution was made by representatives of eastern Kazakh leaders, meeting in Verny (now Alma-Ata) under the leadership of M. Tanyshbaev.[45] The ideologist of both these groups was the editor of *Kazakh*, Baitursunov, who initiated an election campaign which brought victory to the Kazakh Kadets. (Kazakhs and the European settlers in Kazakhstan voted separately at the elections for the Duma.[46])

In view of the young, though well-established, tradition of the Kazakh intelligentsia, which followed the precepts of Valikhanov, Altynsaryn, and Abai, it is not astonishing that Kazakh leaders were cool toward cooperating with the Turkic national movement led by the Tatars and toward its organization, Ittifak. Their indifference toward religion prevented them from becoming enthusiastic over the Pan-Islamic slogans uttered by *Tarjuman* and Ismail bey Gasprinsky, while their cautious attitude regarding Tatar officials, mullahs, and traders kept them reserved toward Tatar claims for leadership and cultural supremacy. The Kazakh tongue was more distant from Ottoman Turkish than from the Tatar, and it was quite natural that the Kazakhs should prefer their own newborn literary language to Gasprinsky's import from Ottoman Turkey.

No prominent Kazakh leaders participated in the First and Second All-Russian Moslem Congresses of 1905–1906. In the Third Congress a Kazakh from the Horde of Bukei, Shah Mardan Koshchegulov, a member of the Duma, took part in the deliberations and was elected to the presidium of the stillborn Moslem People's Party.[47] But he, as well as most Kazakhs of the Horde of Bukei, maintained little contact with the bulk of Kazakhs in northern and eastern Kazakhstan, and did not belong to the group of intellectuals forming around Baitursunov, Bukeikhanov, and Tanyshbaev. These intellectuals, who cooperated with the Kadets and actively supported Baitursunov's newspaper *Kazakh*, became the nucleus of the Kazakh nationalist party, *Alash Orda*, which took more definite shape in 1917.

RUSSIAN COLONIZATION IN KAZAKHSTAN

Until the beginning of the revolution of 1917, Kazakh leaders continued their close cooperation with the Kadets in the hope of solving their most serious problem of the early twentieth century, that of the colonization of the Kazakh steppe by settlers from European Russia. Russian agricultural colonization in Kazakhstan began to attain sizable proportions only in the 1890's. Until that time the Russian population in the region had consisted primarily of Cossack settlements along the Ural and Irtysh rivers and in the semimountainous lands of Semirechie, on the outskirts of the Kazakh steppe. There were 77,000 Ural Cossacks in 1857, and only some 30,000 "Semirechian" Cossacks at the end of the century.[48] After the drought and crop failure of 1891–1892 in European Russia, the number of new settlers increased rapidly, forcing the Russian government to expropriate the "surplus" lands of the nomads. (The Russian government readily accepted the viewpoint of traditional Moslem law, the Shariat, in considering these lands the property of the state.) The main regions of new settlement were the rich lands of black earth in northwestern, northern, and eastern Kazakhstan, where the climate and the soil were favorable for agriculture.

Establishment of the Resettlement Administration in 1904 and the rapid development of the Russian economy after the revolution of 1905 resulted in a second, far larger, wave of settlers. The agrarian policy of Russian Prime Minister P. A. Stolypin, who attempted to reduce the agricultural population in Great Russia and the Ukraine, also was propitious for an intensification of resettlement. In the years 1906–1912 over 438,000 Russian and Ukrainian peasant families moved to Kazakhstan, which led to the further expropriation during those years of another 43,000,000 acres of nomadic lands.[49] By the beginning of World War I the Kazakh steppe had already become an important supplier of grain for Russia.

The growing tempo of expropriation, in turn, resulted in a substantial change in the Kazakh economy. Some nomads began to settle, but lack of agricultural experience and the nomads' traditional aversion for settled occupations hampered their conversion. Most of them moved to the poorer and more arid lands of central and southern Kazakhstan, being obliged to leave to the settlers not only their grazing lands but also the pastures which provided winter forage for their cattle. Consequently, nomadic livestock herds dwindled, and famine conditions developed among the Kazakhs.

As early as the middle of the nineteenth century, at the time of the formal integration of the Kazakh steppe into the Russian Empire, it was evident that pacification of the steppe and the subsequent growth of population there were making it difficult for the Kazakhs to preserve their ancient nomadic economic system. Russian explorers of the steppe in the 1860's–1870's pointed out that a large part of the nomads were in a permanently undernourished condition. By 1896 about half of the total livestock of the steppe was in the possession of 7 per cent of the Kazakh population, while 50–70 per cent of all Kazakh nomads belonged to the poorest group of the population.[50] After the beginning of Russian agricultural settlement, economic differentiation proceeded still further. The rapidly deteriorating conditions of the Kazakh population alarmed Kazakh leaders, who considered that only the complete cessation of Russian colonization could save the nomads. Conferences of Kazakh representatives were held in 1907 in Troitsk, Orenburg, and Kustanai, which brought together data relating to peasant colonization of the Kazkh steppe and its disastrous effect upon the economic and social conditions of the Kazakhs. Recommendations were adopted demanding the immediate cessation of settlement in nomadic lands and the restoration of Kazakh representation in the Duma, which had been abolished in 1907. These requests were supported by Russian liberal parties, but the government simply declined to discuss the problem of colonization with them, considering it impossible to leave the rich lands of the Kazakh steppe in the domain of an antiquated and nonrentable economic system. Resettlement meant a substantial source of grain for Russia as well as an easement of the situation of the overcrowded Russian village.

Colonization of the steppe inevitably resulted in tension between the nomads and the newly arrived agriculturalists. Friction also frequently arose from the fact that the Russian administration depended upon elected Kazakh elders, clerks, and translators, who served as

Kazakh Steppes and Central Asia before the Revolution of 1917

intermediaries between the Kazakh nomads and the Russians. Consequently, the needs of the mass of Kazakhs went unexplained to the administration.

Also, among the elected Kazakh officials there were often unscrupulous elements, and the village (*aul*) or regional elders themselves were under the pressure of tribal leaders and local moneyed interests. The democratic elections introduced by Russian authorities could not take hold among the still tribally organized nomads, and as a result elections became a farce and the elected administration a fiction and an abuse.[51]

Russian authorities, too, were frequently to blame for the situation which had arisen. It was not always the best representatives of the Russian bureaucracy who came to Central Asia and Kazakhstan. Among them were many who could not get on in European Russia and who sought rapid advancement by any means. With insufficient supervision by the central administration and the backwardness of the local population, malpractices and illegalities were often committed by those in power in the Russian Middle East.[52] However, the nomad's unconcern and submission to fate, to the prestige of the empire, and to the "White tsar" did not permit dissatisfaction to manifest itself openly.

CHAPTER VI

Uzbek Liberals and the Young Bukhariotes

In no Moslem area of the Russian Empire did the penetration of European culture and the new liberal spirit meet with such intransigent resistance as in Ceneral Asia, which Russia conquered in the period 1865–1876.[1] The persistent enmity of Central Asian natives and their leaders toward all new intellectual currents, however, was not owing to the primitiveness of the native population but rather to the stagnation of their once brilliant culture. As W. Barthold, the most authoritative scholar of Central Asian civilization, has remarked, "In contrast to the Middle Ages, nineteenth-century Turkestan belonged to the most backward countries of Islam."[2] This region, which centuries before gave the world such brilliant medieval thinkers as Al Farabi and Ibn Sina (Avicenna), such outstanding men of science as Al Biruni and Al Khwarizmi, and such great poets as Rudaki and Navoi, began to petrify culturally and economically in the early sixteenth century, when the discovery of a maritime route to the Far East undermined the monopolistic position of the Central Asian oases in continental trade with China and India, bringing about an abrupt decline in their prosperity. The simultaneous collapse of the Eurasian empire created by Genghis Khan further disrupted commercial relations between China and the Middle East. At almost the same time, the triumph of the Moslem Shiites in Persia deprived their Sunnite rivals in Bukhara and Samarkand of continued intercourse with the Moslem Mediterranean world.[3] This ever-growing isolation of Central Asia, already remote geographically, resulted in the region's spiritual stagnation.

Of no less significance for the cultural decline of Central Asia were its many conquests by Turkic nomads. Between 1000 and 1500 A.D. three major waves of Turkic invaders overran this primarily Iranian land. In the course of these invasions, irrigation systems and urban centers were destroyed and a large part of the sedentary population of the oases was annihilated and replaced by nomads possessing a less developed culture. Particularly important were the repercussions from the last of these invasions, that in the late fifteenth century by the Uzbeks, who remained lords over the oases between the Syr and Amu Daria rivers for three and a half centuries.[4] This new contingent of Turkic warriors accelerated the Turkization of the indigenous Iranian population, and from the very outset of their supremacy in Central Asia the Uzbeks demonstrated the most intransigent religious fanaticism and opposition to all foreign or new ideas. The rulers of the Uzbek khanates opposed any change in their traditional way of life and any deviation from the most conformist Sunnite behavior. Medieval philosophy and sciences were banished and replaced by a rigid scholasticism which sterilized Central Asian thought and resulted in the land's cultural lethargy.[5]

COMPOSITION OF THE CENTRAL ASIAN POPULATION

In Central Asia, Russia encountered not an ethnically homogenous state or system of states, but a scattering of feudal principalities and tribal territories of the most complex national composition. The central agricultural mesopotamia between the Amu and Syr Daria rivers, and the fertile valley of the Ferghana, were divided at that time into three main khanates—Bukhara, Kokand, and Khiva—as well as numerous smaller vassal and independent despotisms. In all of these khanates and principalities, Uzbeks formed the aristocracy and dominant political group. Permanent warfare, unstable boundaries, and decadent rulers and dynasties typified the political life of Central Asia during the centuries preceding Russian conquest.

In addition to the ruling Uzbeks, the population consisted of the still Iranian-speaking Tajiks, their Turkized brothers, the Sarts (who are now also called Uzbeks), and remnants of older Turkic groups which had preceded the Uzbeks in conquest of the Central Asian oases. This sedentary core, located between the Syr and Amu Daria rivers, was surrounded by the tribal territories of other Turkic-speaking nomads: Turkomens in the west, Kazakhs in the north, and Kirghiz in the east, all of whom jealously guarded their grazing grounds and occasional cultivated fields from encroachment by the Uzbek khans. There also existed substantial distinctions in religion and culture. The sedentary population strictly observed the Shariat, Islam's written law, while the nomads were only nominal Moslems and preserved the Adat, the customary law of Islam. Within the khanates there were religious minorities of Shiite Moslems and Jews, the former composed mainly of Persian slaves.

The complex ethnic structure and linguistic mosaic of Central Asia naturally hindered the development of any clearly national consciousness. In prerevolutionary times, identification with the religion and culture of the Islamic world was stronger among the Turkic-speaking Uzbeks and Iranian-speaking Tajiks than in any other Moslem group of the Russian Empire, and this obscured or replaced any national concept. The problem of language further complicated any possible national awakening. Although the Turkic language dislodged Iranian to a great extent after the Turkic conquests of the eleventh to fifteenth centuries, the Iranian Tajik tongue continued to play a disproportionately important role in Central Asian cultural life. In poetry and chronicles, Tajik was used as often as old Uzbek—Chagatai—and the emir of Bukhara and his administration preferred Tajik to Uzbek. The literate population and intellectuals knew both languages, as was the case with Abdul Rauf Fitrat, the prominent Uzbek* nationalist and scholar, who began his literary career in Tajik and then switched to Uzbek after World War I.[6] The opposite transition—from Uzbek to Tajik—was made by a veteran of the Jadid movement in Bukhara, Sadreddin Aini, president of the Tajik Academy of Sciences, who died in 1954.[7] Many regions, particularly those of Bukhara, Katta-Kurgan, Samarkand, southern Bukhara, and the western part of the Ferghana Valley, were bilingual, and both languages underwent changes in structure and vocabulary under the other's influence.[8] A large part of the Central Asian population, even Uzbek-speaking inhabitants, have preserved an Indo-European physical make-up, and only in the regions of Tashkent, eastern Ferghana, and Kashka Daria do Turkic features predominate.

RUSSIAN ADMINISTRATION IN CENTRAL ASIA

As the Russians advanced toward the south, in order to avoid provoking the animosity of England—their greatest rival in Asia—they did not directly annex all of the Central Asian territories. The bulk of the lands of Bukhara and Khiva remained outside the Russian

---

* The term "Uzbek" is used here and further on in this study in its present meaning—the whole Turkic population of the Uzbek SSR and not the tribal group that came into Central Asia around 1500. In 1939 there were 4.8 million Uzbeks and 1.2 million Tajiks.

boundary until 1920, and continued to be ruled by their own khans, who acted independently in their internal affairs but who were, in effect, vassals of the Russian crown. The annexed region of Central Asia was organized into the Turkestan General Governorship, headed by a military governor general in Tashkent. The General Governorship, in turn, was divided into three provinces: Ferghana, Samarkand, and Syr-Daria.[9] In these new Russian provinces no major changes in the social organization of the natives were made after Russian conquest, and many traditional features in their administrative system were preserved. While the higher administrators—the governors of the provinces, their staffs, and heads of the districts—were Russians and European Russian subjects (Ukrainians, Tatars, or Baltic Germans), the lower administrators, officials of the Moslem villages and towns, were natives, elected as before by the local population. The same principle applied in the courts. Only lawsuits involving non-natives and unusually serious criminal cases came under the jurisdiction of the Russian crown courts. Most civil suits, particularly those concerning family and commercial law among the natives, and minor criminal offenses were settled by Moslem judges (kazi), also elected by the natives.[10]

From the very beginning Russia's policy toward Central Asians was one of noninterference in their cultural and religious life. The fact that Central Asian Moslems were not subject to compulsory military service, which was introduced throughout the Russian Empire in 1876, helped them to avoid Russification and assimilation. The Russian government recognized the Islamic religion as the faith of the Central Asians at the time of their conquest, and General K. P. Kaufman, the first Governor General of Turkestan (1867–1882), even prohibited Orthodox missionaries from entering the Central Asian provinces during his administration.

General Kaufman's policies were aimed at strengthening Russian rule in Central Asia without antagonizing the natives. It was his belief that the stagnant Moslem culture would eventually disintegrate and the population would turn of itself to the more advanced culture of Russia.[11] He was a military administrator, however, not a professional *Kulturträger*, and considered his main task the preservation of peace and order throughout the region, with no attempt at bold and premature cultural reform. In these early years of Russian administration in Central Asia, the government's main objectives were preservation of the *Pax Rossica*, suppression of slavery, and eradication of banditry and feudal warfare.[12]

THE MOSLEM SCHOOLS IN CENTRAL ASIA

A similar policy of tolerant noninterference was adopted toward the local Moslem schools. During fifty years of tsarist administration in Central Asia, no serious attempt was made to introduce the Russian language in the native schools or to influence their spirit and program. Both the parochial maktab and the collegiate madrasa preserved the system of scholastic religious education created in the late Middle Ages.[13] It was, however, this educational system, adhered to in all the traditional Moslem schools, which hampered cultural evolution in prerevolutionary Central Asia. According to statistics of 1911, there were 6,000 maktabs and 328 madrasas in Central Asia, with a total enrollment of over 100,000 students. In the khanate of Bukhara, there were an estimated 120,000 students in 6,440 maktabs, and 13,200 in the madrasas.[14] For the approximately 2,500,000 sedentary inhabitants in the three provinces of Russian Central Asia, the 6,000 native Moslem schools is not a low figure.[15] It has also been found that not all of the schools which actually existed were officially registered.

The rate of literacy among boys of school age (seven to thirteen) was estimated in some districts in 1910 to be 32 per cent. Although this data does not characterize the whole of the General Governorship, it does show definite progress since the year 1897, when the census revealed 7.8 per cent literacy among the male and 2 per cent among the female population of all the Russian Central Asian provinces. In Bukhara before the revolution the rate of literacy was much lower, estimated at 2 per cent, and even 0.1 to 1 per cent in its eastern parts (present Tajikistan).[16] The curriculum in these schools, as in the other Moslem schools of Russia at that time, was dominated by the study of religion. Instruction in Arabic created an initial obstacle which had to be overcome by the native Tajik or Uzbek pupil, while a study of the local native language, both reading and writing, was minimized.[17] The Arabic texts were learned by rote. Descriptions of Moslem schools left by Russian and European travelers show that these traditional schools did not change between the mid-nineteenth and early twentieth centuries. N. V. Khanykov, who visited the

Bukhara khanate in the early 1840's, before Russian conquest, related, "Hence it happens that, traversing the streets of Bukhara, we are informed of the vicinity of the school before we reach it, so loud is the diligence of the students." Much the same is the description given by A. Polovtsoff, who was in the city of Bukhara in 1918 during the revolution: "The pupils squat on the floor, swaying to and fro and shouting their lessons at the top of their lungs. The main object is to learn the *suras* of the Koran by heart, even if their exact meaning in Arabic is not clearly understood." [18]

Monotonous rote learning, as well as insufficient preparation of teachers, resulted in the fact that graduates of the maktabs were often unable to read the very text they had studied, and many remained practically illiterate. In 1914 a group of rich Tajik merchants from Bukhara wrote to the Russian diplomatic agent in the khanate, "We studied in the traditional schools for seven or eight years, and still we remained illiterate. We did not benefit from having attended the schools." [19] Most descriptions of the old Moslem schools in Central Asia point out the extremely poor progress made by the students. Only a few were able to read and write after attending the maktabs for seven or eight years, and no more than 10 to 12 per cent of the pupils continued their education in the madrasas, preparing themselves for careers as *mullah* (learned man), *imam* (priest), *mudarriss* (professor), *kazi* (judge), or *rais* (censor of morals).[20]

In the madrasa neither sciences nor the humanities, nor even the history of Islam, was offered. Professional education other than theological or juridical was nonexistent, although some knowledge of medicine could be gleaned from the medieval books of Avicenna.[21] The student's training consisted of reading and scholastic discussion. In spite of their one-sided program, many of the madrasas of Central Asia, particularly those of Bukhara—like the renowned Mir Arab— offered excellent theological, legal, and dialectical training, and were famous throughout the entire Islamic world, even in the nineteenth century, as the most orthodox educational institutions. The fanatically pious emirs of the Mankit dynasty, Shah Murad (1785–1800) and Haydar (1800–1825), contributed especially to Bukhara's fame as the guardians of Islamic orthodoxy.[22] The city's reputation for its strict observance of the law of Islam attracted students to it from China, India, Afghanistan, the Kazakh steppe, and European Russia.

RUSSIAN EDUCATIONAL DIFFICULTIES

Eager to spread Russian cultural influence among the native population, the Russian government made substantial efforts to attract
Moslem students into the Russian schools of Central Asia. Recruitment of Uzbek and Tajik students to the schools which were opened
for the local Russian population failed completely in view of the
strong opposition on the part of Moslem society toward educating
their children in Christian schools. Although the government offered
various incentives, including special Russian–native boarding houses
and scholarships, the total number of Moslem students in the purely
Russian schools, after some initial success, decreased steadily, and by
1912 out of a total of 14,000 students in the Russian secondary schools
of Central Asia, there remained only 197 Moslems.[23]

Greater success was achieved, however, by another type of governmental school patterned after the program recommended by
Ilminsky in the 1860's. In these schools instruction was conducted
in the lower classes in the native language, and in Russian in the upper
classes. This bilingual school trained students for careers as inter-
preters, local administrators, and judges. In 1909, in 89 such bilingual
schools there were 2,552 Moslem students. By 1911 the number of
such schools had grown to 120,[24] and the number of applicants considerably surpassed the admissions quota. The spread of these schools
was hindered in certain instances, however, by the reluctance of the
Moslem municipalities to allocate subsidies for the bilingual educational network. When Russian authorities advised the Moslem upper
classes of Central Asia to send their children to these bilingual schools,
there were cases where parents hired the children of poorer families
to attend these schools in place of their own children. In 1905 one of
the major points in the Moslem petitions to the Russian government
was the closure of the bilingual schools and discontinuance of governmental support to children who wished to continue their education
in them after completing their studies in the maktabs.[25] This reluctance among the native Moslem population to enter the Russian-
native bilingual schools noticeably subsided shortly before the beginning of World War I, when the enrollment in Tashkent schools
greatly exceeded their facilities. The efforts of the Russian administration were thus finally rewarded.

This change was at least partly due to the attempts made to popularize Russia and its culture in Central Asia by N. Ostroumov, editor of the government newspaper published in Uzbek in Tashkent. An orientalist well acquainted with the problems of Central Asian society, Ostroumov for decades published translations of Russian writers and articles on Russian life, economy, and culture, and won the cooperation of some prominent liberal Uzbek writers. Verses, stories, and articles by Muhammed A. Kh. Mirzakhoja-Mukimi (1850–1903), Zakirjan Khalmuhammed Furkat (1859–1919—not to be confused with the Jadid ideologist, Abdul Rauf Fitrat), Abdullar Salikh Zavki (1853–1921), Khoja Muhitdin Muhtyi (1835–1911), and other well-known Uzbek writers won a wide circle of readers for Ostroumov's publications. Ostroumov also helped these writers to travel in the European parts of Russia, and their reports and articles further helped to spread knowledge of Russia among the native population.[26]

INCEPTION OF UZBEK LIBERALISM

Enactment in 1907 by the Duma of a bill for compulsory education throughout the empire, which was to have been achieved by 1920, forced Russian educators in Central Asia to look for a new type of school, acceptable both to the native population and to the government. A special conference in the Ministry of Education elaborated a plan for reforming the traditional maktab and making it the basis of a new educational system. Such subjects as mathematics, history, and geography were to be introduced into the maktab, in the native language, while the Russian language was to be taught in its upper classes.

For the evolution of the native society, however, the very fact of Central Asia's inclusion in the Russian state and its economic system was of far greater significance than the efforts made by Russia to further education in the region. Removal of barriers fostered by the cultural rigidity of the Central Asian khanates before their conquest was decisive for their further development. After its annexation, Central Asia became exposed to ideological currents emanating from Russia, from Western Europe, and from Moslems in the Near Eastern countries. Russian, Tatar, Persian, and Turkish books and journals made their way into Central Asian cities, while natives found themselves in continual personal contact with Russians, Tatars, and Europeans.

Finally, in the last quarter of the nineteenth century, the Central

Asian provinces became an integral part of the economic life of the empire, and the growth of Russia's textile industry put cotton in such demand that it became the main product of native Central Asian agriculture. From 1888 to 1916 the cotton fields in Russian Central Asia increased from 68,000 to 533,000 desiatines (one desiatine equaling about 2.7 acres). In these twenty-eight years cotton production grew by 750 per cent. In six years alone, 1910–1916, it increased more than 50 per cent—from 9.3 million puds to 14 million puds (one pud equaling about 44 pounds). In the khanate of Bukhara there were 110,000 desiatines of cotton fields by 1916, and 60,000 in the khanate of Khiva. Cotton exports in both khanates increased from 1.6 to 4.4 million puds, or 275 per cent, in 1911–1914. The over-all expansion of trade corresponded to that of agriculture, and in 1914 Russian Central Asia exported to European Russia and abroad products totaling 301 million rubles, while its imports amounted to 271 million rubles. Central Asian imports and exports per capita and per square kilometer surpassed the average for the whole Russian Empire by four times: in 1914 Russia's trade averaged 15.2 rubles per capita and 98 rubles per square kilometer, and in Central Asia these averages were 71.5 rubles and 390 rubles. Toward the end of the nineteenth century, cotton ginneries appeared even in Bukhara, where the economy also was developing rapidly. By 1913 there were 26 ginneries in the khanate. By 1916 in the city of Bukhara there were six branch offices of Russian banks which, in turn, sent out a network of agencies throughout the khanate.[27]

The growth of trade turned the Central Asian economy from an isolated, self-sufficient rural economy into a market-oriented one, and, with its strengthening, the wealth and prestige of the native middle class also grew. Composed primarily of cotton ginners and buyers, merchants and moneylenders, the middle class developed into a significant and influential part of native society after the turn of the century. Eager to displace feudal and tribal chieftains in leadership, and vying with the Moslem clergy for influence, the Uzbek and Tajik middle class, supported by liberal Moslem students, formed a new stratum in Central Asian society which was particularly receptive to new ideas.

One of the first heralds of a new trend of thought in Central Asia was a Bukhariote statesman and poet, Ahmad Mahdum Donish (1827–1897), who had visited Petersburg as secretary to the khan's ambassador after Bukhara's defeat by Russia. Donish was profoundly impressed by Russian schools, women without purdah, the abundance of books and periodicals, the Russian intelligentsia, and the higher standard of living, and he returned to his land as one of Central Asia's first Westernizers. In a politico-philosophical treatise, "An Unusual Journey," Donish appealed to the Bukhariotes to create a new way of life for themselves. In his writing, this new order appears as an admixture of enlightened absolutism and Utopian socialism. In another work Donish attacked the reigning Mankit dynasty, the clergy, and the land's ignorant administrators. "The Emir and the Vizirs, the clergy and the aristocracy, are all alike. You, reader, should find out what kind of man the Emir himself is, the sovereign of orthodox Moslems and your sultan. Look around and you will see that he is a libertine and tyrant. His Supreme Kazi is a glutton and hypocrite. Of the same kind are the Rais and the head of the police. The latter is simply a perpetually drunk gambler and consort of brigands and thieves." [28] Donish's words were taken up by Bukhariote liberals in the late nineteenth and early twentieth centuries as the main arguments in their struggle against the corrupt and backward regime of Bukhara.

Donish's principal disciples were the poets Abdulkadyr Savdo (1823–1873) and Shamsiddin Mahmud Shohin (1857–1893), and a historian, Somi Bustomi (died, 1908), head of the emir's personal chancellery.[29] While these writers and their supporters, such as the preacher, Yahia Haji, and Mullah Sherif, a watchmaker, limited their oppositional activity to criticizing the regime, other liberals, such as the *damullahs* Ikram and Evez, sought constructive reform, particularly in education. Bukhara's emir, Muzaffar ed Din (1860–1885), who reigned in the time of Russian conquest and succeeded in consolidating his khanate only with Russia's help, vigorously combatted opposition and the infiltration of new ideas. Persecuted by the emir, most of Bukhara's early liberals were obliged to leave the khanate. Some, such as Isa Maksum and Inayet Maksum, fled to Samarkand and Tashkent, while others, like Sherif Maksum, became émigrés in Constantinople. Only after the death of the old emir and the accession of his son, Abdul Ahad (1885–1910), were they able to return to Bukhara.[30]

The reign of Abdul Ahad coincided with the cultural revival of Moslem society in European Russia and with the activities of Ismail

bey Gasprinsky. Gasprinsky's new liberal ideas were brought to
Central Asia via the Tatar settlements there, though the native Uzbeks
and Tajiks were less receptive to them than the Tatars had been. The
first Central Asian protagonists of the Moslem liberal movement
came into sharp conflict with the conservative majority. While the
liberals regarded modernization of education and changes in the traditional way of life as the only means of rescuing Moslem society
from decay, the conservatives, of course, considered such changes
the greatest danger to family life and to Islamic civilization.

THE JADID MOVEMENT AMONG THE UZBEKS

The clash of these two conflicting ideologies found its most overt
expression in the struggle over the schools. In the late 1890's, when
Gasprinsky's *Tarjuman* and similar periodicals in European Russia,
Turkey, and Persia had won some readers among the Uzbeks and
Tajiks, the influence of liberal thought grew stronger. In 1893 Gasprinsky visited Central Asia personally, bringing with him his ideas
for educational reform. Several reformed schools were opened in
the Kazakh steppe by the Tatars, and in some cities of northern
Central Asia. In 1901 Munevver Kari, a former student of the
Bukhariote madrasas, opened the first Uzbek reformed maktab, patterned after the reformed Tatar schools, and two years later Mahmud
Hoja Behbudi opened a second one in Samarkand. [31] Behbudi, an
able educator and passionate journalist who had initiated a campaign
for educational reform, simultaneously attacked the traditional Moslem clergy for its obscurantism, accusing it of distorting the Islamic
faith and law.

The persistent efforts of Munevver Kari and Behbudi, as well as of
other enthusiasts for enlightenment, began to bear real fruit after the
abortive Russian revolution of 1905, in which Central Asian Moslems
took little part.[32] The constitution of 1905 granted Central Asians
representation in the Russian Duma, and the elections of 1906 were
important for Uzbek and Tajik political development. Despite the
fact that the Moslem deputies from Central Asia belonged to conservative groups, with the single exception of Mullah Abdul Kariev,
the delegate from Tashkent, this short parliamentary experience aided
the liberal movement, which had the wholehearted support of Tatars
in Central Asia. It was the Tatars who instigated the first political
rallies in Tashkent and Samarkand, where petitions were drawn up

requesting reorganization of the Moslem Administration, greater native representation on municipal boards, and cessation of Russian agricultural colonization in Central Asia. These meetings were attended by influential representatives of the Moslem population—merchants, clerics, and members of the native administration.[33] Tashkent, the administrative and cultural center of Russian Central Asia, became the rallying point for liberals.

Encouraged by the success of revolutionary activity in Russia, the liberal movement in Central Asia, led by Munevver Kari, Ahmejan Bentimir, Ismail Abid, Abdullah Avlani, and Abdullah Hojaev, began to spread throughout the urban population. In Tashkent the Jadids started publishing several periodicals, the main ones being *Khurshid* (The Sun), *Shuhrat* (Glory), *Asia*, and *Sada-i-Turkestan* (Voice of Turkestan). Tatars in Tashkent also published *Tarakki* (Progress), a newspaper intended to propagate liberal ideas among the Uzbeks. Because of its proximity to the khanate of Bukhara, Samarkand became a second important center for Jadid activity. Here Behbudi and his friends put out *Samarkand* and *Aina* (The Mirror). The movement also took root in Ferghana, where the Jadids were headed by Nasirkhan Tora in Namangan, and by Abujan Mahmud, Ashur Ali Zakir, and Sali Pulat in Kokand. The latter published *Sada-i-Ferghana* (Voice of Ferghana), *El Bairagi* (Fatherland's Banner), and *Yurt* (Fatherland). These Jadid publications began to appear after promulgation of the Russian constitution of 1905, which brought a lessening of censorship. Most of them were of short duration, but they played an important part in the spread of reformist thought.

Uzbek publishing houses and the appearance of a national Uzbek theater were other effective tools for the dissemination of liberal and national ideas. Tashkent and Kokand publishers made available the works of national poets and writers, among whom the sixteenth-century poet, Navoi, was particularly widely read. Along with poetry and prose, the religious and philosophic works of such seventeenth- and eighteenth-century Central Asian thinkers as Jassavi, Mirza Bedil, and Suphi Allajar gave a new impetus to Jadid thought. The young Uzbek intelligentsia saw these writers as the heralds of native religious thinking, and they were as highly esteemed as the Arabic and Persian thologians. Uzbek readers were not limited during these years of Jadid successes to local publications. A large number of books imported from Persia and Turkey acquainted them with ideas of other Middle Eastern Islamic countries which themselves had only recently experienced political and intellectual revolution.

The Tatar dramatic groups "Sayer" and "Nur," as well as Azerbaijani ones, began to tour Central Asian cities in 1911, making accessible to local spectators the achievements of the modern Turkic stage, and contributing as well to a growth of inter-Turkic cultural and linguistic ties. The Jadid press warmly supported Uzbek interest in a national stage, which, after some initial difficulties, found an extremely sympathetic audience. Behbudi's play, "The Patricide," became the first "hit" of the national theater. The appeals of this leading Jadid writer for the need for enlightenment among the Central Asian peoples, and the need to form an Uzbek intelligentsia, found a warm response.

A further step toward the strengthening of Jadid groups was taken in 1909 when the Jadids organized a cultural society, "The Aid," devoted to furthering the liberal press, spreading liberal thought by means of lectures, and educational reform. Founded with the permission of Russian authorities, The Aid made new Uzbek, Tatar, and Turkish literature available in bookstores throughout all the important cities of Central Asia.[34] Through its efforts, also, the number of reformed schools grew. In 1908 there were ninety-two Jadid maktabs in the entire Turkestan General Governorship, thirty-five of them in the cities of Tashkent, Samarkand, Kokand, and Andijan. By 1912 there were twelve in Tashkent alone, with over one thousand students.[35]

In Tashkent the danger of liberal agitation by Tatars had long been recognized. As early as the 1870's, General Kaufman had rejected the claims of the Tatar Ecclesiastic Administration to place Central Asia under its jurisdiction, and in 1886 Tatar influence was further curtailed when non-Christian settlers in Central Asia were prohibited from purchasing real estate. In 1907 the administration of the General Governorship took measures to combat Tatar propaganda by increasing censorship and suspending many Jadid publications. The Tatar paper, *Tarakki*, the most radical in all Central Asia, was suspended after the appearance of its seventeenth issue.[36] Tatar settlers' influence in education likewise drew the administration's attention, and in January 1911, several reformed maktabs founded or conducted by Tatars in the Ferghana province were closed. In June of that year a new regulation was enacted requiring teachers in Moslem schools to belong to the same national group as the students, so as to withdraw the Uzbek, Kazakh, and Tajik children from Tatar tutelage. The Russian government further called upon officials and educators in Central Asia "to pay particular attention to the infiltration of newcomers from other regions and from Turkey or Persia who might be contaminated by revolutionary ideas."[37] These new measures did not halt the growth of reformed schools, however, but in effect accelerated the preparation of Uzbek and Tajik teachers to take the place of Tatars. The final unexpected result of the administration's struggle against Tatar influence was the quickened and independent development of native Uzbek and Tajik reformed schools.

In opposing Jadid influence, the Russian government sought the support of conservative Moslems and looked with greater favor on the conservative Moslem schools and clergy. Russian authorities in Tashkent became sympathetic toward Moslem traditionalists, who resented Jadid activities even more than the Russian government and for whom the Jadids were but one more hostile group in Central Asian society. When the radical Tatar newspaper, *Tarakki*, had attacked conservative schools and teachers in the summer of 1907, it aroused the ire of the traditionalists, or Kadimists, and at an assembly of the Moslem clergy of Tashkent, *Tarakki*'s editors and supporters were proclaimed unbelievers and were banished from the mosques.[38] It is understandable that Central Asian Moslems participated very little in the All-Russian Moslem Congresses of 1905–1906 and in Ittifak. Before the 1917 revolution, the Kadimists still represented the majority of Central Asia's urban population and the whole of the rural districts, where the preponderantly urban Jadids had no roots; in the three provinces of the Turkestan General Governorship the Jadids controlled only some hundred schools with six thousand to eight thousand students, while the Kadimists maintained over six thousand schools, with one hundred thousand students.[39]

JADID SCHOOLS IN BUKHARA

In the khanates of Bukhara and Khiva, which were outside the borders of the General Governorship and hence beyond the reach of Russian law, the situation was even less favorable for the Jadids. The ideological duel between liberals and traditionalists—which here, too, took the form of a struggle for the schools—was fought more intensely than in the Russian provinces. In Bukhara, particularly, the clergy's influence was unlimited.[40] The rulers of Bukhara were little inclined toward liberal thought, and the Jadids found propitious soil only in Russian extraterritorial settlements within the khanate, such as the city of New Bukhara. Here, protected by Russia from Bukhara's fanaticism and sometimes even supported by the Russian diplomatic agent, the reformed school made its appearance. After an unsuccessful attempt by Mullah Jurabay in Pustinduzom in 1900, the first new-method school was opened in 1902 by a Tatar teacher, Karimov, for the Tatar children of the Russian settlement in New Bukhara. This school closed after a few months, but in 1907 another was organized by Sabinov and Burnashev, also Russian Tatars.[41] This one had immediate success among the inhabitants of the settlement, and its effective methods of teaching aroused interest in Bukhara's capital.

An influential member of Bukhara's clergy, Mufti Ikramutdin Uron, ventured an opinion that the Jadid school in no way undermined the teachings of Mohammed, though the majority of the Bukhariote clergy opposed it as contradictory to the Shariat. Under pressure from liberal elements of Bukhara's bourgeoisie, and from Ismail bey Gasprinsky himself, the emir of Bukhara granted permission for such a school to be opened in the capital city for the children of his subjects.[42] It opened on October 8, 1908, and was conducted in Tajik —at that time the preferred literary language in Bukhara. Examinations given the students at the end of the year were open to the public and revealed that the students of the reformed school had made far greater progress than those in the traditional maktabs. Fearing that the success of the reformed school would undermine the standing of conservative schools in Bukhara, the clergy enjoined the emir to prohibit the school's continuance and instigated a wave of religious fanaticism in the capital city which led to severe riots in January 1910, between the Sunnite and Shiite inhabitants. Order was reestablished only after the intervention of Russian troops sent to Bukhara at the emir's request.[43]

The new maktab continued to interest the people of Bukhara, however. In addition to cultural considerations, commercial advantages offered by the reformed school lay behind the persistence with which Bukhara's merchants exercised their influence with the emir to reinstate the outlawed school. The merchants, themselves only semiliterate, saw benefits in the reformed school's program, which included both Russian and Uzbek (or Tajik), elementary mathematics, and geography. All these subjects were necessary tools for successful commercial relations with Russia and other countries, and none had ever been offered in the traditional maktab. Consequently, pressed by the bourgeoisie and fearing Russian intervention, the emir re-authorized creation of a new-method school in Bukhara in 1912, and by 1913 there were ten such schools among the Sunnite and Shiite inhabitants of the city. The towns of Kerki, Shahrisiab, Karakul, and Gijuan followed suit, and it seemed that the Bukhariote clergy had finally become reconciled to the Jadids' victory. But this, too, was only a short period of tolerance.

The emir and clergy had yielded because they had to reckon with both Russian and Moslem political circles. The arbitrary regime in Bukhara had aroused the indignation of progressive groups in Russian society, and in the 1910's a number of books were published in Russia criticizing the khanate of Bukhara for inhuman treatment of its peasants and for its medieval methods of ruling. One of the most pointed of these books, written by an eminent geographer, Colonel D. N. Logofet, appealed directly to the Duma for Russian intervention in the khanate.[44] Actually, Bukhara's regime, based on the rule of Uzbek chieftains, reactionary clergy, and unpaid—consequently corrupt —government officials, had not progressed since the time of Uzbek conquest.[45] Tatars and Moslems in European Russia were equally aghast at conditions in the khanate, and supported Russian intervention in Bukhara's internal affairs. Ismail bey Gasprinsky wrote in *Tarjuman*, "If only Tashkent and Petersburg would try seriously, it would be possible to make of Bukhara a better organized and cultured land with a well-adjusted administration."[46] Another Tatar, S. Maksudov, head of the Moslem caucus in the Duma, stated in 1910 after a visit to Central Asia that the situation in Bukhara, as contrasted to that in the Russian Central Asian provinces, was intolerable.[47]

After the death of Emir Abdul Ahad in 1910, the Russian Governor General of Turkestan proposed annexation of the khanate of Bukhara to Russia, but the tsarist government, fearing British irritation at a change in the status quo of Central Asia, postponed action.[48] The new emir, aware of the Russian administration's intentions, hesitated to provoke further antagonism by persecuting the Jadids or resisting introduction of the reformed maktabs. His acquiescence in this instance was neither voluntary nor lasting, and at the first relaxation of Russian attention he and the clergy retaliated against the liberals.

In 1914, after the assassination of Archduke Francis Ferdinand in

Sarajevo, the political situation on Russia's western border became tense. The emir of Bukhara took advantage of this opportunity to recover the concessions he had made to the liberals two years earlier, and he "yielded" to the clergy in its request to close the Jadid schools. In his manifesto of July 18, 1914, the emir announced closure of all schools which adhered to the new methods in their programs. Many educators were deported to eastern Bukhara and some, such as S. Aini (later president of the Tajik Academy of Sciences), fled to Russia. Prohibition of reformed education could not be completely enforced, however, for by this time liberal thought and new educational methods had taken root among the Bukhariote upper classes. Children of wealthy families remained under the private tutelage of Jadid teachers, and so the processs of enlightenment continued.[49]

THE YOUNG BUKHARIOTES

In Bukhara, as in the Russian Central Asian provinces, the movement for educational reform, which was the expression of the minimal demand of liberals, was followed closely by political activity. Participating in this were such wealthy Bukhariote merchants as the Maksumov and Hojaev families, later allies of the Bolsheviks and administrators of the Bukhara Peoples' Republic. Frustrated students of the madrasas also furnished teachers and propagandists for the liberal movement. Many of the movement's leaders, such as Behbudi, Aini, Munevver Kari, Nasirkhan Tora, and Abdul Rauf Fitrat, were themselves products of the Bukhariote madrasas, where their training in scholastic debate prepared them for dialectical and speculative thinking.

Their acclaimed ideological leader was Fitrat, who, after completion of his studies in Bukhara, had been sent by wealthy Jadid supporters to Constantinople for further education. In the Ottoman capital, Fitrat became associated with the Young Turks, and his first publication, *Munizira* (A Talk), became the manifesto of the Bukhariote Jadids. In this treatise Fitrat accused his former teachers of destroying the strength of Islam by isolating the Moslem world from cultural and technical progress and bringing about its spiritual stagnation. "Consider the blow you have inflicted upon our religion," he wrote. "What a misfortune befell us because of your ignorant exposure of the law of Mohammed. Yes, the decline of Moslem greatness is the work of your hands. Because of you, the complete downfall of Islam will soon come. You have hindered progress and have spread a great cloak of ignorance over Moslems." Fitrat also held the clergy and the madrasa educators responsible for Islam's weakened military power, charging, "You have limited the armament [of our land] to daggers and swords, to bows and arrows, . . . forbidden the manufacture of cannons, rifles, bombs, dynamite and other munitions. . . . You have divided the Moslem nation into Sunnites, Shiites, Zeydits and Wahabis, and made them enemies of each other. . . . You have sacrificed the Holy Writ of Koran to your own vile and untamed passions." In another pamphlet, Fitrat censured not only Bukhara's clergy, but the emir himself.[50]

Along with the program for enlightenment and struggle over the despotic and lawless regime of the emir, there were also anti-Russian and Pan-Islamic motifs in the propaganda of Behbudi, Fitrat and other young Bukhariotes. Fitrat continually lamented the conquest of Moslem lands by Europeans and censured both "clerical obscurantists" and the Bukhariote administration for being unable to defend Central Asia from Christian ascendancy. He recalled that Mohammed had declared the Holy War an obligation and pointed out that enlightenment would help "prepare arms and bullets for defense of Islam and freeing of the fatherland from infidels' hands." [51]

Although, like Fitrat and other young Bukhariotes, the Jadids urged that children be sent to school in Constantinople, the program of Central Asian Jadids before the revolution was Pan-Islamic rather than Pan-Turkic (see Chapter IV). Fitrat's native Bukhara was holy to him, and outside of it he revered all Islam, not just the Turks alone. His appeals were addressed to his "compatriots and brothers in religion." For the young Bukhariotes, Islamic faith and civilization, and the multinational cultural world of all Central Asia, still took precedence over Pan-Turkic feelings.[52]

Fitrat's activities resulted in an intensification of Jadid political action in Bukhara. Embittered by the unfulfilled promises of the new emir, Seid Alim (1910–1920), who upon coming to the throne had proclaimed his intention of reforming the administration, prohibiting bribes, reorganizing the system of taxation, and improving the madrasas, the Jadids organized an underground oppositional society.[53] This society continued the struggle against illiteracy, ignorance, and abuses by the clergy and judges, vowing to defend the victims of injustice. It further agitated for denunciation of the emir's policies and court as well as for limitation of his expenditures. Above all, it pointed out the need for a moral revival and struggle against superstition, prejudice, and fanaticism. The Jadids' program met with the approval of liberal Sunnites and Shiites, particularly of the latter, although they formed the minority in the khanate. The underground society collected funds from its wealthy supporters to continue sending Bukhariote students to universities in Turkey and Constantinople, where, with the help of Turkish sympathizers, Bukhara's political émigrés founded an analogous organization.[54] In Constantinople, also, Bukhariotes became better acquainted with the Young Turk movement and witnessed its successful revolution and ascendance to power. The Bukhariote liberals adopted the name "Young Bukhariotes" in imitation of the Young Turks.

Influenced by the Young Turks' political program and ideology, the Young Bukhariotes undertook the distribution of political literature in Central Asia. The first issue of *Bukhara-i-Sherif*, a camouflaged Jadid paper in Tajik, appeared in the Russian extraterritorial settlement of New Bukhara on March 12, 1912. It was soon followed by its Uzbek counterpart, *Turan*. Both periodicals were authorized by the Russian diplomatic agent in the khanate, who issued licenses to their editors, Mirza Muhiddin and Mirza Sariji Hakim, unaware of their connection with the Jadids. As was the case with most liberal undertakings in the khanate, these papers were soon closed at the insistence of the emir, but despite their premature end, they were the most effective instrument of the Young Bukhariotes.[55] In 1912–1913 the two organizations, *Ma'arifat* (Enlightenment) and *Barakat* (Success), were founded, ostensibly occupied with trade and the import of books and periodicals from abroad but actually concerned with the distribution of liberal propaganda throughout the khanate.

The emir's manifesto of 1914, which had closed the reformed schools in the khanate, was intended at the same time to suspend the activities of liberals in general. The measure was apparently directed against the Young Bukhariotes, who, although clandestinely organized in the khanate as a political party, held their meetings openly in private groups. Prohibition of their gatherings did not suppress the movement, however, but only drove it further underground, and despite deportations and emigrations the Young Bukhariotes continued their agitation and activity. At the beginning of the World War in 1914, many Bukhariote students and émigrés returned from

Constantinople to Tashkent, which became their stronghold for further struggle against Bukhara's regime. Among these returned émigrés was Fitrat.[56]

In the other vassal khanate, Khiva, the Jadid movement also took root in the first decade of the twentieth century. The liberals there found two influential sponsors, close advisers of the khan: Islam Hoja and Hussein Bek. The latter founded a reformed madrasa in the capital city of Khiva. A Russian orientalist, A. M. Samoilovich, discovered in Khiva in 1908 four Jadid maktabs, with Tatar teachers.[57] Khiva, however, was less concerned with educational problems than Bukhara, a fact which contributed to the prompt failure there of new-method schools. Intense rivalry between the Uzbeks and Turkomens dominated the political scene in Khiva, which was saved in 1912 from Turkomen plunderers, bent on overthrowing the khan, only with the assistance of Russian troops.

Hence, on the eve of World War I and the Russian revolution of 1917, Islam continued to dominate the life and mind of Central Asians. The inconsistent attempts of the tsarist government to carry Russian culture to the Uzbeks and Tajiks were relatively unsuccessful, while the development of a liberal national movement among them was checked by conservative forces. The Jadids' initial successes were largely due to the Tatars' assistance and were limited to regions controlled by the Russian administration, where imperial authorities, intentionally or not, protected liberals from the wrath of Moslem fanatics. When and where it was exposed to an open struggle with traditionalists, the progressive national movement in Central Asia proved itself still too weak to overcome the structure and spirit of Central Asian society. Moreover, the Central Asians' nascent Turkic nationalism was obscured by their hope for reforming and resurrecting Islam.

CHAPTER VII

Azerbaijani Awakening

One of the most salient traits of the cultural and political development of Russian Azerbaijan in the course of the nineteenth century was its overcoming of Iranian influence. As we have seen, cultural "de-Iranization," which was initiated in Constantinople, was a common feature of the Turkic national revival both inside and outside Turkey. Among all the Turkic regions of Russia, it was of particular importance for Azerbaijan, where Persian influence had been intense and long-lasting.

Situated between the Caspian Sea, the Caucasian range, the Armenian uplands, and the Araks River, which separates Azerbaijan from Iran, this small country of eastern Transcaucasia had belonged to the realm of Iranian culture for two and a half millenniums, even though the basic core of its population was not Iranian, but of Caucasian-Japhetic origin. In the sixth century B.C., during the reign of the Achaemenides, the first Persian dynasty, the territory that is now Azerbaijan became a part of the Persian empire, and from that time on Iranian culture and language penetrated the country deeply.[1] Despite numerous subsequent conquests and migrations, Azerbaijan preserved its Iranian character for nearly fifteen hundred years. Its inclusion in the Arabian caliphate in the seventh century A.D. and the infiltration of Turkic nomads beginning in the eighth century did not substantially alter its ethnic structure.[2] An Arabian, Ibn Haukal, wrote in about 950 A.D. that nearly the entire population of Azerbaijan "speaks Persian, and only the merchants speak Arabic." [3]

The situation changed in 1054, when the Seljukid Turks, coming through Persia from Central Asia, appeared in the Near East and conquered Azerbaijan. Togrul Bek, the Seljukid sultan, integrated Persia, Iraq, Syria, Azerbaijan, and Asia Minor into his empire, laying the foundation for the strong Turkic state which later, under the Ottoman dynasty, became a world power. With the appearance of the Seljukids, the Turkic nomads became sufficiently strong to Turkize the population of Azerbaijan and secure their rule in Persia and Transcaucasia for four hundred years.[4] The process of the Turkization of eastern Transcaucasia has lasted almost up to the present time, for the number of local inhabitants speaking Iranian or Caucasian languages has progressively decreased, while the number speaking the Azerbaijani Turkic tongue has increased. In 1926, for instance, Turks comprised 62 per cent of the entire population of Azerbaijan; those speaking the Iranian dialects of Talysh and Tat comprised only 5 per cent, and Caucasian mountaineers, 2.4 per cent. The remainder were Russians and Armenians. In the period 1926–1939, assimilation of non-Turkic peoples raised the number of Azerbaijanis to 2.3 million, an increase of 33 per cent, while the average population increase for the entire USSR during those fourteen years was only 15.9 per cent.[5] Even those non-Turkic people still speaking Caucasian languages often regarded themselves as Azerbaijanis: in 1926 over 30,000 mountaineers speaking Caucasian-Japhetic dialects declared themselves Azerbaijani Turks.[6]

Despite this process of Turkization in Azerbaijan, which began as early as the sixteenth century, the Persians subsequently made another attempt to Iranize the inhabitants of eastern Transcaucasia. In 1501 power in Persia and Azerbaijan was seized by the Safavid dynasty, which professed Shiism. The Safavids began to eradicate the orthodox Moslem Sunnites of Azerbaijan, and under Shah Abbas the First (1587–1628) the struggle with the Sunnites and the process of Iranization took an especially sharp form. The Sunnite leaders of Turkic tribes were either executed or expelled from Azerbaijan, while thousands of Azerbaijani Turks were liquidated or resettled in Persia.[7] Toward the end of the eighteenth century, the administration, clergy, schools, and a large part of the aristocracy and merchants were again using the Persian language and became Shiites, while only in the western part of Azerbaijan, where the Turkic nomadic element was particularly intense, did the population remain Sunnite. By 1916 over 60 per cent of the Moslem population of present Azerbaijan were Shiites.[8]

In 1804 the Georgian prince Tsitsianov, commanding tsarist troops in Transcaucasia, began Russian conquest of the land between the Armenian plateau and the Caspian Sea. In 1805 Baku was taken, and in accordance with the terms of the Gulistan treaty of 1813, much of present Azerbaijan became a part of the Russian Empire. Nakhichevan and western Azerbaijan were conquered in 1826 and officially incorporated into the Russian Empire under the Turkmanchai treaty of 1828. Despite Russian conquest, the Persian language remained the main language of the administration in these provinces until the reforms of 1840. The local authorities themselves were either Persians or local aristocrats who spoke Persian, and the Persian tongue continued to be spoken in the courts until the 1870's. The Shiite clergy, which controlled the schools and the courts, was the main perpetuator of Iranian influence.[9] Persian also remained the language of the upper classes and of literature.

TURKIC REVIVAL IN AZERBAIJAN

Iranian influence began to decrease noticeably in 1860–1870, when interest in the Turkic language arose among the Azerbaijanis. In 1859 several comedies were published in the Azerbaijani tongue, written by the Azerbaijani satiric dramatist, Fath Ali Akhond-Zadeh, who also took up a campaign against the bigotry and religious fanaticism of the Shiite clergy.[10] Akhond-Zadeh urged Azerbaijanis to become acquainted with Russian and West European culture, and even suggested replacing the Arabic alphabet by Russian-Latin letters of his own invention. His call to enlightenment, his anti-clericalism, and his writings in the native language had an especially strong influence on the native population after the creation of an Aberbaijani national theater, of whose repertoire Akhond-Zadeh's plays became an integral part.[11]

The publication of the first newspaper in the Azerbaijani Turkic language was of no less importance. In 1875 Hassan Melikov-Zarbadi, a teacher in the Russian secondary school in Baku—whose efforts had made possible the appearance of Akhond-Zadeh's plays on the Azerbaijani school stage—began to publish *Akinchi* (The Plowman). Although *Akinchi* lasted only two years, it was nevertheless important for the development of the Azerbaijani literary language. In his paper Melikov-Zarbadi, too, sharply attacked the fanatic Shiite clergy, and his anti-Iranian agitation was so outspoken that it aroused the local nobility and clergy against him. Persian-speaking nobles attacked him, also, for publishing his newspaper in a "peasant dialect," which they considered the native Azerbaijani Turkic tongue to be.[12]

In the period 1870–1883 this remote corner of the Russian Empire suddenly became a part of the world economy. Oil promoted Baku to an international industrial center. While in the 1840's the output of oil was no more than 250,000 puds a year, in 1885 it jumped to 115,000,000, and in 1895 to 377,000,000 puds.[13] Completion of the Baku-Batum railroad in 1883 connected Azerbaijan with the markets of Russia and Western Europe, facilitating contact with Constantinople, and led to a strengthening of Turkish influence in Azerbaijan. At the same time, the growth of Baku's industry complicated relationships between the various national groups of Azerbaijan, contributing in turn to a rise in Turkic national feeling. Armenian and Russian workers streamed into the new oil centers, while foreign businessmen and entrepreneurs nearly gained a monopoly in Baku's oil industry. Baku itself was transformed from a quiet Asiatic town into a noisy economic center. Eastern Transcaucasia became divided into a multinational industrial region in urban Baku and a Turkish agricultural countryside, where patriarchal relationships persisted between the old, formerly feudal, aristocracy and the peasantry.[14]

Toward the beginning of the twentieth century, a local intelligentsia, already oriented toward Baku, began to emerge from the Azerbaijani nobility and merchant class. This new group of intellectuals began to show its Pan-Islamic and Turkic consciousness quite early. Ismail bey Gasprinsky's *Tarjuman* had awakened among Azerbaijanis the feeling of belonging to the Islamic and Turkic world, which had lain dormant for so long under Persian and Shiite hegemony. The contrast between "international" Baku and the surrounding Turkic villages, the prevalence of foreign and Armenian capital in industry and trade, and clashes between Turks and Armenians in eastern Anatolia and Constantinople all helped to sponsor anti-Russian and anti-Armenian feelings in the newly awakened intelligentsia. Hostility toward Persian cultural dominance and toward Shiism, which was separating Azerbaijan from Sunnite Turkey, grew no less rapidly.[15] The satiric journal, *Mullah Nasreddin* (the name of a character in Near Eastern folklore), founded in 1906, resumed the anti-Iranian and anti-Shiite tradition of Akhond-Zadeh's *Akinchi*.

One of the first propagators of liberal ideas and Turkic nationalism in Azerbaijan was Ali bey Hussein Zadeh, an energetic political leader and writer educated in Baku and Petersburg. In 1889 he went to Turkey, where he came into close contact with the Young Turks. He participated actively in Turkish political life there, and when liberal winds again began to blow in Russia in 1905 he returned to Baku, where he began publishing a popular weekly, *Fiyuzat* (Prosperity), which took a liberal-nationalist position. He also contributed to several other Azerbaijani newspapers in Baku.

Another prominent and dynamic Azerbaijani, Ahmed bey Agaev (Aga-Oglu), also returned to Baku in 1905 after a fifteen-year absence from Russia. Like Hussein Zadeh, Agaev had studied in Baku and Petersburg, and then in Paris, where he was a student of the French historian, Ernest Renan, and the orientalists, James Darmestaeter and Barbier de Meynar. The nationalist and political theories of Renan, who taught that a nation is "a natural group determined by race," [16] produced a particularly strong impression on the young Azerbaijani, who later became one of the main proponents of the unification not only of all Turks, but of all the Uralo-Altaic peoples, whom he called "Turanians." In Paris Agaev wrote on subjects touching Persia, Turkey, the Near East, and Islam, in such distinguished periodicals as *Journal des Débats*, *Revue Bleue*, and *Nouvelle Revue*. He also cooperated there with the Young Turks, who had established a center in Paris. Agaev's journalistic talent won him a favorable reputation in Paris, although his later Pan-Turkic and anti-Russian concepts were not yet apparent in the articles he published there. In his contributions of 1891–1893 to *Nouvelle Revue*, for instance, he displayed greater interest in modernizing Iranian culture than in the Turks, and even made some anti-Turkish remarks which aroused a storm of indignation among the Young Turks residing in Paris. Further, he expressed at that time open admiration for Russia, and claimed that he had found in Iran three times more friends of Russia than of England. Such Russian popularity in the Near East he attributed to the absence of racial prejudice and to the inherent "good nature" of the simple Russian. Like most liberals of his time, he strongly attacked the Moslem, and especially Shiite, clergy's exploitation of ignorance and superstitition, and considered the clergy's domination over the cultural and social life of Moslems the cause of the poverty of Moslem countries. Agaev took a similar position in his articles published in Baku in *Kaspii* and *Kavkaz*, in which he urged reform of Moslem society and emancipation of Moslem women. He also protested in these articles against the Moslem clergy's "complete distortion of religion." [17] In Baku, along with Hussein Zadeh, Agaev contributed to Turkic and Russian newspapers, including *Kaspii*, the Azerbaijani paper in Russian. *Kaspii* had been established by the Baku

millionaire, Zeinulla Abdin Tagiev, who, though a Persian by ancestry, became the leading supporter of the newly born Turkic national
movement in Azerbaijan. Thanks to the wide support of this Maecenas, there existed not a few Azerbaijani publishing houses, schools,
charitable organizations, and theaters.

A third notable contributor to *Kaspii* was Ali Mardan bey Topchibashev, the attorney who presided over Ittifak in 1905 and who was
at the head of the Moslem caucus in the Second Duma. Topchibashev
considered that, awakened under the impact of European civilization,
Western imperialism, and modern nationalism, the Moslem world
would inevitably become united. This end was served both by the
agitation of Pan-Islamists and by the activities of those Moslems who
completed their education in Russian or European schools.[18] During
the short period of Azerbaijan's independence in 1918–1920, Topchibashev was one of the country's most active politicians, and he subsequently became the president of the Azerbaijani Republic.

THE PRESS

The Azerbaijanis, suprisingly enough for a people only recently
introduced to Western civilization, proved themselves to be capable
journalists. The new Baku press was overflowing with talent, and
during the liberal period from 1905 to 1908 the Azerbaijani press
mushroomed. Besides the newspapers *Ziya* (Aurora), *Keshkyul* (Cup
of Alms), and *Ziyai Kafkaz* (Aurora of the Caucasus), there were
added after 1905 *Seda* (The Voice), *Seda-i-Vatan* (Voice of the
Country), *Seda-i-Hak* (Voice of Justice), *Seda-i-Kafkaz* (Voice of
the Caucasus), *Hakikat* (Truth), *Yeni Hakikat* (New Truth), *Ikbal*
(Success), *Malumat* (Knowledge), *Gyunesh* (The Sun), *Tarakki*
(Progress), *Negat* (Salvation), and many others.[19] The majority of
these periodicals did not last very long, due to absence of necessary
funds and a sufficient reading public, severity of censorship, and in-
experience, but where some closed down, others opened up. Only
Kaspii, thanks to the support of Tagiev, existed almost up to the
arrival of the Bolsheviks in Baku. Nevertheless, these journals played
an important role and greatly contributed to the growth of a Turkic
nationalist mood among the Azerbaijani intelligentsia, bourgeoisie
and aristocracy. Besides Hussein Zadeh, Agaev, and Topchibashev,
there were other journalists who stood out in the press, such as
Hashim bey Veziri, subsequently leader of the Azerbaijani national-

ists, Mehmed Emin bey Resul Zadeh, and Mehmed Aga Shahtahvili. The words of Shahtahvili, that Azerbaijanis "should love the Turkic world above anything else," [20] illustrate best of all the Pan-Turkic views shared by these writers.

Of all the Turkic groups in Russia, it was among those of Azerbaijan that the movement for equality of women started the earliest. The woman's journal, *Ishik*, edited by the Azerbaijani suffragette, Hadijé Hanum, energetically fought for the full emancipation of Moslem women. Hamidé Hanum, wife of the publisher of *Mullah Nasreddin*, and Saadat Hanum, wife of the future Prime Minister of Azerbaijan, Nassip bey Usubbekov (Yusufbeyli), among others, also actively participated in the press and in social activity.[21] With the exception of clerical periodicals, the entire Azerbaijani press supported the struggle for emancipation of Moslem women.

AZERBAIJAN IN 1905

Involved multinational antagonisms and social unrest lent a tragic aspect to the revolutionary years 1905–1907 in Azerbaijan. After 1900 the Social Democrats succeeded in infiltrating labor in the Baku oil fields, and by December 1904 they were strong enough to call a general strike. Stalin himself participated there in the organization of revolutionary groups, in the dissemination of propaganda, and in the strike movement. In 1904 the Social Democrats in Baku created a special Moslem group, *Hemmet*, whose leaders were the Azerbaijanis, Narriman Narimanov, Effendiev, and Meshadi Azizbekov. After the revolution of 1917, Azizbekov became the Bolshevik boss in Baku and figured prominently in the Sovietization of Transcaucasia.[22]

Terrorist activities, murders, riots, and demonstrations between Armenians and Moslems also characterized the years 1905–1907 in Baku. Agitation by the Social Democrats and the Armenian revolutionary society *Dashnaksutiun*, as well as Moslem countermeasures, developed into mutual massacres. It should be stated, however, that the Azerbaijani Turks were the least revolutionized part of the Transcaucasian population, and only in rare instances displayed real anti-Russian hostility, while Azerbaijani landowners cooperated with the Russian administration and took the initiative in forming counter-revolutionary security detachments. Liberal nationalists maintained close ties with the Russian Kadets. Among the workers, however, this "fraternal cooperation" between Azerbaijanis and Russians found

its expression in anti-Armenian riots, and mobs of these two nationalities participated in the frequent looting of Armenian shops and
enterprises.[23] Aside from such clashes, complaints about anti-Russian
or antigovernmental activities on the part of Azerbaijanis can be
found in only a few reports of the Russian police and administrators,
and even in these reports Azerbaijani conservatism is stressed. Russian-
Azerbaijani "anti-Armenian" collaboration, however, disappeared
some ten years later when the revolutionary events of 1917–1920
reversed the situation, and the growth of Turkic nationalism led to
an alliance between Russian and Armenian forces in Baku.

In 1906 a welfare society, *Neshir i Sherif*, was founded in Baku,
concerned with philanthropic activities and with the growth of
literacy. Tagiev, Melikov-Zarbadi—the former editor of *Akinchi*—
and other representatives of the Azerbaijani bourgeoisie and liberal
clergy gave it their warmest support. The society's operations at the
beginning were financed by Tagiev, and several new Moslem schools
were indebted to the society for their existence. After two or three
years, however, enthusiasm for educational progress diminished, and,
running out of money, *Neshir i Sherif* drastically curtailed its undertakings.[24] This society, nevertheless, laid the foundation for the unification of Azerbaijani liberal national forces and was the protoype
of a purely Azerbaijani national party.

Azerbaijani liberals participated very actively in the All-Russian
Moslem Congresses in Nizhni Novgorod and Petersburg, and in the
formation of Ittifak. Topchibashev, who presided over some of these
meetings and who headed the Moslem caucus in the Second Duma,
distinguished himself as one of their ablest and most tactful politicians.
After the dissolution of the Second Duma and the reduction of Moslem parliamentary representation, Azerbaijani liberals lost interest in
Duma politics and relaxed the ties which had bound them with the
Kadets in the parliamentary elections, even displaying some indifference toward Ittifak. They concentrated, instead, on local Azerbaijani
affairs and resumed their relations with Constantinople. After the
Young Turks' upheaval, Pan-Turkism prevailed over a preoccupation
with social and religious problems among the Azerbaijani intelligentsia
and bourgeoisie, and they intensified Pan-Turkic propaganda.

After the quelling of revolutionary disturbances, when the administration began to scrutinize more closely the political activity of the
local population of Transcaucasia, even curbing the work of many

parties, some Azerbaijani leaders decided to leave Russia. They went to Turkey, eager to mount the band wagon of the victorious Young Turks, with whom they had not lost touch.[25] Among those who left Russia were Agaev, whose pan-Turkic publications were prohibited in Russia and who came to Constantinople in 1908, and Hussein Zadeh, who followed him in 1910.

MUSAVAT

Definite formation of the first Azerbaijani political party came about only in 1911–1912, when a handful of intellectuals, led by Mehmed Emin bey Resul Zadeh, created an underground left-bourgeois party, *Musavat* (Equality). Like Agaev and many other Azerbaijanis, at the beginning of his career Resul Zadeh was more a liberal protagonist of Moslem unity than a Turkic nationalist. After participating with Stalin in creating the Social Democratic group, Hemmet, and in antigovernment agitation in Baku, Resul Zadeh escaped to Persia, where he assisted in promoting the struggle against the absolute monarchy of the shah. He was a good example of the bilingual, and even "binational," intellectual, for in Teheran he became editor of two Persian periodicals, *Irane Ahad* and *Iran Nev*. Defeated on the battlefield of the Iranian revolution, however, Resul Zadeh migrated once more, this time to Constantinople. Here he joined the Pan-Turkic movement and cooperated with the Young Turks, who were now in power. He contributed to the radically nationalist *Türk Yurdu* (Turkic Fatherland), which had been founded in Constantinople by his revolutionary colleague from Baku, Agaev. Extremely enthusiastic over the cause of Pan-Turkic unity, Resul Zadeh returned to Baku in 1910 or 1911 and immediately became prominent in the local political life.[26]

Despite its name and the Social Democratic affiliations of its founders, Musavat was rather a Turkic national, or Pan-Islamic, party than a socialist one. In a manifesto published on the occasion of the party's founding, Musavat's central committee recalled that "once the noble people of Islam reached out one hand to Peking . . . and with the other built at the opposite end of Europe the palace Alhambra." It lamented that once "having been the ruler of such huge parts of the world as Asia, Europe, and Africa, Islam has now disintegrated into tiny pieces." Nonetheless, the leaders of Musavat did not lose heart, and advised, apparently recalling the former feats of Turkic horsemen, "All possible means of repulsing the enemy are being made ready—even horses." [27]

The basic points of Musavat's program were less concerned with equality than with the unification of all Moslems, by which was meant, of course, Turks. Its program called for the following:

(1) Unification of all Moslem peoples, regardless of nationality and religious doctrine.

(2) Restoration of the Moslem countries' lost independence.

(3) Rendering of moral and material assistance to Moslem countries struggling to preserve or restore their independence.

(4) Aid in developing the defensive and offensive strength of the Moslem peoples.

(5) Removal of all barriers hindering the spread of these ideas.

(6) Establishment of contact with those parties seeking Moslem unification and progress.

(7) Establishment where necessary of contact and exchange of opinion with foreign parties working for the prosperity and progress of mankind.

(8) Strengthening all means of struggle for Moslem existence and the development of their commercial, industrial, and economic life.[28]

Musavat's manifesto and program were badly adjusted admixtures of national, religious, and social slogans. Firuz Kazemzadeh, in his excellent study of the revolution in Transcaucasia, points out that Musavat's program was characterized by "no well-defined ideology" and "lack of any systematic political philosophy," and that it remained "rather vague." [29] While the party's name and the more belligerent points in its program echo the revolutionary past of Resul Zadeh, its work was still less social than purely nationalistic. According to its program, Musavat's energies should have been directed toward the liberation of the Turkic peoples and creation of a new Moslem Turkic empire extending from the Atlantic Ocean and Morocco to the Pacific Ocean and Mongolia, all under the aegis of Constantinople.

In reality, however, Musavat's political activity was much more peaceful than its program. Before 1918—that is, before the appearance of Turkish troops in the Caucasus—Musavat's leaders did little to transform Azerbaijan into an independent state or to join it to Turkey. The Azerbaijani intelligentsia was certainly attracted to the second idea—political union of the population of eastern Transcaucasia with its coreligionists and fellow Turks of Turkey. But in 1910–

1914 few historical or economic premises existed for the creation of an independent Azerbaijan or, more correctly, for propaganda urging the creation of such a state. Musavat found supporters mainly among the bourgeoisie and intelligentsia, while the peasantry and nobility were more inclined toward the conservative ideas of Pan-Islamism and did not fully trust the leftist intellectuals. In general, it was easier to arouse the peasantry of Transcaucasia in the name of Islam and the old patriarchal relationships than with an abstract political program they did not readily understand. The Russian Kadet, Baikov, who lived in Baku and knew the situation there very well, wrote in his memoirs that the party organization was very weak and consisted only of a few hundred persons, "while beneath them was a conglomeration of Tatar masses which had been accustomed since time immemorial to doing whatever the khan, bek, governor or leader told them to do." [30] But Baikov was only partly justified in his conclusions. A party machine in the majority of cases consists of just such a small group of political leaders, while the masses' political indifference is in general typical of Near Eastern countries. (The success and fall of Mossadegh in Iran in 1953, the oscillation of the Iranian masses in their relation toward the Moslem leader, Kashan, or toward the Tudeh party in 1945–1953, as well as the rise and fall of a "soviet" republic of southern Azerbaijan in Iran, are recent demonstrations of the flexibility and passivity of the Russian Azerbaijanis' closest neighbors, who are capable of manifesting their political moods only spasmodically.) Baikov was mistaken in stating that the supporters of the Musavat Party constituted only a few hundred people. The power-thirsty Azerbaijani intellectual, the merchant disturbed by Armenian competition, the khan, bek, or agha (aristocratic landlord) desirous of more prestige—of such there were thousands standing behind Musavat's rather hazy principles. Turkic religious and national solidarity, the alluring prospect of union with their kinsmen of Turkey, and understandable resentment at being ruled by "foreign Russian Christians" were all reasons for Musavat's success.

Hopes aroused by the Young Turks' seizure of power in Constantinople also were a factor in the strengthening of pro-Turkish sympathies in 1908–1914. To Moslems the world over it seemed that a new power had been born which could re-establish the former glory of the East and force Europe again to respect the religion and culture of the peoples of Asia. Actually, however, the leaders of Musavat were simply pro-Turkish at heart, rather than clearly Pan-Turkic, and more acutely interested in the future of Constantinople and Turkey than in the destinies of their Tatar or Uzbek brothers. A demonstration of this pro-Turkish mood occurred at a conference in 1913 in the Turkic town of Baiazet, at which Azerbaijan's delegates, Agaev, Resul Zadeh, and Topchibashev were present.[31] Their discussions of the future unification of the Turkic peoples, however, amounted to no more than mere fantasies and political conjectures. Musavat's pledge to maintain the strictest secrecy in its undertakings was no more, in effect, than the masking of its hesitancy to openly challenge the administration. This is well illustrated by one of the party's instructions: "At the present time it is best to continue to guard our existence with the severest secrecy, and Musavat . . . warns its members against openly criticizing the government and its agents." [32] This attitude did not change even at the beginning of World War I.

Although Musavat quickly became the leading party in Azerbaijan, there were several opposing groups in the country, especially among the upper strata in Turkish Azerbaijani society. The Shiite clergy, which had been connected with Persia for centuries, looked with especial disapprobation upon the growth of sympathy for Sunnite Turkey. Mullahs and other conservative Moslems also did not approve the militant secularization of the supporters of a Moslem–Turkic empire. The Western fashions popular among Musavatists contradicted the traditional views on the Moslem family and society, which, accustomed to the harem and purdah, regarded suffragettes and feminine equality with horror. The attraction of new modes, Western literature and art, interest in the theater—which affected attendance in the mosques—the study of French and modern Turkish literature and language, instead of Arabic and Persian classics, all contributed to destroying the old tenor of the Moslem social order. Hats replaced turbans, new furniture and pictures changed the appearance of the Moslem home, and traditional religious views disappeared under the influence of Russian, French, or Turkish ideas. Despite the promises made by the liberal and Musavatist intelligentsia about the future glory of Islam, the clergy saw in their innovations the end of the old order and customs. Furthermore, for the supporters of the old order—educated in the spirit of religious universalism—the cosmopolitan, international faith of Islam stood above national limitations, and they were disturbed by the narrow racial and linguistic theories of the Pan-Turkists. Musavatists, echoing the words of Yusuf Akchurin and Agaev, decidedly placed the Turkic racial and national ideal above the religious, and consequently many conservative Azerbaijani groups preferred preservation of the existing order with the help of Russia to the new liberal order promised by Pan-Turkists. This antagonism frequently became open enmity, with the mullahs proclaiming liberals to be heretics and defectors.

Musavat also lost during the war and the revolution some of its support in the left sector of Azerbaijani political life. The Social Democratic Hemmet, to which Resul Zadeh and many of his followers had belonged, was still more popular among Azerbaijani workers than was Musavat. Also, Hemmet was not yet divided, despite the schism between Mensheviks and Bolsheviks, and was able to overcome the casualties of the period 1905–1907. However, in the less boisterous prewar years, 1908–1914, Hemmet also lost much of its former revolutionary ardor and curtailed its agitation and propaganda.

Thus, revolutionary and nationalist agitation in Azerbaijan was strongly curbed by the counteraction of Russian authorities, headed by the Viceroy, I. I. Vorontsov-Dashkov, and during the last decade of the imperial regime Transcaucasia quieted down after the violence of the 1905 Revolution. As elsewhere in the Russian Empire between 1907 and 1914, rapid economic and educational progress distracted the attention of Azerbaijani social leaders from purely political problems. Even the involvement of Turkey on the side of the Axis powers in World War I did not change the superficial quiet of Transcaucasian life.

CHAPTER VIII

Pan-Turkists and the Tatarists

On June 3, 1907, finding it impossible to cooperate with the Second Duma effectively, the tsarist government, led by P. A. Stolypin, dissolved it. At the same time, a manifesto signed by Nicholas II changed the electoral law. Stolypin's "constitutional upheaval" signified the beginning not only of a new parliamentary period in Russian history, but a new era in the political life of Russian Turks as well. The new electoral law deprived the steppe region and Central Asia of representation and sharply diminished the number of Moslem deputies from the Caucasus and the Volga-Ural provinces. Moslems could send only nine deputies to the new (Third) Duma,[1] and in the Fourth Duma the number fell to seven, owing to local administrative shifts.[2] The government sought reduction in the number of Moslem deputies for two reasons: first, it would thus deprive the Kadets and labor caucus of thirty members, and, second, it would inflict a blow upon the prestige and influence of the growing Moslem—rather, Turkic—political movement.

The growth of Turkic political activity in the years 1905–1907 had alarmed the Russian government. It was evident that the Tatars were working stubbornly for unification and leadership of the Turkic peoples—in fact, of all the Moslems—of Russia. The success of the Tatar schools and press, and of the Moslem congresses, showed that the Tatars had become a significant force definitely oriented toward Turkey. The resolution of the Third All-Moslem Congress to introduce the Ottoman Turkish language in Russian Moslem schools clearly indicated that Tatar nationalists wanted to subject all Russian Turks to an influence foreign and even hostile to Russia. Even more, they sought to include under their Moslem—Turkic aegis other non-Turkic Moslem peoples of the Russian Empire, such as the mountaineers of the Caucasus, the Central Asian Tajiks, and the Moslem Finnish population of the Volga region. The defection back to Islam in 1905–1907 of forty-nine thousand Volga Tatars who had become

Christians in the eighteenth century was further cause for alarm. It seemed that Islam and Turkic nationalism had gained a brilliant new victory at the very gates of Moscow.[3] Bishop Andrew of Mamadysh (Prince Ukhtomsky) wrote the government, "Conquest by the Moslem Tatars of Kazan and the entire Volga region is proceeding slowly and quietly, but persistently, before our very eyes. . . ." [4]

Concern on the part of the government and some Russian nationalist circles for the fate of the Volga region—the very heart of the empire—also explains attempts in 1905–1907 to place Moslem schools under government control.[5] Later, in 1909–1912, the Ministry of Education organized a special commission "to study means for combating Tatar-Moslem influence in the Volga region," and a number of conferences were held to discuss possibilities of strengthening Russia's cultural impact in the eastern parts of the empire.[6]

Reduction in the size, and consequently in the strength, of the Moslem faction in the Duma and the government's more severe limitation of political propaganda, congresses, and demonstrations had a twofold result. On the one hand, some extreme nationalists—Pan-Turkists—transferred their activity to Turkey, and their work at home acquired a clandestine character which led to radicalism. At the same time, however, the curtailment of open Turkic nationalist agitation led to the general appeasement of Russia's eastern areas, particularly of the Tatar territorities.[7]

TURKEY AND PAN-TURKISTS

Hindered in their political undertakings, in the years 1908–1910 a number of Turkic leaders emigrated to Turkey, and Constantinople once again became the main center for Russian Pan-Turkists. After the Young Turks' coup in 1908, the Turkish government radically changed its attitude toward Turkic émigrés from Russia and became more favorably inclined toward the idea of common Turkic unity which they propagated. While Sultan Abdul Hamid had been suspicious of all political émigrés, fearing their revolutionary spirit, the Young Turks—themselves former conspirators—after coming to power demonstrated greater sympathy for the Tatar and Azerbaijani nationalists. The Young Turks rejected Pan-Islamism, which was so close to the heart of Abdul Hamid, and adhered to the doctrine of Ottoman state ideology—that is, the unification of all the empire's nationalities under the Ottoman dynasty. Not initially Pan-Turkists, they did come to accept more and more the Pan-Turkists' ideas. Pan-Turkism, already voiced in 1904 by Yusuf Akchurin, was caught up by the young Turkish publicist, Ziia Gökalp, who, despite his Kurdic origin, became a dynamic new herald of the Turkic national idea. He and his friends, Ata Günduz, Abdulla Jevdet, Hussein Jahid (editor of *Tanin*), and Halidé Edib Hanum,[8] established an influential, strongly nationalistic society, *Yeni Lisan* (New Word), which had the following aims:

(1) The purging from Turkic life of foreign and pernicious influences, revival of the old Turkic (Asiatic) culture, and purification of the Turkish language by eliminating Persian and Arabic loan words (whence the society's name—"New Word").

(2) Scientific determination of the ethnic and cultural community of all "Turanians"—that is, Turks, Mongolians, Tunguz, Finno-Ugrics, and other Uralo-Altaic peoples.[9]

The society's organ, *Genç-Kalemlar* (Young Quills) soon became the Pan-Turkists' leading trumpet. Based first in Salonika, long a Young Turk center, the society later moved to Constantinople, where it could more easily exert its influence. At the plenum of the central committee of the Young Turk Party in 1911, the society effected the passing of a resolution—which in principle departed somewhat from Ottomanism—calling for "the spread of the Turkish language as an excellent means for establishing Moslem suzerainty and for assimilating non-Turkic elements."[10] Another step toward recognizing the ideological and racial unity of all Turkic peoples was taken when the Young Turks elected to their central committee three well-known Russian Turkic nationalist leaders: Ismail bey Gasprinsky (Crimean), Ali bey Hussein Zadeh (Azerbaijani), and Yusuf Akchurin (Tatar).[11] About this same time another Azerbaijani, Ahmed bey Agaev, was named general inspector of all educational institutions in Constantinople.

Ismail bey Gasprinsky was still living in Bakchisarai, but Agaev, Hussein Zadeh, Akchurin, and Resul Zadeh, along with other Crimean, Azerbaijani, Tatar, and Uzbek émigrés and students from Tashkent and Bukhara, worked together in Constantinople. Akchurin became their leader, and on March 25, 1912, he founded a new organization, *Türk Oçagi* (Turkic Home), which soon had affiliated groups throughout all of Turkey. Akchurin also organized special groups of propagandists to disseminate Pan-Turkic ideas in Russia.

Thus, in the five or six years before the beginning of World War I, Constantinople became a rallying point for Pan-Turkism and for a consolidation of the forces of Turkic emigration from Russia. In 1908 the Union of Crimean Students[12] had been founded, in 1909 came the Bukhariote Society for the Spread of Knowledge in Constantinople,[13] and in 1911 Turkic Unity,[14] the Society of Tatar Emigrants, and the Society of Turkic Students from Russia, as well as others.[15]

THE TURANIAN NATIONALIST MYTH

On December 7, 1911, Akchurin's Pan-Turkic journal, *Türk Yurdu* (Turkic Fatherland) began to appear. Its success was so great that the first issue was printed in four editions, the second in three, and the third and fourth in two.[16] In almost every issue the movement's ideologist and theoretician, Agaev, who completely abandoned the Iranian inclination he had held in his student days, discussed and further developed the Pan-Turkic theories which Akchurin had formulated in 1904. Although both Akchurin and Agaev were closer to the older generation of Gasprinsky,[17] it was no longer Islam and its culture, but Turkism—or "Turanism," as it came to be called—which inspired the founders of *Türk Yurdu*. In his articles Agaev wrote of Turkic unity and the Turks' role in world history and civilization. He considered that the seventy to eighty million Turanians (both Turks and the related Finno-Ugric and Mongolian peoples of Europe and Asia), if united, could form a powerful empire, which he urged them to do.[18] He had a high regard for Turkic cultural possibilities, and—forgetting the culture of China, India, Iran, and Arabia—wrote, "We can say that among the peoples of Asia, with the exception of the Japanese, the most progressive and most cultured people are the Turkic peoples." [19]

Although the Pan-Turkists followed in the footsteps of Ernest Renan in considering that "the basic factor of nationality lies, first, in language; second, in religion, morals, and customs; and third, in a common history, fatherland, and fate," and pointed to Islam as the Turkic national religion, nevertheless they were neither clericalists nor Islamic traditionalists. "We do not know Islam," stated Agaev. "Or, to put it more correctly, no one has taught us Islam properly. . . . In many places (Turkey, the Caucasus, and Central Asia) Islam manifests itself only in the utterance of pious expressions, and there are not a few Moslems who do not know even these religious phrases." [20] In the eyes of Agaev, who remained faithful to his early anticlericalism, Islam should be cleansed of superstitition and meaningless rites, and become a more rational religion.

The culture and traditions of Islam actually held little interest for this new school of Turkic national thought. Pan-Turkists regarded neither Islamic nor Ottoman Turkish cultural and political traditions as the genuine products of the Turkic national genius, and their reasoning was justified to a considerable extent, since Ottoman Turkey was mainly the historical and geographical heir to Byzantium. Furthermore, Islamic culture was more a product of Arabian and Persian traditions than the fruit of purely Turkic intellectual and artistic talents. Therefore, indifferent to the glory of the Arabian and Ottoman caliphates, the Pan-Turkists (or Pan-Turanists) sought inspiration in the "Turanian" (or Turko-Mongol) past. The heroic feats of Attila and Oguz Khan, of Genghis Khan and Tamerlane, furnished the necessary material for creating a historical and national myth. Recollections of the past empire of the Huns and Mongols, which once had stretched from the Sea of Japan to the Mediterranean, and from the plains of Hindustan to the North Russian forests, were an irresistible attraction for them. A return to such a Turko-Mongol, Turanian empire, and the creation of a new Turanian state, to include all the Turkic, Mongol, and even Finno-Ugric peoples and to encompass the former territories of Genghis Khan's and Attila's nomadic nations, became an intellectual obsession with the Young Turks in 1908–1918.

In his poem *Türkluk* (The Turkish People), which became very popular with young Turkish patriots, Ziia Gökalp described the patriotic fervor of his compatriots and urged them not to forget the legendary land of their ancestors:

> They listen to the Occident, and the Occident
> Lends its ear to the voice of their glory.
> They let their heart speak, they let their heart cry,
> But never, never do they forget, these children of Oguz Khan,
> This land called Turan, and the very name of Turan.

> And you, enemies of the Turks, turn your eyes on these books,
> Learn who were Farabi and Ulugh Bek.
> Do not forget the origin of Avicenna
> And do not forget heroic Attila.

The same sentiments could be found in another popular poem of Ziia Gökalp, "The Turan":

> The fatherland of Turks is neither Turkey nor Turkestan,
> It is a great land, a land eternal. It is called Turan.[21]

In their enthusiasm, Agaev, Ziia Gökalp, and their fellow nationalists were not aware that their glorification of Turan as the legendary original home of the Turko-Mongol peoples was based on an unfortunate literary and scientific misconception. The term "Turan" had been erroneously used throughout the late nineteenth and early twentieth centuries to designate the Turko-Mongol land of Central Asia. The error was to a great extent due to phonetic similarities between the words "Turk" and "Turan." In its original meaning, as used in the Iranian epic tradition and in Firdousi's epic poem, *Shah Nameh* (The Book of Kings), the word "Turan" did not mean the ancient home of the Turko-Mongol peoples, but rather of the north Iranian population which occupied all Central Asia until the sixth century A.D. Consequently, the entire Pan-Turkist terminology and all the attempts to represent an "ancient, glorious land of Turan" as a national symbol were the product of the misuse of an obsolete geographical term.

On the political level, in the 1910's Pan-Turkists placed their hopes not only in the regenerative power of their national myth, but also in the military power of Ottoman Turkey and Germany. Their respect for the Constantinople government did not go unappreciated by the Young Turks and their puppet sultan, who wrote to the Pan-Turkists on the occasion of the appearance of the first issue of their *Türk Yurdu,* "The favors which the journal *Türk Yurdu,* its founders, and editors have shown the Turkic race are worthy of recognition. I particularly greet them." Upon receipt of the sultan's message, the editors responded that "That day was a historic date for the Turkic nation" and that the sultan had shown that "the Turkic race is a nation unified spiritually, ideologically, and internally by its leaders." The pro-German leanings of Turkic nationalists also manifested themselves at this time. In the same issue of *Türk Yurdu* in which the sultan's message was printed, the editors wrote that the "rulers of the universe have always been the representatives of only two great nations—Turks and Germans," and that only they would be worthy of ruling the world in the future. In his turn, Akchurin also declared that a renewed alliance between the Ottoman Turks and the Germans was of the greatest importance for the successful development of the activities of Russian Turkic students in Constantinople.[22]

Many Ottoman Turkish periodicals even surpassed the nationalistic dreams of *Türk Yurdu* by preaching a purely political Pan-Turkism and visualizing the formation of a Turanian nation extending from the Mediterranean to the Pacific. A nationalist journalist of this type was Kachen Zadeh, who included in the future Turanian, or Turko-Tatar-Mongol, state: Asia Minor, Iraq, northern Iran, Azerbaijan, Crimea, all the plains between the Volga and Urals, the Kazakh steppe, Central Asia, Mongolia, western China, eastern Siberia, the Irkutsk, and the banks of the Amur River to the Pacific coast.[23] Although Ziia Gökalp was one of the leading enthusiasts of Turanism, he was more cautious in his political projects than his friends. He outlined three consecutive phases of Turkic nationalism and expansion. First, the Ottoman Turks had to consolidate their grip over their empire and Turkize its minorities. In the second, "Pan-Turkic," phase, the closest relatives of the Ottoman Turks—the Azerbaijanis of Russia and Persia (the southeastern group of Turkic peoples)— were to be taken into the Turkic state. The third step would be the uniting of all the Turanian people of Asia around the Turkish core.[24]

The climax of Pan-Turkic political agitation was reached on the eve of World War I. Patriotic journalists already envisioned the fall of Russia and the rise of a Turanian empire on its ruins. The massacre in 1914–1916 of one and a half million Armenians was largely conditioned by the desire of the Young Turks to eliminate the Armenian obstacle which separated Ottoman Turks from the Turks of Azerbaijan, and to prepare the way for the territorial unification of the "Oguz," or southeastern group.

TÜRK YURDU AND RUSSIA

Despite their efforts at Turkic unification, the group of Akchurin and Agaev avoided open anti-Russian propaganda during the years preceding World War I, and did not demonstrate hostility toward the Russian government. *Türk Yurdu* insisted that it was a cultural, not political, journal, and more than once it complimented Russian schools, literature, and language. Akchurin, for instance, wrote that everyone "wishing to study Turkic history should certainly learn

Russian, because there are more works about the Turks in Russian than in any other European language." [25] Other writers in the journal praised the organization of Russian schools, the pedagogical system of Ushinsky, the teaching and idealism of Tolstoy, and showed that, in Russia, Turkic national consciousness had developed earlier and more strongly than among other Turkic groups. They noted the "beneficial results of coexistence in Russia of Moslems and Russians." [26]

Thanks to this comparatively moderate tone, the Russian government did not oppose the dissemination of *Türk Yurdu* in Russia. The respectable journal of Russian orientalists, *Mir Islama* (The World of Islam), even welcomed the appearance and success of *Türk Yurdu* as "an outstanding demonstration of the new stage of development of Turkic national culture." [27] Russian orientalists, however, noted a confusion in meaning of the terms "Turkism" and "Turanism," as well as a naive enthusiasm on the part of the journal's publishers.

THE "TURKIST-TATARIST" CONTROVERSY

The theories of Akchurin, Agaev, and Ziia Gökalp were also reflected in the Turkic press in Russia, where they called up a polemic on the theme, "Who are the Tatars? Are they a separate Tatar nation or only a local group of the same Turkic people as the Ottoman Turks?" The leading Tatar newspaper, *Vakyt* (The Time), published in Orenburg by Rameev, a gold industrialist and poet, even added the subtitle, "A Turkic Newspaper." In *Shura* (Council), the literary supplement to *Vakyt*, a professor at the Huseinieh madrasa in Kazan, Jemaleddin Validov, urged Tatars to consider themselves Turks, since their language was Turkic. He believed that Tatars should regard themselves as a separate nation (*millet*) not because they *differed from the Russians* in custom and in religion,[28] but because they *spoke a Turkic dialect* similar to Ottoman Turkish. Other writers in *Shura* reiterated this viewpoint. One, under the pseudonym "Türk Oglu" (Son of a Turk) even stated, "We should be convinced that we are not Tatars, but Turks, and that all the Turkic peoples of Russia stem from the same root." [29]

This Pan-Turkic viewpoint of Tatar journalists found considerable support among Kazan's and Ufa's historians. In 1907–1909 two textbooks on Turkic history were published for Tatar primary schools by the historian Hasan Gaty, who divided all humanity into the Aryan (Indo-European) and Turanian groups. To the latter belonged the Turks, Mongols, Japanese, Chinese, Finns, and other peoples of eastern Europe and Asia, all of whom, according to Gaty, had a common origin racially, linguistically, and culturally. He displayed particular interest in the Japanese, recently victorious over Russia, and even found them the Turks' closest kinsmen. Both peoples had great military and diplomatic aptitude, and had been predestined for close collaboration, in Gaty's opinion. Gaty also called for the cementing of close ties among all the various Turkic peoples.[30] A Bashkir, Ahmed Zeki Validov (later a professor of history at the University of Istanbul, writing under the name Zeki Velidi Togan; not to be confused with the above-mentioned Jemaleddin Validov), also published a history of the Turkic peoples which won considerable success among Tatar and Bashkir readers. These publications clearly reflected a growing interest for the Turkic problem among the Moslem population of the Volga-Ural region, as well as the progress of Pan-Turkic propaganda.

Devoting its pages wholeheartedly to the Turko-Tatar issue, *Shura* also published the articles of anti-Turkists, such as the "Tatarist," Galimjan Ibragimov, and the Tatar journalist, Hadi Maksudov. "The persistent assertion that we are not Tatars, but Turks, is contrary to logic," uttered Ibragimov. "No one denies that we are Turks—Turks are a large race, divided into many branches, from which each receives its name. We constitute one of these branches, and, therefore, besides the common name 'Turkic,' we also have the particular name 'Tatar.' ... If a Slav can be a Russian, then a Turk can be a Tatar. ... No, we are Tatars! Our language is Tatar, our literature is a Tatar literature, our problems are Tatar problems, and our future civilization is a Tatar civilization." [31]

A third group of Tatar thinkers followed the theories of the first Tatar reformer, Shihabeddin Merjani (see Chapter III), whose works had first been published in the 1890's. It proclaimed that the Tatars actually were "neither Tatars, who were Mongols, nor Turks, but Bulgars." This was supported by the historian, Gainudin Akhmarov, whose "History of the Bulgars" was published in Kazan in 1909. Akhmarov maintained that the Tatar khanate of Kazan (1438–1552) was a "continuation of the ancient Bulgar realm, in which the once independent Bulgar princes were replaced by intruders from the

Golden Horde. . . . The population itself has remained." These Bulgars were given the new name of Tatars by the khans of the Horde, and the present Tatars have faithfully preserved the ancient cultural and economic traditions of the Bulgars, according to Akhmarov. They have nothing in common with the nomadic Turks and are an authentic sedentary population. Akhmarov added that many Moslems in the Volga region continued to call themselves Bulgars, and not Tatars.[32]

Two other historians, Abdulbari Battal and A. Zabirov, whose works also appeared during the years of this controversy, lent some support to the theses of Akhmarov and Merjani. They regarded the Bulgars as a people of complex Turkic and Finno-Ugric origin, very different from the later Mongol-Turkic invaders of the Golden Horde. Both writers expressed rather anti-Russian and Tatar nationalist feelings, considering Russia's conquest of Kazan in 1552 a disaster and insisting on the superiority of Bulgar-Tatar culture. They pictured medieval Russian princes as subservient sycophants and the cunning vassals of Tatar khans. The ony Russian ruler whom they praised was Boris Godunov, whose Tatar ancestry they carefully stressed.[33]

THE PROBLEM OF THE LITERARY LANGUAGE

Closely related to the problem of the Tatars' national identity was the question of their literary language. The idea of a single common Turkic written language as recommended by Gasprinsky and Agaev met unexpected opposition on the part of Kazan's Jemaleddin Validov (not to be confused with the Bashkir historian, Ahmed Zeki Validov), who supported the Turkic national identification of the Tatars but argued that a common Turkic literary language would be impracticable. "Its introduction would be a hindrance both in education and in literature, where it would restrict writers in their creative efforts. Works written in a tongue alien to the majority of the population would not find any readers. Furthermore, which of the Turkic dialects should be selected for literary purposes—that of Gasprinsky's *Tarjuman* [Ottoman Turkish], or perhaps the Tatar language itself?" Although Validov supported the importance of Turkic solidarity, he rejected the concomitant assumption that this solidarity required a common literary language.

J. Validov was backed by Nushirvan Yanyshev. "No one, with the exception of the Azerbaijanis can understand the language of *Tar-juman*. The farther north you go, the fewer the people who read *Tarjuman*." Yanyshev suggested creating a literary language based on the common linguistic features and words shared by all the Turkic tongues throughout the world.[34]

The problem was more than a mere theoretical one. During these years some writers and newspapers followed the recommendation of the Third Moslem Congress to use Ottoman Turkish, while others —such as Galimjan Ibragimov, J. Validov, Yanyshev, and the Tatar poet, Abdulla Tukaev—preferred to write in the Tatar tongue, which Nasyri had been the first to use in literature. During the Duma years, 1907–1917, colloquial Tatar continued to develop as a literary tongue, differing greatly both from ancient Chagatai and from Ottoman Turkish.

The poet Tukaev, whom Tatars called the "Tatar Pushkin" and whose verses were known by the entire Tatar younger generation, greatly contributed to the popularization of the new literary use of the Tatar tongue. Tukaev's lyric poetry rings with a deep love for his people, and he did much to foster Russian-Tatar understanding by translating Russian lyric poetry into Tatar. The Tatar press explained Tukaev's success by the fact that he was the first popular poet to write in a popular tongue, purified of Arabic, Persian, and Ottoman words.[35] His premature death in 1913 was deplored by the entire Tatar press, even by *Tarjuman*, which regretted that this gifted poet was unknown to the southern Turks, Azerbaijanis, Crimeans, and Ottoman Turks—all of whom, of course, did not understand Tatar.[36] *Tarjuman*, however, lamented the fact that the absence of a common Turkic literary language deprived Tukaev of a wider public, but simultaneously recognized the failure of Ottoman Turkish to take hold among Russian Turks. *Türk Yurdu* also regretted that young Tatar authors wrote in their native language rather than in Turkish: "The desire of each Turkic people to create its own language is in agreement with democratic principles, but it is harmful for the future."[37]

The future which *Türk Yurdu* and the Pan-Turkists visualized was, of course, a broad political union of all the Turkic peoples, strengthened by a common literary language. Tatars were to be included in this federation, and hence both their independent national evolution and their exposure to Russian influence were opposed by the advocates of Pan-Turkism. The Tatarists, however, preferred to deal with reality and firmly defended their own identity, considering that Russian-Tatar cooperation was historically inevitable.

In 1913, the year of Tukaev's death, Russian Turkic émigrés in Turkey brought an end to the long feud in their milieu between the Tatarists (*Tatarchilik*) and the Turkists (*Turchuluk*), deciding it in favor of the latter. This decision, which completely disregarded the actual evolution undergone by Turks in Russia, was pushed through in the form of a resolution proposed by Akchurin at a meeting of Moslem students from Russia on January 22, 1912.[38] This was an important step in the direction of political, as well as cultural, Pan-Turkism, toward which the increasingly radical Turkic émigrés were headed (as became particularly evident after the outbreak of war). Life itself, however, disregarded the vociferous demands of Constantinople émigrés to rule the evolution of the written language, and literary Tatar rapidly won the lead in its competition with Ottoman Turkish. Indicative of this turn in the course of developments was the switch to Tatar in the publications of the proceedings of Russia's Moslem congresses. In accordance with the resolution of the Third Congress in 1906, which recommended the use of Ottoman Turkish by Russian Moslems, the proceedings of that years' congresses were published in this "imported" language. Despite a similar resolution by the first free and democratic Moslem convention in 1917, the proceedings of that year were published in Tatar, and that language had already been adopted by most Tatar creative writers and political pamphleteers.

The linguistic and literary disputes had not prevented the further growth of Tatar literature and publishing activities. During 1905–1914, over three thousand titles of "Moslem," mostly Tatar, books were published. Only ninety-one of these three thousand dealt with political questions, perhaps indicative of no great interest in politics on the part of Tatar readers.[39] Popular literature, textbooks, and religious publications dominated the Turkic press during these years.

DECLINE OF POLITICAL AGITATION

Interest in *national* problems remained, however. Sympathy for Ottoman Turkey continued to be a salient trait of Tatar cultural and political orientation, but aside from the Crimea and Azerbaijan,[40] this was merely a platonic and sentimental attachment to a country of the same religion and a related tongue. Aside from some minor exceptions, it did not lead to activities directed against the political unity of the Russian Empire. Tatars, Bashkirs, and Kazakhs became more and more preoccupied with cultural, social, and economic problems of their own, as well as with those of Russia. The subjects treated by popular prose writers, such as the Tatars Ibragimov and Iskhakov, as well as Tukaev, dealt primarily with the social and cultural aspects of their compatriots' lives.[41] This detachment of the bulk of the Tatar people from political problems and a growing interest for their relations with Russia—which, despite the Pan-Turkists' dreams, remained their country—was reflected in the intellectual evolution of J. Validov. A Turkist during the years 1911–1912, in 1914 Validov published a significant work, "Nation and Nationalism," in which he summed up the arguments proffered by the adherents of Turkism and Tatarism. He offered a compromise solution for the Tatar national problem, suggesting the name "Turko-Tatars," which satisfied both parties and was officially accepted by the Tatars in 1917. He also rejected Agaev's and Ziia Gökalp's glorifications of past Turkic culture: "Because of patriotic considerations, our historians have attempted to prove that we have a great and ancient culture, but they are not able to determine when and where such a culture actually flourished." In place of an inflated national myth and the dream of unifying all Turanian peoples, Validov offered the more sober and practical aim of strengthening Tatar culture and the Tatars' position within the Russian Empire. "The words 'Tatarism and Russian citizenship' must be the basic slogan for our way of life," concluded this Tatar historian and literary critic.[42]

Interest in Turkic national problems began to decline around 1908, and was especially felt in Tatar and other political activities after 1911. Ayaz Iskhakov, the most prominent leader of the strongly nationalist Tatar Socialist Revolutionaries, later explained this declining interest for popular Turkic political parties as owing to the fact that Turkic parties borrowed their programs from the Russians:

The Russian reaction of 1908–1914, in a way, was healthy for the Turks of Russia because all their political parties—which had been created as replicas of Russian political organizations [Ittifak—Kadets, Tangists—Socialist Revolutionaries, Uralchelar—Social Democrats, etc.]—pined away, not being genuine Turkic national phenomena. In their place, an unofficial center was organized which directed all the national affairs of

Turkic people in Russia. During World War I, the official organ of this center was the bureau of the Moslem caucus of the Duma.[43]

Such an assertion, however, was a strong exaggeration, because no clandestine center actually existed, and the Duma caucus itself was very passive after 1907. Its six to nine representatives in the Third and Fourth Dumas could do little more than attempt to defend the religious rights of Moslem communities.

The head of the Tatar caucus in the Duma period was Sadri Maksudov (Sadreddin Maksudi),[44] who traversed Russia in 1912 for the purpose of organizing the Russian Turks. In his speeches in the Duma, Maksudov claimed that the Tatar faction represented twenty million Russian Moslems[45] who were ready to guard their religion and national culture by all possible means, but he emphasized that the Tatars, like all the other Moslems of the empire, supported the unity of the Russian Empire, and he denied the existence of secessionist tendencies among them.[46] The general lessening of political activity among Russian Moslems was reflected even in Tatar circles, which became slack in supporting their Duma faction. In 1913 M. I. Jafarov, a member of the Fourth Duma, complained that Russian Moslems were not able to collect the two hundred rubles needed for the delegates' secretariat, and that the caucus itself was without funds.[47] *Vakyt, Tarjuman, Yulduz,* and other Turkic newspapers called upon Moslems several times during 1912–1913 to support their Duma faction, which needed only two thousand, four hundred rubles a year for its work. *Ikbal* wrote that the Moslems' indifference toward political work and toward their caucus had attained its height: "Moslems are not supporting any relations with their faction, nor do they even advise it of their present affairs or needs."[48] The deputies, in turn, became apathetic and sometimes were not heard for entire sessions of the Duma.[49] They were dissatisfied with their electors and accused them of complete indifference toward Duma elections.[50]

In order to strengthen the faction and enliven its work, in 1914 a group of Kadets and other deputies of the Duma's center, together with the Moslem caucus, attempted to restore representation in the Duma from the steppe region and Central Asia, which had been curtailed in 1907. Their project was submitted to the secretary of the Duma for transmission to G. I. Goremykin, president of the Council of Ministers, but it was rejected on the grounds that it was "not in keeping with the times."[51]

GROWTH OF RUSSIAN CULTURAL INFLUENCE

The lessening concern for political and national questions soon affected the situation of the schools. While in the 1890's and the years 1900–1907 Russian Moslems had vociferously clamored in their press for their own national schools, in the period 1910–1914 they became more and more favorable toward the Russian schools. Even the sharply nationalist Tatar organ, *Vakyt*, began to express preference in certain cases for Russian as against Tatar schools. Tatar papers were particularly sympathetic toward the founding of Russian-Tatar elementary schools, although they had opposed this type of school earlier, and in the years preceding the 1917 revolution the number of Tatar students in Russian educational institutions grew rapidly. *Vakyt* wrote in 1912, "Go to whatever schools you like— Tatar madrasa, Turkish, Arab, Russian, European—but the most desirable for us is training in the Russian schools, in order that we might later serve in the local self-government, in city councils, and teach in our maktabs." [52] Other correspondents in *Vakyt* pointed to the growing numbers of Tatar children in Russian schools and appealed to the Tatar bourgeoisie to grant scholarships to Tatar students attending Russian universities and gymnasiums. A certain Khasanov, speaking for the older generation of Moslem clerics, stressed with satisfaction the growing number of Tatar boys attending Russian schools and the maktabs, and pointed out that the Russian tongue was an indispensable and useful tool for Tatars. A progressive organ of the Tatar clergy, *Baian ul Hakk*, congratulated the zemstvo, Russian local self-government, for its initiative in building up the network of special Russian schools for Tatars and for publishing modern Tatar textbooks. In 1914, when the zemstvo temporarily slowed down its program for constructing Russian-Tatar schools and its distribution of textbooks, the Tatar press, significantly, did not rejoice at the interruption of "Russification," as they called such undertakings in the nineteenth century, but—to the contrary—complained about it. [53]

This new mood in the Tatar press and society did not necessarily mean a rejection of the Turkic national idea or the capitulation of the Tatar national movement, but was simply the result of a more practical approach to the solution of Tatar and Moslem educational problems. In effect, however, both Tatar press and Tatar society were disavowing the activities of their leaders and Duma deputies, who were seeking to guard Tatars and other Russian Turks from the influence of Russian schools and language.[54]

Russian Turks, and especially the Tatars, began to realize that the further development of their culture and schools, their enlightenment in general, was unavoidably dependent upon Russia. This was particularly true in the case of the Tatars because they lived in the very midst of the Russian population. The growth of government-native schools, absorption of the native population in the national economy, Russian and Ukrainian settlement of the vast eastern regions, Tatar migration to Russian centers, the Donets Basin, Siberia, and the Far East—all completely disrupted the centuries-long isolation of Moslems from Slavs. Russian books were being read by Tatars and other Turks more and more, either in translation or in the original, and began to exert an influence on Russian Turkic literature. In the descriptions of life in Kazan, Ufa, or Tashkent, depictions of Volga and Ural landscapes, portrayals of the peasants and merchants of the steppes, and pictures of revolutionary activity among the various peoples of the empire, Tatars and Kazakhs found more themes and heroes in common with Russian literature than with Ottoman Turkish. The very spirit of Russian writers was closer to them than was that of the writers of Constantinople or Cairo. Increasingly, Russian words were introduced into the Turkic languages through daily contact with Russians via the press, the courts, business, or even common signboards. Although politicians recommended studying the Ottoman Turkish language, life itself demanded a knowledge of Russian, and Russian mercantile, technical, literary, and political terms were adopted by Russian Turks in ever-growing numbers. The Tatar newspaper, *Ikbal*, affirmed the fact that Tatars were adhering to their own literary language and refused to introduce Ottoman Turkish, but it objected at the same time to the adoption of too many Russian loan words by the Tatar language. *Ikbal's* correspondent observed that in a four-minute conversation, two Tatars used fifty Russian words. He found over twenty borrowed Russian words and expressions in an article published by one of his colleagues in Kazan's newspaper, *Yulduz*.[55]

Perusal of Tatar publications reveals a generous appropriation of Russian political terminology. A check of random pages of the proceedings of the Moslem congresses of 1906 and 1917 shows the frequent use of the following Russian words (many of them "international" words in their Russian spelling): *zemstvo, doklad* (report), *Duma, komisia, plan, parlament, partia, telegrama, protokol, monastyr, autonomia, programa, firma, komitet, konfederatsia, sobranie* (meeting), *kuria-lar, zhandarm-lar, tovarishch-lar* (the three latter being the Turkic plural), *soldatsoviet, kolonia, nakaz* (instruction), *sessia, sektsia, okhranka,* and even the word so popular in revolutionary days, *doloi* ("down with").[56]

RUSSIAN TURKS ON THE EVE OF WORLD WAR I

In reviewing Russian-Turkic relations during the last decades of the tsarist regime generally, it can be said that despite isolated instances of antagonism—on the part of both Russians and Turks—the situation was rather compatible. The Tatars, who at that time occupied the leading position among Russia's Turkic peoples, realized that Russian schools would not eradicate their language or their Islamic faith and culture, just as the Koran could not turn them into Arabs, but, on the contrary, would offer them a number of educational advantages. Indeed, most of their leaders, such as Agaev, Gasprinsky, Iskhakov, and Hussein Zadeh, had emerged from these Russian schools. In turn, it also became clear to Russian society over the years 1912 to 1917 that Tatars were not a danger to the Russian state and its culture. Continual contacts between Russians and Tatars in the Duma, the schools, zemstvos, and economic life, which became especially frequent after 1905, laid the ground for mutual understanding. In Central Asia, however, these ideas were less shared, as would be illustrated in 1916. On the eve of World War I, then, Tatar social and cultural achievements were already very considerable, and by 1917 Moslems' civil rights were about on a par with Russians'. By 1912 the number of schools conducted in Turkic tongues had reached 25,000, and, in that same year, 608 books were published in the "Moslem languages;" of these only four were altered by the censor.[57] Kazan became the main Turkic publishing center in Russia, and, in 1912, 466 Turkic titles were published there, in over 3.2 million copies.[58] Scores of Turkic journals and newspapers had sprung up throughout Russia, from Petersburg to Baku and from Bakchisarai to Omsk. Moslem societies and mosques had grown up in Arkhangelsk, Vladivostok, Chita, Irkutsk, Petersburg, Vilno, Moscow, and elsewhere, and madrasas or maktabs appeared in previously completely non-Turkic parts of the empire.[59] Generals Chingiz, Enikeev, Makhmendarov, Yuzeforich, Sulkiewicz, the khan of Nakhi-chevan, and others were equal to Russian generals in their commands, and the Husseinovs and Tagievs remained among the wealthiest people of Russia, while scores of other Moslem industrialists and merchants were no less successful in their undertakings than their Christian competitors. It is true that Russian Moslems had been unable to attain more independence and power for the Moslem Ecclesiastic Administration,[60] but the Russian Orthodox Church itself was controlled to an even greater extent by the government, since all nominations of bishops and priests had to be approved by the government. The efforts of Russian clergymen to convene a national church council and to elect their Patriarch were no more successful than were the Moslems' attempts to elect a Mufti of their own choice.[61]

The achievements of the Tatars in the last decade of the imperial Russian regime were facilitated also by the absence of racial prejudice against them in all levels of Russian society. A Tatar intellectual, merchant, or student was unhesitatingly accepted by his Russian colleagues or comrades as an equal. The idea of social discrimination for reasons of race was hardly conceivable in any group of Russian society. The officers of the most selective regiments of the Imperial Guards were not in the least disturbed when the khan of Nakhi-chevan, a Moslem Azerbaijani, was appointed commander of the elite Guard Cavalry Corps by Nicholas II. Another Moslem general, Eris Khan Aliev, who headed the Second West Siberian Corps during the Russo-Japanese War, assumed command of all the Russian fighting forces in Manchuria when General Linevich fell ill, and he was highly respected by officers. In the Kadet Party Russians, Tatars, Kazakhs, Jews, and Poles shared the leadership alike. A Cossack or an aristocratic officer both wore with pride uniforms and arms patterned after those of the Caucasian mountaineers, while such Russian writers as Pushkin, Lermontov, Tolstoy, Dostoevsky, and others sympathized with the heroic attempt of Russia's Moslem mountaineers to maintain their freedom.

CHAPTER IX

World War I and the Central Asian Revolt of 1916

The beginning of World War I did not disrupt the conciliatory character which relations between Russia and her Turkic peoples had assumed during the years 1907–1914. Like the rest of the country, caught up during the first weeks of war by a patriotic enthusiasm, Russian Turks were quick to express their feelings of loyalty to the state and to participate in organizing aid for the wounded. The old veteran of Ittifak and former Duma member, Seid Girey Alkin, was one of the first Tatar leaders to urge Moslems through the press to contribute to the setting-up of infirmaries, to support the government, and to give a correct interpretation to the events of the war. He recalled that when a fire had recently broken out in the Tatar section of Kazan, Russians were no less ready than Tatars to help the victims.[1]

Moslem newspapers, muftis, and social organizations all responded to Alkin's call, and financial contributions were forthcoming from the Moslem regions of the empire. The Tatar paper, *Turmush*, wrote, "Since time immemorial Russian Moslems have been loyal to the government and at difficult moments have lent their assistance. Russian Moslems played a large part in the expansion of the Russian state and the annexation to it of foreign lands. They are bound historically to their Russian compatriots. Therefore, in difficult moments on the battlefield they are capable of demonstrating even greater self-sacrifice than the Russians."[2]

Tatar and other Turkic political leaders proved no less loyal in their attitude toward Russia and the government. Following Alkin's example, representatives of a number of other Turkic political and social organizations added their voices to the call to support the government's military efforts and to help organize infirmaries. The Moslem faction in the Duma sent out two appeals urging Russia's Moslem people "to fight to the end for the honor and integrity of Russia," for Moslems, too, "are sons of the great fatherland." [3] Social organizations gathered funds for the wounded. Even small rural Moslem communities collected some 70–100 rubles in the first few days of the war, and such wealthy Tatars as A. N. Nakiev or Z. Tagiev individually contributed checks more than once for 100,000 rubles.[4] Tagiev financed the formation of Azerbaijani volunteer units to fight against the Germans and personally supported a large military hospital in Baku. The peoples of Central Asia and Kazakhstan contributed 2,400,000 rubles, and supplied 70,000 horses, 12,797 camels, 40 million puds of cotton, 300,000 puds of meat, and many other commodities.[5] Moslem assistance to military hospitals became organized in December 1914, when a special all-Russian Moslem congress was convened. In this congress Tatars and Azerbaijanis, some of whom had only recently supported Pan-Turkism, were widely represented.[6] Making up the committee for aid to the wounded were such outstanding Russian Turkic leaders as the Duma delegate, I. A. Akhtiamov, A. Davletchin (former laborite delegate), S. G. Alkin, K. M. Tevkelev, Sh. Syrtlanov, S. Shatgupov (Ittifak), Mufti Zadeh, and Yu. Jafarov (Azerbaijani).

Russian Moslems expressed their readiness to give not only their money but also their lives in defense, as Alkin wrote, "of our great fatherland, Russia." This readiness was demonstrated by an influx of volunteers into the Russian army. A cavalry division of six regiments, called the "Savage Division" (*dikaia divisia*)—which performed heroically on the Austrian front—was formed of volunteers from among the Moslem mountaineers of the Caucasus, who did not legally have to serve. Moslem generals proved themselves on the battlefield. An Azerbaijani, General G. Mehmendarov, commanding the Second Caucasian Corps, was one of the best commanders of the war. Another Azerbaijani Turk, the khan of Nakhichevan, commanded the Russian Guard Cavalry Corps, consisting of sixteen regiments composed of members of the Russian aristocracy. In the turbulent days of February 1917, the khan was among the few commanders who offered his troops and personal forces to Nicholas II.

Crimean Tatar and Turkomen cavalry regiments also stood up well in action, as did Tatar and Bashkir soldiers fighting in the lines of regular Russian regiments. The testimonies of officers commanding Tatars are laudatory and mention the high degree of discipline, endurance, and fighting qualities of these and other Russian Moslem soldiers and officers.

Russian Moslems were united in their stand regarding the war with Germany and Austria. German imperialism and the Kaiser encountered no sympathy either among the liberals of Ittifak, who had always been oriented toward republican France, where many of them had resided, or among Moslem left-socialist factions. The situation regarding war with Turkey, however, was more delicate, since their coreligionists there had long been a source of inspiration for Russian Turks. But here, again, the common sense and inherent caution of the Tatars came to the surface. On August 24, 1914, in Petersburg, where the extreme rightist circles of the Moslem clergy had always been strong, there was a demonstration by local Moslems against Turkey's intention to break its neutrality and enter the war against Russia. This group sent a telegram to the Turkish sultan protesting Turkey's entrance into the war.[7] Despite the fact that it expressed the view of only a limited group, the telegram undoubtedly reflected the mood of most Russian Moslems, who, as Russian subjects, could understandably have felt a duplicity of allegiance.

When the attack by the German ships *Goeben* and *Breslau* on Russian shores provoked Turkey's declaration of war against Russia, Mufti Muhammed Yar Sultanov offered Russian Moslems a successful formula for allaying their consciences: "A handful of people at the head of the Ottoman government, under the influence of Germany, have caused Turkey to begin war with Russia and attack her. . . . All Russian Moslems must guard our fatherland from the enemy." [8] This was quickly supported by the patriotic Seid Girey Alkin, who added that "Pan-Islamism preaches the spiritual, and not blood, kinship of Moslems. . . . Moslems are obliged to defend their coreligionists only in a fight for the faith, and not for political interests." Since Turkey had attacked Russia, then, with political rather than religious motives, in the words of Alkin, Russian Moslems were not under any obligation to help either their brother Turks or the sultan-caliph.[9] Telegrams, demonstrations, and declarations by Moslems in Baku, Orenburg, Petersburg, Tiflis, Kazan, and other cities supported the words of the Mufti and of Alkin.

Kaspii, the journal of Tagiev and Topchibashev, which stood close to the Azerbaijani nationalists of Musavat, in turn called upon Russian Moslems to join Russia in the fight against Germany and Turkey, pointing out that Russian Moslems, like the Moslems of India, should not consider the Ottoman sultan-caliph the head of all Moslems since he had not been chosen by all Moslems. Other Turkic newspapers in Russia declared that the Moslems of India, Egypt, and Algiers also stood united against the aggressors—Germany, Austria, and Turkey—and with this, the last doubts of zealous Moslems were lulled.[10]

The definite desire of Russian Moslem leaders to preserve an even keel in the country and not to utilize the war for purposes of agitation was best illustrated by the actions of Resul Zadeh, the head of Musavat, who had only recently urged Azerbaijanis to keep their horses in readiness for the struggle to resurrect the Moslem world from Peking to Alhambra.[11] In October 1915, Resul Zadeh published in the Azerbaijani paper, *Achyg Soz*, a new program summing up the desires of local nationalists. These modestly amounted to the following:

(1) Opening of new governmental primary schools and introduction of education in the national language of the population.

(2) Establishment of state-supported Moslem theological seminaries.

(3) Permission for Moslem parishes to elect their clergy without any control or pressure by the Russian administration.

(4) Turning over to the Moslem clergy funds and real estate confiscated by the Russian government from Moslem churches and other organizations.[12]

In this program there was no trace of former Pan-Turkic or Pan-Islamic dreams. It repeated almost exactly the desiderata of the Third All-Russian Moslem Congress of 1906 concerning the autonomy of Islamic religious organizations and the Moslem school system in Russia, which Ittifak likewise had always supported. During the war years, Ittifak's representatives in the Duma also stepped forward with this program but, aware of their faction's weakness in the parliament, acknowledged that time of war was not particularly propitious for reform.

Among the approximately seventeen million Moslem inhabitants of Russia, however, there were some cases which disrupted this generally calm atmosphere. Police records for 1914–1916 reveal that Tatars in various places throughout the Crimean peninsula were leading "intense agitation for the unification of all Crimean Moslems and for helping Turkey."[13] In Kazan and its environs there were instances of defeatist agitation, and the Tatar Socialist Revolutionaries there disseminated leaflets urging Tatars "to wake up while it is not too late." [14] Such leaflets—whose source is indicated by their appeal to help the Ottoman Turkish caliph-sultan and "to act now, or Moslems never will free themselves from the infidel Russians"—appeared in Ferghana, where they were distributed by German and Turkish agents who had infiltrated through Persia and Afghanistan.[15] In Khiva, apparently under the influence of enemy agents seeking to arouse disturbances throughout all Russia, the Turkomen nomads began military action against the khan of Khiva and the settled Uzbek population there. In April 1916, after suffering heavy losses, the khan called in Russian troops, who saved his throne and preserved peace in ancient Khiva.[16] With the exception of the occurrences in Khiva, however, these events did not seriously disturb the government or the police. They did not affect the over-all peaceable situation reigning in the Moslem provinces of Russia, with the exception of Central Asia.

RUSSIAN TURKS IN CONSTANTINOPLE

The stand taken by the small but active group of Russian Turkic political émigrés abroad, particularly those who resided in Turkey, was very different from the cooperative attitude of their fellows in Russia. In 1915 the émigrés in Constantinople, who had been rallied around Yusuf Akchurin and his *Türk Yurdu* since 1911, formed a Committee for Defense of the Rights of Moslem Turko-Tatar Peoples of Russia. Besides Akchurin, the committee included R. Ibragimov, who had initiated Moslem cooperation with Russian liberals in 1904, the Azerbaijanis Hussein Zadeh and Agaev, Mulla M. ch. Jihan (Crimean), and Mukim Edin Beijani. The Young Turks, who hoped to annex to Turkey all the Turkic regions of Russia in the case of a victory by the Central Powers, were most sympathetic toward this committee. When Turkey entered the war, the Young Turks' central committee sent out a circular to all the party's local branches explaining, in the following terms, Turkey's entrance on the side of the Central Powers:

Could we possibly have remained silent and done nothing, when our natural allies [the Germans and Austrians] found themselves at war with Russia, our sworn, irreconcilable, eternal enemy? . . . We should not forget that the reason for our entrance into the world war is not only to save our country from the danger threatening it. No, we pursue an even more immediate goal—the realization of our ideal, which demands that, having shattered our Muscovite enemy, we lead our empire to its natural boundaries, which would encompass and unite all our related peoples. [17]

That the Young Turks' mood was shared by most of the members of the Committee for Defense of Moslem Rights is emphasized by the fact that some of the latter belonged to the central committee of the Young Turk Party, and Hussein Zadeh himself conducted an energetic propaganda campaign urging Turkey's declaration of war against Russia.[18]

At the end of 1915 the Committee for Defense of Moslem Rights extended its activity to Central Europe. In December of that year its leaders were received by the Austrian prime minister, Count Stürgkh, and by Count Forgach of the Ministry of Foreign Affairs, to whom was submitted a memorandum stating the committee's desires. In the committee's opinion, the further development of Russian Turks was

possible only through full independence. . . . We Turko-Tatars, bearers of culture up to the present time, believe that Western culture, with the help of the Turko-Tatars, will conquer Russian-Byzantine culture in all Asia. . . . We hope that today's standard bearers of Western civilization—Germany, Austria, and Hungary—will shortly change the future of Asia. Restoration of the east European and Central Asian khanates will be the beginning of this program. . . . With uplifted hands we ask the allies and friends of the leader of Islam, the Caliph and Great Sultan—the emperors of Germany and Austria, the rulers of Hungary and Bulgaria and their heroic peoples: Free us from Russian designs.

The memorandum also insisted on the neutrality of the Volga River and the Caspian Sea.[19]

The delegation was also heard by Count Tiszo, the Hungarian prime minister, and by German authorities, and the German press supported the committee quite energetically.[20] The German and Austro-Hungarian commands permitted the committee to carry on activity in camps of Turkic prisoners of war from Russia, among whom, with the committee's help, they began to recruit volunteers for a special military unit composed entirely of Russian Moslems. Some twelve to fifteen thousand Tatar prisoners of war were concentrated in Zossen, near Berlin, where they were subjected to intensive propaganda by the members of the committee. It was planned to organize a special legion composed entirely of Tatars from Russia, but only a few of the Tatars volunteered for the Turkish army, which was operating against the British in Mesopotamia.[21] No Tatars were sent to the Russian front since, apparently, there were no volunteers among them to fight against the Russians. These meager results were perhaps indicative of the political mood of Russian Turks during World War I.

The Committee for Defense of Moslem Rights likewise held lectures and speeches, and in 1916 it organized in Lausanne, Switzerland, a Congress of the Peoples of Russia. In the committee's declarations, however, could be discerned either an internal division or a duplicity of policy. In contrast to the committee's memorandum, Akchurin in his lectures indicated only the desirability of full Moslem equality by law with the Russians and demanded cultural autonomy for the Moslems of Russia. The same demands were put forward in the committee's telegrams to President Woodrow Wilson and other Western leaders.[22] All four Turkic émigré leaders, Akchurin, Ibragimov, Agaev, and Hussein Zadeh, appeared at the Lausanne conference and, in the name of all Russian Moslems, demanded the religious and cultural autonomy of the latter, the lifting of the remaining legal discriminations against Russian Moslems, and changes in Russia's electoral system. There are some indications that they even expressed hope for the federative union of Russian Turks with the Ottoman Empire.[23]

The committee's agitation and its proclamations met a sharp rebuff, however, by the Moslems of Russia themselves, particularly from the Moslem faction in the Duma. The deputy from Ufa, K. M. Tevkelev, categorically declared (with the support of all the other members of the Duma's Moslem caucus), that "not one Moslem organization in Russia was connected with the committee, and Russian Moslems would fulfill their duty toward Russia and her allies." Musavat's leader, Resul Zadeh, wrote in a similar vein on October 22, 1915, and until the October upheaval, excepting only some defeatist speeches by Musavat leaders in 1917, the Moslem organizations of Russia actually did stand firmly behind continuation of the war with Germany and the Axis powers.

While the émigré Pan-Turkists and foreign agents failed to stir up Russian Turks against the government, however, the negligence dis-

played by the Russian administration during the war years in its
dealings with its Turkic peoples was directly responsible for a sharp
conflict between some groups of Russia's Moslem population and the
administration. This conflict was the bloodiest, most tragic, and, at
the same time, most incongruous event in the history of Russian-
Turkic relations and was a clear indication that the Russian administration neither fully understood the empire's Turkic problem nor was
sufficiently concerned over it.

MOBILIZATION OF CENTRAL ASIAN MOSLEMS

The heavy losses sustained by Russian troops in 1914–1915 had
forced the Russian government to mobilize a significant percentage
of the population. In all, 15.8 million men (including 40 per cent of
all the industrial workers of Russia) had been drafted into the
army.[24] As a result, it later became apparent that the number mobilized was too large, and the concentration of reserve soldiers in the
cities—especially in Petersburg, where, at the beginning of 1917, there
were more than 300,000 of them—was one of the reasons for the
rapid development of the February Revolution. But in 1915–1916
the military command was anxious both about military reserves and
labor reserves. To fulfill the needed labor contingents, it suggested
mobilizing the Moslem population of Transcaucasia, Kazakhstan, and
Central Asia. During the years of Russia's conquest of the Caucasus
and Central Asia, when a military draft was introduced throughout
most of the empire, the Russian government had promised not to
call Moslems of new Russian provinces for military service. This
promise was confirmed by a law in 1886 which reorganized the administration of Central Asia. Therefore, despite its fear that military
reserves would be insufficient, the government decided to mobilize
Russian Moslems in labor battalions behind the lines, for the construction of trenches, barracks, and infirmaries. News of the forthcoming mobilization aroused alarm among the Moslem population,
and improbable rumors began to spread among the groups which
gathered, according to custom, in the marketplaces of the cities and
villages to discuss the decree. Although badly informed because of
inadequate communications, the population's reactions to the proposed plan began to appear on the pages of the local Turkish press.
Kazakh, the main newspaper of the steppes, was especially heated in
its judgment of mobilization. It remarked that mobilization was un-

avoidable, and demanded only that Kazakhs be compensated for it and have the possibility of serving under appropriate conditions. The Kazakhs' main desires were for the cessation of colonization and restoration of their representation in the Duma. Many insisted that Kazakhs serve in the cavalry rather than in the worker battalions.

"It is impossible to assume that Kazakhs will forever be free from military service. But if the question of military service is to be decided, then it would follow that this decision come with the participation of the Kazakhs themselves," wrote Salmak bey Kesmetov in *Kazakh*. "If Kazakhs must be called, will they serve in the infantry or in the cavalry? . . . We think that it would be very opportune to raise simultaneously with the question of military service, the question of Kazakhs' participation in the Duma and the distribution of their lands." In the same issue of *Kazakh*, Ahmed Jantaliev insisted that "in case Kazakhs are taken to military service, then it is necessary that they be given the same advantages which those peoples who have always served in the army already have. Kazakhs must also be given the rights which Cossacks enjoy and they should serve in the cavalry. Furthermore, Kazakhs should be allotted lands equally with the Cossacks." The author joined with other Kazakh leaders in relating the question of military service with restoration of Kazakh representation in the Duma. Mustaki Maldybaev, in the same issue of *Kazakh*, pointed out that "as a result of the absence of birth certificates and other documents among the Kazakhs, it is very difficult to determine their ages and clarify who is liable for call. It is necessary first to remove this obstacle . . . and introduce birth certificates." Other Kazakh leaders voiced their opinions in the same tone. Various Turkic newspapers in Russia, especially *Vakyt* and *Turmush*, supported the Kazakh point of view, considering that liability for military service should be accompanied by equality of all political and economic rights.[25]

The government's land policy, however, was a source of even greater dissatisfaction for Kazakhs and Kirghiz than the question of military service. As long as Kazakhs and Kirghiz had not been required to serve in the army as were the Russians and other peoples of the empire, the confiscation of their lands had seemed to have some, however small, justification. Now even this consolation was withdrawn, and for this reason Kazakh leaders related military service with the land question in their articles. Finally, swayed by rumors,

Moslems began to fear that during their terms of service in worker battalions, settlers would seize not only their lands and cattle but also their families, and that they would be fed with pork in the labor squads. For many, especially the nomads, unaccustomed to walking and to physical labor, service in worker battalions was a humiliating offense. All of these factors, in addition to the long-standing dissatisfaction over the land question, contributed to the creation of a tense situation.

Kazakh leaders, after conferring, finally sent a delegation, on February 3, 1916, to Petersburg, headed by A. Bukeikhanov, A. Baitursunov, and N. Begembetov. In Petersburg this delegation interviewed a number of officials for the purpose of clarifying the question of Kazakh mobilization. During their talk with the Minister of Defense, General Polivanov, the delegation attempted to convince him that the Kazakh draft was complicated by a number of technical and psychological difficulties. They pointed out that Kazakhs would prefer serving in the army, especially in the cavalry, rather than in labor brigades. Also, they requested the same conditions, rights, and privileges which Cossacks enjoyed.[26] Two other Kazakh delegations, headed by a former member of the First Duma, A. K. Kalmenev, and the Kazakh administrator, G. Nukashev, sought to prevent mobilization of Kazakhs altogether.[27]

The Kazakh delegations were given no definite answer, but they must have been somewhat encouraged, since *Kazakh* wrote that the draft would not be enacted. Nevertheless, disagreement on and discussion of worker mobilization continued both in the press and in the villages, and rumors even began to spread that Kazakhs and other Moslems would have to dig trenches not behind the front, but between the fronts, under enemy fire.

The manifesto decreeing conscription of Moslems of the Caucasus and Central Asia was signed June 25, 1916, and was soon published. It was written, in the words of General Kuropatkin, "in such a hurried and indefinite form that it caused utter confusion in the minds of the population." [28] It was completely unclear how this draft would be carried out and who, exactly, between the ages of nineteen and forty-five, should be called. "Confusion in the minds of the population," contradictory reports in newspapers, promises and rumors let loose by adroit businessmen and German or Turkish agents finally resulted, after the selection began, in the population's agitation. The natives knew neither whom to trust nor for what definite purpose they were being called. The compilation of lists led first to misunderstandings, and then to disorder.

REBELLION IN JIZAK

The first disturbances began in the Uzbek parts of Central Asia, among the urban population. On July 4 riots began in Khojent, and then spread to other cities. Two days before the official day for the call, July 13, disorders began in Jizak, where they were of an especially serious nature. The Moslem population declared to the local regional head, Rukin, that it would not respond to the summons. Rukin answered with threats. Five days later a large crowd of Moslems from the old part of the city set out for Jizak's new settlement, where the administration was located. Rukin and the Moslem authorities who went to meet them were killed. The appearance of a detachment of soldiers resulted in clashes with the crowd, which proceeded to rout the Jizak railway station, setting fire to gasoline tanks. Heading for Samarkand, the mob destroyed bridges, railways, and telegraph lines, and the uprising quickly spread throughout the district. Eighty-three Russians were killed and seventy persons were taken captive. All captured women were raped. Religious fanaticism played the main role in this uprising, and the insurrectionists declared a holy war upon the Russians. The governor general of Turkestan sent an armed expedition from Samarkand and Tashkent against them, and by July 21 the rebellion was put down. Disorders spread to other cities in the Uzbek part of Central Asia, but there they did not reach the pitch they had in Jizak. In the Kirghiz mountain regions, however, where many of the Kirghiz people took part in an organized military movement, the rebellion assumed the character of a spontaneous mass uprising.[29]

KIRGHIZ IN REVOLT

The Kirghiz nomad population living on the slopes of the western Tien Shan Mountains, in the valleys of northern Semirechie, and in the eastern foothills of Ferghana had suffered even more than Kazakhs from the expropriation of their lands for Russian and Ukrainian settlers. The fertile lands of Semirechie, with their rich harvests and moderate climate, particularly attracted colonizers from the Chernigov and Poltava regions of the northern Ukraine, so similar in soil and climate to Kirghizia. "The promised land, Pishpek," as this part of Kirghizia was called (after one of its most attractive cities), was the center from which settlers penetrated further into the land of the nomadic Kirghiz. The consequent reduction in grazing lands resulted in decreased cattle production, after which, as among the Kazakhs, came the impoverishment of the Kirghiz. The density of both the new and old populations in Kirghizia, whose area was less than Kazakhstan's, had led to friction between the colonizers and the Kirghiz natives even before the proclamation of mobilization, and the announcement of the draft in Kirghizia brought the situation to a head. The Kirghiz were especially afraid that after the call, when Kirghiz men would leave for the front, the settlers would seize their lands; furthermore, in the rebellion they saw a means of getting back their former holdings. In mid-July part of the Moslem population of Semirechie decided to evade mobilization by entering China, and on July 13 a group of Dungan (Chinese Moslems) who had emigrated to Russia from China in the second half of the nineteenth century went back to China. The uprising itself began in Kirghizia on August 6 around Pishpek, quickly spreading to other regions and eventually throughout all Kirghizia. The natives murdered colonizers, burning their houses and fields. On August 14, the Kirghiz laid siege to the village of Tokmak, holding it in complete isolation for eight days, at the same time continuing military operations against other settlements.[30] The approach of Russian troops put an end to the Kirghiz' armed operations and in the beginning of September the revolt ceased, but the Kirghiz began to leave for China. The losses of Ukrainian and Russian colonizers were quite high: in all, 2,222 settlers, with their wives and children, perished at the hands of the rebels; in addition, several Russian women were taken by the Kirghiz to China. Around 80 Russian soldiers and officials also perished.[31] Kirghiz losses are unknown, but in any case the losses they sustained during the suppression of the uprising by troops and at the hands of angered colonizers who revenged the murder of their kinsmen were two or three times greater than the losses among the latter. Furthermore, the Kirghiz nomads who moved into China, fearing military call and repressive measures, lost both people and property in their flight. A large number of cattle perished. The approximate number of nomads who went to China, as determined by official Russian data, was very large—300,000 persons, nearly one third of the entire Kirghiz population. Only in the winter of 1916 and after the revolution of February 1917, did the Kirghiz return home, ruined and weakened by epidemics.

The Kirghiz uprising assumed such a broad and organized character because it was headed by the tribal leaders, the *manap*, the last representatives of the old tribal organization. Mukush Shabdan and his family—children and grandchildren of Kirghiz tribal chiefs of the mid-nineteenth century, when Kirghizia had still belonged to the Kokand khanate—were the main organizers of the movement. Other Kirghiz tribal aristocrats joined it, such as Kanaat Abukin, Batyr Khan Nogai, and others, hoping to resurrect the old tribal order destroyed by the Russian administrative system.

In those districts where the tribal chiefs did not participate in the uprising—for instance, central and southern Kirghizia—the movement was very weak and soon ended. In some places it took on the aspect of a social movement by the oppressed and poorer classes of the population, and some Russian peasants even participated in it. A peasant, Mark Vlasenko, headed one group of rebels in the village of Folbaumovka, and the Russian district elder of the Preobrazhensky district, I. V. Karashaev, took part in the uprising in the Kirghiz lines, for which he was later executed.[32] There were several cases of this kind, but they were not characteristic and, in general, the Kirghiz uprising remained a revolt against Russian administration and Russian colonization. The murder of more than two thousand Russian settlers clearly gave proof of this.

DISTURBANCES IN THE KAZAKH STEPPE

In Kazakhstan, considering the size of its population and the number of colonizers—which exceeded the number in Kirghizia by several times—the uprising was only of a local nature and did not spread so widely. There were disturbances among the Kazakhs in the Lepsinsk, Ust-Kamenogorsk, and Karkarala districts of the Semipalatinsk province, where some native district administrators were killed.[33] Here, too, a small group of Kazakh nomads, not desiring to be mobilized, moved into China. More serious were the disorders in the Turgai and Irgiz districts of the Turgai province. In the desert steppes of these regions, the future Kazakh Communist leader, Amangeldy Imanov, had already gathered sizable detachments by the end of June 1916. In late September 1916, Amangeldy engaged in a skirmish with a

Russian detachment under Colonel P. Tkachenko, and on October 18 his partisans—numbering over two thousand—pushed back the Russian detachment to Irgiz.[34] In November, Amangeldy laid siege to the city of Turgai, which controlled the central steppe region. A detachment under General N. Lavrentiev was sent against Amangeldy, and succeeded in driving off the insurgents. Amangeldy held out until February 24 in the sands of Tusum in the Batlakkara region, between lakes Sabti Kul' and Kara Kul, forty kilometers to the south of Turgai. On February 24, 1917, Batlakkara was taken by the Russians, and after the revolution, when the Provisional Government proclaimed a general amnesty, Amangeldy laid down his arms.[35]

It is necessary to mention the exceptionally restrained behavior and understanding shown by Kazakh leaders throughout this period. Before the publication of the manifesto, they did all they could to prevent worker mobilization. After its proclamation, they tried to lighten the conditions of the draft, succeeding in obtaining some postponements, and they intervened between the administration and the Kazakh population. On July 7, after the beginning of disturbances, a conference was held in Turgai by Kazakh chiefs and administrators, under the leadership of A. Bukeikhanov, O. Almazov and M. Dulatov. This group requested the tsarist administration to postpone the draft and recommended several measures to facilitate the procedure, many of which were later accepted by the Russian authorities.[36] During the uprising, these same Kazakh leaders, always close to the Kadets, did their best to calm the population, stop the disorders, and avert bloodshed. Thanks mainly to their efforts, the movement among the Kazakhs resulted in fewer victims than had the uprising among the Kirghiz. Kazakh losses could be counted in the hundreds, including those who perished from epidemics in China, while Kirghiz losses amounted to tens of thousands. Furthermore, as a result of *Kazakh*'s appeals and the mediation of Kazakh leaders, less bitterness was nurtured in the hearts of the Russian and Kazakh populations of the region than among the other peoples of Central Asia. During the uprising, *Kazakh* urged its readers, "Restrain yourselves, submit to law. Away with ill-intentioned provocators. Guard the people of Allah from a calamity inspired by an evil spirit." [37] After the uprising, the editor of *Kazakh*, Baitursunov, and his colleagues, urged reconciliation. M. Dulatov wrote, "Kazakhs have been ruined in this senseless disorder. The cause of this terrible disaster lies in the

Kazakhs' backwardness and their lack of culture." He understood that, despite all the difficulties of colonization, the land question, and the mistakes of the administration and of the Kazakhs themselves, the main reasons for the casualties among the Kazakhs were, nevertheless, the absence of a common language and the inability of the Kazakhs to deal with facts and events. The Kazakhs themselves also realized this, and throughout the revolution and the Civil War they maintained their confidence in their leaders. In 1917 Baitursunov received an overwhelming majority in the elections to the Constituent Assembly.[38]

The Russian administration was, to a great extent, responsible for the spread of the uprising and its tolls. The manifesto decreeing mobilization and the regulations for selecting Moslem workers were incoherently written. Despite a number of liberal features—such as determination of those to be drafted by representatives of the population and the right to send substitutes—confusion and dissatisfaction were rendered unavoidable by the indefiniteness of some of the decree's points and by the short period of time which elapsed between the manifesto's publication and the actual call—only a month. The administrators concerned were not the best, and the higher officials knew neither the language nor customs of the natives. During the half-century of Russian suzerainty in Central Asia and Kazakhstan—even a century and a half in some parts—the Russian government had not propagated Russian culture and language sufficiently among the Moslems. Russian society, in turn, had never been sufficiently concerned with the Moslem question, and during the war it was occupied with the political struggle. Very little attention was paid to the preparations for Moslem mobilization. It is true that when the uprising first began and General A. N. Kuropatkin was appointed governor general and commander of the troops in Russian Central Asia, the Duma sent a special commission to Central Asia, headed by A. F. Kerensky and K. M. Tevkelev, the Tatar representative of Ittifak in the Duma. The commission submitted the results of its investigation to the Duma, but it was already too late and the government took no further heed of the Duma's inquiries regarding the uprising.

Scores of books have been written about the rebellion, but it is still difficult to determine exactly what its ultimate goals were. That the movement was organized only locally is witnessed by the fact that disturbances began in different places at different times, from the first of June to the first of September. The Jadids did not take part in it anywhere, despite the fact that some authors ascribe the uprising's organization to them. Perhaps a few students who took part in the disturbances in Jizak were associated with nationalist-liberal circles.[39] The movement's leaders were wholly responsible for the deaths of their fellows, since they should have known that isolated uprisings would be quickly and easily suppressed by the Russian administration and troops. There were actually no chances for the insurrectionists' success. Therefore, it is difficult to characterize this movement as anything more than a rather senseless carnage in the steppes, resulting from mutual misunderstanding on the side of the Turks and Russians.

CHAPTER X

Russia's Moslems in the Revolution of 1917

The February revolution of 1917 ignited enthusiasm and hope in all strata of Russian society. Everyone was convinced that a new era in the democratic evolution of Russia had begun, giving promise of a further development of the nation's spiritual and economic forces. It seemed that the old slogan of the French revolution of 1789— Liberty, Equality, Fraternity—was once again inspiring a considerable part of humanity. These words were the guiding star which illuminated a free and democratic future for all the freedom-loving peoples of Russia. Never before in the history of eastern Europe had so many speeches, petitions, and declarations been written and voiced as in the chaotic eight months between February and November 1917. Men and parties were intoxicated with the ideals of democracy and social justice, while only a few, if any, realized that for the construction of a happy future practical considerations and simple toil were just as necessary as ardent professions of faith.

Not only the Russians, but all the peoples of the late tsarist empire were seized by optimism and enthusiasm during these weeks, and Russia's Moslem leaders participated no less than anyone else in celebrating this "great and bloodless liberation from the chains of autocracy." Moslem leaders also believed, together with the leaders of Russia's other national groups, in the democratic reconstruction of the newborn republic, and visualized the unification and cooperation of all the Moslems of Russia. In 1917, when the need to camouflage purely political and nationalist aims with religious slogans came to an end, Russian Turks—as well as other non-Turkic Moslems—continued to be united by the religion and culture of Islam, and Islam revealed itself to be stronger than any national or racial program.

In the early period of the new Russian republic, the promoters of Islamic unity in Russia were the experienced, though slightly outdated, veterans of 1905–1906, the leaders of the now defunct Ittifak. Two weeks after the abdication of Nicholas II, their representatives in the Duma called a conference in Petrograd of Russia's Moslem leaders. The conference convened March 15–17. It elected a Provisional Central Bureau of Russian Moslems and decided to hold a new—this time, unhindered—all-Russian Moslem congress in early May 1917. The conference elaborated some basic rules for the election of deputies to the new congress, and set up an agenda. The electoral rules provided that:

(1) All Moslem nationalities of Russia must be invited to participate in the forthcoming congress.

(2) The principle of proportional representation should be adhered to as far as possible.

(3) The representatives of all Moslem cultural and educational associations, of students' societies, credit unions, cooperative societies, and similar organizations be summoned to take part in the new all-Russian Moslem congress.

The Moslem members of the Duma, as well as members of the newly created Central Bureau and representatives from Moslem regiments, were also invited to participate in the congress. The "all-Moslem" rather than Turkic national character of the forthcoming congress was stressed by the election not of a Russian Turk, but of a Daghestani, Ahmed Tsalikov, to the chairmanship of the twenty-eight-member Central Bureau. The congress' agenda included consideration of Russia's new constitution and state organization, the cultural autonomy of Moslems, educational problems, reorganization of the Moslem Administration, labor and agrarian questions, resettlement, and the colonization of the eastern provinces.[1]

Following the pattern of development of Russians and other peoples in the European part of the empire, supporters of radical social experimentation also began to appear and grow among Russian Moslems. The strengthening of the radical left, particularly noticeable among the Tatars, Bashkirs, and Azerbaijanis, soon led to clashes with the traditional nationalist-liberals. The first of these conflicts occurred in the first week of March, over the question of the administration of the Kazan province. The Duma's Moslem caucus wanted to keep at the head of the province its former governor, P. Boyarsky, with whom the caucus had worked satisfactorily before the revolution. The workers' and soldiers' soviets in Kazan, however, which were composed to a great extent of Russians and other peoples from the European part of the empire and of which the Tatars composed only a minority, insisted on dismissing all the former tsarist administrators. On March 4 the soviets, dominated by Socialist Revolutionaries and Mensheviks, demanded the arrest of the local military commander, General K. Sandetsky, his assistant, General A. Komarof, and other high-ranking officers. On March 6, Governor Boyarsky was dismissed.[2] Thereupon the Tatar socialists in Kazan organized a special Moslem Socialist Committee, headed by Fuad Tuktarov and R. Halfin, which cooperated closely with the local soldiers' and workers' soviets and which became the rallying point for all Tatar extremists. At this committee's first meeting, held on March 7 in Kazan, a Tatar Social Democratic speaker, Mullanur Vahitov, urged all "toiling Moslems" to participate in the coming social revolution. He pointed out that a deep chasm separated Tatars of the bourgeois Moslem union, *Ittihad*, from the "masses" of the Moslem Tatar proletariat.[3]

The formation of Moslem socialist committees in Kazan and other cities and the speeches of Mullanur Vahitov and his socialist associates were the first clear signs of the rapid disintegration of Moslem social and political unity and of the progressing radicalization of the Moslem population of European Russia and the Caucasus. The Moslem political front became divided into many factions. On the extreme right were the clericals and conservatives, still powerful in the northern Caucasus and Central Asia. The central position remained occupied by the moderate bourgeois liberals of the late Ittifak, newly organized as *Ittihad* (Unity), whose uncontested leader was the Duma deputy, Sadri Maksudov.[4] On the left, the socialist flank rapidly expanded, the most popular group within it being the Moslem brand of Socialist Revolutionaries, who were more concerned with national and agrarian questions than with workers' problems. On the extreme left, a group of internationalist Mensheviks and Bolsheviks was crystallizing, but in the spring of 1917 this radical wing was still very weak.

CENTRALISTS AND TERRITORIAL AUTONOMISTS

Another obstacle to Turkic political unity in Russia at this time was the conflict between territorialists and centralists. The Turkic leaders of the borderlands—especially of the Caucasians, Crimeans,

Kazakhs, Bashkirs, and the Moslems of Central Asia—supported the principle of national territorial autonomy. They wanted to organize the Crimea, Azerbaijan, Bashkiria, and other Moslem borderlands as autonomous national subdivisions of a federated Russian republic. The Tatars opposed this principle, proposing instead the centrally directed cultural autonomy of all Russian Moslems. They aimed at preserving Moslem-Turkish unity and wanted to create a central administrative organ for all the Moslem peoples of Russia. Disregarding their territorial distribution, Moslems would be organized in one national-cultural body, whose supreme organ would be an autonomous part of the central Russian government.

Such a centralized Moslem administration would be the only suitable arrangement for the Tatars, who were not concentrated in any one area but were scattered throughout all of Russia. Only the administrative centralization of Moslem life could effectively include all the Tatars in any autonomous organization. Furthermore, having become accustomed in the course of the past century and a half to playing the leading role in the empire's Moslem affairs, they hoped to preserve this role in a centralized Moslem administration. Kazan had long ago become the leading cultural center for Russian Moslems, but the Tatars realized that with the territorial autonomy of various regions and national groups, Kazan would lose its importance and become a center only for the Tatars in its immediate vicinity. In the Kazan area there remained no more than one third of the total number of Tatars in Russia; the rest were dispersed throughout other provinces of the Volga-Ural region, where they formed about 15 per cent of the population, and throughout other parts of Russia.[5]

THE FIRST ALL-RUSSIAN MOSLEM CONGRESS

The second half of March and the month of April were spent in preparing for the new all-Russian Moslem congress, and this time the delegates were to represent nearly all the political, social, and national groups of Russia's Moslem population. Local conferences were held in most Moslem regions during this period, at which delegates to the coming congress were elected and questions concerning cultural and religious life were discussed. Along with the Tatars and other Turkic national groups, non-Turkic Moslems of Russia, such as the Caucasian mountaineers and Central Asian Tajiks, were also to participate in the congress.

Two fundamental points were taken up in all the local conferences: reconstruction of the Moslem Ecclesiastic Administration and organization of the national-cultural life of each region. The most significant of these gatherings was the Tatar conference in Kazan on April 10–15. Plans for reorganizing the Moslem Ecclesiastic Administration in Ufa and for the creation of centralized all-Russian Moslem cultural autonomy were elaborated, and delegates were elected for the First Congress.[6] The Bashkir conferences were primarily concerned with the question of colonization, and they sought means for returning to Bashkirs the lands expropriated from them for the benefit of the settlers from European Russia.[7] The conference of Central Asian Moslems in Tashkent also was concerned with the problem of settlement, but here the conservative clergy put in first place the question of church funds (*vakuf*), strengthening of Islamic influences among the local population, and the schools.[8]

In the Crimea, the conference of local Tatars in Simferopol on March 25 elected a new Mufti for the Moslems of Crimea and Lithuania; in addition, it set aside church funds for the Crimean Moslems' use and formed a special executive committee of forty-five members to work out the practical realization of the Crimean Tatars' cultural and territorial autonomy.[9] The selection as Mufti of Mulla M. Ch. Jihan, member of the radically nationalist group *Vatan*, which was closely associated with pro-Turkish circles, determined from the very beginning the orientation of the Crimean Tatar leaders.

The First Congress, which convened in Moscow and in which some nine hundred Moslem delegates from all parts of Russia participated, was opened on May 1, 1917, by Musa Bigeev, one of the most popular and progressive of Tatar clergymen. After the reading of some suras from the Koran, Ahmed Tsalikov, head of the Provisional Central Bureau of Russian Moslems, pronounced the inaugural speech. Tsalikov, a left Social Democrat and member of the Petrograd Soviet of Soldiers' and Workers' Deputies, combined in his address the customary Moslem aspirations with the new revolutionary goals. He congratulated the deputies for inauguration of "this historical convention" and for "liberation from the chains of tsarism."

The dark jail of the nationalities, in which we suffered for centuries, is crushed under the blows of the people's revolt. Our meeting in this hall is illuminated by the rays of the dawn of freedom. The feeling of happiness which fills our hearts, however, should not muffle a sense of political responsibility and a consciousness of the centuries' historical lessons. Up to now the Moslems have been trampled under the feet of Christians and treated as citizens of the second, and even third, category. . . .[10]

Following Tsalikov's speech, the assembly elected to its presidium Topchibashev, Akhtiamov, Dosmuhammedov, Abdullah Hojaev, Tsalikov himself, and seven others. Then came a series of addresses by representatives of various parties and political groups, all keynoted by a fervor of enthusiastic hope for a democratic future. Serge A. Kotliarevsky, head of the Department for Non-Christian Denominations, greeted the congress in the name of the Provisional Government, and warned the deputies of the responsibility before them in undertaking to reorganize the cultural and political life of Russian Moslems.[11]

Topchibashev rose to respond to the government's representative. He thanked Kotliarevsky for his good wishes and recommendations, but pointed out somewhat bitterly that Kotliarevsky would be able to find

in the acts of his department the reasons which would explain why the many million Moslems of Russia had remained so silent for centuries. . . . But now the sun of liberty is above us, and we will demonstrate to the world what we are really able to do once liberated from the yoke of the police. . . . We want first of all complete religious liberty—and you, the delegate of the Russian government, should transfer to us in the shortest time all authority for the administration of Moslem affairs.

Further, Topchibashev insisted upon educational freedom for the Moslem schools, although he admitted that the Russian language—the language of the state—should have due place in the curriculum of Islamic schools.[12] The Tatar socialist, Iskhakov, who took the floor after Topchibashev, reminded the delegates of their duties toward the "thirty million Moslems" and urged them to achieve "greatness for Islam." [13] A labor delegate, Hojaev, introduced a note of dissonance into the generally enthusiastic tone of the speeches by insisting that "liberty was won through the efforts of the workers" and that, "unfortunately, in each nation there still exist the classes of the oppressed and the oppressors." [14]

Spending the first two days in salutations and the election of commissions, the congress took up more serious considerations only on May 3. The principles of organization of Moslem autonomy and the future political structure of Russia occupied the attention of the congress during the following days of its work.

PROBLEMS OF AUTONOMY

The centralist theses elaborated by Sadri Maksudov and his Tatar associates were cautiously presented to the congress—not by a Tatar or even by a Turk, but by the Daghestani, Tsalikov. With all the vigor of his Caucasian temperament, Tsalikov started his speech by castigating the Western powers and accusing them of imperialism and of exploiting the peoples of Islam.

Up to now all the European governments have adroitly disguised their pernicious intentions and deeds by beautiful speeches declaiming liberty and democracy. . . . Now, with the recollection of the many wars organized by the European powers, there comes to mind the saying, "Those who sow the wind, reap the tempest." . . . Thanks to you— the Europeans—humanity has bled and been defiled for the last three years. . . . The Russian revolution, like a thunderbolt from heaven, is predestined to chastise Europe and cleanse humanity from the filth with which the West has covered it. . . . This revolution has awakened the Islamic world, from the Mongolian steppes to the Atlantic Ocean. This world of Turko-Tatars, of the peoples of Asia and Africa, long ago accepted Islam, and they are firmly bound by the Moslem culture. We Russian Moslems are the most progressive of all the nations of Islam, and it is our duty to set the example of uniting for the sake of liberty. . . . Today the Islamic world is backward, but this is the result of the European bridle. At the present time this world is collecting its strength. . . . We Moslems are united, on the basis of the holy and great book of Islam, on a community of thought, legends, and traditions. . . . The time is near when all Moslems will rise in defense of their faith and civilization and will initiate the struggle against the Europeans, who continue to regard themselves as rulers of the universe. It is often said that the people of the Near East slumber and that silence reigns over their lands. Now this slumber has ended. The Iranian and Young Turkic revolution, the revolt in Tripoli, and, finally, our participation in the Russian revolution have demonstrated that the Orient is awakening. . . . Europeans still misunderstand the situation in Islamic countries, but the time is at hand when they will be forced into a defensive position and will have to exert their supreme effort against [the revolt of] those who were subservient to them and whom they exploited." [15]

Thus concluding his anti-Western harangue, the head of the Moslem Central Bureau took up the problem of autonomy. He pointed out that all nations are entitled to independence. He added, however, that "at the present time there are no political groups of importance among Russian Moslems which strive for secession from Russia." Tsalikov then enumerated the basic principles for federation, or autonomy—these two concepts being frequently confused at that time in many minds: "Today the most popular political system is federation based on territorial autonomy. Supporters of federation claim that this system will solve all of Russia's national problems and guarantee the nationalities the widest opportunity for the development of their selfhood." Analyzing the various types of autonomy and federation to be found, from the Norddeutscher Bund to the United States of America and Australia, Tsalikov expressed his doubt as to whether territorial autonomy corresponded to the real needs of Russia's Moslem peoples, since the creation of numerous autonomous territorities would divide them into separate and isolated national groups. He recalled the principle of *divide et impera*, "which was so successfully used by tyrants for the purpose of subjugating the people," and came to the conclusion that it would be more practical for Russia's Moslems to unify themselves not on territorial bases but rather on socio-cultural principles. In such a manner, despite their geographic dispersion, the Moslems of Russia would form a united, centralized cultural-religious community, having its own legislative, executive, and judicial organization. Its national parliament, the *Mejilis*, would be elected by the entire Moslem population of Russia.

The Azerbaijani leader, Resul Zadeh, spoke out in support of federative, or autonomous, organization. His sober and logical exposition strongly contrasted wtih Tsalikov's impassioned and frequently contradictory speech. Resul Zadeh agreed with Tsalikov's basic postulate that the Moslems of Russia should preserve political ties with the Russians and, together with them, organize a democratic people's republic:

But how could it be possible to organize successfully the democratic administration of so vast a land, extending from Kamchatka to the Black Sea, and from Arkhangelsk to Iran—one sixth of the surface of the entire continent, and encompassing a population of some one-hundred and seventy million inhabitants? . . . when, in one part of this nation, the sun rises, in the other part people are retiring. Only decentralization and autonomy can satisfy the aspirations of Russia's peoples, and even many

Russians themselves support the principle of decentralization. . . . In the future, according to my opinion, Russia should be a federation consisting of autonomous territories. Russia's future political organization must satisfy all of its peoples, each one of whom should have its own national home. . . .

All the nations of Islam, however, might form a cultural federation within Russia—which would be easily accomplished, since the strongest national group among them are the Turko–Tatars. We are Turks, and the sons of Turks, and we should be proud to be so. We want and must create a Turkic culture, form a Turkic selfhood, and not forget that of the thirty million [sic] Moslems of Russia, twenty-nine million are Turks. . . . Russia's Turkic peoples have been divided for centuries, but now they are voicing their firm intention not only to unite but also to affirm their own national existence. . . . There are already various Turkic tongues, however. The Volga Tatars have their own language, literature, publishing houses, and schools. The Turkestanis have their Chagatai literary language and their rich literature. The Kazakh language likewise is making its way toward further development, while the Azerbaijani Turks, with the help of God, have created their own culture and a literature in their own tongue. . . .Thus, all of these peoples have their own ways . . . although sometime these various Turkic rivers, which are already flowing in the direction of a common Turkic ocean, will form this Turkic sea. . . .

We want national Turkic autonomous local statehood [*milli mahalli muhtariat*]. . . . To concretize my suggestions, I recommend the creation of autonomous Azerbaijan, Daghestan, Turkestan, Kazakhstan, etc., since all these people have their specific local particularities. . . . Each of these autonomous states should govern its local affairs and have its own national administration. . . . For the purpose of coordinating the religious and cultural development of these autonomous territories an All-Russian Moslem Council should be formed.[16]

The centralists, represented primarily by the Tatars and led by Sadri Maksudov, together with their Caucasian associates headed by Tsalikov, were so indignant at Resul Zadeh's project for national-territorial autonomy that they walked out of the hall, sabotaging a vote on the resolution.[17] To prevent a final rift between the territorialists and centralists the presidium decided to postpone voting until May 7, to relegate further study of Tsalikov's and Resul Zadeh's motions to the constitutional commission, and to allow additional discussion by an equal number of speakers for both sides.

The battle opened on May 7, with a speech by the Kazakh delegate, Dosmuhammedov. In his opinion the centralist thesis was basically opposed to any conception of autonomy. Expressing his fellow delegates' apprehension of Tatar ambitions for spiritual and political dominance over the other Turkic peoples of Russia, the Kazakh leader bitterly attacked Tsalikov: "Do you have any idea what a nationality is? It is the unity of blood, spirit, culture, traditions, language, customs, and territory. You cannot create a 'Moslem' nation on the basis of a non-territorial, centralized autonomy. Are you not, incidentally, a Pan-Islamist? We know that behind Pan-Islamism there are concealed the machinations of one nationality to dominate the other!" [18] (Here Dosmuhammedov clearly hinted at the Tatar claims for leadership.)

The Turkestani delegate, Abdullah Hojaev, energetically supported Dosmuhammedov and Resul Zadeh. "We Turkestanis want autonomy because it is the only way to maintain national identity. Our traditions are quite distinct from Russian traditions. We desire to live within the boundaries of our national territory." Hojaev cited the American system of government as the best illustration of a territorial federation which in no way contradicted the democratic principle. Territorial autonomies, in his opinion, would not divide the Moslems because the doors of one autonomy would always be open to the inhabitants of another. Further illustrating his argument, Hojaev reminded his audience that despite the political borders between Russia's and Turkey's Moslem peoples, they had always sympathized with each other.[19]

The only Tatar speaker of distinction to support territorial autonomy was Fuad Tuktarov, who attempted to persuade his Tatar comrades that adoption of the centralist motion would lead inevitably to abandonment of the congress by the Central Asian and Caucasian delegates and result in the collapse of this Moslem convention—the first one to be really free in its deliberations. This would amount to a real crime against Moslem interests. Tuktarov felt that the Tatars must prove that they had been working not merely for their own autonomy and Kazan's supremacy but also for a genuine autonomy of the Moslem borderlands. Moreover, adoption of the centralist thesis would furnish an effective propaganda weapon to the Russian government, enabling the latter to prove that the Moslems themselves were opposed to territorial autonomy.[20]

One of the most vehement defenders of the principle of territorial autonomy was Ahmed Zeki Validov, himself a Bashkir, although this time he was representing not the Bashkirs but the Central Asian Moslems. "In order to understand our problems," said Validov, "we must realize that there is not a Moslem nation in Russia." An orientalist as well as a politician, Validov reminded that, keeping in mind ethnological facts, the Moslems included both Turks and non-Turks:

The former are themselves divided into the eastern, central, and southern Turkic groups, each with its distinct language, culture, and history. . . . In some parts of Russia, as, for instance, Central Asia, Turks form from 61 to 96 per cent of the total population of the province. These provinces should unquestionably be granted national territorial autonomy, and even form a federation within Russian frontiers. . . . If we want national autonomy, and not merely a national fiction, we must organize our self-governments on historical and ethnic bases . . . bearing in mind the national-geographic boundaries of these Turkic peoples.[21]

Vociferous applause greeted Validov and the veteran of the Turkic movement in Russia, Topchibashev, mounted the platform to congratulate him.

While the conservative delegates from Turkestan, Kazakhstan, and the Caucasus continued to support the federative, or territorial-autonomist, motion, the Tatars and socialist deputies backed the centralist resolution almost unanimously. Ibrahim Hatasov, a Tatar socialist journalist, posed the question whether the federalists seriously believed that Russian Moslems were rich enough to be able to pay the expenses which would be entailed by a multitude of national administrations. "In the case of Russian Moslems' division into autonomous territories, various political parties would certainly benefit, but the people would have to pay for its administrators. Moslems should unite and cooperate with the workers' class." The exploitation of the population by parties and politicians should be prevented, "since parties should be for the people, and not people for the parties," finished Hatasov, under the indignant outcry of the federalists. The general tumult which followed Hatasov's diatribe nearly led to a new suspension of the session, and the delegates recovered their calm only after the chairman's energetic intervention.[22]

The absurdity of the strict application of Validov's and Resul Zadeh's territorial and linguistic principles in organizing Moslem autonomy, however, was demonstrated by Iskhakov, who simply pointed out that if such prerequisites were strictly followed, there would then be forty-eight autonomous republics in the Caucasus and twelve in Central Asia.[23] Thereafter Tsalikov again took the floor to defend his project. In his mind, only the wealthy strata of the population in Turkestan would profit from territorial autonomy, since power would be seized by the upper classes. In a centralized autonomy, however, the workers and peasants would be better represented and protected, since the Russian socialists—who then dominated the Provisional Government—were, according to Tsalikov, the supporters of the Moslem lower classes as well. Only a centralized Russian republic in which Moslems would participate in the central administration and have their own cultural autonomy would satisfy the Moslems' aspirations.[24]

Of the women delegates present, most were in favor of centralized autonomy. Fatima Kul Ahmedov voiced Moslem women's support of Tsalikov's resolution. She felt that only a centralized administration could guarantee the emancipation and liberation of Moslem women, many of whom, especially in the eastern provinces, were still sold to their prospective husbands and inhumanly treated. She also protested to the assembly that during the last conference of Caucasian Moslems in Baku, despite the fact that Baku was considered the most progressive Moslem city in Russia, the women delegates were mistreated, prohibited from taking the floor, and finally expelled from the convention.[25]

The final vote on the resolution concerning Moslem autonomy in Russia took place in an atmosphere of tension and mutual distrust. The ballot boxes were guarded by Dosmuhammedov and Ilias Alkin themselves. A strict check of the votes found Resul Zadeh the incontestable victor, his resolution polling 446 votes against 271 for Tsalikov's centralist motion.[26] The final text of this resolution, which was forwarded to the Provisional Government as the official political plank of Russian Moslems, recommended the following:

(1) Autonomous democratic republics based on national, territorial, and federative principles.

(2) Those Moslem peoples not possessing their own separate territory should be granted national-cultural autonomy.

(3) A central Moslem administration should be created for regulating and coordinating the cultural and religious affairs of all the Moslem peoples of Russia.

It might have been expected that the project for autonomy, which had divided the convention into two conflicting camps, would have

been the most controversial subject on the congress' agenda. Unexpectedly, though, it was the question of women's emancipation
that evoked the most heated debate. Fatima Tutash, who was the
official reporter for this question, bitterly complained of the sub-
ordinate and humiliating position of the woman in the Moslem family,
and she presented a motion demanding the complete political and
social emancipation of women in Moslem society, as well as prohibition of polygamy.[27] The resolution, supported by Musa Bigeev, Hadi
Atlasov, and the entire liberal wing of the convention, won a majority of the votes, but on May 10 the conservatives, collecting their
forces, launched a violent counterattack requiring revision of the
motion. Abdullah Hojaev, an imam, speaking in the name of "ten
million [sic] Central Asian Moslems," declared that the problem was
too serious a one to be solved in one day, and that the resolution
contradicted the moral foundation of the Moslem religion. "How
would I be able to appear before those who sent me to this congress?"
asked the indignant and alarmed delegate. "What can I tell them if
this motion is not revised?" Thereupon a written protest was delivered
to the congress by some 195 imams, and several other Central Asian
and Caucasian delegates supported them.[28]

The congress accepted with little or no debate a project for reorganizing Moslem religious administration, which would be completely separate from the supervision of the state. The new Moslem
religious administration recommended by the congress consisted of
a Mufti and six kazis (judges) elected by a special Moslem assembly.
Although this project was not yet approved by the Russian government, the congress proceeded to choose their new Mufti: Galimjan
Barudi, the well-known leader of the liberal Tatar clergy and a
theologian who had participated in all the Moslem political conferences since 1905. His election, however, showed that the progressive
Tatar wing of the Moslem clergy still had to reckon with a substantial
traditionalist and anti-Tatar opposition, since of the 900 delegates
present, only 292 voted for Barudi; 257 deputies opposed his election,
while a large number abstained from voting altogether.[29]

Reorganization of the Moslem educational system was also decided
upon without undue disagreement. According to a program elaborated by the commission on schools and presented by Teregulov,
Moslem education would be placed exclusively under the jurisdiction
of an organ of the Moslem national autonomy. The curriculum of the

Moslem schools was supposed to be parallel to that of the Russian educational program in order to provide the graduates of Moslem schools access to higher Russian educational institutions without special entrance examinations. Part three of this resolution was of great significance, for it introduced, at the insistence of the Tatar and Pan-Turkic wing, the "local national language" in the Moslem primary and secondary schools, and "common Turkic" (actually Ottoman Turkish) as a compulsory subject in the secondary schools and as the main teaching language to be used in higher schools. Russian was to be taught as a compulsory subject in the secondary and higher schools, but was relegated to a far more modest position than both the local national language and common Turkic, or Ottoman.[30]

THE REVOLUTIONARY MOVEMENT AND ANTI–IMPERIALISM

Evident unwillingness to continue the war—an effect of left-socialist defeatist propaganda—was clearly manifested by the majority of the delegates during Tsalikov's speech on foreign affairs, in which he revealed himself a brilliant popular tribune. No other speaker at the convention won such enthusiastic ovation as this Daghestani Social Democrat. His speech was to a large extent a repetition of his diatribe against the "European imperialists" with which he had begun his report on the constitutional status of Moslem autonomy. He accused the Allies of preparing the dismemberment of Turkey and demanded immediate publication of all secret treaties existent between Russia, France, England, and Italy, according to which the allied Great Powers intended to annex considerable pieces of the Ottoman Empire. Tsalikov recommended conclusion of a peace treaty without the annexation of new territories, and without the payment of any indemnities to the eventual victors. Further, he recommended including the principle of self-determination in the future peace treaty, and insisted that coming peace conferences should satisfy not only the European nations but also those of Asia and Africa.[31] "The key to the present world carnage lies in Europe," said Tsalikov. "The ruling classes of Europe aim at dominating all humanity. . . . Moslem nations have already become the victims of European imperialists. . . . Therefore we should protest against continuation of the imperialistic war and join in the manifesto of the socialist parties which convened recently in Stockholm. . . . We should also adhere to the proclamation of the Petrograd Soviet of Soldiers' and Workers' Deputies, which was addressed to the representatives of world democracy." [32]

Tsalikov's theses were unanimously accepted by the jubilant congress, which recommended that greetings be telegraphed immediately to the pacifist congress in Stockholm. Most of the delegates after Tsalikov's harangue were in a state of delirium, and Tsalikov was carried on their shoulders to the presidium; the entire congress greeted him with a storm of applause.[33]

On May 11, its last day of sessions, the congress ruled to present a common ticket, under the name of the "Moslem Democratic Bloc," in elections to the All-Russian Constituent Assembly. Coalitions with Russian socialist parties were recommended.[34] Until the autonomous Moslem administration was set up, the coordination of Moslem political action in Russia was entrusted to a Provisional National Shuro (Council).[35] The Tatar and Pan-Turkic faction of the convention sought to name this Provisional Council the National Turko-Tatar Council and recommended that the city of Kazan be its permanent seat. This proposal caused a general tumult and the congress' majority rejected it, ruling that the council be named the All-Russian Provisional Moslem National Council (*milli merkezi shuro*). Petrograd became the permanent residence of this organization.[36]

Notwithstanding the compromise decision in the question of national autonomy and Resul Zadeh's hopes for an eventual "common Turkic sea," [37] reality saw not the unification of Russia's Turkic peoples but the complete disintegration of their already shaky unity. The All-Russian Moslem Council created by the congress soon proved to be a field of discord and, in general, a stillborn child. The Moslems of Russia in 1917 were subject to the same disease as the rest of the country—unreality of political concepts. All wanted to be free and equal, and went so far in that direction that, in fact, they discarded real opportunities for social and state construction. Democratic individualism quickly degenerated into anarchy. Of submission to principles or personalities, there could be no thought. The love of freedom turned into a denial of all duties, of all bonds of a social or governmental character.

SHURO'S WORK IN 1917

In June the struggle between the various national groups represented in the Shuro reached such a critical point that Iskhakov concluded, "The council stands before the historic decomposition of the unity of the Turko-Tatar peoples." [38] The Tatar and Kazakh representatives drew near still greater conflict at the Shuro sessions of June

25; the Kazakhs wanted to organize their own Kazakh congress, while the Tatars protested that a second Moslem congress should take the place of any local organizations or conferences. Sadri Maksudov considered, in general, that Shuro itself was practically an executive power for all Moslems. This point, in turn, was sharply disputed by the territorial autonomists.[39] But Maksudov's efforts were in vain, for local centripetal forces continued to grow. At the Second Moslem congress, held in Kazan, one of the council members, M. Sultangaliev, complained that of Shuro's thirty members, only half had participated in its last sessions, and that of the five persons making up the central committee, only three were working. Shuro's executive committee was so skeptical toward its own members that when the Provisional Government asked it to find a chairman for the Turkestan committee, it offered a Russian candidate rather than a Moslem for the post.[40]

Shuro was no more successful in dealing with the Provisional Government and Russian political parties. Members of Shuro participated only twice in the deliberations of the Cabinet of Ministers, and this was limited to the discussion of lesser non-political, religious, or regional matters. But they did take part in the work of the commission for the preparation of the elections to the Constituent Assembly, where they defended the interest of Turkic and other Moslem minorities.

SHURO AND THE PROVISIONAL GOVERNMENT

The most significant contact between Shuro and the Provisional Government occurred in July after the beginning of the pro-Soviet demonstrations by the soldiers of the demoralized Petrograd garrison and the withdrawal of the Kadet ministers, when the Moslems made Prince Lvov an offer to cooperate. Headed by Tsalikov and Iskhakov, Shuro's negotiators paid a visit to the head of the precarious government. They offered Lvov both the cooperation of the Moslem parties and the support of Moslem soldiers, whom the Russians and Shuro both considered as particularly resistant to revolutionary agitations. Tsalikov and his friends counted on obtaining at least two posts in the new coalition government: they hoped that the Kazakh politician and agricultural specialist, Tanyshbaev, would be appointed to the Ministry of Agriculture, and that Tsalikov himself, as head of Shuro, would receive a ministry without portfolio. The Crimean leader,

Seydamet, the moderate Baku lawyer, Topchibashev, and the veteran of Tatar bourgeois politics, Maksudov, were Shuro's best candidates for the position of undersecretary in three other ministries. Lvov, harassed by the demonstrations and wearied by the struggle with the socialists, was sympathetic toward Shuro's offer of alliance. When, however, he undertook to consult Chkheidze, chairman of the Petrograd Soviet, this Georgian politician categorically vetoed Moslem participation in the government on the ground that not nationalities but parties should compose the government. Tseretelli, another Georgian Menshevik in the Petrograd Soviet, likewise threw the full weight of his political prestige against Moslem participation in the government. When the new coalition under Kerensky was formed, none of the Moslems found themselves in the cabinet. Tsalikov later ascribed this unexpected intervention by the two Georgian Menshevik leaders to the historical animosity between Georgians and the Caucasian mountaineers (Tsalikov himself being the latters' representative in Shuro).[41]

This conflict between Shuro and the Georgian leaders of the Petrograd Soviet did not, however, prevent their later collaboration when both eagerly aligned themselves against General L. Kornilov, who planned to take the power out of the hands of Kerensky and clean house in Petrograd. Shuro even sent its agitators to the Caucasian cavalry (the so-called Savage Division), when at the end of August Kornilov's troops began their march against Petrograd and succeeded in demoralizing even this staunch formation.

The last appearance of Shuro and Tsalikov on the all-Russian stage took place in September when the so-called Democratic Convention of socialist parties started deliberating in Petrograd. In an impassioned speech, Tsalikov demanded the convention take immediate measures in order to protect the Kirghiz and Kazakhs from deserters and settlers, requiring the immediate cessation of agricultural settlement in the Kazakh steppe. Further, he asked the socialists to support creation of a Moslem State Secretariat with the rank of a ministry, immediate convocation of the Constituent Assembly, and the resignation of V. M. Chernov, whom, as Minister of Agriculture, Tsalikov held responsible for the misdeeds of settlers in Kazakhstan and Kirghizia. He received, however, little support from the socialists, who were preoccupied with their own demagogical activities. Tsalikov's disappointment with the Russian and Georgian socialists was instru-

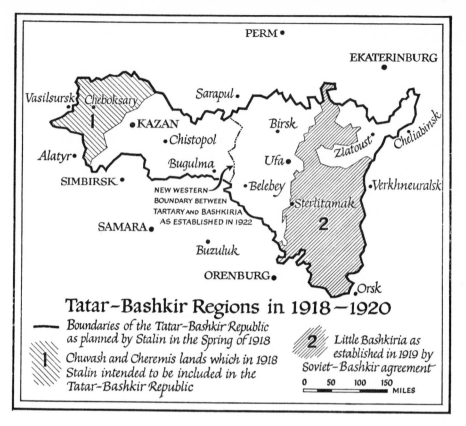

Tatar–Bashkir Regions in 1918–1920

— Boundaries of the Tatar–Bashkir Republic as planned by Stalin in the Spring of 1918

1 Chuwash and Cheremis lands which in 1918 Stalin intended to be included in the Tatar–Bashkir Republic

2 Little Bashkiria as established in 1919 by Soviet–Bashkir agreement

0   50   100   150
MILES

mental in his subsequent short-lived flirtation with the Bolsheviks and his contacts with Stalin, whom he knew from mutual collaboration in the Caucasian Social Democratic organization. [42]

TATAR AUTONOMY

Because of the dissension among the representatives of Russia's various Turkic nationalities at the Second Moslem Congress, meeting in Kazan on July 21, only the delegates from the Volga and Ural regions appeared. Those from Azerbaijan, Kazakhstan, and Central Asia boycotted it, not wishing to cooperate with the Tatars. This congress concluded the short-lived front of Russia's Moslem-Turkic peoples. At the congress even the Bashkirs broke with the Tatars and returned home to Ufa. They protested the Tatars' refusal to recognize them as a separate Turkic people and rejected the new name, "Tatar-Bashkir Autonomy," thrust upon them by the Tatars.[43] Even after the Bashkirs' exit, the Second Congress carried through a decision not only in the name of the Volga and Ural Moslems, but in the name of "all the Moslems of central Russia and Siberia." This time, however, the Tatars relinquished their aims for all-Turkic leadership, and relegated organization of the Turkic territories of the borderlands to the Kazakhs, Azerbaijanis, Uzbeks, and Crimeans.[44] At this session, which was joined by participants of two other Moslem congresses being held at that time in Kazan—military and clerical—the cultural autonomy of the Moslems of central Russia and Siberia (actually of the Tatars) was officially proclaimed.[45] The declaration was met by the cries, "Long live our people! Long live Idel-Ural!" *

The project of cultural autonomy was worked out and submitted by Maksudov, a persistent defender of centralization. Its basic feature was the principle of national and cultural autonomy. According to the project:

(1) Moslems of central (European) Russia and Siberia constituted a separate national group, with all the rights of a legal national body and with legislative power over its members in religious and cultural questions.

(2) The administrative organ of the autonomy was to be the National Parliament (*Milli Mejilis*), elected by local assemblies in the districts where Tatars lived. Each region or district of Russia with a sizable Moslem population was to form a local assembly, on the basis of one deputy to five thousand Tatars. Wherever Tatars lived, they were to submit to the National Parliament in cultural questions and to the regular Russian authority in administrative or judicial questions. In its turn, the National Parliament had no jurisdiction over non-Moslems, even in the predominantly Moslem provinces.

(3) The governing organs of the Moslem autonomy were to be the Moslem Ecclesiastic Administration in Ufa and special Moslem commissariats (*Nazarats*) for education and finance. The Commissariat for Finance was to care for the cultural needs of Moslems and for the organization of schools. Financial aid would be obtained, proportionately to the size of the Moslem population, through govern-

* The term "Idel-Ural" was created by a Tatar socialist, G. **Sharaf** (Mende, p. 12). "Idel" is the ancient Turkic name for the Volga, and hence Idel-Ural is equivalent to Volga-Ural.

mental and local Russian institutions and from special taxation of the
Moslems. The Commissariat for Education would direct the Moslem
school system.

(4) Moslems of European Russia and Siberia should have propor-
tionate representation in the Russian parliament, and there should be
a special secretary for Moslem affairs, with the rights of minister, in
the Russian governmental apparatus.[46]

According to this project, Russian Moslems would be guaranteed
autonomy in their cultural life, without the creation of independent
autonomous territories, and their central administration would be
given jurisdiction over the Moslem peoples of European Russia and
Siberia. The congress informed the Provisional Government of its
decisions and resolved "not to wait for convening of the Constituent
Assembly but to proceed immediately" to realization of their cultural
autonomy.[47]

One of the congress' resolutions dealt with the forthcoming elections to the All-Russian Constituent Assembly, and the relations of
Moslems with the Russian political parties. The strengthening of leftist radical tempers among Moslems was indicated by adoption of
the name, "All-Moslem Democratic Socialist Bloc" for the Tatar
electoral ticket. The resolution also recommended introduction of an
eight-hour working day and nationalization of landlords' estates.
Further, alliance with Russian socialist parties was recommended.
All cooperation with bourgeois organizations was categorically rejected. The congress resolved to call a "people's parliament" (the
Milli Mejilis) in the historical Bashkir city of Ufa in the fall of 1917.
These resolutions and the congress' unanimous vote for establishing
Tatar (Moslem) autonomy were a definite step toward clarification
of Tatar national consciousness and limited Tatar political activities
to their immediate kinsmen, in an abandonment of Tatars' long-
cherished plans to unite all the Moslems of Russia.

Simultaneously with the sessions of the Second Moslem Congress
beginning July 17 in Kazan, there was also held an all-Russian Moslem
military congress which, in effect, was only a congress of deputies
from the predominantly Moslem units of the Russian army for the
Moscow and Kazan military districts. This group decided to create
an All-Russian Moslem Central Military Council (*Harbi Shuro*) and
to establish separate military units for Moslems. To the Council were
elected Ensign Ilias Alkin (president), Ensign H. Tokumbetov, Lieu-

tenant Asadulov, Lieutenant Colonel Prince Kugushev, A. Mana-syrov, and others. Before the Council met, Alkin, formerly president of the Provisional Moslem Military Council, had already sought Kerensky's permission to form Moslem units, pointing out that "Moslems have always walked hand in hand with the Russian people." Now, in July 1917, the military congress once again turned to the government with this request, adding that in case the government refused, Harbi Shuro "would not submit to it, in view of the extreme urgency for Moslems to have their own military force." But permission was granted, and soon Moslem soldiers were drawn together in special units and sent to the Rumanian front, under the command of the Moslem general, Suleyman Sulkiewicz, while Tatar reservists were transferred to the Kazan military district.

This was the last Tatar congress to convene before the October Revolution, and while the Tatars were preparing for the opening of their National Parliament, the Russian Provisional Government collapsed under the blows of the Bolsheviks.

THE BOLSHEVIKS' NATIONALITIES PROGRAM

The upheaval of October 26, 1917, which transferred to Lenin and the Soviets power over the central administration in Petrograd and, theoretically, over all Russia, at the beginning did not affect the Tatars' national activities. The reaction of Russian Moslems to the Bolshevik upheaval was not at all inimical, even though only a few educated Tatars and Azerbaijanis were acquainted with the theories of Marx and Lenin or had ever read some of the voluminous writings of these apostles of the proletarian revolution. Of course, the Moslem liberal bourgeoisie, headed by Sadri Maksudov, did not conceal its misgivings toward the victory of "the toiling class," but it was no longer the most powerful group, even among the Tatars. A number of Moslem politicians sympathized with the Bolsheviks' proclamations regarding the national question in Russia and considered them the true friends and supporters of the non-Russian peoples of the late empire. In reality, no Russian party had such a radical program for the nationalities problem as the Bolsheviks'. As early as 1913–1914, Lenin had come out with a number of articles and declarations on the nationalities question in which he advocated supporting the national aspirations of all the peoples of Russia. This cunning tactician saw in the non-Russian nationalities very useful tools for the achievement of

Communist goals, and carefully prepared a program to win their allegiance. The so-called "summer meeting" of the Central Committee of the Russian Social Democrat Labor Party (Bolshevik faction) in 1913 had issued a special resolution on the nationalities problem in which it announced that "the right of all nationalities forming part of Russia freely to secede and form independent states must be recognized. To deny them this right or to fail to take measures guaranteeing them its practical realization is equivalent to supporting a policy of seizure and annexation." These words became widely known in Russia, while the next passage, which practically annulled this declaration, received less publicity by politicians. Lenin carefully added that "the right of nationalities to secede must not be confused with the expediency of secession of a given nation at a given moment. The party of the proletariat must decide the latter question quite independently in each particular case from the standpoint of the interest of the social democracy as a whole and the interests of the class struggle of the proletariat for socialism." [48] Hence, the self-determination of the nationalities was, in Lenin's mind, to be conditioned not by the desires of the nationalities themselves, but by the decisions and needs of the Communist Party.

Returning in 1917 from Switzerland to Russia, Lenin immediately reactivated the nationalities program of his party, and at the Petrograd City Conference of RSDRP(b) [the name "Communist Party" was adopted only in March 1918], held on April 14–29, 1917—on the eve of the First All-Russian Moslem Congress—the resolutions of 1913 were solemnly confirmed and the right of all peoples of Russia to self-determination, and even secession, was again proclaimed. This time Lenin's clauses of reservation concerning self-determination and autonomy were even more carefully elaborated than in 1913. He protested against the projects of "cultural autonomy," considering that national cultural autonomy "leads to a strengthening of ties between the workers and the bourgeoisie, while the aim of social democracy consists in the development of an international culture of the world proletariat." [49]

These reservations, however, were not repeated for tactical purposes in the resolutions of conferences held by Bolshevik military organizations on June 16–23, and the slogan of self-determination received particularly wide publicity, along with demands for peace, transfer of power into the hands of the Soviets, and immediate confiscation of all landowners' estates for the benefit of the peasants.[50] The Bolsheviks' propaganda slogans were effectively disseminated among the Tatars by Mullanur Vahitov, in *Kzyl Bairak*, the organ of the Moslem Socialist Committee in Kazan.[51]

Immediately after its rise to power, on November 2, 1917, the first Soviet, or, as it was then called, the Provisional Workers' and Peasants' Government—issued its famous Declaration of the Rights of the Peoples of Russia, a product of Lenin's and Stalin's collaboration.[52] This declaration proclaimed:

(1) Equality and sovereignty of the peoples of Russia.

(2) The right of the peoples of Russia to free self-determination, even to secession and formation of independent states.

(3) Annulment of all national and religious privileges or limitations.

(4) Free development of national minorities and ethnic groups which populate the territory of Russia.[53]

At the time of the formation of the first Soviet governmental body, Lenin and his comrades paid close attention to the nationalities problem, and Stalin became the head of a new Commissariat for the Affairs of the Nationalities (*Komissariat po delam natsionalnostei*, or *Narkomnats*). The national question became, and remained for many years, a problem for his special care and endeavor. Since Stalin himself was not Slavic, but Georgian, Russia's eastern problem was closer to his heart than to many others in the Soviet government. On November 20, 1917, at Stalin's instigation, the government published a manifesto to "all the toiling Moslems of Russia and the Orient." Addressed to their Moslem "comrades and brothers," this brilliant piece of political demogogy ignored all the atheistic and internationalist elements of Marxist and Leninist teaching and appealed to the Moslems' religious and national feelings:

Domination by predatory plunderers, who have enslaved the peoples of the world, is coming to an end. Under the blows of the Russian revolution, the old system of serfdom and slavery is cracking. . . . A new world, a world of the toiling and newly freed peoples, is being born. At the head of this revolution stands the workers' and peasants' government of Russia. . . . Moslems of Russia, Kirghiz and Sarts of Central Asia and Siberia, Turks and Tatars of Transcaucasia, Chechens and mountaineers of the Caucasus—all those whose mosques and prayer houses were destroyed, whose beliefs and customs were trampled under foot by the tsars and oppressors of Russia . . . from now on your customs and beliefs, your national and cultural institutions, are declared free and inviolable. Organize your national life freely and unhindered. You now have the right to do it. Know that your rights, exactly as the rights of all the peoples of Russia, are now protected by the entire might of the revolution and its organs—the soviets of workers', soldiers', and peasants' delegates. Support this revolution, it is your government. . . . Moslems of the Orient, Persians and Turks, Arabs and Hindus—all those whose lives, property, fatherlands, and liberties were the objects of speculation by the predatory robbers of Europe, whose lands were seized by the spoilers who started the present war. . . . Our banners carry the liberation of all the oppressed people of the world.[54]

In order to prove that these proclamations were not mere empty words, Stalin took some easy and effective steps. The ancient Koran of Khalif Othman, a historical book particularly venerated in the Islamic world, was returned from the former imperial public library in Petrograd to the Moslems.[55] In January 1918, Narkomnats gave the order to transfer to the local Moslem national committees the historic Tatar monuments, the tower of Princess Suyumbeka in Kazan, and the ancient Karavan Serai in Orenburg. Further, a special Committee for Moslem Affairs was set up within Narkomnats on January 19, 1918 (N.S.).[56]

Originally Stalin had intended to entrust the direction of Moslem affairs to Sagid Engalychev, a Tatar socialist from Saratov, but the latter at the outset compromised his office by arresting three leading Moslem personalities, among whom was the nephew of Shamil, the famous Daghestani fighter for the independence of the Caucasian mountaineers, whom he wanted to prevent from participating in the electoral campaign to the Constituent Assembly. At that time Ahmed Tsalikov, who in his capacity as chairman of Shuro maintained contacts with Narkomnats, advised Stalin to replace individual administration by Engalychev with a committee.[57] Stalin followed Tsalikov's recommendation and created the Committee for Moslem Affairs, appointing as its chairman the veteran Social Democrat and fanatic of social revolution in the Orient, Mullanur Vahitov, head of the Moslem Revolutionary Headquarters in Kazan, who since March 1917 had urged the Moslems to take part in the proletarian upheaval. The second member was the prominent Tatar novelist and philologist, Galimjan Ibragimov, a firm supporter of Tatar-Bashkir territorial autonomy. The third, Sharaf Manatov, an acolyte of the Bashkir revolutionist, A. Z. Validov, was, to the contrary, the partisan of a solely Bashkir autonomy and the enemy of Bashkir-Tatar collaboration. Suspected by Iskhakov and many other Moslem leaders as being an Okhrana spy in Turkey in 1913,[58] Manatov was a disrupting element in the committee and often hampered the action of Vahitov and Ibragimov.

These steps taken by the Soviet government, and the skillful propaganda which accompanied them, led to the rise of a unique movement in which Islam and Marxism merged. This was the movement of the Soviet Shariatists (Soviet supporters of the Shariat). Their leader in Daghestan was a certain Tarko Haji; among the Chechens, Sultan Mulla; and in Kabardinia, Katkhanov. A. Rasulaev propagated Soviet Shariatism among the Tatars of the Volga-Ural region.

More serious and pregnant with political consequences, however, was the movement for autonomy or secession from the Soviet government which grew with increasing momentum soon after the rise of Lenin. National leaders throughout Russia sought to sever connections with the Bolshevik system, and interpreted the Declaration of the Rights of the Peoples as a carte blanche for political secession. The first national group to exercise this right was Finland, which proclaimed its independence on December 6, 1917. The Finns' act of separation from the Russian state was greeted by Stalin, at that time in Helsinki, with the assurance that mutual confidence between the Russian and Finnish peoples would be "inconceivable if the right of the Finnish people to free self-determination were not firmly recognized." And, Narkomnats added, it was not important that verbal recognition be "confirmed by an act of the Council of Peoples' Commissars, to be put into effect without delay".[59]

Following the Finnish example, other peoples of Russia also began to count upon "recognition without delay." On December 11, 1917, Lithuania proclaimed itself a sovereign state; on January 12, 1918, Latvia; on January 22, the Ukraine; and on February 24, Estonia. Not only these national groups, but also purely Russian areas, or regions with a mixed population—sometimes small districts or even villages— hurried to put the principle of self-determination into practice and escape Soviet control. Among these peoples were the Moslems, who took steps toward proclaiming their national autonomies. The Bashkirs announced their autonomy from Russian and Tatar authority on November 15, 1917, and the Kazakhs on December 10. Representatives of the Moslem and Russian populations of Central Asia, who met in Kokand, decided to proclaim their autonomy on November 27, and the more cautious Tatars followed in December. Only in Transcaucasia, where historical ties with the Russian state were strongly felt, did local national bodies postpone a decision regarding the political status of their region.[60] After pressure was exerted by the Turkish and German high commands, however, Transcaucasia, too, claimed its right to self-determination and independence on April 25, 1918.

Most of these independent, autonomous states did not last very long, The Soviet government was quick to realize the centripetal effect of its original national program and soon put into application the clauses of reservation elaborated by Lenin in 1913 and 1917, which provided for suspension of the right to self-determination "in the interests of the class struggle of the proletariat for socialism." [61]

CHAPTER XI

Idel-Ural Dreams

The Bolsheviks' seizure of power in the Volga-Ural region occurred simultaneously with the upheaval in Petrograd. By October 26, Kazan and Ufa were entirely in the hands of the Reds. In Kazan, the Bolsheviks had started organizing political and military groups as early as March, under the leadership of A. Tikhomirnov, and Lenin's slogans on peace, transfer of power to the workers' and soldiers' soviets, and immediate confiscation of landowners' estates for the benefit of the peasantry had been skillfully propagated among Kazan Tatars by Vahitov, editor of *Kzyl Bairak* (The Red Banner).

A Latvian Communist, Karl Grassis, led the Bolshevik *coup d'état* in Kazan, where power was secured by the Bolsheviks on October 26 after a short struggle of only a few hours. Among the Bolshevik supporters were a few regular Tatar detachments, formed by the Moslem Socialist Committee, and a small troop of Tatar Red Guardists under the command of Z. Bulushev, Kamil Yakubov, Yakub Chanyshev, and I. Akhtiamov, father of Tatar Social Democrats.[1] There were several other Tatar units located in and around Kazan, but these did not step out either for the Provisional Government of Kerensky or for the Soviets, following the instructions of the Moslem Military Council (Harbi Shuro) to maintain neutrality. A few days after their seizure of power, the Bolsheviks proclaimed the Kazan Soviet Republic, with the president of the Council of People's Commissars of Kazan, Jakob Sheinkman, at its head. A Tatar, Said Galiev, became Commissar of National Affairs.[2] Other leaders of the Kazan Republic were Gersh Olkenicki, Karl Grassis, and Yakub Chanyshev. Both factually and formally, the Kazan Republic was simply a Kazan "province," and the new Council of People's Commissars (*Soviet narodnykh komissarov*, or *Sovnarkom*) little more than a new local, self-governmental, zemstvo organ. In the revolutionary jargon of 1917, "republic" was, in effect, equivalent to "Soviet authority," meaning merely "popular power" rather than an actual independent, or at least autonomous, state.

In Ufa the change-over took place still more quietly, without any armed struggle, and a local regional Sovnarkom was also formed there. On October 26 (November 8, N.S.), a combined meeting of the Ufa councils of workers' and soldiers' deputies resolved "to proceed immediately to the organization of power on a revolutionary-democratic basis," taking the power into their own hands.[3] A Revolutionary Committee (*Revkom*) was created, under the chairmanship of a well-known Bolshevik, Alexander Tsiurupa. On October 29 (November 11, N.S.), after some hesitation, the Ufa Moslem Military Council also decided to go over to the side of the Soviets.[4] This decision, based on a resolution suggested by the council's president, Shagid Hudaiberdin, placed on the side of the Reds—or at least neutralized—numerous Moslem military detachments in the Ufa region, which counted over five thousand bayonets. The propagandistic activities of two dynamic Moslem Communists, Bagau Nurimanov and Sh. Huseinov, who succeeded in winning over a number of Bashkir social leaders and workers' groups for the Bolshevik cause, considerably strengthened Soviet influence in the Ufa region in just a short period of time.

The Reds' seizure of power in Ufa and Kazan was followed by the development of awkward relations between the Soviet central government, the local Soviet authorities in Kazan, and the Cultural-National Autonomy of the Moslems of Inner Russia, as the new Tatar national administration was called. For about two months these bodies coexisted harmoniously, without interfering in each other's affairs. The autonomous Tatar Nazarats for education and finance which had been set up paralleled the provincial soviets in Ufa, Kazan, and some other cities of the region, but the population itself continued to go about its own affairs, not greatly affected either by the Moslem or by the Communist administrations. Neither the Tatar nationalists nor the Soviet authorities had any actual power, and neither side had formally recognized the other. It was a coexistence without cooperation. It seemed, however, that the Soviet government *de facto* recognized the local Tatar authorities, since, on the occasion of the transfer of the Koran of Othman to the Moslems, a decree signed by Stalin (as Commissar for the Affairs of the Nationalities) mentioned Usman Tokumbetov as "vice-president of the Moslem

Military Council" and Kerim Sagadov as "member of the [Tatar] national parliament." [5] But these were just incidental cases of contact which did not in the least indicate either official acceptance of the Tatar national organs in Kazan and Ufa by the central government, or *de jure* recognition of Lenin's regime by the Tatar Mejilis (parliament) and the Nazarats.

DECLARATION OF THE RIGHTS OF THE TOILING AND EXPLOITED PEOPLE

In January 1918, the Soviet government issued a new "Declaration of the Rights of the Toiling and Exploited People," which was officially accepted on January 25, 1918, by the Third All-Russian Congress of Soviets as the platform for the future reconstruction of the empire. It was sympathetically greeted by Tatars and other nationalities and considerably eased their apprehensions toward the Soviets. Article Two of Part One of this declaration provided that "the Russian Soviet Republic is established according to the principle of the free union of free nations, as a federation of Soviet national republics." Another passage, from Part Four, repeated the Bolsheviks' theories on the nationality problem and reaffirmed that the government was "leaving it to the workers and peasants of each national group to decide independently at their congresses of soviets whether or not they wished to participate in the federal government and in the other Soviet federative institutions, and on what terms." [6] The optimists among Tatar political leaders took this declaration at its face value and hopefuly believed that now they were officially authorized by the Soviet government to decide freely whether they would cooperate with Lenin's regime or not.

It was important for the Soviets to avert possible hostility on the part of Tatars and other nationalities in Russia, since the Bolshevik government did not actually have at its disposal any sizable forces outside Moscow and Petrograd. Theoretically, the Tatar "autonomy" was perhaps stronger than the central Soviet authority, because Harbi Shuro had access to tens of thousands of Moslem soldiers mobilized under the tsarist regime and stationed in the Volga-Ural region, plus the steady stream of Moslem troops deserting from the German-Austrian front and returning home. These Tatar troops were nominally under the command of Harbi Shuro, located in Zabulachie, the Tatar section of Kazan beyond the Bulak River (the source for the appellation, "Trans-Bulak Republic," which the Tatar autonomy was popularly called).[7] The Tatar socialists, who formed a majority in Harbi Shuro, were, for the most part, suspicious of their more radical and successful Bolshevik competitors, and were not in a hurry to submit to the authority of the new proletarian victors. In addition, in November 1917 the newly created Tatar National Parliament (Milli Mejilis) in Ufa, set up according to the decision of the Second Moslem Congress in Kazan, began its deliberations.[8]

THE BASHKIR QUESTION

Ufa was selected as the place for the Tatar Mejilis to convene for two reasons. The Moslem Ecclesiastic Administration, the highest religious administrative organ for Tatars, was located in Ufa, and the city was likewise an old Bashkir center. By meeting there, Tatars demonstrated their desire to include Bashkiria in their planned autonomous administration. The Bashkirs, however—headed by their tribune, A. Z. Validov—convened their own pre-parliament (*Kurultai*) in Orenburg, the third most important Moslem city in the Volga-Ural region. Power in Orenburg, in contrast to Ufa and Kazan, was not in Soviet but in anti-Communist hands. On October 27, 1917, the Orenburg "Committee for the Salvation of Fatherland and Revolution" [9] decided not to recognize Lenin's seizure of power, and gave authority in the city to the ataman of the Orenburg Cossacks, General Alexander I. Dutov, who readily cooperated with Bashkir and Kazakh nationalists.

On November 20 the Tatar Mejilis in Ufa opened its first (and last) session. In his inaugural speech Sadri Maksudov hailed "the first national Mejilis of Turko-Tatar Moslems of Inner Russia and Siberia" and voiced the hope that "their endeavor will bring lasting and long-lived results." He affirmed his confidence in a "happy future" based on the "ancient Turko-Tatar culture of Ulugbek" and on such recent attainments of their civilization as madrasas, publishing houses, schools, and social organization.[10] Soon after the opening of the Mejilis consultations, three political caucuses came into being. The more moderate elements, supported primarily by the clergy, bourgeoisie, and liberal intelligentsia, united around Sadri Maksudov and formed the centralist faction, which supported the nonterritorial cultural autonomy of all the Moslems of Russia. This faction counted slightly over fifty of the ninety-six members of Mejilis, among whom besides Maksudov the most prominent were Ayaz Iskhakov (Iskhakov was a socialist but the convinced enemy of territorialists), Omer Teregulov, and Gadi Atlasov. They called themselves *turkchilar-turkists*, stressing by this their unwillingness to limit cultural autonomy to the Volga Tatars. The left, more clearly socialist, group had some thirty delegates and was headed by Ilias Alkin, Galimjan Sharaf, Galimjan Ibragimov, and Nazib Halfin. They insisted on the creation of an autonomous state (*shtat*)[11] of the Volga-Ural (Idel-Ural) region, and planned to include in their territorial autonomy not only Tatars but also Bashkirs. Finally, seven to ten Tatar and Bashkir delegates, among whom should be mentioned Engalychev and S. Atnagulov, formed the extreme left wing of this constituent convention.[12] They openly sympathized with the Soviet regime and advocated immediate recognition of Lenin's government. However, neither their persistence nor a telegram from Ahmed Tsalikov inviting Mejilis to establish contacts with the central Soviet government swung the majority of the delegates from their neutralist position.[13] The attitude of the socialist-territorialist deputies toward the Communist government of Russia, however, was not clearly defined. In the following month they vacillated between collaboration and armed opposition, but after the collapse of Mejilis and, especially, after the end of the Civil War, most of them, including such prominent leaders as Ilias Alkin and Galimjan Ibragimov, closely cooperated with the Soviet regime and even joined the Communist Party.

Maksudov, as head of the moderate national group, succeeded in taking into his hands the administration of the Nazarats, including that for finance.[14] The presidium of Mejilis likewise consisted primarily of Maksudov's centralist and bourgeois supporters. Harbi Shuro, however, and the Constitutional Commission of Mejilis set up at the Second Moslem Congress in Kazan in August—for the purpose of organizing the Tatar autonomous state—were both in the hands of the socialist supporters of territorial autonomy. Realizing that the activities of a separate Bashkir legislature would undermine the prestige of their own "parliament" and doom Tatar efforts to create a larger Idel-Ural autonomous state, the Tatar territorialists did their best to tip the Bashkir leaders to their side. They sent one of their leaders, Galimjan Ibragimov, to Orenburg to convince the head of the Bashkir nationalists, A. Z. Validov, and his adherents to return to Ufa. The Bashkirs refused once more to join Mejilis, but some weeks later, having gone to Ufa on private business, Validov agreed to appear in the Tatar assembly. He refused, however, to negotiate with Mejilis for Bashkiria's inclusion in the Idel-Ural state and remained unwilling to cooperate either with Maksudov's centralists or with the territorialists supporting Ibragimov and Sharaf. Moreover, Validov's visit to Mejilis led to a sharpening of the tension between the Bashkirs and the Tatars. His appearance at the session of Mejilis in high felt boots and winter travelling attire was interpreted by the Tatars as a deliberate offense to their high assembly and caused a storm of indignant protests.[15]

After Validov's exit, the Tatars finally came to an agreement with a small Bashkir group participating in Mejilis and headed by the left socialist, S. Atnagulov. On the basis of this agreement—which Atnagulov signed in the name of "the entire Bashkir nation," although he was not authorized to do so by the Bashkirs' pre-parliament—Bashkiria was to join the future autonomous Tatar state of Idel-Ural, receiving within it its own autonomy. This "autonomy within an autonomy" was to apply to the solution of questions concerning local Bashkir affairs and the agrarian and colonization problems. Thus, the question of Bashkir autonomy received simultaneously two different solutions: in Orenburg, Kurultai proclaimed an "independent autonomy" on November 15, while in Ufa a small pro-Tatar group of Bashkirs in Mejilis agreed to Bashkiria's entrance into the Idel-Ural autonomous "state" and to the "autonomy within an autonomy." The Tatar-Bashkir controversy and the dispute between centralists and territorial autonomists took so much time that neither Mejilis nor its Constitutional Commission were able to complete elaboration of the statute for Tatar autonomy before the dissolution of Mejilis by the Bolsheviks in March 1918, even though the national autonomy of the Moslems of Inner Russia was proclaimed in December 1917.[16]

CONSOLIDATION OF RED FORCES

In January 1918, Harbi Shuro and the Constitutional Commission moved back to Kazan, while Sadri Maksudov, the Nazarats, and the presidium of Mejilis remained in Ufa. During these decisive weeks of the consolidation of Soviet power, the Tatars did not support either the Whites or the Reds—"neither Kornilov nor Lenin," as it was put at the time. Right-bourgeois Tatars wanted to adhere to the Kazakhs' and Bashkirs' agreement with Dutov and other anti-Communist forces, while the leftists, who were becoming both louder and stronger, were firm in their belief in the logic and justice of the revolution and hoped for an agreement with the Soviet regime. The Reds, meanwhile, lost no time in liquidating their opposition. On January 6 (January 19, N.S.), 1918, the All-Russian Constituent Assembly in Petrograd was dissolved, and on January 27 the Black Sea fleet occupied Simferopol and put an end to the Crimean Tatar autonomy there. Four days later the Red Guardists took Orenburg and liquidated the central executive councils of the Kazakh and Bashkir autonomies, and chased the small troop of General Dutov's supporters into the steppe. In the beginning of February, an attempt to create an anti Bolshevik Siberian government was forestalled, and all Siberia fell to Red control. On February 8, the Central Rada (Council) of the Ukraine abandoned Kiev in the face of the Red Army, and at the end of February the White Army gave up Rostov and Novocherkask, retreating into the north Caucasian steppes. Finally, on February 20, Soviet troops stormed Kokand and dissolved the executive organs of the Central Asian Moslem autonomy. Thus, by the end of February 1918, all the territory of the former Russian Empire, except the Transcaucasian administration, the White armies of Generals Dutov, Popov, and Alekseev in the Kazakh and north Caucasian steppes, and the Tatar Mejilis, had officially submitted to Soviet power.

Tatar nationalists—both Sadri Maksudov in the right, liberal, wing, and Alkin and Sharaf in the left, socialist, wing—now realized that while they argued about cultural or territorial autonomy and the Bashkirs, the Reds were rapidly seizing more and more power throughout all Russia. Before their very eyes the Reds' position was becoming stronger even in Kazan and Tatar territory, and the authority of the Tatar autonomous administrative bodies was being undermined.

At the time of the Soviet upheaval, the Tatars still represented considerable strength: Mejilis and Harbi Shuro were backed not only by densely populated Moslem Tatar regions, but also by numerous Moslem regiments in the area. The number of Moslem soldiers in the Volga-Ural region in early winter of 1917 was still some tens of thousands.[17] The appearance of these Moslem units on the side of General Dutov and other anti-Communist Russian forces (who in these months often operated with only some hundred soldiers) might have been a decisive factor in deciding the further fate of Soviet power. Submitted to Bolshevik propaganda during the following months, however, these troops began to show signs of decomposition. Desertions from the Russian army, as well as from Moslem troops, reached such a proportion that whole divisions and corps vanished in a period of months. The Moslem Corps, for instance, which was formed in Bessarabia and Odessa by the Russian high command late in the fall of 1917, under General Suleyman Sulkiewicz, and which numbered originally twenty-eight thousand, melted away over the winter. By early spring of 1918 only its headquarters remained.[18] Tatar national leaders, for their part, suffered from the same illness as their Russian colleagues of the center and the left: lack of decisiveness and a hesitancy to step out against the Bolsheviks, who were proclaiming themselves "defenders of the people's freedom and rights." Probably, Tatar politicians were not very sure even of their own soldiers. The verging of the masses to the left took place very quickly, and Tatars experienced the contagion of anarchy and radicalization to the same degree as the Russian population. Troops at that time were rather mobs of armed workers and peasants in uniform than real military units, while the civilian population was also in a state of anarchy and rapidly progressing political radicalization. In the city elections in Kazan held on October 12, Tatar Communists received six votes and the socialists eleven, while Tatar bourgeois groups received only one vote. In elections to the Constituent Assembly, of eight elected Moslem deputies from the Ufa region, six belonged to socialist groups. By December 14, 1917, all non-Communist newspapers in Kazan were closed, and on January 28, 1918, the city council was dissolved.[19] A pro-Soviet "first Moslem socialist infantry regiment" was formed.

Upon its return from Ufa to Kazan, Harbi Shuro faced a new and rapidly deteriorating situation: the Reds, feeling the ground more secure under their feet, changed their tone and prepared to eliminate altogether their Moslem competitors from the local administration. Therefore, to strengthen its shaky position and to mobilize Tatar military forces, Harbi Shuro called a new "all-Russian Moslem congress," in reality simply a Tatar military conference. Moslem officers were instructed to recruit Tatar soldiers for elite shock troops, which later became known as the Wolves' Detachments and the Iron Squads. Contacts were established with Russian officers' groups, which, under the leadership of General L. Rychkov, succeeded in concentrating in Kazan over five thousand former tsarist officers and cadets.[20] The lack of financial resources for setting up troops and for administration led Tatar politicians to the doubtful task of sequestering private capital through Kazan banks, which had already been nationalized by the Soviet government. Tatar commissars were appointed to all banks and savings unions.[21]

The renewed activity of Tatar nationalists alarmed the Kazan soviet, which attempted to conquer the Tatar autonomy from within. At the Moslem military congress held in Kazan—more exactly, in Zabulachie—the Tatar Bolshevik faction, headed by Kamil Yakubov and Yakub Chanyshev, presented a motion meant to sway the congress toward officially recognizing Soviet power. At the same time, the Constitutional Commission of Mejilis, at the instigation of the Bashkir Communist, S. Atnagulov, and the Tatar, Fatyh Saifi, voted to reorganize the Tatar autonomy along Soviet patterns and to recognize the Soviet regime. This decision was protested by Ilias Alkin's national caucus in the commission, and Harbi Shuro repealed the commission's resolution to recognize the Soviets. It also decided to merge the commission with Shuro.

COUNTERREVOLUTION IN ZABULACHIE

These measures and countermeasures were followed on February 17 by a break in the ranks of the Tatar organizations. Finding it impossible to impose recognition of the Soviets upon the military congress and the Tatar autonomous administration, the pro-Bolshevik faction walked out of the congress and the Constitutional Commission, joining forces with the pro-Soviet Moslem Socialist Committee in Kazan. This committee, dominated by Vahitov (Stalin's assistant in Narkomnats) and Said Galiev (Kazan Commissar of National Affairs), cooperated unceasingly with the Soviet government and was the main instrument for Communist activities among the Tatars.[22]

The conflict on February 17 between pro- and anti-Soviet Tatar groups signified the beginning of open warfare over the undivided authority of the Soviets in the Volga-Ural region and led to liquidation of the last traces of Tatar autonomy (which had never been officially recognized anyway). The leaders of Harbi Shuro made a last-minute effort to organize a defense for the Tatar national autonomy, and entered into negotiations with Socialist Revolutionaries, Russian officer organizations, and with the White Army of General Dutov. Tatar units, the Wolves' Detachments, and the Iron Squads began to concentrate around Kazan,[23] and Zabulachie became an armed camp. At the Tatar military congress,[24] one of the leaders of Harbi Shuro, H. Tokumbetov, turned to the Bolsheviks with an angry speech: "It is not your concern to teach us how to govern ourselves. That is our own business. If you intend to interfere in our business, then know that behind us are a million [Tatar] bayonets."[25] But Tukumbetov's "million bayonets" did not frighten the Reds, for they were the first to strike: the leaders of Harbi Shuro, including Tukumbetov himself, Alkin, et al.—some two hundred persons—were arrested. In reply, the Tatar troops, fortified in Zabulachie, brought in reinforcements and formed the so-called Provisional Revolutionary Staff, composed of Iskhakov, Manasyrov, and other Tatar anti-Communists. A few days passed in skirmishes and indefinite movements by both sides, but on February 28 a truce was signed, according to which the Reds freed those Tatars they had arrested. The Tatars, for their part, were obliged to:

(1) Cease temporarily organization of the Idel-Ural state.

(2) Recognize that in Kazan and in the "Kazan Republic" full power belonged to the Soviets.

(3) Unarm their units.

(4) Give up to the Reds those White Russian officers who had supported Harbi Shuro.[26]

THE SHAKY TRUCE

The Kazan truce of February 28, 1918, gave the Tatar autonomy, or better to say the "Trans-Bulak Republic," the possibility to exist a few more weeks. The Bolsheviks had agreed to the truce not because they sought some sort of agreement with the Tatar nationalists, but, rather, merely to gain time, since they did not want to begin military operations against the Tatars before the conclusion of a peace treaty with Germany, Austria, and Turkey. At that time a Soviet delegation led by Trotsky was conducting negotiations in Brest-Litovsk with representatives of the Central Powers, but owing to the difficult conditions laid down by the Berlin and Vienna governments, these negotiations were suspended. On February 18, finding it impossible to come to terms with the Soviet delegation, the German high command began an offensive along the entire front against the remnants of the demoralized Russian army. The Soviet government was preoccupied during these days with the problem of stopping the German offensive, and not with the Tatar situation. All available Bolshevik armed forces were sent to the front. In his proclamation, "The Socialist Fatherland is in Danger," Lenin and his government appealed to the peoples of Russia: "The German militarists want to strangle the Russian and Ukrainian workers and peasants, to return their lands to the landlords, mills and factories to the bankers, and power to the monarchists. . . . The German generals seek to establish their 'order' in Petrograd and in Kiev. . . . The Socialist Republics of the Soviets are in the greatest danger." [27] At the same time, the government announced the new mobilization of all military and economic resources.

Some days later, under the pressure of Lenin, the Central Committee of the Bolshevik Party and the Soviet government decided to accept the terms of the German and Austrian peace proposal. The conclusion on March 3, 1918, of the Treaty of Brest-Litovsk by the Soviet delegation, headed no longer by the irreconcilable Trotsky but by the tactful old diplomat Georgi Chicherin, gave the Bolshevik government freedom of action. The peace treaty was ratified March 6–8 by the Seventh Party Congress of RKP(b) and on March 14 by the Fourth Extraordinary Congress of the Soviets. Their hands untied, the Soviet government now proceeded to liquidate all remaining internal enemies.

A SOVIET COUNTERPROJECT

Preparations for dissolving the Trans-Bulak Republic and the entire Tatar national autonomy were begun with the creation of a new—this time, pro-Soviet—Tatar "people's movement." The pro-Soviet members of Harbi Shuro and of the Idel-Ural Constitutional Commission, who in February had advised Tatars to recognize the Soviet government and, with the blessing of Sovnarkom and Narkomnats, had joined the Kazan Bolsheviks, now summoned an extraordinary regional congress of the soviets in which Tatar delegates from all the Volga-Ural governments were invited to participate. The congress decided to create a Soviet Moslem autonomous republic of the Ural-Volga region.[28] One of its resolutions attacked the Tatar nationalists and proclaimed, "The stratification of the Moslem masses has begun, indicating that the hour has drawn near when all social barriers created between the proletariats of various nations by the bourgeois pseudo-nationalists will definitely collapse." This resolution clearly reflected the whole duplicity of the national policies of the Bolsheviks at that time. Despite their "solemn proclamation of the principle of self-determination by the people," they stressed simultaneously that the revolution denied the sense of the existence of nationalities.

The local soviet of workers', soldiers', and peasants' delegates in Kazan at its meeting on March 6 resolutely supported the decision of the extraordinary regional congress. The soviet proclaimed its "steadfast support of the principle of national determination up to secession" and appealed to the Ufa and Orenburg soviets to start the necessary steps for establishment of the promised Soviet Moslem Ural-Volga Republic.[29] A special commission, organized as a replica of the Constitutional Commission of the Tatar Mejilis, in contact with and under the supervision of Stalin's Narkomnats and Vahitov's Committee for Moslem Affairs, began to draw up plans for the new republic. By March 20 the first project was ready and submitted for Stalin's preliminary examination. On March 22, at Stalin's recommendation, the Council of People's Commissars of the RSFSR published a decree which announced the forthcoming creation of a Tatar-Bashkir Soviet Republic: "Having decided to grant the desire of the Tatar-Bashkir revolutionary masses, and in conformity with the decisions of the Third Congress of Soviets, which proclaimed Russia a 'Federation of Soviet Republics,' the People's Commissariat for the Affairs of the Nationalities, in agreement with the Council of People's Commissars, has laid down provisions for setting up a Tatar-Bashkir Soviet Republic. . . . The constituent congress of the soviet of this republic . . . will elaborate the definite form and details of its statute." [30]

Further on in this decree it was pointed out that the future Tatar-Bashkir Republic of the RSFSR would be formed from the territory of the southern Urals and middle Volga region. The entire Ufa, Orenburg, and Kazan provinces (except for the Chuvash and Mari districts) and substantial parts of the Perm, Viatka, Simbirsk, and Samara provinces were scheduled for inclusion in the new Moslem Soviet republic. Relations between the eastern, Bashkir, part and the western, Tatar, part of the projected republic were supposed, according to the decree, to be determined later by a constituent congress of the republic's soviet. The Committee for Moslem Affairs of Narkomnats, under Vahitov, was commissioned with the actual carrying out of this decree and the convening of the constituent congress of the Tatar-Bashkir Soviet Republic. At the bottom of the decree were the names of its initiators: Stalin, Vahitov, and Ibragimov.[31] By setting up this projected autonomous Tatar-Bashkir Soviet Republic, the Bolsheviks competed very advantageously with the Tatar nationalists, whose timid plans for cultural-national autonomy had never been carried through. The new decree, elaborated at Stalin's instigation, officially proclaimed an autonomous republic, and its boundaries were far vaster than had ever been envisioned even by the most radical Tatar nationalists. In the new projected republic were to be included not only all of Bashkiria but also extensive parts of the Volga-Ural region in which the Turkic population formed a minority. In May 1918, despite their protests, it was decided that even the Chuvash and Cheremiss (Mari) should be included (see map on p. 156). [32]

Thus, Narkomnats successfully challenged the aspirations of Tatar nationalists and out-trumped them with their own weapon of national autonomy. The Tatars' organs of administration, their Mejilis, Constitutional Commission, and Harbi Shuro, became obsolete and unnecessary, in view of the formation of the projected Tatar-Bashkir Republic.

THE END OF IDEL-URAL AUTONOMY

Having ideologically and tactically disarmed the Tatar nationalists, the Communists initiated steps for the final liquidation of Tatar national organizations. A Soviet proclamation published in February, during the German offensive and the conflict with Harbi Shuro, bluntly told Tatar nationalists what to expect. Appealing to "brother Moslems," the proclamation stated, "Damned should be those who dare to fan the flame of the counterrevolution. Comrades, Moslems, brethren! Summon all your spiritual and physical forces under the banners of the Moslem socialist army. What a wonderful, solemn finale will resound when the last enemy of the Russian revolution is defeated. In the name of liberty and in the name of your national development, hurry into the ranks of the manful defenders of the fortress of the revolution." [33]

By the end of March 1918, the "fortress of the revolution" was prepared not only to "damn its enemy" but also to crush it. On March 26 the People's Commissariat for the Affairs of the Nationalities issued a decree signed by Stalin and Vahitov which dissolved the All-Russian Moslem Harbi Shuro and, together with it, the entire Trans-Bulak Republic.[34] Two days later, on March 28, a few hundred Red sailors arrived in Kazan, sent at the order of Stalin and Lenin, and the Kazan soviet demanded the unconditional surrender within four hours of Harbi Shuro, which was meeting in Zabulachie. Some defenders of Tatar autonomy defected to the Reds, but Harbi Shuro and the remaining Tatar detachments decided to resist, whereupon the sailors moved up the Bulak River and a Red armoured car crossed the bridge to Zabulachie, cutting off its line of defense. The Red Guard advanced upon Zabulachie from other sides, and street fighting lasted several hours. On March 29 the Zabulachie bulwark of Tatar autonomy and Harbi Shuro were liquidated.[35] The Tatar Nazarats in Ufa were discontinued on April 12, and the Tatars' efforts to create a genuinely national autonomy came to an end, unnoticed even by the majority of the Volga-Ural population. On April 25 the Moscow office of Harbi Shuro was dissolved, and a decree issued on May 22, 1918 by Narkomnats liquidated the All-Russian Moslem Council, under Tsalikov, whose formation had been heralded with such enthusiasm and hope at the May 1917 All-Russian Moslem Congress.[36]

CHAPTER XII

The Road to Red Tatary

In spring 1918, after the dissolution of the Tatar national administrations, Moslem Communists set about the organization of an autonomous Soviet Tataro-Bashkiria and its working basis, a separate Moslem Communist Party. At their head, along with Vahitov, stood Sultangaliev, Galiev, Ibragimov, Ismailov, and other Tatar intellectuals, many of whom had left the ranks of the Tatar nationalists to join the band wagon of the Moslem revolutionaries after Stalin and the Soviet government promised to carry through the "Soviet autonomy of the Moslem peoples." Stalin himself was behind them and wholly supported their plans for creation of the first Autonomous Soviet Republic and of a pro-Soviet Tatar-Bashkir political organization, as he wrote in an article published in *Pravda* on March 23. For Stalin, who, at the Third Congress of Soviets in January 1918, had first initiated the federative principle for reconstructing Soviet Russia, Tataro-Bashkiria represented an important testing ground, "the only region whose revolutionary organizations have outlined a definite plan for federation with Soviet Russia. We are referring," he continued, "to that clear-cut general outline of the organization of a Tatar-Bashkir Soviet Republic about which everyone is now talking and which was elaborated by the influential [*sic*] Soviet organizations of the Tatars and Bashkirs." [1]

Of course, both Stalin and the Communist Party were interested in Tataro-Bashkiria as a trial balloon, the first case of the application of a new system which they hoped would win the sympathy of the entire eastern region. Along with its publication of Stalin's statement regarding the status of Tataro-Bashkiria, *Pravda* revealed that analogous plans were being worked out for the other peoples of eastern Russia, particularly of Central Asia and the Caucasus. [2] But in 1918 Stalin was not yet the all-powerful master of Russia which he became in the late 1920's, and, therefore, despite his support, various oppositional circles in the party caused first postponement and then com-

plete revamping of his plan for the autonomous organization of the
Volga-Ural region. His desire to create a large Moslem republic
there can certainly be explained to a large extent by his desire to
gain control, as Commissar for the Affairs of the Nationalities, of a
vast territory and a powerful new administration. Therefore Stalin
not only wholeheartedly supported the plans of the Tatar Communists
but even sought to include in the planned Tatar territory the regions
of such other national groups as the Bashkirs, Maris (Cheremiss), and
Chuvash. The Bashkirs, the left-internationalist Communists, and
some Russian Communists stepped out against Stalin's plans for setting
up his own Volga–Ural feudal apanage. All Tatar Communists, however, were of course in favor of creating a united Tatar-Bashkir Soviet
Republic.

Toward the beginning of 1918, after the taking of Orenburg by
Red troops, a Bashkir Communist group which had formed in Ufa
in November 1917 extended its activities to Orenburg, where, with
the help of local fellow travellers, it organized in early February a
Provisional Revolutionary Council of Bashkurstan (PRCB), "Bashkurstan" being the Turkic name for Bashkiria (see Chapter XIII).
This organ proclaimed Bashkiria a Soviet autonomy on February 20,
1918,[3] the first such Autonomous Soviet Republic to be declared. In
March, PRCB sent a delegation to Moscow, where the Bashkirs found
a zealous supporter of separate Bashkir autonomy in the person of
Sharaf Manatov, one of Vahitov's assistants in the Moslem Committee.
Along with the president of the Bashkir delegation, Shafeev, and its
other members, Manatov himself was sharply opposed to a Bashkir-
Tatar union, and only Stalin's personal support in March–April 1918
provisionally saved the project of Tatar "unificationists." In this instance, Bashkir Communists, as well, adhered to the anti-Tatar line
of A. Z. Validov and other Bashkir nationalists.[4] In July the Bashkir
Commissariat in Ufa published an open letter to Stalin in which it
declared that "not one Bashkir should participate in the constituent
congress of the united Tatar-Bashkir republic," [5] and in 1920 the
Tatars' and Stalin's attempts to lay their hands on Bashkiria led to
open rebellion against Soviet power by Bashkir nationalists.[6]

No less categorically opposed to a Tatar-Bashkir Autonomous
Soviet Republic were the left Communists, who basically rejected the
idea of any type of national autonomy. This wing was especially
strong toward the end of the Civil War, when many of its members

—future Trotskyites—considered that the world revolution was just around the corner and that precious time should not be wasted over the organization of national autonomous territories. Various Moslem left Communists, such as Atnagulov and Shamigulov,[7] sided with them, as well as representatives of those national groups which did not have their own national territory wtihin Soviet Russia, such as the Latvians, Germans, Jews, and Poles living in Russia. Karl Grassis, Goldberg, Milkh, Sheinkman, Veger, Izrailovich, Zwillinger, Chodorowski, Olkenicki, and many other leaders of the Kazan and Ufa Communists in 1917–1920 belonged to this antiautonomist, centralist group in the party. They believed that the proletariat alone should lead the revolution, and since there were very few proletarians among Moslems, then the proletariat of other nationalities must legally seize power and form a proletarian dictatorship over the country.

Finally, the Moslem autonomists were also opposed in Bashkiria, Kazakhstan, and other regions of eastern Russia by representatives of the right peasant and labor wing of the Russian Communists, who feared that the Bashkirs and local Turkic peoples would take back from the peasants the lands the latter had just settled. In Central Asia, Russian workers sought to prevent Moslems from gaining power, for the reason that "the Moslems have not yet matured enough for autonomy."[8]

THE IDEOLOGY OF TATAR COMMUNISTS

The Tatar Communists, however, were united and resolute in their support of Stalin's projected Tatar-Bashkir Republic. They saw in it the triumph of the Tatar idea and believed that the revolution would spread from Tataro-Bashkiria to the entire East, freeing the latter from the European colonial yoke. The fact that the Communist Party and Soviet government needed them for propagandistic purposes as the oriental "show-window" for Islamic Asia made them confident of their luck and strength. Tatar Communists were united by a marriage of reason with the Central Committee of the Communist Party, which they themselves needed for the achievement of Tatar autonomy. It is difficult to suppose that these Moslem Communists felt themselves Communists in the regular Marxist, international, and proletarian sense of the word. Their devotion to the revolution was wholehearted, but they visualized it, first of all, as the revolt and triumph of the East—particularly the Moslem East—over European

colonizers. In the 1920's a Tatar writer, K. Kasymov, in describing
one of Stalin's first Moslem collaborators, Mullanur Vahitov, wrote:

Vahitov was certain that the influence of ancient Arab culture on the
universal culture which would emerge as a result of world-wide socialist
reconstruction would be immense. In his dreams he pictured this Islamic
culture—whose impact extended from Arab lands to the sacred river,
Ganges—as great, beautiful, and profound in its content. He could not
conceive of its possible disintegration or disappearance and dreamed
that in the future it would . . . illumine all humanity. Of this he was
convinced.[9]

For Vahitov, the Tatar revolutionary experience was just the beginning of the general political awakening of all Asia, as was revealed by
his first speech in Kazan on March 7, 1917, when he spoke of the
future socialist Tatary as a springboard for Asian revolt.

   Equally attached spiritually to the East and Islam was Vahitov's
Communist assistant, the popular Tatar novelist and philologist,
Galimjan Ibragimov, who also wrote at one time that "in accordance
with the type and evolution of their culture, Tatars should orient
themselves toward the East." Ibragimov in his writings even warned
his kinsmen against the possible influence of Moscow over Kazan.[10]
A third influential Tatar Communist, M. Sultangaliev, in a series of
articles for the official publication of Narkomnats, "The Life of the
Nationalities," in 1919, pointed out that only the Moslem East could
ensure the victory of the revolution.[11] Therefore, according to
Sultangaliev, they, Tatar Communists, were the true "revolutionaries
of the East and of Islam," and their prime concern was not the world
revolution but the freeing of the East from the shackles of "European
exploiters."

   Stalin, who sponsored their publications and speeches during these
years, was well aware that the ideology and aims of Moslem Communists differed immensely from those of European Communists,
and in 1918 or early 1919 he told his assistant, S. M. Dimanstein,
"Sultangaliev long regarded us askance, and has only recently become
somewhat tame." [12] But in the difficult days of 1918, the Bolsheviks
picked up support wherever they found it. They accepted as allies
anyone who was for the international revolution or who was eager
to fight against the White armies and the last representatives of the
old, anti-Communist, national Russia. Therefore, despite opposition
on the left and, probably, despite his own distrust of his Tatar allies,

Stalin did his best to help them. On March 31 he called a joint session of Vahitov's Moslem Committee and the Bashkirs, at which, despite the Bashkirs' desperate opposition, Stalin made public his "Statute on Soviet Tatary."

THE SOVIET AUTONOMY

On May 10–16, Stalin convened a conference of Moslem Communists for the purpose, as was indicated in the invitations to the meeting, of "organizing a commission for convening a constituent congress of soviets [and] . . . to determine the boundaries and outlines of the Tatar-Bashkir autonomy." The importance of this first large meeting of Moslem Communists in Moscow was emphasized by the fact that the invitations were sent out in the names of Lenin and Stalin.[13]

The conference opened with a speech by Stalin, in which he clearly indicated that the autonomy would be under Soviet control, and that the nationalists would never be permitted to play any role in Tataro-Bashkiria.

Nearly everywhere, in all the regions, bourgeois autonomous groups were formed which set up "National Councils," split their regions into separate national curiae, with national regiments, national budgets, etc., and thus turned their countries into arenas of national conflict and chauvinism. These autonomous groups (I am referring to the Tatar, Bashkir, Kirghiz, Georgian, Armenian, and other "National Councils") —all these "National Councils" were out for one thing only, namely, to secure autonomy so that the central government should not interfere in their affairs and not control them. . . .

It goes without saying that the Soviet power cannot sanction autonomy of this kind. To grant autonomy in order that all power within the autonomous unit may belong to the national bourgeoisie, who insist upon noninterference on the part of the Soviets, to surrender the Tatar, Bashkir, Georgian, Kirghiz, Armenian, and other workers to the tender mercies of the Tatar, Georgian, Armenian, and other bourgeois—that is something to which the Soviet power cannot consent.

Autonomy is a form. The whole question is what class content is put into this form. The Soviet power is not at all opposed to autonomy. It is in favor of autonomy—but only such autonomy in which the entire power belongs to the workers and peasants, and in which the bourgeoisie of all nationalities are debarred not only from power, but even from participation in the election of government bodies.

Such autonomy will be autonomy on a Soviet basis.[14]

At the conference, Stalin—in the best style of such Tatar Communists as Vahitov and Sultangaliev—emphasized that future Tataro-Bashkiria should be the avant-garde of the revolution in the East: "Let this autonomous republic serve the Moslem people of the East as a beacon, lighting the way to liberation from oppression." According to Stalin's proposal, the conference decided to include within the boundaries of the Tatar-Bashkir Republic the Chuvash and Cheremiss (Mari) regions, and it elected a commission of eight[15] to prepare for the constituent congress of Tataro-Bashkiria, to be held in Ufa on July 1, 1918. Vahitov was elected chairman of the commission.

The Tatars were delighted with the pending fulfillment of their desires. Soviet Tatary or Tataro-Bashkiria was to become a powerful multinational state on the Volga, with some eight to ten million inhabitants, under the command of a Tatar minority, and Vahitov could say with sincerity, "Great thanks to comrades Lenin and Stalin, who understood . . . that fulfillment of the hopes of the Moslem proletariat is a magnificent revolutionary deed." [16]

THE CIVIL WAR

When Stalin had appeared at this conference, he could, of course, not foresee that a few days later the revolt of Czecho-Slovak Legions and Russian anti-Communist forces would set off civil war throughout entire eastern Russia. The Czecho-Slovak Legions[17] were retreating from the German front and crossing Russia to the free harbors of the Far East. Their echelons extended by May 1918 along the railroads from Penza to Vladivostok, and on May 25 they went into action against the Soviet government. On June 8, with the help of former tsarist officers' organizations and Socialist Revolutionaries, they took Samara, which became the center of an anti-Communist movement. A conference of members of the former Constituent Assembly in Samara organized a new government, the Committee of the Constituent Assembly (*Komitet Uchreditelnogo Sobrania* or *Komuch*). On July 4, Red troops vacated Orenburg, on July 6 they left Ufa, and at the end of July Komuch's anti-Communist White Russian and Czecho-Slovak units stood at the approaches to Kazan. Shortly afterwards, all the eastern provinces of Russia from the Volga to the Pacific fell to anti-Soviet forces.

The unfolding situation, it would seem, should have forced the Communists to forget, at least temporarily, about the Tatar-Bashkir autonomy, Moslem Communists, and revolution in the East. But, to the contrary, danger only whetted their energies and increased their readiness to seek out new allies. Vahitov began to manifest his talents in a new field—the organization of military forces. On May 2, 1918, shortly before the beginning of the Czecho-Slovak "insurrection," when the threat of civil war was already in the air, Narkomnats and its Moslem Committee, in agreement with the Commissariat for Military Affairs, had decided to create a "Moslem workers' and peasants' army." A few days later Vahitov stood at the head of a newborn Moslem military commission, under the Commissariat for Military Affairs and the Revolutionary Military Council (*Revvoensovet*),[18] and immediately began the formation of Tatar-Bashkir regiments. In his appeal to the provincial Moslem commissariats of June 13, Vahitov wrote, "At this moment of threat to the Soviet republic, all Moslem proletarians should rise to defense. All Red Guardist Moslem units should mobilize without delay for the struggle against the counterrevolution." [19]

THE MOSLEM COMMUNIST PARTY

Along with the creation of a Soviet Moslem army, Vahitov worked feverishly to set up a Moslem Communist Party capable of inspiring the "defenders of revolution" and leading them into battle. He called the first conference of Moslem Communists in Kazan on June 17–20. This group resolved to organize an All-Russian Party of Moslem Communists (Bolshevik) on the basis of the program of the RKP(b), and elected a central committee for it.[20] This new Moslem party was the culmination of a systematic preliminary campaign conducted by Vahitov and his aides among the Tatars and Bashkirs during the winter of 1917–1918. In Ufa on October 15–18, 1917, a congress of Bashkir and Tatar Social Democrats had been held, under the presidency of Bagau Nurimanov—a member of the Bolshevik faction of RSDRP—and this had been the first Moslem pro-Soviet conference ever to convene. This congress had created the Tatar Social Democratic Workers' Party, which merged with the internationalist Social Democrats and the Bolsheviks, but was nevertheless short-lived.[21] Also, in the fall of 1917, a pro-Soviet Tatar Socialist Committee had been set up in Kazan. Communist Moslem groups had likewise been created, at Vahitov's instigation, in Astrakhan, Samara, Moscow, and some other cities of Russia. Thus, Vahitov's new Moslem central committee did not initiate, but organized the movement, unifying and placing under stricter control various groups of Moslem Communists not previously attached formally to RKP(b). Sovnarkom of the RSFSR gave wide support to Vahitov's efforts, and Lenin decreed the setting-up of special Moslem Socialist Committees in all provincial and district centers of "those regions having a Moslem population." Moreover, participation in these committees was not limited to Communists, but extended to all "left-revolutionary Moslem organizations standing either on a Communist platform or a left Socialist Revolutionary one." [22]

There was divergence, however, concerning the formal organization of the Moslem Communists. The majority of Tatars favored the creation of a separate Moslem Communist Party, such as Vahitov himself, Sultangaliev, Fedovsi, Ibragimov, Galiev, and other co-workers in Stalin's Commissariat for the Affairs of the Nationalities. The left, internationalist, Moslem Communist wing, headed by Atnagulov and Shamigulov, was opposed to any independent Moslem Communist organization, although Vahitov's plan was carried through.

THE BATTLE FOR KAZAN

With the approach of the Czecho-Slovak and Russian anti-Communist troops toward Kazan, Vahitov left Moscow to organize the defense of this Tatar city. In his last speech, delivered on July 22 to the Moslem Communist congress in Kazan, he once again urged Moslem workers to defend the city, pointing out that only the workers' proletariat could play the decisive role in liberating the East.[23] On August 4 the First Tatar-Bashkir Battalion—most of which eventually perished in the battle over the city—arrived in Kazan.[24] The Red defense of this old Tatar city assumed a cosmopolitan flavor with the arrival of reinforcements: Vahitov's First Tatar-Bashkir Battalion was joined by a Moslem socialist reigment (under the command of an experienced Tatar officer, M. Alimov), a Serbian regiment, various Latvian regiments (including the Fifth Zemgali Rifle Regiment, which particularly distinguished itself), and several Russian, Cheremiss, and Chuvash Red Guard troops. Jakob Sheinkman, the local party secretary, was the moving force behind the defenders, while the White offensive was conducted by Colonel Kappel, commander of the Russian regiments, and Colonel Svec, in charge of the

Czech and Slovak detachments. Kazan fell on August 7 to the anti-Soviet forces, and the following day Vahitov was captured by the Czechs in the village of Borisov. A special *troika* (three-man tribunal) condemned him to be shot. One of the members of this tribunal was mullah A. Apanaev, who had participated with Vahitov at the first Moslem revolutionary meeting in Kazan one and a half years earlier. Despite the attempts of friends to gain the intervention of Ilias Alkin, Tatar commissar of Komuch in Kazan, and of Tatar national leaders connected with Komuch, Vahitov was executed on August 19.[25] His death and the continuation of the Civil War were among the factors which brought about a two-year postponement of the proclamation of an autonomous Tatar Soviet Republic.

TATARS AND THE RUSSIAN COUNTERREVOLUTION

An interesting and, at the beginning, promising attempt at Turkic-Russian political cooperation in the anti-Bolshevik struggle was made by politicians from two groups who joined the anti-Soviet Komuch government in May–June 1918. Tatar socialists began to gather in June in Samara and met there with their Russian socialist colleagues—mainly Socialist Revolutionaries, who comprised about half of the former Constituent Assembly. These two groups rapidly came to a provisional agreement, and the Tatars—headed by members of the defunct Mejilis (Fuad Tuktarov, Omer Teregulov, Fatyh Tuhvatullin, Ayaz Iskhakov, G. Fakhredinov, and M. Akhmerov)—formed a committee which collaborated closely with Komuch. They were soon joined by Kazakh, Bashkir, and Uzbek leaders who had managed to escape Bolshevik prisons.[26] Moslem anti-Communist military groupings also began to form, some of which participated actively in operations against the Red Army, often fighting against their own pro-Bolshevik Moslem brothers.

Turkic-Russian socialist collaboration reached its climax in early September 1918, when Komuch organized a conference of anti-Soviet collaborators in Ufa. This conference was attended primarily by socialist and other leftist groups, while bourgeois liberals and Russian rightist organizations preferred not to cooperate, regarding these groups as morally and politically responsible for the revolution and for the Bolsheviks' success. Six Turkic politicians were elected to a twenty-member presidium of the gathering: Mustafa Chokaev, former head of the Central Asian autonomy, Kh. Dosmuhammedov,

chairman of the western Kazakh government, M. Agdaev, representative of the Bashkirs, and the Tatars Teregulov, Akhtiamov, and
A. Chembulov.[27] The conference issued a declaration regarding the
future organization of the Russian state, elaborated by a joint Turkic-
Russian commission. "The future organization of liberated Russia
will be based on the wide autonomy of all her regions, formed according to geographic, economic, and ethnic principles. The final political
structure of Russia will be determined on the basis of federation by
an authoritative and legally elected Constituent Assembly." The next
paragraph promised cultural autonomy to those people not bound to
specific territories.[28] This declaration was signed by delegates from
all the Turkic autonomous administrations, elected by their various national congresses during the turbulent months of October–
December 1917.[29] They all demonstrated their willingness to support
a new anti-Communist All-Russian Provisional Government, or Di-
rectorate, presided over by N. D. Avksentiev. However, cooperation
between Avksentiev's anti-Bolshevik government, set up in the beginning of October 1918, in Omsk, and the Turkic politicians did
not last long. On November 4, Avksentiev suspended Kazakh autonomy, finding the Kazakh government unable to check Communist
infiltration and effectively administer its region. The same fate befell
the Bashkir administration. The Tatars, likewise, never succeeded in
carrying through the provisions of the Ufa declarations, since their
territory had been occupied by the Red Army even before the conference met.

The Omsk socialist government, however, proved no more effective than the Kazakh and Bashkir administrations. Growing anarchy
in the anti-Communist regions, and dissatisfaction among officers—
the only real power at the time—led to a coup by White Russian
officers' organizations and the arrest of Avksentiev's government.
Admiral A. V. Kolchak, former commander of the Black Sea fleet,
was declared Administrator of Russia. Although his immediate supporters belonged to rightist parties, Kolchak himself was not hostile
to limited Turkic autonomy; but he considered that until an authoritative Russian government was formed, no one had the power to
recognize or sanction the secession of Russian territories from the
state, or the creation of national autonomous administrations in
regions formerly composing the Russian Empire. Consequently, he
refused to acknowledge the principle of Tatar, Bashkir, or any other

autonomy. This rigid, legalistic point of view, shared by Kolchak with other White Russian military leaders, doomed cooperation between the Russians and non-Russian nationals during the Civil War and considerably undermined the strength of the anti-Soviet forces.

TATARS IN THE RED ARMY

In the meantime, the Moslem Communists renewed their efforts to create a Soviet Tatary. After the death of Vahitov, leadership of revolutionary Moslems was transferred by Stalin to Mustafa Sultangaliev, Vahitov's earlier co-worker in the Moslem Socialist Committee in Kazan.[30] As long as Kazan itself, part of the Volga region (until autumn 1918) and the Urals (until autumn 1919), remained in the hands of the White armies, the problem of organizing the Tatar autonomy was provisionally relegated to second place. Of first importance was the question of recruiting Tatars and Bashkirs for the Red Army. The draft of Moslems into Red units and the formation of Moslem regiments kept Narkomnats and its Moslem Soviet Military Council busy. Sultangaliev was most active in these undertakings. Kazan, Ufa, and, particularly, Astrakhan, as well as Moscow, became the main centers for Moslem recruitment into the Red Army. Astrakhan provided the Soviets with tens of thousands of Moslem soldiers from the Volga region and the Caucasus. During the years of 1918–1919, the First and Second Tatar Infantry Brigades, two separate infantry regiments, and numerous companies and battalions were formed. The Kazan Moslem reserve battalion, for instance, supplied the eastern front during the Civil War with over seventy reserve companies. Sultangaliev asserted that, at times, up to half of the Red soldiers fighting on the eastern front against Admiral Kolchak's armies were either Tatars or Bashkirs and that the Red Fifth Army, under the command of M. Frunze (later renamed the "Turkestan" Army), consisted of over 70 per cent of Moslem soldiers.[31] Moslem Red Army units and, especially, the First Tatar Brigade, played an important role in the campaigns against the Basmachis in Central Asia, and the Tatar and Bashkir regiments provided the first military instructors for Red Central Asian units.

SOVIET REOCCUPATION OF KAZAN

After Red Fifth Army divisions retook Kazan on September 6, 1918, the civilian administration of the city was placed under the

local Revkom (Revolutionary Committee). The Kazan Revkom consisted of five persons, all henchmen of Trotsky, who was in charge of
military operations on the Volga front. These men were Bochkov,
Kieselstein, Milkh, Smidovich, and Rubov (not a single Tatar among
them). Trotsky himself, despite his prolixity, never mentioned in his
voluminous speeches and writings on the war in the Volga region the
problem of the Tatars and their autonomy.[32] In general, among left
Communists of the Trotskyite callings, no interest was manifest for
the Tatar autonomy, and Tatars reappeared in the Kazan soviet only
after the local elections of September 25–27, 1919. Even then, out
of the twenty-five members of the soviet, only three were Tatars.[33]

MOSLEM COMMUNIST CONGRESSES

In November 1918, a congress of the All-Russian Party of Moslem
Communists (Bolshevik) was held in Moscow, attended by forty-six
delegates. The main aim of this congress was the unification of the
Moslem Communist Party with the main body of the Russian Communist Party (RKP[b]). After their rupture with left Socialist Revolutionaries and the latter's rebellion of July 6–8, the Bolsheviks had
no desire to endure—even if only formally—further independent
political organizations in the country. It was resolved at this new
congress that "the central committee of Moslem communists be renamed the 'Central Bureau of Moslem Organizations of RKP(b).'
Local Moslem organizations are to be associated with the general
organization of the party by means of representation in the local
committees by one of their delegates. The Central Bureau is to be
bound with the Central Committee of RKP(b)." [34] The congress'
resolutions were all very flexible, for, although submitting Moslem
Communists to discipline and control by the party, the Central Committee of RKP(b) still left local organizations, and even the Central
Bureau, a certain autonomy, as well as their very name, *Moslem*
Communists. A few months later, in March 1919, this Central Bureau
of Moslem Communists was reorganized into a wider and more
promising organ, the Central Bureau of Communist Organizations
of Peoples of the East.

This comparatively liberal attitude shown by the Russian Communist Party toward Moslem Communists could be explained by the
needs of propagandists, who were presenting RKP(b) as the liberator
of the peoples of the East. In his articles on the occasion of this congress, Stalin continued to claim that

the October Revolution is the first revolution in world history to break the age-long sleep of the laboring masses of the oppressed peoples of the East and to draw them into the fight against world imperialism. . . .

The great world-wide significance of the October Revolution chiefly consists in the fact that . . . it has widened the scope of the national question and converted it from the particular question of combatting national oppression in Europe into the general question of emancipating the oppressed peoples, colonies, and semicolonies from imperialism. [Thus] . . . the October Revolution, having put an end to the old, bourgeois movement for national emancipation, inaugurated the era of a new, socialist movement of the workers and peasants of the oppressed nationalities, directed against all oppression—including, therefore, national oppression—against the power of the bourgeoisie, "their own" and foreign, and against imperialism in general.[35]

Even in time of civil war, Stalin said, "To forget the East is impossible, even for a minute, if only because the East remains an inexhaustible reserve and most reliable hinterland of world imperialism." [36]

The struggle for autonomy continued until the beginning of 1920. Tatars insisted not only on the creation of an autonomous Tatar Republic but even on a united Tataro-Bashkiria. When the front moved from the Volga and Urals to Siberia, and the Civil War was nearing its end, voices began to be raised among Tatar Communists and army officers demanding the final establishment of the autonomous Tatar Republic. In the fall of 1919, in the November issue of *Kyzyl Armia*, a Tatar officer, Minhadus Konov, complained that "the revolution has given nothing to Tatars" as long as Stalin's decree of March 1918, creating an autonomous Tataro-Bashkiria, was not put into effect.[37]

At the end of November 1919, the Second Congress of Moslem Communists convened in Moscow, and one of the main questions placed before it was the creation of Tataro-Bashkiria. The majority of the delegates once again took a position favoring the inclusion of the Bashkirs in the autonomous Tatar Republic. This congress, too, was opened with a speech by Stalin. Once again he emphasized the task of Moslem Communists to work for "the awakening of the peoples of the East."

if our Red forces have advanced eastward so swiftly, not the least factor contributing to this, of course, has been your work, comrade delegates. If the road to the East is now open, that too the revolution owes to the supreme efforts of our comrades, the delegates here, in the work they have latterly accomplished. . . .

Let us hope that the banner raised at the First Congress, the banner of the emancipation of the labouring masses of the East, the banner of the destruction of imperialism, will be borne with honour to the goal by the militants of the Moslem Communist organizations. [*Applause.*] [38]

Further, Stalin gave his approval to a united Tataro-Bashkiria. But the Bashkirs continued resolutely to oppose their union with the Tatars. A Bashkir Autonomous Soviet Republic had already legally existed since February 1919, when Bashkir units abandoned the White armies and joined the Reds, and the Council of Peoples' Commissars, on March 20, 1919, had officially recognized the Bashkirs' autonomy.[39] It seemed that the Bashkir-Tatar controversy would last indefinitely.

CONTINUED TATAR-BASHKIR DIFFICULTIES

In December 1919 and early 1920, the question of Tatar or Tatar-Bashkir autonomy was again discussed in vain in the Central Committee of RKP(b). Finally, in February 1920, at a gathering of Communists from the Volga-Ural region, in which both Lenin and Stalin personally participated, the old Statute of the Tatar-Bashkir Republic of March 22, 1918, was altered to set up a separate Tatar Soviet Republic excluding Bashkiria. The prolonged disagreement was due to the fact that the Tatar Communists were stronger and more influential than the Bashkirs, and neither Stalin nor the Central Committee of RKP(b) wanted to go against the Tatars' hopes. On the other hand, the Bashkirs, already having their own autonomy, as well as their own troops, did not want to compromise with the Tatars and were prepared to resist Tatar ambitions with arms in their hands, if necessary. Neither Stalin nor the government desired an additional conflict with the Bashkirs, since relations with them were already very tense.

OPPOSITION TO TATAR AUTONOMY

Another serious obstacle to the final formation of a Red Tatary was the opposition to it of the Kazan Communist Party organization. Tatars constituted only 19.8 per cent of the local party membership in 1922, and probably less in 1920. There were by that time only 612 Tatar members out of the total 3,125 Communists in the Tatar territory. In 1922, however, Tatar strength in the all-Russian party organization was higher, since there were 3,943 Tatars in the RKP(b) then. Of these, 85 per cent were affiliated with RKP(b) organizations outside the Tatar Republic. The reason for this phenomenon was twofold: many Tatar Communists were serving with Moslem or Red Army military units, or with the Soviet administration in other Moslem regions of Russia, where they were the main bearers of Communist propaganda. Also, for several generations Tatars had been migrating from their original Volga homeland to the borderlands—the Urals, Kazakhstan, and Central Asia—where they settled in the cities, and these "proletarianized" Tatars furnished the main reserve for Moslem Communist cadres. In 1926, of 2,916,268 Tatars, 451,415 (15.2 per cent) were city-dwellers, but only 64,905 (14.4 per cent) of them actually lived in Tatar lands. In 1920, when, as a result of famine and civil war, many of these urban Tatars returned to the country and settled on lands expropriated from the nobility, and the proportion of the Tatar urban population was at its lowest, there were only 41,300 Tatars living in the cities in Tatar territory. Thus, the Volga Tatars' preponderantly rural or peasant background, as well as their religious and social conservatism, caused them to refrain from joining the party—a factor which, in turn, resulted in the Communists' apprehension toward their projected autonomy.[40]

The urban European population—which was almost six times as strong as the urban Tatar population in Tatar territory—resented the possibility of being placed under the tutelage of "peasant" Tatars as much as did the Communist leadership. Moreover, the Kazan Communists, led by Grassis and Chodorowski, considered that a national group without its own proletariat should not be given the commanding position. This argument was presented in April 1919 by Chodorowski, who regarded Tatar autonomy as "unnecessary, harmful, and unfeasible," since "there were not enough disciplined and experienced Tatar Communists to organize an administration in the republic." He feared that the establishment of such a Tatar autonomy would result in anarchy throughout the Volga region, which would seriously endanger Russia's economy.[41]

Lenin and Stalin, however, bearing in mind the fruitful work performed by Tatar Communists in other Moslem areas, as well as the strategic importance of a Red Tatary for their projects of Asian revolution, supported Tatar autonomy. As Lenin logically pointed out in a conversation with Chodorowski, "It is not admissible to place narrow, transitional, and purely utilitarian local interests above the interests of the party as a whole" (and above the final goal of world revolution). Consequently, when, in January 1920, the situation in such important Moslem regions as Bashkiria, Kazakhstan, and Central Asia became unstable, the Central Committee decided to counter the dissatisfactions of Turkic nationalists and entrusted M. Sultangaliev with the task of carrying out the project for autonomy. He was even appointed to the three-member board of Narkomnats.[42]

THE FINAL SOLUTION

On May 27, 1920, a decree of the Central Committee of RKP(b) finally announced the official creation of the Tatar Autonomous Soviet Socialist Republic. Two weeks later, the Republic's Revkom was established, composed of Said Galiev (president), Chodorowski, Goldberg, Bochkov, and Muhtarov.[43] On July 25, in the name of the autonomous Tatar Republic, Revkom took over the reins of government from the Kazan Provincial Executive Committee of the soviets. In mid-September elections were held for delegates to the soviets of the newborn Tatar Republic, and on September 25 the First Constituent Congress of the republic's soviets elected its Central Committee and Council of Peoples' Commissars (Sovnarkom). At the head of the Central Committee was placed a rather obscure Tatar Communist, Burkhan Mansurov, while Vahitov's former aide, Said Galiev, became head of Sovnarkom. The latter also included such veteran Tatar Communists as Ismailov, Sultanov, Iskhakov, and Muhtarov. The long-awaited Tatar Autonomous Republic finally became a reality, although, as Stalin had promised in May 1918, it was not a national autonomy but a Soviet one. Stalin himself, most probably, was no less overjoyed than the Tatar Communists: a new republic had been created in spite of the opposition of Trotsky's left Communists. The idea for its creation had originated in Narkomnats, among Stalin's fledglings, and a new stage in the creation of the Stalinist apparatus within the country and the party was reached. Tatar national aspirations were also satisfied, although the Tatars' optimism prevented them from realizing that a Soviet autonomy would never be a national one as they understood the latter to be.

CHAPTER XIII

Validov's Little Bashkiria

Creation of an autonomous Tatary limited to the Volga-Tatar area and excluding Bashkiria, as a result of the Bashkirs' desire to form their own autonomous state apart from the Tatars, was a serious blow to Turkic political unity in Russia.[1] Before the revolution of 1917 no antagonism had been observed between the Bashkirs and Tatars. Part of the Moslem population of the Ufa, Orenburg, and other eastern Ural provinces had even vacillated in its national identity, at times calling itself Bashkir and at times Tatar.* After the beginning of the revolution, however, the Bashkir leaders began to display their own brand of nationalism and a firm intention to solve the local problems of their territory without becoming involved in Tatar politics.

Since the late nineteenth century, the Bashkirs' fundamental problem was the colonization of their lands by peasants from European

---

* The Bashkirs, a Turkic people very closely related to the Tatars, have lived in the southern part of the Urals at least since the ninth century. The Tatars began their penetration into Bashkiria only in the sixteenth to seventeenth centuries after the Russian conquest of the Kazan khanate. Most of the Bashkirs remained seminomadic until the end of the nineteenth century, while all of the Tatars were sedentary peasants. In 1789 the Russian government created a special privileged "Bashkir Voisko," an autonomous military organization, and since that time many Tatars registered as Bashkirs, and began to call themselves Bashkirs. After the dissolution of the Bashkir Voisko and the termination of their special privileges, the Tatars of Bashkiria once more began to call themselves Tatars. This "registration" of Tatars with the Bashkir Voisko was one of the main causes of confusion in the population statistics of Bashkiria. So, for instance, there were only 95,000 Bashkirs in 1767, 1,493,000 in 1897, 741,000 in 1926, and of the latter only 393,000 spoke Bashkir while the remainder used Tatar. These nomadic and "Bashkir-speaking" Bashkirs formed the core of the Bashkir national movement. The antagonism between the Bashkirs and the Tatars arose mainly on a social and cultural basis—the old problem of nomads versus peasants. The Tatars considered the Bashkirs merely as one of their nomadic and backward tribes, and this attitude was bitterly resented by Bashkir politicians and chieftains.

Russia. The Bashkirs particularly resented those agricultural colonizers who had settled their lands after the 1905 Revolution as a result of the agrarian policy initiated by Stolypin. Under this program, some 180,000 peasants and their families received lands during 1905–1911 in the Orenburg and Ufa provinces, whose eastern parts were inhabited by the Bashkirs. The enforced sale of lands to the incoming colonizers considerably undermined the living standard of the Bashkirs, who in 1897 were 99.3 per cent, and still in 1926, 97.9 per cent, a rural, seminomadic people.[2] Therefore, immediately after the February revolution, the Bashkirs raised the question of re-examining land tenure in their region at the very first political meetings of Moslems in the Ufa and Orenburg provinces in the spring of 1917. At a conference of Moslems of the Ufa province held April 14–17, the Bashkirs requested the province's commissar "to halt the peasant movement and deforestation of the mountains in the Birsk district." [3] Even as early as this first gathering, the influence of the Bashkir socialists, who were close in their agrarian program to the Russian Socialist Revolutionaries, became predominant.

Contrary to the Bashkirs' expectation, the First All-Russian Moslem Congress in Moscow in May 1917 did not endorse their land program. This congress' resolutions concerning the agrarian question—"All the land to the people"—were not in accord with the notions of the Bashkirs, who insisted on the principle "All the lands of Bashkiria only to the Bashkirs." Furthermore, the congress decided that solution of the agrarian question in the Ufa and Orenburg provinces was outside its jurisdiction.[4] In July 1917, when the Tatars convened the Second All-Russian Moslem Congress in Kazan, the Bashkirs, objecting to Tatar aspirations for tutelage over Bashkiria, organized their own First All-Bashkir National Conference in Orenburg. At this conference, attended by over seventy Bashkir delegates,[5] Ahmed Zeki Validov—who was not only the energetic politician we have seen but also a promising orientalist[6]—was the moving force behind its decisions. It would be no exaggeration to say that the entire Bashkir national movement of the years 1917–1920 was to a large extent the product of Validov's efforts. Without Validov, the Turkic national movement in the Volga-Ural region would have assumed quite another character, and the sharp conflict between the Bashkirs and Tatars might have been avoided. At Validov's instigation, the Bashkir conference adopted a rather radical program which demanded the creation of a national territorial autonomy, the setting-up of Bashkir military units, and the return to the Bashkirs of all lands taken by incoming settlers after 1898. The congress further announced that "Bashkirs, judging by the character of their language, differ from other Moslems who have settled the Bashkir region"—that is, from the Tatars—an additional reaffirmation of the Bashkirs' desire to live a life apart from the Tatars.[7]

NATIONAL AUTONOMY

After the Soviet seizure of power in Ufa on October 26, 1917, when all Bashkiria was drawn into the sphere of Soviet influence, Bashkir nationalists, wishing to collaborate neither with the Tatars nor with the Bolsheviks, transferred their seat of activity from Ufa to Orenburg.[8] Under the military protection of General Dutov and his Cossacks (see Chapter XI), a Bashkir pre-parliament (Kurultai) was convened on November 8 by Sharaf Manatov and Validov, in the historic building of Karavan-Sarai in Orenburg. A week later, on November 15, Kurultai proclaimed the national territorial autonomy of Bashkiria.[9] As initially announced, the autonomy included all of "Great Bashkiria"—that is, most of the Orenburg and Ufa provinces and parts of the Simbirsk, Samara, Perm, and Viatka provinces.[10] The total number of Moslem inhabitants, including both Tatars and Bashkirs, formed only 20–30 per cent of the population in these territories. Therefore in the next weeks Kurultai reconsidered its decision and limited its claims only to "Little Bashkiria"—the northern part of the Orenburg province and the eastern part of the Ufa province, where Bashkirs still preserved their native language and nomadic way of life. The local Tatars,[11] however, continued to work against the Bashkir nationalists and even provoked some minor clashes, but the Bashkirs succeeded in eliminating them from Kurultai and elected a new central committee led by Validov and Manatov.[12]

In the initial struggle between the Whites and Reds, Bashkirs took a semineutral position, as was announced in the first manifesto of the Bashkir central committee published November 11, 1917: "We are neither Bolsheviks nor Mensheviks, we are only Bashkirs. On which side should we be? Not on any side. We are for ourselves . . . the Soviet government grants nationalities the right even to secede from Russia. As a supplement to this right, however, it gives them also disorder, illegality, and excesses." [13]

THE YEARS OF THE CIVIL WAR

When Soviet troops took Orenburg on January 31, some of the members of the Kurultai openly capitulated to the side of the Soviet government. Manatov even accepted Stalin's and Vahitov's invitation to join the Committee for Moslem Affairs of Narkomnats in Moscow, and became its vice-chairman.[14]

In February 1918, the idea of Bashkir autonomy was unexpectedly exploited by this enterprising Moslem leftist group. Enjoying the warmest support of Orenburg's Soviet boss, S. M. Zwilling, they organized the Provisional Revolutionary Council of Bashkurstan (PRCB), which recognized the Soviet regime in the name of the local Moslem population.[15] Two days later, on February 20, PRCB announced Little Bashkiria to be an autonomous part of the Soviet Russian federation[16] (see Chapter XII). This proclamation had little practical significance, since power in Orenburg and Bashkiria remained in the hands of Zwilling and the Red Revolutionary Military Council. It would have been an insignificant political maneuver had it not received publicity as the first case of "a sovereign and self-determined Moslem nation's expressed desire to federate with the Soviet government." As such, it came to be regarded by Stalin's Narkomnats as the first application of the Soviet national policy. PRCB subsequently sent a Bashkir delegation from Orenburg to Moscow, where, through Manatov himself, the Bashkir "plenipotentiaries" gained access to Stalin.[17]

THE COUNTERREVOLUTION

Validov and other Bashkir nationalist leaders fled Orenburg on April 3 and stubbornly continued their work for creation of an autonomous Bashkiria. After the revolt of the Czecho-Slovak Legions and the taking of eastern Russia by the anti-Communists, these Bashkir nationalists met in Cheliabinsk, where they concluded an agreement with the Komuch (Committee of the Constituent Assembly).[18] This agreement provided for organization of the Bashkir autonomy within a future non-Soviet Russian federation, and for the formation of Bashkir troops. Maneuvering adroitly between socialists from Komuch, seated in Samara on the Volga, and the more moderate Siberian government, the Bashkirs succeeded in obtaining supplies to fit out their detachments.

With the November 1918 coup of Admiral A. V. Kolchak in Omsk, however, the attitude of the Russian anti-Bolshevik forces toward Turkic autonomies changed completely. Witnessing their inability to organize an administration and their close cooperation with socialists in Komuch—who were conspiring to overthrow Kolchak's administration in Orenburg [19] Kolchak refused to recognize the Bashkirs' autonomy, and their military detachments were partially disarmed. Angered, the Bashkirs decided to realign themselves politically, and on December 6, 1918, they met with representatives of the Kazakh *Alash Orda* government. Both of these autonomous groups, aware of Admiral Kolchak's unwillingness to support their national autonomies, decided to go over to the Reds.[20] When the Bolsheviks reoccupied part of the Urals on January 30, 1919, the Bashkir and Bolshevik representatives opened negotiations. Learning of the Bashkirs' intention to join the Soviet forces, the Red high command asked Moscow's advice. The problem was important not only militarily—for the Soviets would strengthen their ranks by several Bashkir units—but also politically, since the Bashkir's transfer to the Soviet side involved recognition of their autonomy and the granting of amnesties to Bashkir opponents of the Soviet regime. The Council of People's Commissars gave its answer without delay. On February 6, 1919, a telegram signed by Lenin and Stalin informed the Ufa Revkom that it could "agree to amnesty, provided that Bashkir regiments join with the Soviet army in forming a united front against Kolchak. The Soviet government fully guarantees national freedom [to the Bashkirs]. . . ." [21] Two days later, Bashkir military and political leaders decided to leave Kolchak and accept the Soviet conditions. In all, 6,556 Bashkir soldiers and military personnel were to join the Reds.[22] This was considerable military strength, in view of the limited numbers of both Red and White fighting units. During the winter of 1918–1919, which was so decisive for the future of the Soviet regime, the Red and White armies which faced each other along the endless Ural front each comprised only some 100,000 men.[23]

On February 19, 1919, the Bashkirs, led by Validov, concluded a political "preliminary agreement" with the Soviet command. This document lay at the basis of the official agreement countersigned by the Council of Peoples' Commissars. It determined Moscow's relations with the Bashkirs and the exact territory to be included in this first Soviet Turkic autonomous republic. Article 13 provided that, until

the Bashkir Congress of Soviets convened, administration in Bashkiria
should be placed under the Provisional Bashkir Revolutionary Committee (Bashrevkom) composed of two Bashkir members, two members appointed by Moscow, and one member co-opted by mutual
agreement. Later, the republic's government would be organized
according to the Soviet constitution promulgated at the Fifth All-
Russian Congress of Soviets on July 10, 1918. According to this
agreement, the Bashkir army was supposed to be subordinated to the
Soviet high command.[24]

BASHREVKOM IN EXILE

The agreement was concluded on the eve of Admiral Kolchak's
last great offensive, as a result of which all Bashkir territory was again
taken by the White Army, while Bashrevkom, under Validov's
leadership, was transferred to Saransk (now capital of the Mordovian
ASSR) to the west of the front. In Saransk also there soon appeared
representatives of the Soviet government—the Bashkir, Kh. Yumagulov, and a Pole, Zarecki, who organized there a special bureau of
RKP(b) for the recruitment of Bashkirs into the Communist Party.

The Bashkirs, however, and particularly Validov, joined the Communist Party with reluctance. They would have preferred creating
their own national Communist Party, which they wanted to call *Volia*
(Freedom). In his long conversations with Zarecki during his Saransk
"emigration," Validov pointed out that "whether or not Volia will
enter the Comintern is unknown, but it will be farther left than
RKP(b)." [25] This assertion, of course, revealed Validov's unfounded
political optimism and misunderstanding of the situation. Never, since
summer 1918, even in time of civil war, did the Bolsheviks counte-
nance political organizations other than the RKP(b). The termination of their short-lived collaboration with the left wing of the Socialist Revolutionaries in 1917–1918 clearly indicated that there was room
in the Soviet state only for the RKP(b).

In talks with his Communist co-workers, Validov did not hide the
fact that one of the fundamental points in his program was creation
of an antonomous Bashkiria in which the Bashkirs would be the actual
ruling political force. To facilitate Bashkir national development,
Validov wanted not only to stop Russian colonization but also to
regain the former Bashkir landholdings from new settlers who had

encroached upon the nomadic domain in accordance with Stolypin's agrarian policies. Validov wanted to resettle this area with Moslem Turks and thus create a purely Turkic territory.[26] This tendency toward national segregation was not only the product of prerevolutionary friction, but was also the result of recurrent incidents between Soviet and Bashkir troops and conflicts between Bashkir and non-Bashkir Communists. The Soviet command was apparently unsure of the Bashkirs' loyalty and feared their possible defection back to Kolchak. Therefore, some Bashkir detachments had been disarmed, and additional tension arose between them and the Soviet troops. Such incidents actually caused the return of some Bashkir units to the Whites, and led to the first discord between Bashrevkom and the Soviets.

RETURN TO BASHKIRIA

In the summer and fall of 1919 the Civil War in the Urals was nearing its end. After the failure of Kolchak's spring offensive and the subsequent retreat of his armies beyond the Urals, the autonomous government of Bashkiria returned to its own territory. The town of Sterlitamak, although actually outside the boundaries of Little Bashkiria, was selected as the republic's provisional capital since there were no large settlements in the mountains and steppes of rural Bashkiria. During the first few weeks after Bashrevkom's arrival in Sterlitamak, railroad and telegraph communications between Bashkiria and the rest of Russia were so precarious that the Bashkir government remained in a state of almost complete isolation. This prevented the Moscow government from exercising any control over the situation in the newborn republic.

The Bashkirs, both the Communists and the nonparty leaders, kept aloof from their Russian and Tatar comrades, forming their own party cells. There are no data available on the number of Bashkir Communists in 1920, but apparently, despite the fact that Validov and his aides joined the party, they hardly numbered more than 150–200. Even in 1922 there were only 272 Bashkir and 256 Tatar Communists in the entire Bashkir Republic.[27] Thus, unhampered by Communist supervision, Validov and his associates promulgated their Decree No. 1, in which they proclaimed their autonomous local administration and economic independence from the Moscow government. Further, Bashrevkom declared itself the only legal authority in the republic and forbade the export of agricultural produce beyond Bashkir boundaries.[28]

PROLETARIAN AND PEASANT OPPOSITION TO BASHREVKOM

Bashrevkom's clearly demonstrated intention to liberate itself from insistent Soviet tutelage, together with growing difficulties in obtaining agricultural supplies for distribution among workers in the iron mills and factories, aroused suspicion among local Communists and within the Soviet regional administration.[29] Editorials in Ufa's *Izvestiia* reflected growing uneasiness among local Soviet administrators, and among the Russian peasants and workers of the region as well. Particularly vociferous were the new peasant settlers (*novosioly*), who feared the expropriation of their lands by the Bashkirs. This group was very influential with the Ural party organization. Having received their lands less than a decade before, the novosioly were not yet economically well off and formed the most radical part of the local population. They had lent their support to the Bolshevik cause since the earliest days of the revolution, and many of them joined the Communist Party. The unusually high percentage of peasants in the local party organization—55 percent of the total membership[30]— was a clear reflection of the novosioly's revolutionary temper and their importance in party politics. Therefore their voice was listened to with attention by the Soviet administration in the Urals and even in Moscow.

The complaints of southern Ural Bolsheviks set the Soviet government into motion. In the beginning of October it sent to Sterlitamak a new representative, F. Samoilov, to organize Communist forces in the Bashkir Republic. The first conference of the Communists of Bashkiria, which convened November 7–13, dealt a heavy blow to Validov's Bashkir "national Communist" faction, and tended to alienate them. Election to the local party bureau of a Tatar—Ismailov —and a vociferous Bashkir antiautonomist—Shamigulov, a personal enemy of Validov—was accepted by Validov's faction as a challenge to Bashkir independence by the Tatars, who, they feared, would still succeed in gaining a unified Tataro-Bashkiria encompassing Little Bashkiria. In Validov's eyes, the Tatar promoters of such unity still remained the sworn enemies of Bashkir liberties. Therefore, the Bashkirs fought desperately to put through a motion at this conference demanding the "condemnation and expulsion from the Communist Party of the main Tatar offenders" against Bashkir independence.

VALIDOV AND BASHKIR-KAZAKH UNITY

These apprehensions on the part of Bashkir autonomists were not unfounded. The Second Congress of Moslem Communists, held late in November 1919 in Moscow, and dominated by such Tatar supporters of a united Tataro-Bashkiria as Sultangaliev and Galiev, declared itself in favor of this union (see Chapter XII), although for tactical reasons Little Bashkiria was not mentioned officially.[31]

To counteract this Tatar "imperialism," Validov put forward a new project for a Bashkir-Kazakh federation. Bashkirs had been in close contact with Kazakh leaders since their first attempts to break with Kolchak and join the Red Army in the winter of 1918–1919.[32] On the eve of the above-mentioned Second Moslem Congress, Validov had wired his representative at the congress to raise the question of "creation of a common Kazakh-Bashkir conference in Moscow for the purpose of considering such a federation." The seminomadic Bashkirs and their Kazakh neighbors in the steppe were certainly more akin to each other both in spirit and way of life than to Tatar or Russian peasants and workers. Both peoples shared the same problems: settling of the nomads, resistance to Russian peasant colonization, defense against the Tatar cultural and economic hegemony, and the strengthening of their own "selfhood."

At the instigation of the Tatars and the party's Central Committee, this new Kazakh-Bashkir conference rejected Validov's plan.[33] Moscow's strained relations with the Bashkirs and the Kazakhs were also poor incentive for approving a Kazakh-Bashkir union. But Validov, who in the meantime was engaging in personal negotiations with the Kazakhs and even with the Central Asian Moslem Communists, did not give up his objective and continued clandestinely to pursue his project for Kazakh-Bashkir federation.

THE COUP OF JANUARY 1920

The tension in Sterlitamak grew steadily. The Bashkirs were irritated by the failure of their project for union with Kazakhstan, by the ascendancy of Tatar Communists, and by the tightening control of Moscow. Bashrevkom lost its temper in mid-January 1920, and decided to free itself from control by the local delegates of the central government and Tatar Communists. At night on January 15, at the order of Bashrevkom's chairman, Yumagulov, Bashkir armed patrols arrested local supporters of federation with the Tatars—Ismailov, Shamigulov, Murzabaliev, Mustafin, and Valiev—on the grounds that they were conspiring against the liberties of the Bashkir people.[34]

Bashrevkom, naively enough, hoped that it would succeed in freeing itself from the annoying supervision of local Communists without provoking the wrath of the Soviet government. But the Soviet military machine was set immediately into action. In agreement with Frunze, who commanded Soviet troops in the southern Urals, orders were given to isolate the only sizable Bashkir unit, the cavalry brigade of M. L. Murtazin, which some days later was transferred outside of Bashkir territory. The garrison in Sterlitamak was placed under the direct command of the Red Army and Bashkir units were forbidden to move.[35] Thus isolated in Sterlitamak, Bashrevkom yielded and released the arrested Tatars, while Bashrevkom's chairman, Yamagulov, was called back to Moscow.

THE END OF BASHKIR AUTONOMY

During this entire January tumult Validov remained in Moscow, where he continued his attempts to convince the party's Central Committee, Narkomnats, and Stalin himself of the need to change Soviet policy toward the Bashkirs and other Turkic peoples. It seems that he placed his main hope in Stalin's personal support of his cause, which fact Stalin frankly admitted three years later.[36] Validov was successful in one important point. Early in January, the government finally put an end to its prolonged deliberations on Tataro-Bashkiria and decided to create an autonomous Tatar Republic not including within it the Bashkir territories. The Bashkirs' joy over their exception from the Tatar Republic was of short duration. A new attempt to limit their autonomy, this time directly by Moscow, was made in late spring of 1920. On May 19, a Decree on the State Organization of the Bashkir Autonomous Republic was promulgated, without previously consulting the Bashkirs. All Bashkir economic agencies were subordinated to the respective central administrative organs in Moscow. Bashkir military organizations and troops were placed under local Soviet regional military command. Only the departments of education, public health, social welfare, and similar "politically harmless" branches of administration remained under the jurisdiction of the autonomous Bashkir government. The decree also provided that the Soviet central government supervise and regulate all the economic and political activities of the Bashkir self-government.[37] Bashkir national autonomy became a fiction.

THE SOUTHEASTERN FEDERATION

At the time this decree was published, Validov was in Moscow, where he had come on April 30 at the Soviet government's invitation. It is not difficult to imagine the state of fury into which this perseverent politician must have been thrown. For three years he had labored to carve out of the Turkic territories of the Volga and Urals an autonomous Bashkiria, over the destiny of which he would preside, but now his ambitions for political leadership were effectively shattered. Soon, however, a new and far more grandiose project than the independence of nomadic Little Bashkiria was born in Validov's mind. He began to conceive of a vast southeastern federation of the Soviet Turkic peoples, constructed either on a genuine autonomous basis within the Soviet system or, if necessary, as an independent, non-Communist, nation.

The moment for its conception seemed to him to be at hand. In Kazakhstan the leaders of Alash Orda—united around their national leaders Baitursunov and Bukeikhanov and the energetic Russian Social Democrat, Sedelnikov—were struggling for an autonomous state. Uzbek Communists in Tashkent, mainly former Jadids and the comrades of Validov's youth, were in control of most of the Soviet apparatus in Central Asia and were exploring possibilities for carrying through Lenin's dream of Asian revolution. With the hope of consolidating their position and widening the scope of Tashkent autonomy, the Uzbek Communists came to Moscow in early June 1920 to see Lenin.

Validov now hoped for the materialization of his project for organizing a Turkic Communist Party, *Volia*,[38] which, comprising all Moslem Communists and socialists of Russia's southeast regions, would be a full-fledged member of the Comintern, and not merely a territorial section of the Russian Communist Party. The most promising factor in Validov's planning and timing was the rapidly deteriorating military and diplomatic situation in which the Soviet government then found itself. The Poles were pushing into the Ukraine, and having taken Kiev, were preparing for further offensive. General P. N. Wrangel's White Army, reorganized over the winter, was initiating an attack from the Crimea into the southern Ukraine and the Caucasus. In Central Asia, the rapidly growing Basmachi movement controlled a sizable part of Ferghana, while the remnants of Kolchak's army were being regrouped in the Russian extreme Far East under the protection of Japan. Soviet Russian resources and the Red Army were exhausted. All indications seemed to point to June 1920 as the most propitious moment to achieve wider autonomy and, simultaneously, the federation of the Turkic peoples of Soviet Russia. But again, despite his firsthand experience, Validov underestimated the strategic skill of Soviet leaders.

Lenin, seeking to avoid complications while in armed conflict with Poland, postponed his decision regarding wider Turkestan autonomy and referred Validov to Stalin, who was organizing the defense of the Ukraine. Stalin, no worse a tactician than Lenin, refused to give any definite answer to Validov's and the Uzbek Communists' ambitions.[39] Very soon the Soviet government had a free hand. Toward July the Poles retreated from the front, and finally the answer came. It was, of course, negative. The Central Committee refused to allocate wider power to the Uzbek Communists, and the Bashkir problem was declared to be fully resolved. The only alternative for Validov and his allies was armed resistance.

BASHREVKOM'S EXIT

In a letter written early in June to his aides in Sterlitamak, Validov warned his political associates that he considered further cooperation with the Soviet regime senseless, and that Bashrevkom should be prepared to abandon the Bashkir capital and go underground in the fight for the Bashkir and Turkic national cause. Validov still had some hope that Turkic resistance would force the Soviets to take a more conciliatory attitude and permit decentralization. In his opinion, RKP(b)'s policy of centralism would undermine all possibilities for the revolution's success in Asia, and he regarded the present Soviet plan for autonomy even "worse than the administration of Nicholas II and Stolypin." [40] Bashrevkom followed Validov's instructions in early June. Bashkiria's temporary capital at Sterlitamak was abandoned, and the stupefied republic remained without committees, commissions, soviets, boards, and councils for some ten days. National Bashkir

Communists, headed by Bashrevkom and assisted by some Russian anti-Soviet allies, moved to the mountain village of Novo-Usmanovo. The final rift with Moscow was consummated in view of the impossibility of cooperating further with the Soviet government on the basis of its decree of May 19. Bashrevkom's members decided to leave for Central Asia, where they would continue their struggle for Bashkiria and the Moslem world, and for creation of a genuine Asian Communist Party of liberation.

Neither Validov's maneuverings in Moscow nor the exit of Bashrevkom from Sterlitamak was successful politically. All military units in the southern Urals were warned of Bashrevkom's flight, and a number of Bashkir nationalists were intercepted. Bashkir troops could not intervene because they were all fighting the Poles in the Ukraine. The Moslem Communists of Kazakhstan and Central Asia did not want to commit themselves, and raised neither arms nor voices on behalf of the Bashkirs. The Tatars were only too happy at the defeat of the Bashkir autonomists, who had frustrated Kazan's project for Tatar-Bashkir unification. On June 26 a new, conformist, Bashrevkom was created, with Validov's implacable opponent, the left Communist and antiautonomist, Galim Shamigulov, at its head.[41] Thus, as Richard Pipes has pointed out in his detailed study of the Bashkir national movement, "the Bashkir republic . . . had no native in his [Shamigulov's] government. The party, in close alliance with Tatars and Russian colonists, who now filled the key positions, and in intimate contact with envoys from the center, had emerged victorious." [42]

It was, however, neither the end of the Bashkir national movement nor of the plight of this little republic. Uprisings of Bashkir peasantry, raids by Red and White partisan bands, and operations of the Communist punitive expeditions continued to shatter Bashkiria. In 1921 the great famine, which spread over entire Russia, seized the Ural and Volga lands. In Bashkir territory alone, the population diminished by 25.1 per cent during the period 1917–1922. While Russian and Tatar agricultural areas in the Urals lost from one fifth to one sixth of their population, among the seminomadic Bashkirs nearly one third of the people starved to death.[43] In the most decisive way, famine undermined whatever possibility remained for Bashkirs to resist, and ravaged both their population and their seminomadic economy.

A final blow to the Bashkirs' hopes for a genuine national autonomy within their ethnic boundaries was dealt in 1922. The Soviet decree of June 4, 1922 nearly doubled the size and population of Bashkiria by joining to it four districts of the Ufa and three of the Cheliabinsk provinces.[44] The acquisition of new fertile lands improved the economic situation of mountainous Bashkiria. The Bashkirs, however, became proportionately diluted by the addition of new Russian and Tatar population, and Bashkir influence in "Great Bashkiria" dropped to nothing.

Thus ended the short existence of Little Bashkiria, for whose national autonomy Validov and Bashkir patriots had struggled for almost four years. In place of it was created a Bashkir Autonomous Soviet Socialist Republic, "socialist in content" but only one quarter Bashkir.[45]

CHAPTER XIV

The Civil War and the Kazakhs

In few parts of Russia did the happenings of the revolution and civil war reflect so clearly the population's geographical setting and social structure as in the Kazakh steppe. * The 1,011,111 square miles of Kazakh territory—almost a third of the United States'—stretched 1,800 miles from the Volga to the Altais and 900 miles from Omsk in the north to Tashkent in the south; and the sparsity of its population as well as the poor means of communication rendered any effective organization of national administration impossible. One third of Kazakhstan's population consisted of Russian and Ukrainian peasants or city dwellers; the other two thirds were nomadic or seminomadic Kazakhs, of whom, in 1920, less than 1.5 per cent lived in the cities and no more than 5 per cent were literate.[1]

The nomadic way of life, a low rate of literacy, and a rigid tribal system doomed the Kazakhs to political passivity in the era of the "proletarian revolution." The Kazakh upper strata consisted of a few idealistic intellectuals, the tribal elders, and the so-called *bais* (nomadic nouveaux riches and merchants). The intelligentsia was not numerous enough to play a leading role among the Kazakhs, while the backward tribal elders and bais were unable to fathom the revolutionary events and preferred to avoid the hazards of political struggle. The average Kazakh nomad was even less prepared for any political activities than the Tatar or Bashkir peasant, and, consequently, during the years of civil war, Kazakh territory was more an area

*The Kazakh republic and the Kazakh nationality were officially called, until the publication of the decree of April 19, 1925, the Kirghiz, and from 1925 to 1936 the Kazak (in 1936 the final "k" was replaced by "kh"). In order to avoid misunderstanding, however, I apply in this chapter uniformly the term "Kazakh." In quotations from official decrees dating from 1917–1925 and in the names of the congresses, both terms—Kazakh and Kirghiz—are used. See M. Sapargaliev, *Vozniknovenie kazakhskoi sovetskoi gosudarstvennosti* (Alma-Ata, 1948), pp. 88–89.

of conflict between the Red and White Russians than of any national action by the Kazakhs themselves. News of political events reached these cattle breeders of the steppe very slowly, and the various ideological slogans had little meaning for the nomads, who still lived according to the *Weltanschauung* of past centuries. Therefore, despite conventions, resolutions, and programs, the majority of Kazakhs remained apart from the events of 1917–1920.

However, the fundamental problem of Kazakh life—that of Russian colonization—preoccupied both the Kazakh intellectuals and the nomads in 1917. Despite the war and the uprising of 1916, the stream of settlers into the steppe had continued ever-increasingly, disrupting native economy and threatening the very existence of many nomads. Although some of the Kazakhs were also gradually settling along the outskirts of the steppe, the process of their "sedentarization" was not rapid enough to solve the underlying problem of their adaptation to new conditions. Conferences and congresses in spring 1917 fully reflected the Kazakhs' anxiety over their future. Resolutions were passed demanding a cessation of colonization, the redistribution of confiscated lands to the Kazakhs, and the improvement of cattle breeding.[2]

The Kazakh intellectuals, who since 1913 had gathered around the newspaper *Kazakh*, organized a moderate Kazakh national party, Alash Orda, in March 1917.[3] This party was close in its program to the Kadets, and its leaders realized that the nomadic order could not be indefinitely upheld under the conditions of the twentieth century. They were also aware that centuries-old nomadic habits were an almost unsurmountable obstacle to the rapid mass settling of the Kazakhs. They considered, however, that forced settling would lead to the extinction of their people. An attempt by the Soviet government in the 1930's at the forced mass settling of Kazakhs, which resulted in a sharp increase in mortality, proved how right they were in this prognosis.

Concerned primarily with the agrarian problem, the first Kazakh conferences of 1917 gave little attention to purely political questions. National and constitutional problems were not taken up until the "All-Kirghiz" (Kazakh) Congress was convened in Orenburg on April 28, attended by representatives from the entire Kazakh steppe. This congress' resolutions stressed the desirability of introducing the Kazakh language in grade schools and in the local administration and courts, of increasing the educational network, and of establishing a zemstvo self-government in the provinces inhabited by the Kazakhs. The congress also gave its support to the Provisional Government and to "the war's continuation to a victorious end." [4]

The party of Alash Orda, under the leadership of A. Bukeikhanov, A. Baitursunov, M. Dulatov, and Kh. Dosmuhammedov, formed the dominant political grouping among Kazakhs. Its members participated in the First Moslem Congress in Moscow in May 1917, and in its executive organ, the All-Russian Moslem Council. Both Kazakh delegates in the council, Kh. Dosmuhammedov and V. Tanachev, fought stubbornly against Tatar encroachment, defending the Kazakhs' independent political development. When the Tatars opposed the convening of a Kazakh conference, claiming that the Second All-Russian Moslem Congress would take up Kazakh problems, the Kazakhs held out and organized their own national conference.[5]

This Second All-Kirghiz (Kazakh) Congress took place in Orenburg July 21–26, 1917, simultaneously with the Tatar congress in Kazan. In this way, Kazakhs, together with the Bashkirs, demonstrated their desire for independence from Tatar leadership. This time more discussion was devoted to national-political questions, and resolutions insisted on Russia's reconstruction along a democratic and federative basis. Unlike the congresses of other national groups in Russia, however, this conference did not demand either a national autonomous government or the unification of provinces inhabited predominantly by Kazakhs. The introduction of zemstvo self-government and of the Kazakh language in the lower administration, courts, and schools satisfied, for the time being, the national aspirations of the Kazakhs. These modest demands clearly reflected the Kazakh leaders' realistic understanding of the peculiarities, needs, and background—both geographically and socially—of Kazakhstan. They realized too well that their people were still too immature for autonomous government and that the vastness of their steppes, which had always tended to divide the Kazakhs into separate hordes, created a serious obstacle to the administrative unification of the provinces.

Nor did this conference care about the introduction of a common Turkic language in their schools—as did the Tatar-sponsored All-Russian Moslem Congress—but advised the teaching of Russian on the secondary level. The conference also recommended the establishment of a separate Kazakh ecclesiastic administration, distinct from

the Tatar Moslem administration in Ufa.[6] At about the same time
the Provisional Government appointed two Kazakhs to vacant posts
as provincial governors: Bukeikhanov to the Turgai province, and
M. Tanyshbaev to the Semirechie.[7]

SOUTHERN KAZAKH OPPOSITION

While Alash Orda was the leading Kazakh political party, it still
was not without opposition. A southern Kazakh group, whose voice
was the Tashkent newspaper, *Ush zhuz,* also participated in the
Kazakh conference, where it opposed the tactics of Alash Orda. This
was a heterogeneous group representing Pan-Islamic clerics, left
radicals, and nationalists who adhered to a more anti-Russian position
than Alash Orda. This group, however, lacked influential leaders;
only candidates of Alash Orda were elected to the Constituent Assembly.[8]

At a convention held August 2–5 in Tashkent, the radically anti-
Russian mood of the southern Kazakhs was revealed. The Kazakhs
of the Syr Daria and Tashkent regions had been much less touched by
Russian influence than their kinsmen to the west and north. While
Alash Orda's pro-Russian orientation reflected its animosity toward
the Tatars, the southern Kazakhs did not suffer from such an antagonism. The valley of the Syr Daria had long been a region of common
Kazakh and Uzbek (Sart) agricultural settlement, and these two
national groups—despite some friction—coexisted rather peacefully.
Also, the more civilized Uzbeks had exerted considerable cultural
influence on the southern Kazakhs.

Equally significant for the radicalization of the southern Kazakhs
were the events of 1916, which assumed a more tragic aspect in the
south of the Kazakh steppe. The Kazakhs of the Syr Daria region
sympathized with their kinsmen and the Kirghiz from Semirechie
who had migrated into China in the fall of 1916 and who were now
returning. During their emigration, Russian and Ukrainian settlers
had seized sizable portions of their landholdings, and when the returning nomads resettled on their former lands, the new colonizers responded violently. Looting and murder of the Kirghiz by the Russian
and Ukrainian peasants almost assumed the aspect of guerrilla warfare
in the summer of 1917, and the administration—made up of appointees
of the Provisional Government—lacked the authority and armed
strength to intervene effectively.[9]

The anarchy in Semirechie was the main preoccupation of this August conference. It requested the government's protection from violence at the hands of unruly settlers and the resettlement of nomads returning from China to their former lands.[10] This resolution was supported on August 5 by an impressive demonstration of Moslems in Tashkent, who called for the dispatching of Russian troops to Semirechie to protect their kinsmen. Russian authorities in Central Asia responded and in a telegram to Kerensky announced that they had "resolved to put an end to settlers' violence against unarmed Kirghiz, by sending a commission to investigate immediately . . . as well as by dispatching military units."[11] The commission and troops succeeded in checking the disorders to some extent, but the situation in Semirechie remained alarming.

SOVIET PENETRATION AND COUNTERREVOLUTION IN THE STEPPE

The October upheaval did not have immediate repercussions in the Kazakh steppe. Orenburg, Ural, and Semirechian Cossacks living along the outskirts of Kazakh territory took the government of their regions into their own hands, and Kazakhs were in effect isolated for some months from Soviet infiltration. Like the Bashkirs, after the Soviet upheaval Kazakh leaders decided to establish their own autonomy. Under the protection of General A. I. Dutov and Cossack troops, a Third All-Kazakh Congress was convened in Orenburg on December 5–13 (18–26, N.S.), 1917.[12] On December 10 (23) it proclaimed the autonomy of the Kazakh region and elected an executive committee consisting of Bukeikhanov, Dosmuhammedov, Tanachev, and other members of Alash Orda.[13] Semipalatinsk was chosen as the capital,[14] but, in view of the difficulties of communication, there arose in summer 1918 two friendly, though hardly coordinated, independent Alash Orda governments. The western, having its center in the city of Jambeitu in the Ural province, was headed by Dosmuhammedov. The eastern, under Bukeikhanov, was in Semipalatinsk. Both of these bodies were anti-Communist and were referred to simply as "Alash Orda." The main purpose of the Kazakh autonomy was not so much the creation of Kazakhs' own statehood—for which Kazakhs, in the opinion of their leaders, were not yet ready—but rather, as Dosmuhammedov wrote, "to avoid the penetration of the Bolshevik contagion into the steppe."[15] The first city in the steppe region in which Soviet power was established was Kustanai; it fell on January 7 (20), 1918. Aktiubinsk was occupied on January 8 (21), Orenburg on January 18 (31), and Semipalatinsk on January 21 (February 3). Cossacks held out longest in Semirechie, where the Bolsheviks secured the city of Verny (now Alma-Ata) only on March 3 (16). Even then, anti-communist resistance was not suppressed. General Dutov's troops and Kazakh detachments continued the partisan warfare against Communism in the steppe.

This first occupation of Kazakhstan by the Soviets did not last very long. Two weeks after the Soviet regime was established in Alma-Ata on Kazakhstan's eastern frontier, an anti-Communist Ural Cossacks' revolt flared up in western Kazakhstan. At night on March 29 the Cossacks took the city of Uralsk. In May White Russian and Czecho-Slovak forces initiated operations in the Volga region, and in June all the Orenburg Cossacks joined General Dutov. By summer 1918, Siberia, most of the Volga-Ural region, and almost all of Kazakhstan were liberated from Soviet occupation.

The Kazakhs, shielded from Red troops in the southeast (in Semirechie) and in the west (along the Ural River) by the Cossacks, were more impassive witnesses to, than active participants in, the Civil War, which ravaged along their border for one year. The front in the southeast, against the Bolsheviks of Central Asia—between Lake Balkhash and the Chinese border—was held by the Cossacks of Semirechie. During the period of Soviet occupation, the Alash Orda government had fled from Orenburg into the steppes, where it organized some military units which played a modest part in the fight of the anti-Communist Russian forces against the Soviet government. Dosmuhammedov's western Alash Orda signed, in March 1918, an agreement with the Ural Cossacks on joint administration of the Ural region and military operations against the Red troops. After creation of Komuch in Samara, Dosmuhammedov joined this Russian anti-Bolshevik coalition. In eastern Kazakhstan, Bukeikhanov's government cooperated closely with the "White" Siberian administration. In this eastern part of Kazakhstan the military struggle was limited to operations of the Semirechian Cossacks; some peasant militia in the region supported Soviet power, while Kazakh detachments took little part in the fight.

The fight against Red partisans, both Russian and Kazakh, demanded considerable attention by the anti-Bolshevik Kazakh and Russian forces. In the Turgai province were the Red partisans of

Amangeldy Imanov, one of the leaders of the 1916 uprising, and of A. N. Jangeldin, head of the Kazakh tribe of Kipchaks.[16] In alliance with Red Russian guerrillas, Amangeldy cut off communications between east and west Kazakhstan. In subsequent descriptions by Soviet historians, Amangeldy assumed the stature of a great military leader and folk hero.[17] The historical truth is more modest, since Amangeldy's successes were limited to the village and district scale. Only the centrally located position of his district made it possible for him to gain control of the roads through the steppe. His, Jangeldin's, and the Kipchaks' pro-Soviet orientation resulted to a great extent from the traditional feuds between this tribe and the neighboring nomads. Since the Alash Orda leaders had supported the Russian administration during the uprising of 1916 and the anti-Bolshevik forces in 1918, it was only natural that Amangeldy, Jangeldin, and their Kipchaks should side against the tsarist authorities in 1916 and with the Bolsheviks in 1918.[18]

Another pro-Soviet Kazakh stronghold was located in the Mangyshlak and Buzachi peninsulas on the Caspian Sea, where the Adai tribe also sided with the Bolsheviks and helped Jangeldin supply Red troops fighting on the Aktiubinsk front.[19] The Adais, also, took a pro-Soviet position for "traditional" reasons. During the past two centuries they had been at war with the Ural Cossacks, and had long been an annoyance to the Russian government. When the Ural Cossacks took up operations against the Soviets in 1918, the Adai tribe automatically aligned itself with the Reds.

The third and most important pro-Soviet, anti-Alash Orda group in Kazakhstan was the already mentioned southern union, or party, of Ush Zhuz (Three Hordes), whose organ was the newspaper of the same name published in Tashkent. Here, again, there was longstanding enmity between these southern Kazakhs and the Russian administration, as well as the northern pro-Alash Orda Kazakhs. After the Bolsheviks' seizure of power in Siberia, the Ush Zhuz group accused the Bukeikhanov government of maladministration, and in 1918 furnished a pro-Soviet leadership in the south and southeast of Kazakhstan. The deep-rooted antagonism between various tribes over the grazing lands of the Syr Daria and Semirechie lands also played an important role in political alignments. Hence, it was not ideological considerations alone, but rather ancient tribal relationships and hostilities that determined the pro-Soviet politics of some Kazakh tribes. Such tribal and clan loyalties and hostilities were so vital to the Kazakhs that even in 1951 they still functioned in determining recruitment for the Communist Party.[20]

The Soviets turned serious attention to Kazakhstan as early as summer 1917, when the Petrograd Soviet sent Jangeldin to agitate in his native Turgai region. The participation of the Kipchak tribe in the anti-Russian Central Asian uprising of 1916 indicated that they constituted a dissatisfied element susceptible to Bolshevik propaganda. In March 1918, Jangeldin and S. M. Zwilling, Soviet envoy-at-large in the Urals and Kazakhstan, opened the first pro-Soviet gathering in Turgai. On May 12, 1918, Narkomnats created a special Kirghiz (Kazakh) Bureau, while Jangeldin was appointed commissar extraordinary in the steppe region.[21]

KAZAKH CONFLICT WITH WHITE ARMIES

From summer 1918 to summer 1919, during the Civil War, Kazakhstan was in a state of utter anarchy. Only the cities were controlled by Reds or Whites. The steppe and its villages remained remote, occasionally raided by White, Red, or Green (uncommitted peasant) partisans. The new settlers fought against the Kazakhs; Cossacks and "older" settlers against the new; and various tribes with each other. The Alash Orda government was less than nominal. As Sir Olaf Caroe has correctly remarked, Alash Orda was "never much more than a committee which held congresses and issued manifestoes." [22] At first it relied upon the anti-Soviet, socialist Komuch, later on Kolchak's troops. Together with the Bashkirs and some Uzbeks, Alash Orda also sounded the possibilities for forming an eventual southeastern Turkic-Cossack union under General Dutov, head of the Orenburg Cossacks, which would extend from the Urals to the southern borders of Central Asia.[23] These plans, however, never amounted to more than dreams, since none of these Turkic peoples had sufficient leaders or means even to organize and defend their own territories. The situation of the Alash Orda government became completely hopeless when the Russian socialist, anti-Bolshevik government in Omsk, alarmed by the chaos reigning in Kazakhstan, announced on November 4, 1918 that it would no longer support Kazakh autonomy.

The Omsk government's and, later, Admiral Kolchak's attitude toward Kazakh and other national autonomies had the same result everywhere. Like the Bashkirs, the Kazakhs were discouraged by the suspension of their autonomy, and they began to reconsider their political orientation. Their pro-Soviet temper developed so rapidly that on December 7, 1918, the western Alash Orda government was obliged to suppress a pro-Soviet uprising.[24] Nevertheless, in view of their remoteness from the front, the Kazakhs had more difficulty in going over to the Reds than did the Bashkirs. Jangeldin succeeded in establishing contact with an Alash Orda group in Orsk only in March 1919, and convinced Baitursunov to defect to the Reds.[25] On March 22 Jangeldin, at that time head of the Turgai Soviet administration, telegraphed joyously to Moscow: "Unification is now completed of all the laboring Kirghiz (Kazakh) people under the Red banner of the worker-peasant government." [26] But a few more months would pass before this process of unification actually would be complete. At this time some Kazakh troops at the front retreated to the steppes, but others continued fighting on the side of the Whites. Dosmuham-medov's western Alash Orda recognized the Soviet government only on November 10, after the final defeat of Admiral Kolchak. Some weeks later the eastern Alash Orda, under Bukeikhanov, also joined the Reds.

KIRREVKOM

After signing a preliminary agreement, Alash Orda's Baitursunov and the Soviets' Jangeldin went with a Kazakh delegation to Moscow, where they entered negotiations with Lenin and Stalin over the status of Kazakhstan.[27] As a result, on July 10, 1919, an embryo government of the future Kazakh SSR was created—the Kirghiz (Kazakh) Revolutionary Committee (*Kirrevkom*)—headed by S. Pestkowski and including Jangeldin (Kazakh), Mindeshev (Kazakh), A. Kulakov, J. Khaikus, and S. M. Dimanstein.[28] Theoretically, Kirrevkom's jurisdiction extended to the entire Kazakh steppe, but practically its activities were limited to the so-called Bukeev Horde, the westernmost part of present Kazakhstan between the rivers Volga and Ural. The Kazakhs Jangeldin and Mindeshev were to a great extent merely decorative figures in Kirrevkom. The main roles were played by S. M. Dimanstein, the future right hand of Stalin in Narkomnats, and by S. Pestkowski.

The defeat of Kolchak and cessation of White activities in Siberia and the rest of eastern Russia became apparent in May 1919, after which time White Army units streamed ceaselessly to the east. The Red Ural and Central Asian armies were free to join Red forces in the east, as a result of the liquidation of the Aktiubinsk front on September 13. On December 11 Semipalatinsk fell, and the Whites managed to hold out until March 1920 only in Semirechie. The flames of the Civil War gradually went out. The whole Kazakh territory was in Red hands.

The defection of Alash Orda to the Soviets did not signify the triumph of the Communist cause among the Kazakhs, however. The first attempts to introduce Communism among them showed that there were very few supporters of Soviet power in Kazakhstan aside from the tribes and groups organized by Amangeldy and Jangeldin. At the First Turgai Congress of Soviets held in March 1918, during the Soviets' first occupation of the steppe, the Bolsheviks had received first one, later—with difficulty—three places in the local executive committee, out of a total of 55 members. During the Civil War, Communist cadres did not grow noticeably. In 1927, out of all Kazakh Communists only one had been in the party since 1916 (Jangeldin, himself); 9 since 1917; 148 since 1918; and 345 since 1919. Hence, by 1927 there were only 503 Kazakhs in RKP(b) who had joined between 1917 and 1919.[29] True, some were purged in 1920–1927 and others were killed in the Civil War, but it is doubtful if, toward the end of 1919, the number of Kazakh party members exceeded 700–800 persons. And, too, the majority of Kazakh Communists, as indicated above, joined the party not because of sincere devotion to Marxism, but because of tribal relationships and conflicts. There were few, if any, influential leaders among them. The first Communists, like Amangeldy Imanov and A. Maikotov, perished during the Civil War; others, such as Tunganchin, Jangeldin, and Mindeshev, did not command the authority among the Kazakhs which Baitursunov and other Alash Orda politicians had. Therefore, just as in Bashkiria, where at the beginning the Bolsheviks depended upon Validov's autonomists, so in Kazakhstan the core of administrative and cultural workers among Kazakhs consisted primarily of Alash Orda members.

At the turn of 1919–1920, despite the conclusion of the Civil War in Kazakhstan, the situation remained very tense, as it was in other regions of the Soviet Union. The Soviet government had often to rely upon nationalist fellow-travelers—such as former Tatar socialists, the Validovists, former Alash Ordists, and the Central Asian Jadids, who wanted a broad, genuine national autonomy—as well as on local Russian Communists (mainly workers and new settlers). "A healthy, active core of communists did not exist among the Kazakhs then," wrote a Soviet historian later.[30] Local Russian Communists, supported in the east by other non-Turkic groups, such as Ukrainians, Jews, Latvians, and Armenians, were firmly opposed to autonomy and did their best to counteract the centripetal plans of Turkic nationalists. Between September 1919 and January 1920, the situation changed, however. With the blessing of the Central Committee of RKP(b), Moslem Communists from the ranks of the Jadids came to power in Central Asia. Under Turar Ryskulov and Nizametdin Hojaev, these persons were close ideologically to the Bashkir supporters of Validov and the Kazakh supporters of Alash Orda, and demanded greater freedom of action from Moscow.[31] These circles once again considered projects for creating a southeastern Turkic union, within the Soviet sphere, and they also sought to establish a separate Moslem Communist Party. The resoluteness of some Moslem Communists to proceed in this direction was clearly demonstrated by the abortive Bashkir *putsch* in January 1920 (see Chapter XIII), which called to mind the old ties between Alash Orda and Validov, who had originally conceived the idea of a Bashkir-Kazakh union as a step toward a southeastern Turkic federation.[32] Still, however, the Soviet government did not want to break with the Moslem Communists, and it maneuvered for time.[33] This also explained its delay in resolving the question of Kazakh autonomy.

THE OPPOSITION

A stubborn battle also began in Kazakhstan between die-hard Communists and the former supporters of Alash Orda who had now joined the Communist Party or defected to the side of the Soviets. This struggle was most apparent in Kirrevkom, the main administrative organ of the Kazakh region. On October 11 Kirrevkom met to prepare for a constituent congress of the soviets of Kazakhstan, and discussed the question of electoral laws. A special committee was formed to prepare for the election. Some Communists suggested excluding from the lists of voters all members of the clergy, members of the tsarist and Alash Orda administrations, the rich bais, and former village and tribal elders. Baitursunov vehemently protested, declaring that the deprivation of these persons' political rights was tantamount to "depriving the Kazakh people of its representation, and suspension of its rights to express its own will through its most capable representatives." [34] He succeeded in pushing a motion through to guarantee these social groups the right to vote, but Kirrevkom's chairman, Pestkowski, subsequently altered Kirrevkom's membership, and at a later conference Kirrevkom deprived part of these groups of all political rights.[35]

The main battle between nationalists and die-hard Communists of the Pestkowski group was fought out at a local Communist conference on January 1, 1919. Leading the nationalists were Baitursunov himself and his principal ally, the former Russian Social Democrat, Sedelnikov. Receiving no cooperation from members of the party's local central committee, these two turned to the Central Committee of RKP(b) in Moscow at the end of March 1920. In a letter they proposed a program of reform, outlining a common platform for local party organizations throughout Kazakhstan, Bashkiria, and Central Asia, and demanding that the Central Committee "give effective and real guaranty for the self-determination of the peoples of the Kazakh, Bashkir, and Turkestan autonomous republics." Further, they requested that "the industrial and agricultural policies of the autonomous territories be determined by local economic councils and commissariats for food supply, satisfying first of all the needs of the local populations." As a Soviet writer has very plausibly commented, their final aim was to attain the following from the Central Committee: (1) that the Communist Party should not rule in these republics; (2) that the Soviet government not adhere in the eastern regions to the principle of "dictatorship of the proletariat"; and (3) that local government be relegated to local administrators, or the "bourgeois nationalists," in Soviet terminology.[36]

Soviet sources have often exaggerated the significance of the opposition's actions. The assumption that Baitursunov and Sedelnikov (the first a moderate Kazakh intellectual, the second a Russian) joined the clandestine Turkic national organization of *Ittihad ve Tarakki* (Unity and Progress),[37] in which the Tatar, Sultangaliev, the Bashkir, Validov, and the Uzbek Jadid leaders, Tursun Hojaev and Turar Ryskulov, allegedly participated, is probably also unfounded. Doubtless, however, all these national leaders did have a unity of purpose and were in continual contact with each other. Baitursunov and Validov were very well acquainted personally, and not infrequently expressed their belief in the practicality of a Kazakh-Bashkir federation as a counterbalance both to Soviet power and to Tatar ambitions. Sedelnikov, a Russian anti-Communist, also favored this plan as a means of weakening Soviet control in the east.

Sedelnikov followed up his letter to the Central Committee in Moscow with a personal appeal to Lenin, his former comrade in the Social Democratic Party. He declared that there were no longer any old revolutionaries left in the Communist Party, whose membership now consisted mainly of "March foam"—that is, people who joined after March 1917. He regretted that only "raw recruits" of Communism, such as wartime Bolsheviks (soldiers and racketeers) and "Bonapartists," were now in power in Moscow.

Sedelnikov's and Baitursunov's bold opposition won support from young Kazakh Communists, and the local party bureau informed Moscow that "Sedelnikov has become the leader of Kazakh nationalists and is conducting an open chauvinistic fight against Communism.[38]

CREATION OF THE KAZAKH ASSR

For the time being the Central Committee and the Soviet government left Sedelnikov and Baitursunov alone. The war with the Poles, who began a new offensive in the Ukraine, and with the White Army of General Wrangel, which moved in from Crimea, required all available Red military forces. After the danger on the front lessened, the Bashkir nationalists were dislodged from power and tension decreased in Central Asia. The possibility of a joint Bashkir, Kazakh, and Central Asian opposition or insurrection was eliminated, and the Bolsheviks could proceed to recognizing Kazakh autonomy, which they did by decree on August 26, 1920.[39] Simultaneously with formal creation of the Kazakh (Kirghiz) ASSR, the Central Committee removed Sedelnikov and Baitursunov from Kirrevkom, thus depriving the opposition of its leaders—who had been sitting in the highest body of the germinal republic.[40] (A few months later Baitursunov, as a capitulated national symbol, was reinstated to membership in Kirrevkom, and became People's Commissar for Education of the Kazakh ASSR.) Of the other Kazakhs in Kirrevkom, there remained only five decorative figures. The remaining five members were Russians or other non-Turks.

On October 4–12, 1920, two months after publication of the decree establishing the Kazakh (Kirghiz) Republic, the First Constituent Congress of Kazakh Soviets was held in Orenburg.[41] Over 700 delegates took part, of whom 273 were entitled to vote; among the latter 197 were Communists. Delegates from the solidly Communist Ural and Turgaisk regions—where Jangeldin and Amangeldy had strengthened Soviet influence among the Adai and Kipchak tribes—formed over half of the congress' members.[42] The other Kazakh delegates—Communists and nonparty members alike—were still grouped around Alash Orda's leaders, Baitursunov and Bukeikhanov. One of the delegates, A. Nakhimjan, wrote in his reminiscences some years later:

> We came to the first all-Kirghiz [Kazakh] congress . . . united with the Alash Orda intellectuals, many of whom, under Baitursunov, were delegates. Hence, it is not surprising that we joined the [Communist] party still dominated by an Alash Orda ideology . . . Before going to the [Communist] faction's conference, we usually received directions from our Alash Orda leaders, and after the faction gathering we would report what had happened at the meeting of RKP(b).[43]

The opposition, left leaderless after the removal of the dynamic Sedelnikov, bore itself quietly, realizing that the Central Committee was no longer inclined to permit serious criticism. In an address, Baitursunov even praised the Soviet system.[44] The congress elected a central committee of the republic, as well as a Council of People's Commissars, and published a constitutional manifesto, "Declaration of the Rights of the Laboring Kirghiz (Kazakh) Autonomous Republic." This document sanctioned Kazakhstan's entrance, "as an autonomous member, into the free, federative Union of Soviet Socialist Republics . . . into the common revolutionary family." The main Kazakh problem, that of colonization, was also resolved by the congress. Further peasant settlement in Kazakhstan was forbidden.

Questions bearing on the international situation and Communist propaganda in the East were also taken up in sessions of the Constituent Congress. In a lengthy opening speech, Stalin's envoy and assistant in Narkomnats, Dimanstein, proclaimed that Kazakhs should be the avant-garde of the revolution in the East: "The Kirghiz Republic, by its example and new form of government and social order, will be the bearer of the idea of Communism among the peoples of the East." [45] A special appeal to the eastern peoples urged them to follow the example of the Soviet revolution and throw off the chains put upon them by imperialists. The organization of autonomous Soviet republics in the East was held up as a challenge to President Woodrow Wilson, whose principle of national self-determination had not been pushed through to actualization in Asia. [46]

THE AGRARIAN PROBLEM AND THE UNIFICATION OF THE KAZAKH TERRITORY

Important steps directed at solving the agrarian problem were taken in 1921. A decree of February 2 of that year returned to Kazakh possession all lands held by the state, the church, and the nobility, as well as private trusts. Further, according to a decree of April 19, all land along the left bank of the Ural River was expropriated from the Ural Cossacks and given to the Kazakhs, while the Siberian Cossacks were deprived of a strip of ten versts (six miles) along the Irtysh River which had belonged to them since the seventeenth century. Finally, an additional law restored to the Kazakhs and Kirghiz 470,000 hectares held by Russian and Ukrainian settlers in Semirechie.[47] These decrees, satisfying the long-standing desires of the Kazakhs, struck a blow at the stubborn antagonists of Soviet power—the Cossacks, as well as at some rebellious settlers.

As originally formed, the Kazakh Autonomous Republic included under its administration only part of the areas inhabited by Kazakhs. Large territories in northwestern Kazakhstan and the Kazakh-populated districts of the Akmolinsk and Semipalatinsk provinces remained under the Siberian regional administration, while some of southern Kazakhstan was under the control of Tashkent.

The agrarian reforms, which deprived both local Cossacks and the Russian and Ukrainian peasantry of their landholdings, led to a sharpening of relations between them and the Kazakhs. The peasants also resented the Soviet rule, which they had supported during the Civil War. There resulted a number of peasant uprisings in western Siberia and eastern Kazakhstan against the Soviet regime. On the other side, since the Communist Party and the Soviet apparatus in western Siberia were composed to a great extent of peasants, the latter refused to relinquish to Kazakhstan the Semipalatinsk and Akmolinsk provinces. There were strong apprehensions among the peasants that all their holdings would be expropriated by the Kazakh administration. At the first meeting of the central committee of the Kazakh Republic in early February 1921, the committee's chairman, Mindeshev, announced that although most of the Kazakh People's Commissariats had already intiated their activities, the eastern Kazakh territories were still under Siberian soviets.[48] Toward the end of that month a Kazakh delegation was dispatched to Omsk for the purpose of negotiating with the regional Siberian administration for the transfer of the Semipalatinsk and Akmolinsk provinces to Kazakhstan.[49] The Siberian Communists remained reluctant to give up control in these territories, and refused to relinquish these southeastern lands to the Kazakh Republic until summer 1921, and even then did it only under pressure from Moscow.[50]

The Kazakhs of the Syr-Daria and Semirechie regions remained under the administration of the Turkestan Autonomous Republic for three years more. A congress of southern Kazakhs in Aulie-Ata in the summer of 1921 strove vainly to secure the annexation of these lands to Kazakhstan.[51] Only after the Twelfth Party Congress of RKP(b) [VKP(b)] in 1924, which signified a turning point in the Communist Party's attitude toward the national problem, were the southern Kazakhs incorporated into their own republic.[52] The republic's present name, Kazakh SSR, was given it in 1925.[53]

The unification of all Kazakh territories into one republic, however, was not the triumph of Kazakh nationalist longings. Although the Kazakh nationalists—the Alash Ordists—played an important role in the Kazakhstan administration in the republic's early years, the Communists were sufficiently vigilant not to permit nationalism to manifest itself. The famine of 1921, from which over two million Kazakhs suffered, weakened Kazakh strength just as it did Bashkir strength. The conflict between nationalist and internationalist Communists continued unremittingly, and the Kazakh language itself did not become the state tongue of the Kazakh autonomy immediately.[54] With the exception of lower officials and clerks, the government remained mainly in the hands of Russian and non-Turkic Communists. Only after the Twelfth Congress of RKP(b) were serious attempts made to draw more Kazakhs into the Soviet apparatus. Still, however, the Kazakhs continued to hope for an independent national development of their own. A Kazakh nationalist Communist wrote in 1922, "Our method in the future should be the following: we are not struggling now for supremacy [in Kazakhstan], but that is still our goal. Even if we were to fight for that, it would not be possible to succeed. Therefore, the greatest effort must be exerted toward educating the youth and preparing it for a future muster of strength." [55]

CHAPTER XV

The Revolution in the Central Asian Oases

Two German historians of contemporary Central Asia write that while supporters of the Soviets were seizing power in Tashkent in October 1917, "the native Turkestanians remained impassive observers of both the Russian and their own revolutionary tragedy." [1] Indeed, from February to October 1917, as well as in the following months, which were determining destinies of the subsequent decades, the great majority of Central Asian Moslems demonstrated very little concern over political developments. This attitude to a very great extent was conditioned by "the oases psychology" of the Central Asian sedentary population. The isolated and scattered oases had caused the settled *dekkhans* (native peasants) to become fragmentized into little-connected and often self-supporting districts, preventing the development of any "national" or regional unity. The fragile system of irrigation canals rendered agriculture, which formed the only substantial foundation for existence in this region, and the supply of water extremely vulnerable, voiding not only the possibility of active resistance but even the willingness to engage in any struggle. Innumerable nomadic invasions during the millenniums of Central Asian history had conditioned the sedentary inhabitants of the oasis region to the inevitability of conquest, resulting in their fatalistic acceptance of domination by alien usurpers. The formation of any clear concept of a legal state and constitutional administration was equally precluded by the medieval regimes of the khans and other feudal rulers who dominated Central Asia until the second part of the nineteenth century, or even until 1920 in the case of Khiva and Bukhara.

In 1917 four fifths of the total population was concentrated in the overcrowded oases of the central mesopotamia between the Amu and Syr Daria rivers. Except for their elaborately organized system of water distribution, few factors entered in to support a consciousness of unity, either among the dekkhans or between them and the urban inhabitants. Tribal bonds existed only among the nomads on the outskirts of the area, while the ancient urban artisan and merchant guilds among the natives were in a process of disintegration, under the impact of new economic conditions which arose after Central Asia's annexation to Russia. The only force which served to unite the native population of this area was the faith of Islam, its clergy and its mosques. Unless the faith was endangered or offended, however, this remained only a passive force, and as long as political or military issues did not involve religious problems, the Moslem clergy and believers maintained neutrality.

The seminomadic and mountain tribes on the outskirts of Central Asia's central mesopotamia—as, for instance, the Yomud Turkomens in Khiva, Kipchaks* in Ferghana, Lokais and Kara Kitais in Bukhara, and Tajik mountaineers of Karategin and Darvaz (southeastern Bukhara)—differed greatly from these settled natives in behavior, mentality, and military preparedness. In the wastes of their arid steppes and highlands, several Turkic and Tajik tribes still preserved in 1917 their patriarchal clan organization and the autocratic rule of elders and chieftains. For centuries these tribes maintained a war-like spirit, resisting the administration of khans, raiding the settled population, and waging continuous warfare over possession of the fertile lands.

These tribes of the steppes and mountains became the main source of difficulty and of armed resistance to the Soviet regime after 1920, and it was largely they who filled the ranks of the guerrilla Basmachi movement which seriously endangered Communist domination in Central Asia. They rose against Soviet rule, however, only when the Bolsheviks began to appear as a threat to their traditional mode of life, which became apparent to them toward the end of the Civil War and after the conquest of Bukhara. During the first two years of the revolution, with the exception of Ferghana, where the Basmachi movement started in the summer of 1918, these tribes were not involved in the struggle between the Communists and the Russian counterrevolutionists. Furthermore, inhabiting the outskirts of the area, they were isolated even from each other by the deserts and high mountain ranges, and were no threat to the main urban admin-istrative centers of Central Asia. Hence, at the beginning, the Soviet

* Not to be confused with the Kipchaks of Kazakhstan. "Kipchak" is a common tribal name among the Kazakhs and Uzbeks, all of whom were called Kipchaks until the twelfth century.

regime had sufficient time to consolidate its grip over Central Asia without becoming involved in any serious conflict with the native population. The facility with which alien conquerors had intermittently gained supremacy over these peoples in previous centuries was hardly diminished even in 1917, and the native population's political torpor and cultural backwardness created a vacuum of power after the disintegration of the tsarist administration which the advocates of Soviet power were quick to fill. Seizing control in Tashkent, they gradually consolidated their authority and imposed their rule over all Central Asia. A further reason for the Bolsheviks' cautiousness was their alliance with the left socialists, who were by far more numerous in Central Asia than the Communists and who dominated the local Tashkent Soviet government until the beginning of 1919.

MOSLEMS' POLITICAL ORIENTATION IN 1917

Moslem political activity in Central Asia was initiated in 1917 by local Tatars (as usual), who convoked a conference of Moslems of the Volga-Ural region—i.e., of Tatars—on April 13–20, 1917.[2] On April 16 this gathering was joined by some Central Asian Moslem intellectuals, mainly Jadids who had united in March around *Shuro-i-Islamie* (Islamic Council).[3] The conference passed resolutions, typical for the period March–April 1917, calling for elaboration of a Russian constitution based on democratic and federative principles, equal rights for Moslems, and improvement of the Moslem clergy's conditions.[4] A union of the Turkestan Moslem clergy, *Ulema Jemyeti* (Board of Learned Men), was also organized, presided over by Sher-Ali Liapin, a mullah from Ak-Mechet, and its activity immediately assumed an extreme clerical-conservative character. At its last session on April 26, the conference set up a permanent executive organ, the Turkestan Moslem Central Soviet (*Turkestan Musulman Merkezi-Surasi,* or TMMS, later altered to "National Center" [*Milli Merkez*]),[5] composed predominantly of Tatars and local Jadids. Their leaders were Mustafa Chokaev (a Kazakh of the Khiva aristocracy and former secretary of the Moslem faction in the Duma),[6] Behbudi (a Young Bukhariote from Samarkand), Ubaidulla Hoja, and Asadulla Hoja.[7] TMMS set up branches in some provincial towns, all of them headed by Jadids. At the head of the Samarkand branch was Behbudi himself;[8] in Ferghana, Nasyr Khan Tiuria; in Semirechie, the influential Kazakh engineer, Tanyshbaev; in Ashkhabad, a Turkomen aristocrat, Oraz Serdar, a colonel in the Russian army. TMMS maintained relations with other Turkic national parties in Russia, although it did not participate in the All-Russian National Moslem Shuro.

Moderateness and passivity characterized the National Center's policy. In the early months of 1917 it did not raise any question concerning Central Asian autonomy, and in its negotiations with the Council of Russian Social Organizations in Tashkent on April 26 it declared that, despite the overwhelming numerical superiority of Moslems in Central Asia, it did not seek the right to a greater number of seats in the local self-administrations than the Russians.[9]

Some friction between TMMS and the Council of Russian Social Organizations occurred in Andijan, whose local branch rejected the nomination of Moslems to administrative posts, claiming that they were politically immature and still attached to the obsolete social system.[10] Russian circles in Tashkent generally shared this attitude toward the Moslems of Turkestan. In a report to Kerensky, then Prime Minister, a group of Tashkent lawyers wrote, "If Moslems are given, at the present time, the privilege of self-determination, then the future presents the picture of a struggle for power among individual tribes, which will amount to bloody carnage." [11] Of all the Russian parties in Central Asia, only the Social Democrats came out for autonomy, and at their June 1917 congress they recommended formation of "a politically autonomous Turkestan based on the national-cultural autonomy of the various individual nationalities populating the region." [12]

After the First All-Russian Moslem Congress in May 1917, the question of autonomy became more acute. The Jadids from Shuro-i-Islam, who dominated TMMS, took up this issue. They believed, as did other Russian Moslems in 1917, in the possibility of solving the nationalities problem by means of autonomy, but they were not for political secession from Russia.[13] They did little to carry out even a Central Asian autonomy. In 1917 the Jadids were more apprehensive of Moslem clerical reaction than Russian power and the revolution, and such fears were well founded. Re-elections to the Tashkent city council in early August, 1917, resulted in the overwhelming victory of the conservatives—even in this most European and progressive city of Central Asia. The reactionary Moslem Ulema, in union with rightist Russian groups, won 60 per cent of the votes; Jadids or other

Turkic nationalists from Shuro-i-Islam, 10 per cent; Socialist Revolutionaries, 25 per cent; the Social Democrats, together with the Bolsheviks, sent only three delegates (among them one Uzbek), out of a total of one hundred, to the council. After this Tashkent defeat, the Jadids realized clearly that the clerical-conservative victory would be even greater throughout the provinces, and they became extremely cautious in their attitude toward Ulema.[14]

Ulema and the clergy were interested neither in autonomy nor in independence, but solely in preserving clerical influence over the Central Asian Moslem population. Their union with Russian rightists was dictated by their hostility toward the Jadids and other leftist parties, whom they condemned as godless renegades. There had even been incidents of murder of some liberal and socialist Moslems in the summer and fall of 1917.[15] When TMMS began drafting a plan for autonomy, Ulema insisted upon the insertion of provisions which would guarantee the clergy's supervision of the autonomy's legislative and executive organs and give them control of the administration.

Since, as indicated by the elections, Ulema represented the overwhelming majority of the Central Asian population and the Jadids from Shuro-i-Islam the small but active group of national intelligentsia, left-socialist Moslem organizations were practically without support. In Tashkent, Ferghana (Skobelev), and Samarkand there were some Moslem workers' organizations with a socialist platform,[16] and Moslem socialists collaborated with the Bolsheviks, but the over-all strength of these groups was extremely limited.[17]

At the Second Moslem Central Asian Conference, which convened on September 3, 1917, the native population was more completely represented than at the First Conference in April.[18] The Second Conference adopted a draft for local autonomy which would organize Central Asia as a part of a democratic Russian republic. The Ferghana, Syr-Daria, Samarkand, and Transcaspian provinces would form an autonomous Turkestan Federated Republic. In accordance with the demand of Ulema, the local Diet would be headed by a Moslem clerical "senate" (*Makhame-i-Sharia*), presided over by a *sheikh-ul-Islam* (guardian of Moslem orthodoxy).[19] The conference recommended introducing a zemstvo self-administration in the Central Asian provinces to safeguard the native population from "the illegal meddling of administrative organs unfamiliar with the local mores." [20] The conference's recommendations were met sympathetically by General Korovnichenko, representative of the Provisional Government in Tashkent. Negotiations began immediately between the Moslems, the administration, and Russian organizations for setting up the new Central Asian zemstvo, but, like all other plans for autonomy, they were interrupted by the Bolsheviks' October coup.[21]

THE OCTOBER UPHEAVAL IN TASHKENT

In contrast to the native Moslems' apathy, the Russian and other European settlers of Central Asia displayed an effervescent political activity. The city of Tashkent, by far the largest urban center in Turkestan, became a beehive for social agitators after the February revolution. The city garrisoned reserve soldiers in its railroad buildings and barracks (many of whom became easy victims of socialist propaganda), and Tashkent grew into the citadel of a revolutionary radicalism which completely dominated the entire Central Asian political scene. When by the end of August 1917 news of the conflict between Prime Minister Kerensky and the commander-in-chief, General L. Kornilov, reached Tashkent, the local radicals decided that their hour had arrived. The Bolsheviks were still very weak in Tashkent, but their allies, the left Socialist Revolutionaries and the left Mensheviks, acted together. On September 12 they elected a new executive committee for the Tashkent Soviet of Soldiers' and Workers' Deputies, consisting of eighteen left Socialist Revolutionaries, ten left Mensheviks, and seven Bolsheviks. This new body arrested the local administration, took over command of the demoralized troops, and assumed power in the name of the revolution, the people's will, and the soviets.

This early dress rehearsal of the Bolshevik's subsequent coup in Petersburg soon misfired, however. While some moderate Russian and Moslem leaders loyal to the Provisional Government escaped to Ferghana and attempted to rally anti-Soviet loyalists in the cities of Skobelev and Kokand, others remained in the Tashkent garrison, managed in their turn to arrest the leftists, and put a quick end to the Tashkent mutiny. The authority of the Provisional Government was restored by September 16.

On October 26, after Lenin seized power in Petersburg, Tashkent's radical socialist leaders, supported by the Red Guards, workers, some regular troops which had been won over to the cause of the socialist revolution, and a few Moslem militiamen once again attempted to take over in Tashkent. The fighting started on October 28, and on November 1 after the capitulation of the Provisional Government's local representative, General Korovnichenko, Soviet authority was proclaimed in Tashkent. Indeed, for the first few weeks this authority was limited only to the city and its immediate vicinity, but the importance of Tashkent as the main city of Central Asia made the revolutionaries more or less the rulers of the entire region. The composition of the Revolutionary Committee of the Tashkent soviet, which was instrumental in both the September misfire and the seizure of power on November 1, clearly indicates that the Moslems had very little to do with the Soviet upheaval. The Revkom was composed of four Russians—Kolesov, Kazakov, Pershin, and Tomilin; one German—Bauman; four Jews—Zwilling, Weinstein, Solkin, and Tobolin; one Moldavian—Cirul; and one Pole —Czerniawski. Politically it was dominated by the left Socialist Revolutionaries, the Communists still being weak and disorganized in Central Asia. This small but resolute group of socialist adventurers, without connections among the natives and unsupported by the larger part of the local Russian population, was to rule Central Asia in the name of the Soviet government for the next two years. The pillars of its power were the railroad workers (the main proletarian force in Central Asia), some regular soldiers who turned Red Guardist, and the Communist, "internationalist" battalions recruited from among the Hungarian, Austrian, and German prisoners of war. These latter mercenaries were to a great extent responsible for the Red victory in Central Asia during the years of the Civil War.

In the weeks following the October Revolution an anti-Communist uprising in the southern Urals, led by the Cossack General Dutov, isolated Central Asia from Moscow and the rest of Russia. Thus, the Red rulers of Tashkent remained self-supporting and practically independent, even from Moscow, until late 1919, while the Civil War was ravaging Russia.

CENTRAL ASIAN MOSLEMS AND THE SOVIETS

Among the Central Asian Moslems very few, if any, actually realized what the Bolsheviks' program promised. Ulema, albeit the most influential group among the natives, had only the passive, unorganized support of the masses of the native population and was lacking any political program. Its slogans were limited to the general defense of the spiritual supremacy of Islam. Shuro-i-Islam and the Jadids were equipped with a program for cultural reform and local autonomy, but their supporters were not a significant force. At the time of the October upheaval, Soviet power was not yet regarded by the Moslems as an inimical rule for Moslems, but rather as the authority of bearers of the idea of equality for all peoples—an administration which would establish conditions propitious for the rebirth of the East and of Islam. Consequently, liberal groups in Central Asia greeted the Bolsheviks' seizure of power with hope. Chokaev, leader of Shuro-i-Islam and, after December 1917, Prime Minister of the Kokand autonomy, subsequently wrote, "There was a time when we were ready to believe, and actually did believe, in the Moscow Bolsheviks." Only later did "Soviet practice destroy our faith in the revolutionary slogans so lavishly displayed by the Communists of all countries." [22] The unions of "toiling Moslems" were even more enthusiastic toward the Bolsheviks, but the most unexpected event was the decision of Ulema to support the new Soviet power and participate in the Tashkent government. Sher-Ali Liapin and the conservative Moslem clerics apparently took at face value the Bolsheviks' nationalist slogans and their appeal for liberation of the East.

On November 15 the Third Regional Congress of Soviets and the Third Moslem Central Asian Conference assembled simultaneously in Tashkent. This Moslem conference, entirely dominated by Ulema, was presided over by Sher-Ali Liapin. Some Moslem socialist groups also participated, but the Jadids and their Shuro-i-Islam were not invited. The conservative majority of the conference made the decision to collaborate with the Tashkent victors of the October coup and proposed to form with them a coalition government consisting of six representatives from Ulema, three from the municipalities, and three from the Tashkent Soviet and Revkom. [23] The Congress of Soviets and Revkom, however, refused this proposal—without "in principle" denying the Moslems' participation in the government. They formed instead a Council of People's Commissars consisting of eight left Socialist Revolutionaries and six Bolsheviks, headed by F. Kolesov. [24] All of them were of Russian or other European origin. By a vote of ninety-seven to seventeen, the Congress of Soviets resolved that:

the inclusion of Moslems in the supreme territorial organ of revolutionary power at the present time is unacceptable both in view of the native population's indefinite attitude toward the rule of the Soviets of Workers' and Peasants' Deputies, and in *view of the fact that there are no proletarian class organizations among the native inhabitants.*[25]

Consequently, similar to the development in Tatary and Bashkiria and thanks to Central Asia's isolation from political centers, a small group of Bolsheviks and left socialists succeeded in excluding the local population from participation in the government.[26]

"THE KOKAND AUTONOMY"

Rejected by the Tashkent Soviet government,[27] Ulema turned to the liberal Shuro-i-Islam for the formation of a unified Islamic organization, to be called *Ittifak-ul-Mislimin* (Union of Moslems). In late November, Ulema and Shuro-i-Islam convened in Kokand the Fourth Moslem Central Asian Conference. The Tashkent Soviet regime would no doubt have preferred to prohibit this conference, but its power was not yet established in all the cities of Central Asia and it was incapable of preventing the gathering.[28] Due to the anarchic conditions reigning in Central Asia in November 1917, it is doubtful whether delegates at the Kokand conference represented a genuine popular vote. In any case, the representation of the various regions was way out of proportion. The Ferghana province (in which the city of Kokand was located) was represented by 150 delegates—nearly three fourths of the total number present; the Syr-Daria and Samarkand regions sent 22 and 23 delegates, respectively; the Transcaspian region, only one; and when the congress opened, Semirechie was not represented at all. There were also several representatives of anti-Soviet Russian—predominantly right Socialist Revolutionary—organizations in Central Asia. When the conference opened on November 25 (December 8, N.S.), 180 delegates were present, and by November 28 the number rose to 203.

The agenda listed four main problems:

(1) The system of administration and nature of relations with the Soviet government.

(2) The attitude to be assumed in regard to General Dutov's proposal to sever all relations with the Soviets and enter into the projected

anti-Communist southeastern union, to consist of the Ural, Orenburg, Siberian, and Semirechian Cossack regions, Bashkiria, Kazakhstan, and Central Asia.

(3) Election of an executive committee.

(4) Creation of a legislature for Central Asia.[29]

The conference decided not to sever relations either with Tashkent or with Moscow. Thus it automatically rejected Dutov's proposal for a southeastern federation, and declined to join the struggle against the Bolsheviks. Like the Tatars and Bashkirs, Central Asians at the Kokand congress neither completely submitted to Soviet authority nor entered into open conflict with it. Even the Tashkent government —no matter how accidentally it was composed, it had the support of Moscow—was accepted by the Kokand conference as an almost legal government. Central Asians at the conference also were loath to expose themselves to Tashkent's wrath and, hence, entered negotiations with Tashkent concerning their mutual relations.[30]

Without waiting for Tashkent's final answer, however, the Kokand conference announced the autonomy of Turkestan on November 27 (December 10, N.S.), 1917.[31] The declaration stressed that the conference proclaimed Turkestan "territorially autonomous within the union of the Russian democratic republic." The proclamation evoked no particular reaction either from the Soviet government or from the anti-Bolsheviks. Since, in their appeals of November 24 to the peoples of Russia and the East,[32] the Bolsheviks had recognized the right of nationalities not only to self-determination but also to complete secession, they could not officially protest the Central Asians' declaration of autonomy. Furthermore, Kolesov's Tashkent government, the only Soviet power in Central Asia at that time, was too weak to take any measures against Kokand. As for the anti-Soviet Russian groups, they welcomed the declaration of autonomy as an expression of opposition to the Soviets. The conference elected members to a new National Council which included thirty-six Moslems and eighteen Russians.[33] Petrograd's Socialist Revolutionary newspaper, *Volia naroda*, reported, with tongue in cheek, "On the basis of the formula of self-determination by the nationalities, as proclaimed by the Bolsheviks, the Moslem territorial congress has formed a provisional government independent of the power which emerged in Tashkent after the October coup and has declared itself the sole authority in Turkestan."[34]

The Kokand conference proceeded to elect an executive committee of twelve, each member in charge of a separate department. The committee, in effect the government of the Turkestan autonomy, was initially headed by the Kazakh leader, Tanyshbaev, then, after his withdrawal on January 17, 1918, by another Kazakh, Mustafa Chokaev. The lack of native Central Asian Uzbek leaders compelled the congress to elect to its committee persons not belonging to the nationalities of Central Asia. The committee included two Kazakhs, two Azerbaijanis, one Bashkir, one Austrian prisoner of war, and four Uzbeks. Baimirza Hajit has reported that Nasyr Khan Tiuria, Commissar for Education, complained at the time that there were barely forty or fifty Uzbeks educated according to European standards and capable of participating in a modern administration.[35]

A situation resulted in Central Asia somewhat analogous to that in Kazan. Despite negotiations, Kokand did not submit to Tashkent, and both administrations operated simultaneously, issuing regulations and exacting compliance. Kokand's city administration, for instance, obeyed only the directions of Tashkent, and recognized the authority of the Kokand executive committee only on the eve of the collapse of the Kokand autonomy, on February 7 (January 25, O.S.).[36] Moscow cautiously did not interfere in the Tashkent-Kokand conflict. When, on December 14, the Moslem Workers' Council of Andijan requested Stalin by telegram to dismiss the Tashkent government, Stalin, knowing that Kokand had no military force, gave a sarcastic answer: "The Soviets are autonomous in their internal affairs. Therefore, the toilers of Turkestan should not turn to Petrograd asking it to dismiss the Soviet commissariat of Tashkent, but should disperse it themselves—if such forces are available." [37]

In December the Tashkent government suppressed an uprising organized there by Russian officers and the conservative Moslem underground,[38] then placed under its authority the Transcaspian region, and dispersed Turkomen military units. In January 1918 it disarmed some Cossack regiments retreating from Persia to the Urals and Siberia.[39] The sphere of influence of the Kokand government, meanwhile, did not grow, since the native Moslem population remained indifferent to the entire conflict. Even in the Ferghana oases the Kokand government had no active support.

The Reds' seizure of Orenburg on January 19, 1918 temporarily opened up communications with Moscow and broke General Dutov's blockade of Central Asia from the northwest, permitting Tashkent to be provided with arms and supplies.[40] Encouraged, the Tashkent rulers began to act. On January 31, the Fourth Regional Congress of Soviets in Tashkent passed a resolution to dissolve the Kokand government. Red Guardists, military detachments formed from Austro-Hungarian prisoners of war,[41] and local Armenian militia units were moved toward Kokand. Rumors that the Moslems of Kokand were slaughtering Russians and Armenians and had demolished the European quarter of the city served to inflame the spirit of the Soviet troops. The Kokand government was supported only by some police units and a mounted Kipchak militia. No other natives, either from the city itself or from other parts of the Ferghana oasis region, took part in the defense. After holding out for three days,[42] the government of autonomous Turkestan fell, on February 19, although the plundering of the city continued.[43] Thousands of inhabitants perished, and only the arrival of a railroad workers' battalion stopped the carnage.[44] The ancient and wealthy merchant city of Kokand was razed, and remained in ruins for many years. The Kokand government was routed, but out of its conflagration was born a native resistance movement. February 19 became the birthday of the Basmachi movement in Ferghana.[45]

With the fall of Kokand, the Tashkent Soviet of Peoples' Commissars gained Semirechie. In March 1918, Kolesov's army attacked Bukhara, expecting support from the Young Bukhariotes, but it was repulsed. April and May witnessed no major military encounters, but in June the Civil War convulsed Central Asia.

THE CIVIL WAR IN CENTRAL ASIA

During the one and a half years of the Civil War, which isolated Turkestan from Moscow for most of that time, the Tashkent Soviet of People's Commissars fought on three fronts. On July 1, 1918, the Soviet army abandoned Orenburg for the second time, under the pressure of Russian anti-Communist armies. Communications with European Russia were severed until September 13, 1919 by the Aktiubinsk front in northwestern Central Asia, extending along the Orenburg-Tashkent railroad.[46] Two weeks after the fall of Orenburg to the Whites, Russian railroad workers, supported by the nomadic Turkomens, initiated in Transcaspia the first anti-Soviet labor uprising in history. Here the struggle was especially prolonged, and this area was secured by the Reds only on February 6, 1920.[47] The third front was in Semirechie, where Cossacks fought Red partisans from July 1918 until March 1920.[48] On all these fronts the fighting was typical of desert warfare, shifting from one oasis to another. It adhered to the lines of communication—the Transcaspian and Orenburg railroads and the Siberian trunkline, which played the same role in Central Asia as the coastal railroad in the Libian desert during the 1941–1942 campaign of General Rommel. The Turkomens and Kazakhs participated only intermittently in the war[49] while the Uzbeks, with the exception of some Basmachi detachments in Ferghana, took no part whatsoever. The armies of both sides were composed primarily of Russians and, in the Soviet case, of "international" battalions, i.e., hired German and Austro-Hungarian prisoners of war.[50] The strength of the forces engaged was minimal: from two to ten thousand on each front.

The Civil War in Central Asia came to an end in the fall and winter of 1919–1920, after which time the struggle became one of passive opposition by the sedentary population, active resistance by the Basmachis, and internal political conflicts within the Communist Party. The anti-Soviet Moslem Basmachi guerrilla movement, which began in Ferghana in the summer of 1918, spread throughout Turkestan in 1921, while in 1919–1920 the Uzbek Jadids attempted to seize power in Turkestan by infiltrating the Communist Party.

CHAPTER XVI

The Jadids and the Communist Party

The rout of the Kokand autonomy by the Tashkent Soviet ostensibly should have eliminated the possibility of cooperation between representatives of the native Moslem population of Central Asia and the Bolsheviks. Soon after the events of February 1918, however, a group of Uzbeks appeared in Tashkent willing to establish contact with the Soviet of People's Commissars there, and this fact largely facilitated Soviet consolidation in Central Asia. These were the Young Bukhariote liberals seeking an ally in their struggle against the emir of Bukhara. In the promising early weeks of the February Revolution, the Young Bukhariotes followed the example of Petrograd revolutionaries in securing the introduction of a constitutional regime in Bukhara. Disturbed by events in Russia, the emir of Bukhara was forced to comply with the demands of the Young Bukhariotes,[1] and on March 17, 1917, he promulgated a manifesto in which he promised reforms and a constitution.[2] His former reactionary advisers were exiled, and it seemed that parliamentarianism and democracy had been born even in medieval Bukhara.

Unexpectedly, though, Bukhariote conservatives proved to be stauncher and more tenacious than their Russian counterparts. Early in April the reactionaries, led by the emir's adviser, Nizametdin Hoja —often called the "Pobedonostsev of Bukhara"—returned from exile and launched an antiliberal campaign.[3] This succeeded in swaying the population, whose mood changed, and new demonstrations began now to demand not a constitution but punishment of the "godless Jadids" and the "apostates of Mahomet's covenants." A wave of reaction overwhelmed the Young Bukhariotes.[4] The majority of them were arrested; others fled, while those who did not escape were tortured or executed by mobs and the emir's henchmen. Only the intercession of the Russian diplomatic agent in Bukhara and his threat of military intervention saved the Young Bukhariotes from extermination.

Not abandoning their hope for overthrowing the emir, however, after the October upheaval a group of Young Bukhariotes went to Kokand, seeking assistance from the Moslem congress there, and then contacted Tashkent.[5] The delegation was headed by Faizulla Hojaev, a member of one of Bukhara's wealthiest merchant families. In early March 1918, Hojaev persuaded the head of the Tashkent Soviet of People's Commissars, Kolesov, to send a military expedition against the emir of Bukhara. This expedition, known in the annals of the Civil War in Central Asia as "Kolesov's adventure," ended in failure. Kolesov and his troops, composed of Austro-Hungarian and German mercenaries, Red Guardists, and some Bukhariotes, barely managed to escape.[6] The surviving Young Bukhariotes left Bukhara in haste and spent the next two years in Samarkand and Tashkent as émigrés, supported by the Tashkent Bolsheviks.[7] They joined forces with the Jadids, among whom they formed a small but firm core advocating cooperation with Soviet authority. The Jadids also began to associate with the Communist Party and eventually, in the years 1919–1920, with Moscow's support, succeeded in winning considerable power within the the party itself.

MOSCOW INTERVENES IN TASHKENT

The unhappy Bukhara campaign, the pillaging of the native population by Red Guardists, and the "unsocialistic" manners of the Tashkent rulers began in spring 1918 to attract Moscow's attention to the situation in Turkestan. The Tashkent ruling group, still composed primarily of left Socialist Revolutionaries and Bolsheviks, was jeopardizing Soviet policy in Asia by its activities. In order to remedy the situation, in April 1918 Moscow sent a special commissar, a certain Kobozev, to Tashkent. A new, Fifth, Congress of Central Asian Soviets convoked by him proclaimed on April 30 the creation of a Turkestan Autonomous Republic, federated with the RSFSR. [8] The congress elected a new Turkestan Central Executive Committee (*TurkTsIK*) of thirty-six members, among whom ten were Moslems, mainly Jadids.[9] The ruling Tashkent group, however, continued to enjoy full freedom of action from Moscow for over a year, without collaborating with the native population.

Under Kobozev's supervision, the work of shaping the framework of the new Autonomous Republic, and of a native Communist organization, continued. On June 17–22 the First Regional Party Congress of RKP(b) assembled, laying the formal foundation of a Communist Party in Central Asia. The composition of this congress revealed the true nature and weakness of the Soviet regime in Turkestan. At the time of the congress, the party listed some 1,500 members in entire Central Asia on its rolls. Of these, 50 were delegates to the congress, but among them only five were Moslems. In the whole city of Tashkent, with its one-half million inhabitants, there were only 261 "European" and 50 Moslem Communists.[10]

Under pressure from Moscow, and guided by Kobozev, this congress passed several resolutions regarding cooperation with the local Moslem population. These required:

(1) Creation of Moslem sections attached to party organizations and to the Soviet of Deputies.

(2) Introduction of the "Moslem" tongue as the state language, on an equal footing with Russian.

(3) Publication of periodicals in the "Moslem" tongue.

(4) Introduction into the administration of experienced workers familiar with local conditions.

(5) Formation of "Moslem" military units.

(6) Publication of Communist literature in the native tongues.[11]

In its turn, the TurkTsIK on July 14 took the following decisions:

(1) Recognition of a "Moslem" language as the state language.

(2) Equalization of the local population's rights with those of Russians and other "Europeans."

(3) Immediate creation of Moslem dekkhan (peasant) and proletarian organizations.

But the Tashkent clique remained reluctant to cooperate with the native population, and the publication of these resolutions was delayed until August 23, one and a half months after the congress closed. For its part, the Tashkent Soviet did not initiate organization either of the local "national" organs or of a Commissariat for National Affairs until November. In July, however, TurkTsIK began publishing the Uzbek journal, *Ishtiraki Yun*, edited by the Tatar, Klevleev, who had come from Moscow with Kobozev, as well as an Uzbek edition of the local *Izvestiia*.

The Civil War, internal discord, the collection of levies and taxes from the local population (which frequently amounted to pillage), and the problem of preserving its own power continued to absorb the time and efforts of the Tashkent government. Lenin's central government, and especially Narkomnats under Stalin, did not relax its attention from Central Asia, being aware that Tashkent rulers were compromising Moscow's plans for an Asian revolution. Moscow's position regarding the half-Socialist Revolutionary, half-Bolshevik Tashkent group in TurkTsIK was a difficult one, in view of Central Asia's military isolation. During the Civil War it was dangerous to push them too far, which could provoke their defection, and consequently Stalin's communiqué to the Soviet deputies and party organizations in Turkestan of February 12, 1919 mentioned only cautiously the need "to attract the working masses of the nationalities in these borderland regions to the general task of building a socialistic state." [12] Soon after this dispatch, Kobozev, commissioned by Moscow to initiate a Communist movement among the local Moslems, reappeared in Tashkent.[13]

This time Kobozev's mission met with greater success. The ranks of the Tashkent veterans were considerably thinned by the mass execution of Soviet leaders during the anti-Communist *putsch* organized by Osipov—the Commissar of Defense in Tashkent—in January 1919.[14] Therefore, the resistance of the surviving group of socialist "conquistadores" toward Lenin's policy of nationalizing the local administration was considerably diminished. The Seventh Congress of Central Asian Soviets, which assembled in February 1919, witnessed a rise in interest in the Communist Party among the native intellectuals, particularly the Jadids. Nearly half the delegates to this congress were Moslems, whom Kobozev immediately integrated into a cohesive and active group.[15] Some days later Kobozev convoked a Second Regional Party Conference which, over the opposition of the remaining Tashkent ruling group, enacted a resolution setting up a Regional Bureau of Moslem Organizations of RKP(b). This bureau, which included such prominent leaders of the former Jadid nationalist movement as Tursun Hojaev, T. Ryskulov, and Nizametdin Hojaev, successfully recruited Moslems into the Communist Party and organized Moslem sections in the RKP(b), where they soon became a leading power.

On May 24–30, 1919 the First Conference of Moslem Communists in Central Asia met. This time Uzbek Communists were really given the opportunity of airing their political grievances, and, characteristic of relations within the Communist Party in 1919, party members spoke out in keeping with the traditions of the time—frankly and, if necessary, critically. Moslem delegates heatedly criticized the Tashkent Soviet of Commissars and TurkTsIK:

We are still obliged to tolerate an openly negligent attitude on the part of representatives of the former privileged classes toward the indigenous working masses. This attitude can be observed even among those who call themselves communists and who—acting like "bosses"—regard the Moslems as their subjects. . . . In the Ferghana region Soviet activity has changed from a struggle against banditry to encouragement of its growth and widespread persecution, not only of the Moslem inhabitants, but also of Moslem Communists.[16]

The Uzbek Communists succeeded at this conference in effecting the disbandment of the Armenian militia units which had participated in the razing of Kokand and which were particularly hated by the Moslems. They also enlisted support of the party and the administration for the local Moslem organizations. Further, the conference issued an appeal to the peoples of the East to support the revolution of "the oppressed toilers of India, Afghanistan, Persia, China, Bukhara, Asia Minor, and Eastern Asia . . . everyone, everyone, everyone!"[17] In this respect, native Central Asian Communists were following the path blazed by Vahitov, Sultangaliev, Validov, and other Moslem Communists, who regarded the revolution first of all as a means of liberating the East from the Western "oppression."

JADIDS COME TO POWER

The persistent efforts of Moscow and her envoy, Kobozev, to recruit more Moslems for the local party organization finally led to the mass infiltration of the Soviet apparatus by the Jadids, who had recently become converted to Communism. At the Third Regional Party Congress in Tashkent, which opened on June 1, 1919, of eleven seats in the Central Asian supreme party organ—the Regional Bureau—four were allocated to the Moslems. Of these, three were old hands of the Jadid movement—Ryskulov, N. Hojaev, and Aliev—while the fourth was a former Ottoman army officer, Effendiev. Three months later, at the Eighth Congress of Central Asian Soviets, this success was extended to the TurkTsIK. A Moslem majority was elected to this ruling Soviet administrative body in Central Asia. Moreover, the congress advised the new TurkTsIK to adhere to the principle of participation by the native population in the Soviet administration, recently proclaimed by the Eighth All-Russian Party Congress of RKP(b) and the First Congress of the Third International.[18] The Fifth Regional Party Conference (mid-January 1920) strengthened the Moslem or, more exactly, the Jadid grip over the Central Asian party apparatus, sending this time an absolute Moslem majority to the party Regional Bureau, whose secretary became the well-known Jadid leader, Tursun Hojaev.[19]

These profound changes in the Soviet Central Asian apparatus were not achieved without the resistance of the original Tashkent ruling clique, which still consisted of the surviving veterans of the October 1917 coup. Before the elections to the Regional Bureau by the party's Third Regional Congress, one of the leaders of this Tashkent clique, Gridnev, announced in the name of the Tashkent Soviet and the city's "12,000 proletarians" that the replacement of this Old Guard by the Moslems would lead to the dissolution of the congress by armed workers. The congress took no heed either of Gridnev's mythical "120,000 proletarians" or of his threats and refused to re-elect Gridnev himself, who soon disappeared, unnoticed, from the annals of the party history.

The Kobozev-Moslem faction at that time had full support from the Central Committee in Moscow, which demanded in a radiogram of July 12, 1919 that the native population be given proportional representation in the administrative organs, and indicated that candidates for positions in the soviets should be candidates of the Moslem workers—not necessarily Communists.[20] It was clear that the Central Committee, having recently come to an agreement with Validov's Bashkir followers and having won over several Kazakh Alash Orda leaders, had resolved to seek an agreement with the Central Asian Jadids as well. Although preoccupied with the southern and western fronts, Stalin did not lose sight of the revolution in the East, in which Central Asia was to play the main role.[21] Furthermore, Red armies moving eastward from European Russia were nearing Central Asia, and Tashkent's isolation was coming to an end. Moscow now could easily dispose of the Tashkent veterans without fear of betrayal.

If the Moscow Central Committee and Council of People's Commissars had had other observers in Tashkent besides Kobozev, they could have been forewarned that Kobozev had gone too far. Certainly he had succeeded in squeezing out the Tashkent veterans of the October coup from leadership in the Central Asian party and administration, since it was they who had compromised the party's policy in the East by their off-hand treatment of the Moslems. But now the "colonizers" were replaced by the far more dangerous Jadid Communists, who, once having the power in their hands, revealed their final aims. The same Fifth Regional Party Congress which gave the majority of seats in the Bureau to the Moslems, together with the Third Conference of Moslem Communists which convened at the same time, decided to proclaim Turkestan officially a *Turkic* Autonomous Republic. It also changed the name of the Turkestan organization of RKP(b) to the Turkic Communist Party.[22] The Moslem Communists did not stop at this. They decided to launch their own revolutionary Communist movement and to undertake the task of unifying all Russia's Turkic peoples into a single territorial and political unit. In this way they were obviously following the pattern of Tatar politicians in 1917, but this time the center of the Pan-Turkic movement in Russia was to be Tashkent instead of Kazan.

In a resolution passed by the Third Regional Moslem Conference, the ultimate goals of the Jadid Communists were set forth. Paragraph six of the resolution somewhat confusedly prescribed

in the interest of the international organization of workers and oppressed peoples, to infuse, through Communist propaganda, the idea of eliminating the inclination of the Turkic peoples to separate in name and substance into Tatars, Kirghiz, Bashkirs, Uzbeks, etc., and to form separate local republics. Instead, we should *unify* them for the purpose of consolidating and attracting other Turkic nationalities—even those that did not constitute a part of the RSFSR—*around a Turkic Soviet republic.* And, where this would be impossible, to unify the individual Turkic nationalities according to their territorial situation.[23]

In other, clearer, terms, the Uzbek Communists sought:

(1) To unify all the Turkic peoples of Russia around a Turkic Soviet Republic, i.e. the Republic of Turkestan.

(2) To draw other Turkic peoples, even those which did not constitute a part of Russia, into this process of political unification (apparently the Turks of Afghanistan, China, Persia, and Turkey).

(3) To consolidate into large territorial units such Turkic peoples of the RSFSR who for geographical reasons could not merge with the Soviet Republic of Turkestan—as, for instance, Tatars or Bashkirs.

This resolution, a veritable manifesto of Turkic national statehood

and Pan-Turkic political objectives, attempted to transform the
Central Asian section of the Communist Party into a nationalist
Turkic "Communist" Party and aimed at transferring its leadership
into the hands of the Jadid Communists. The central government in
Moscow, however, remained unaware that developments in Central
Asia had slipped out of its control, and that the Communist Party in
Turkestan had begun to move in a direction which corresponded
neither to the party's general line nor to the fundamental principles
of Leninism, but rather in accord with the aims of Turkic nationalists.

The Uzbek Jadids who now controlled the party and the administration in Tashkent were, without a doubt, true revolutionaries—
as indicated by their appeals to the peoples of the East to shake off
"the chains of colonialism, clericalism, and feudalism." But their
attachment to revolutionary slogans stemmed more from their two-
decades-long struggle against clericalism and from their aversion for
colonial imperialism than from a desire for social and economic
upheaval. The Jadids, who came either from the merchant class or
from the student milieu of Central Asian madrasas, had very little,
if any, connection with Moslem or Russian workers, and flatly re-
pudiated the theory of class struggle and dictatorship of the proletariat. In this respect they followed Ismail bey Gasprinsky, who, as
early as 1905, stated that the predominantly agricultural Moslem
society of Russia was not stratified into classes, and hence no class
struggle could develop within it. They were the first among the
Turkic nationalist Communists to propound this theory originally
developed by Gasprinsky which, in the 1920's, became the main issue
between them and Communist Party leaders.

The Jadids' belief in Turkic unity and their repudiation of class
struggle rapidly found practical expression in their educational politics
and recruitment of party members. In the new schools, which had
been opened by the Jadid Communist administrators of Central Asia,
national concerns were paramount and students were indoctrinated
not in Marxist theories but in the spirit of Turkic nationalism. Turkic
rather than proletarian unity was being seeded in the schools. The
Commissar of Education under the new Tashkent government was
not even an Uzbek, but the Ottoman Turkish artillery officer and
former prisoner of war, Effendiev. Not Moscow, but Istanbul and
Ankara, where Kemal Pasha had taken up a resistance against the
victorious Western powers, were attracting the sympathies and inter-

ests of the Jadid members of Turkestan's Communist Party organization. The Jadids' speeches did not deal with class struggle and international ideals, but with the future of their own country. As their
leading theoretician, Ryskulov, declared,

> Turkic nationalists must rectify a historical error, namely, that com-
> mitted [by the Communists] in relation to the peoples of Turkestan. . . .
> Turkic Communists are fighting not only for the interests of the factory
> and railroad proletariat [a reference to the two-year dictatorship of
> Tashkent's veteran clique] but also consider it their duty to secure the
> cultural and economic intrests of the peoples who live on the vast ex-
> panses of the thousand-mile-wide deserts and in the kishlaks, by going
> into their midst.[24]

Further, Ryskulov called upon the Kazakhs and Uzbeks to join the
ranks of the party and fill the army with volunteers. In this way, he
intended to strengthen Jadid influence in the Soviet apparatus and
army in Central Asia by filling them with his Turkic patriots.

TURKCOMMISSION AND THE JADIDS

On November 19, 1919, a special Turkestan Commission, (Turk-
Commission), appointed by the Soviet government and the party's
Central Committee, arrived in Tashkent. Its members, inexperienced
in Central Asian affairs, failed initially to understand the true nature
of the Jadids' politics. Consisting of Sh. Z. Eliava, Ya. Z. Rudzutak,
M. V. Frunze, F. Goloshchokov, and V. V. Kuibyshev, this commission came to Central Asia with the purpose of reorganizing the
administration and the party in accordance with the system and
practices of Moscow. The commission immediately purged the Central Asian party apparatus and administration of its remaining "Tashkent veterans," banishing several of them from Central Asia.[25] The
Fifth Regional Party Congress held in January 1920, which resulted
in the Turkic Communists' seizure of control in TurkTsIK, in the
regional administration, and in the party apparatus, did not originally
elicit any reaction from the Muscovite commission.

In the spring of 1920 TurkCommission began to realize, however,
that by having eliminated the last of the Tashkent veterans, it had
transferred power from the hands of socialist adventurers to the
Turkic nationalists.[26] Frunze, as commander of the Red Army in
Turkestan, the only force in the region still entirely controlled by
the Soviet government, was particularly disturbed by the situation

which had evolved and realized its military implications. His forces were very modest and consisted of no more than sixteen thousand men—eleven thousand infantrymen and five thousand cavalry. Most of these troops were located on the outskirts of Central Asia and were engaged in liquidating the remaining White troops in Transcaspia and Semirechie, in fighting the Basmachis in Ferghana, or in covering Tashkent and other urban centers.[27] In notes written at the time, Frunze revealed an understanding of the situation and pointed to the Uzbek Communists' intention to keep "a monopoly of power in the hands of a small group of Moslem party leaders . . . to place only Moslems in the administration," and to oppose "the policy of the Turkestan Commission." He was well aware of their desire "to attain the maximum of independence . . . [which was] clearly revealed in the resolutions of the party conference which formed the Turkic Republic and the Turkic Communist Party." [28]

The Jadid Communists' persistent struggle to substitute a Turkic national plank in Turkestan for the general line of the Central Committee was re-enforced by the support of Moslem Communists in the other Soviet republics. Quite probably they had come to an agreement to cooperate with the Turkic leaders in the Volga-Ural region and in the Kazakh steppe. At any rate, after the Uzbek Jadids' seizure of the party and TurkTsIK, they approached a complete break with TurkCommission, which began to oppose the Jadids' actions. They grew bolder, encouraged by events in other Moslem regions, such as the Alash Ordists' fight for Kazakh autonomy, the success of Tatar Communists in creating an autonomous Tatary, and the unavenged Bashkir *putsch* of January 1920. They were informed of Validov's proposal to the all-Russian Central Committee to form a Kazakh-Bashkir federation, and had in mind plans of their own for an even more ambitious southeastern Turkic union, or republic, as projected at the Third Moslem Communist Conference in Tashkent.

The time for the achievement of these goals appeared favorable. Since May Validov had been in Moscow pleading for the restoration of Bashkir autonomy, which had been curtailed by the Soviets' May 1920 decree. At the Uzbeks' request, Validov attempted to secure a change in the membership of TurkCommission and gain the appointment to it of an equal number of Turkic and non-Turkic Communists. Lenin, with whom Validov and the Turkestan delegation were negotiating, avoided giving a definite answer for weeks. In rough drafts of Lenin's theses for the Second Congress of the Third International, held June 19, his negotiations with these Moslem Communists are reflected. He listed the problems of Bashkiria, Kazakhstan, and Turkestan, mentioning the danger of Pan-Islamism. At the congress itself, however, he refrained from discussing the Turkic Communists' activities and expressed the firm conviction that "the germ of the Soviet movement has been scattered throughout the entire east, over all Asia, among all colonial peoples." [29] To gain time, Lenin referred Validov to Stalin (see Chapter XIII), who, concerned with military operations in the Ukraine, also gave no clear answer. Only toward the end of June, when the Poles had withdrawn from most of the Ukraine, did Validov and the Turkestanis receive a reply.

The Central Committee refused the appointment of any Moslems to TurkCommission, and selected instead the following new members: L. Kaganovich, G. Safarov, G. Sokolnikov-Brilliant, and the notorious Latvian Chekist, Ya. Peters. These men were to act as neutral arbiters, since none of them were either Moslem or Russian. The commission's new composition indicated that henceforth Jadid Communists could expect no indulgence. Peters, with the acuteness characteristic of an experienced Chekist, immediately came to the conclusion that the aims of the Uzbek Communists were (1) to seize control of the Soviet apparatus, (2) to transform educational institutions into centers for nationalist propaganda, and (3) to support the Basmachis.[30] Further, his informers reported that the Jadid Communists had formed a clandestine organization, *Ittihad-ve-Tarakki* (Unity and Progress), which counted among its members the leaders of other Turkic Communist groups in Russia as well as the Central Asian groups.

THE BUKHARA CAMPAIGN

The new TurkCommission and the Red Army, under Frunze, gained in August a victory which radically altered the balance of power in Central Asia and further consolidated Soviet strength locally. This was the liquidation of the emir's regime in Bukhara.[31] The moment chosen for launching the Bukhara campaign was opportune. Triumphs on the western front, where Budenny's and Tukhachevsky's armies were advancing on Warsaw, presaged the end of the Civil War. The Young Bukhariotes, encouraged by the Jadids' rise to power in Tashkent, strove to seize control in Bukhara. Pressed by

TurkCommission and by the Uzbek Communists, they formed a bloc with the Communist Party of Bukhara, with which they subsequently merged. The advance of Red troops on the khanate began August 29, and after an intensive two-day battle the city was in their hands.[32] The emir escaped into the mountains of eastern Bukhara, where he attempted to reorganize his support.

Entering the capital in the path of the Red troops, the Young Bukhariotes set about organizing a government. They proclaimed a People's Republic of Bukhara, but it had little in common with communistic or socialistic rule. Most of the nazarats, or ministries, fell into the hands of two wealthy merchant families, the Maksumovs and the Hojaevs, who had championed Bukhara's liberal movement as early as the time of Donish[33] (see Chapter VI). The Young Bukhariotes supported their program by the authority of the Koran and the Shariat, and kept the populace calm with the promise "to fight with all our strength against the oppression of European socialism," [34] by which they meant European non-Communist colonial forces. Their program for education likewise had not a Communist but a definite Pan-Turkic bias: the native tongue was taught only in lower schools, while the "national Turkic literary language"—Ottoman Turkish— was introduced at the secondary level. The revolutionary points of their program consisted of promises to combat the excesses of clericalism, to eliminate from Asia the "influence of the trade and industry of European manufacturers and factory owners," to improve the administration, and to confiscate the lands of the emir and the aristocracy. Nothing was said either about the dictatorship of the proletariat or the liquidation of private property. The Young Bukhariotes' entire program was characterized more by nationalist slogans than by Communist doctrine.[35]

The political regime introduced in Bukhara, and at about the same time in Khiva, combined the bourgeois structure of contemporary Middle Eastern society with the Communist system of control.[36] It was the first timid experiment with a "People's Democracy," which was subsequently introduced in Mongolia in 1921 and in Central Europe in 1945. The Communists regarded it as a transitional stage, leading to the "normal" Soviet system outlined by Lenin. In any case, the People's Republic of Bukhara eliminated the hostile non-Communist political enclave in Central Asia and precluded utilization of the khanate as a springboard for foreign intervention.[37] Neither the

Young Bukhariotes nor the Bolsheviks could foresee that in less than a year a general Basmachi uprising would transform the young People's Republic into a major threat to Soviet authority in Central Asia.

THE BAKU CONGRESS OF PEOPLES OF THE EAST

The conquest of Bukhara had occurred on the eve of the First Congress of the Peoples of the East, one of the most impressive manifestations of the Bolsheviks' revolutionary forces in Asia. It was attended not only by delegations from all the Turkic and other eastern groups of Russia, but also by representatives from most of the free states and colonies of Asia. Meeting September 1–9, 1920, in Baku, this congress was organized by the leaders of the Third International, G. Zinoviev and Karl Radek. The Bukhara campaign and the congress both contributed greatly to Soviet prestige in the East, the two events appearing as a harbinger of the future rebellion of Asia against European colonialism and the native feudal society. Narbutabekov, one of the Jadid Communist leaders, announced:

We, representatives of the revolutionaries of Turkestan, are not afraid of any Ulema, of any black hundreds of Mullahs. We were the first to raise our banner against them, and we shall not lower it until the end. Either we shall perish or we shall triumph.[38]

Soviet leaders, however, did not escape Narbutabekov's criticism:

The masses of Turkestan have to fight on two fronts. On one hand—in their own midst, with the black Mullahs, and on the other, with the narrow nationalistic bias of local Europeans. Neither Comrade Zinoviev, nor Comrade Trotsky, nor even Comrade Lenin knows the true state of affairs in Turkestan. . . . We demand a genuine realization of the principles of liberty, equality, and fraternity in life, not just on paper.[39]

TAMING OF THE JADIDS

Narbutabekov was deeply mistaken when he suggested that Zinoviev, Trotsky, and Lenin were unaware of the real state of affairs in Turkestan. The Soviet government and the Communist leadership were well informed about the happenings, and it was decided at this time to bring the situation under control. Together with their representatives in TurkCommission—Kaganovich, Safarov, Sokolnikov, and Peters—Lenin and Trotsky drew the appropriate conclusions from Narbutabekov's speech and the Jadids' tactics. The Jadids themselves, rather than the "European colonizers," were soon removed from their leading posts in the Central Asian administration and party. The Jadids had largely completed the task of popularizing Communism and assisting in the growth of revolutionary forces in the East, and their further strengthening would be dangerous. Their speeches in Baku were certainly viewed by Lenin and Trotsky as not only superfluous, but even provocative. Moreover, they were recruiting too many unreliable new party members from among Uzbek nationalists: the party organization itself in Turkestan was becoming more a tool of Turkic nationalism than of international Communism.

Even before the conquest of Bukhara and the Baku congress, shortly after the arrival of the new TurkCommission in Tashkent on June 29, the Central Committee in Moscow had passed a resolution demanding the removal of the last vestiges of colonialism and the "patriarchal feudal heritage" in Turkestan. The actions of the Tashkent October veterans were blamed, astonishingly enough, on "the autocratic, imperialist policy of the tsarist regime," and it was prescribed (1) to banish all the "colonizers," "egotists," and former Russian "bourgeoisie" from Central Asia, (2) to equalize food rationing and land distribution between the native population and the Russian population, and (3) to rout the kulaks' organizations.[40]

This resolution, calling for the liquidation of the Russian "bourgeoisie" and "colonizers" in Central Asia, parried the Jadids' thrust at Soviet centralism. TurkCommission proceeded to "ease" this centralism by conducting the mass arrest and execution of Russian anti-Communists in Central Asia, in a struggle against "Great Russian chauvinism." Presumably, this would soothe the nationalist feelings of native politicians.

Following the liquidation of the "last remnants of Russian imperialism and the bourgeoisie" came the elimination from the Central Asian party apparatus of supporters of "the patriarchal feudal heritage," those Uzbek Communists, mainly Jadids, who refused to accept the theses of proletarian dictatorship and class struggle and who preached instead a Turkic nationalist ideology. In late September, backed by Frunze's army, the commission initiated conferences with TurkTsIK. "The result of these consultations was the removal of all eminent participants in Ryskulov's movement [of the Jadids]," wrote G. Safarov.[41] The Regional Bureau, consisting predominantly of Ryskulov's followers, was dissolved. The new Bureau was not elected by the local party congress, but was appointed by Moscow at the recommendation of TurkCommission. Its new membership included many Uzbeks and Kazakhs, who formed the majority; these men were not intellectuals, as were the Jadids, but such "worker-internationalists" as Tiuriakulov, Atabaev, Sultan Hojaev, Rakhimbaev, and others who adhered obediently to the instructions of the center. TurkTsIK, in turn, eliminated most of its Jadids and elected Rakhimbaev as chairman.

Now, after almost three years of relative liberty, the regional organization of the Communist Party in Turkestan was finally subjected to the undisputed control of Moscow, and became "international" rather than "colonialist" or "Turkic" in spirit. Although the Jadids lost their commanding position in the party and in the government, their fate in the 1920's was not as tragic as that of many Russian anti-Communists. They were withdrawn from leadership but allowed to remain in the party, and most of them, such as Ryskulov, even reappeared in the administrative apparatus, although now supervised by Moscow .

The Ninth Congress of the Soviets of Turkestan and the Fifth Regional Party Congress, which assembled in late September 1920, demonstrated unrestricted cooperation with the center. Tiuriakulov, the main speaker at the party congress, representing "Uzbek workers," insisted on the need to support Moscow's policy line. Another "Uzbek worker," Hakimov, pointed out the inevitability of class struggle in Central Asia. The dekkhans were organized in the Union of Koschi (Union of Poor Peasants) for the purpose of combating the wealthy village bais and "exploiters." TurkCommission and the central government were satisfied with the statement that "everything has been done for the liquidation of old colonizers' and nationalists' groups and for the manifestation of a firm international policy line." [42]

SOVIET AUTONOMY

The further remodeling of the party apparatus and administration in Turkestan continued during the winter of 1920–1921. A number of minor concessions were made to the native population in education and religious life: Friday replaced Sunday as a holiday;[43] the Uzbek language was introduced into the administration and the party, as well as into the postal and telegraph services;[44] and many natives were drawn into the governmental apparatus, although the main organs of the regional administration continued to be strictly controlled by Moscow. On April 11, 1921, the All-Russian Central Executive Committee promulgated a new constitution for the Turkestan Republic, making it an Autonomous Soviet Socialist Republic within the RSFSR. Yet Bukhara and Khiva remained outside the boundaries of the republic until 1924. The 1921 constitution excluded foreign relations, armed forces, and foreign trade from the jurisdiction of the Soviet of People's Commissars in Tashkent, while the commissariats of finance, post and telegraph, and the railroads were subordinated to the corresponding People's Commissariats of the RSFSR. The remaining commissariats were placed under the control of the Central Executive Committee of the Turkestan ASSR.[45]

For the purpose of "maintaining ties with the central administration," a Provisional Commission, including I. Rudzutak and M. Tomsky, was created for regulating the affairs of Turkestan. Its functions were (1) the direction of affairs pertaining to the exclusive control of the central government; (2) adjustment of legislation in Tashkent to that of Moscow; and (3) supervision of the execution of directives elaborated by the central government.[46]

In 1924 the former administrative boundaries between the Russian provinces of Turkestan and the former khanates of Khiva and Bukhara were erased. Four new republics, built strictly on the national principle, were created: Uzbekistan, Kirghizia, Turkmenistan, and Tajikistan. Two of them, Turkmenistan and Uzbekistan, immediately received the status of Union Republic (full-fledged member of the Soviet Union). Tajikistan remained an Autonomous Republic within the Uzbek SSR until 1929, when it too became a Union SSR. Kirghizia stayed under Uzbek tutelage until 1936, when it also was promoted to the rank of Union SSR. This new division was a heavy blow to the Jadids' ambition of unifying Central Asia into one Turkic state. Its Turkic population was now split into three national bodies, each of whose local tongue was promoted to a national language. Of even greater importance for the future of Central Asia was the creation of Tajikistan as a non-Turkic, Iranian-speaking republic. This development put an end to the further Turkization of the land. Thus, the future of Central Asia was clearly determined for many years to come.[47]

CHAPTER XVII

Two Years of National Azerbaijan

The national movements among the various peoples of Russia's "Turkic belt"—stretching from the Volga to the Pamirs and including the Tatars, Bashkirs, Kazakhs, and Central Asian Turks—were closely interwoven because of these peoples' geographic proximity to each other. Located in the southeastern part of the former Russian Empire, all these Turkic peoples were involved in the same process of Civil War between the Soviet and the anti-Communist armies of eastern Russia and Siberia. These factors led to similar and simultaneous developments among them, such as internal conflicts, the first and second Soviet occupations, collaboration with Komuch, and efforts to extend their autonomies in 1920.

Very different was the history during the revolutionary period of the Turkic peoples of Russia located outside this Turkic belt, such as the Crimean Tatars and Azerbaijanis, who had better opportunities to organize their national-political life. In the Crimea the Tatars, although they only numbered some 170–180,000, less than a third of the Crimean population, on two instances demonstrated their desire to organize their own statehood: before the first Soviet conquest of the peninsula in January 1918, and during the subsequent German occupation in April–November. Their leader, Jafer Seydamet, won the support of the German high command and organized a Crimean Tatar government under General S. Sulkiewicz. When the Germans retreated from the Ukraine and from the Crimea, this government collapsed and was replaced by a new one representing the non-Moslem peoples of the Crimean peninsula. In October 1921, however, the Soviet government resurrected the Crimean Tatar Republic, and Tatar became the main language in the administration and in education even for the majority of the non-Turkic inhabitants.[1]

By far more important politically were the events in Transcaucasia, where, isolated by the Caucasian range and protected by the presence of the White Russian armies in the northern Caucasus, national regimes were able to persist from spring 1918 to May 1920. In 1917 the nearness of military operations on the Turkish front, which brought the Caucasians into daily contact with the war, and reminiscences of the massacres and revolutionary excesses of 1905–1907 acted as dampers on the passions of the local population. On March 22 the Provisional Government replaced the Grand Duke Nikolai Nikolaievich, who governed the Caucasus as viceroy, with a four-member Special Transcaucasian Committee (*Osoby Zakavkazskii Komitet*, or *Ozakom*), consisting of representatives of the four major national groups of Transcaucasia. Despite its democratic and multinational composition, however, Ozakom was not endowed with great authority, and the administration of Transcaucasia throughout 1917 was conducted predominantly by local self-governments and municipal administrations.

As might be expected, the main political role among the Azerbaijani population was played by Musavat, which was the strongest Moslem political party in Transcaucasia despite the fact that it had existed only clandestinely since its formation in 1912. From March 1917 on, Musavat to a great extent dominated the political representation of the Azerbaijani population. Its Turkic national feelings abated somewhat during the war, and despite their evident sympathy for Ottoman Turkey, Musavat's leaders preached in 1917 close federative ties with Russia. At the Transcaucasian Moslem congress of April 19–20, Musavat, led by Resul Zadeh, proposed a program for the federative reorganization of Russia, which was officially accepted in May by the First All-Russian Moslem Congress in Moscow. According to this plan, Azerbaijan and the other Turkic territories of Russia were to constitute autonomous units of an "indivisible democratic and republican Russia," organized "in accordance with national-territorial-federative principles." The over-all governmental system was supposed to be linked by "defense, the monetary system, and customs organization." [2] At this conference Musavat advised educational reforms in the Azerbaijani provinces: the Azerbaijani tongue was to be introduced in local lower schools, while the "common Turkic literary language"—Ottoman Turkish—was to be added to the curriculum of secondary and higher schools along with Russian, which was already compulsory. [3] Another resolution called for the support of the policies of the Provisional Government and urged continuance of the war against the Central Powers and Turkey. [4]

Azerbaijani Social Democrats, whom Stalin had organized in Hemmet in 1904 (see Chapter V), and other local socialist groups were skeptical even toward Musavat's modern program for autonomy, which socialists rejected both for its ideological nationalist basis and its organizational principles.[5] Nevertheless, Musavat and the left wing of the Social Democrats, represented by Hemmet and the Bolsheviks —who did not establish their own independent organization in Transcaucasia until summer 1917—were more conciliatory toward each other, for personal and tactical reasons, than toward any other Transcaucasian parties. In March–June 1917 they were the only political organizations in Russia to oppose continuation of the war (although Musavat did not proclaim this openly). While the Bolsheviks regarded the war as an imperialistic collusion aimed at diverting the proletariat's attention from its revolutionary aims, Musavat was just as eager for a cessation of hostilities in view of its pro-Turkish sympathies.[6] The friendly relations between the Bolsheviks and some Musavat politicians also reflected the ties which had been cemented during their cooperation in Hemmet and other Social Democratic organizations in 1904–1907.

In the beginning of April 1917, shortly before the Transcaucasian Moslem congress convened, conservative western Azerbaijanis—mainly the local aristocracy, the so-called *aghalar* (khans, beks, sultans), and clergy—set up in Ganja a nationalist Turkic Federalist Party and elected a rich landowner, N. B. Usubbekov (Yusuf-Beyli) as its chairman.[7] This party held its first "all-Azerbaijani" congress in May and initiated a successful campaign among the Turks of Transcaucasia. More moderate than Musavat, which switched at that time to the left, the new party opposed the nationalization of the aghalar landholdings, was strictly pro-Islamic, and won considerable support among the rural population, where the feudal relationships and loyalties were still adhered to. This party also supported local autonomy and federative ties with Russia and was a serious rival to the more radical and urban Musavat, whose leaders were not always able to find a response among the traditional Moslem peasantry. Consequently, Resul Zadeh decided to come to terms with the Federalists, and at a conference of the two parties, held on June 20, a merger was concluded. M. E. Resul Zadeh, A. M. Topchibashev, M. H. Gajinsky, and N. B. Usubbekov became the leaders of the new united party, which took the name Federalist Turkic Party—Musavat, but was still called colloquially "Musavat." This party elaborated a hybrid plank in which the socialistic tendencies of Musavat—including the demand for a shorter labor day, protection of labor, and agrarian reform—were combined with the more conservative ideology of the Federalists. Formation of an autonomous Azerbaijan dominated by the Turkic population was actually the only paragraph of the program accepted unanimously by both factions of the new party. In October 1917, Resul Zadeh was elected chairman and a general shift of Musavat toward the left became more pronounced.[8]

Real unity between the conservative Federalists and the liberal Musavatists, however, was never actually achieved. The aristocratic "Federalists" from the Ganja province continued to dominate political life in the countryside, while in Baku Resul Zadeh's original urban Musavat group was more inclined to cooperate with socialists and, in some instances, even with Bolsheviks than with conservative Moslems —represented by the rightist Ittihad Party.

AZERBAIJANI INDEPENDENCE

One important feature of Transcaucasian political life characterized its history during the years 1917–1920. This was the almost monopolistic position occupied among Transcaucasia's three main national groups—Armenians, Georgians, and Azerbaijanis—by each of their national parties. In Armenia the revolutionary socialist party, *Dashnaktsutiun,* close in its program to the Russian Socialist Revolutionaries but more nationalistic, entirely dominated the political scene. In Georgia the native Mensheviks occupied a position similar to that of the Dashnaks in Armenia. So, for instance, in the elections to the All-Russian Constituent Assembly in November 1917, the Dashnaks polled 419,887 votes, almost the entire Armenian vote in Transcaucasia; the Mensheviks of Transcaucasia received 660,216, over 80 per cent of the Georgian vote.[9]

Musavat's position in Azerbaijan was not as strong as that of the Dashnaks in Armenia or the Mensheviks in Georgia, but it was still the strongest single Moslem party. In the same elections, Musavatists won 63 per cent of Transcaucasia's Moslem vote—405,917 as against 228,889 received by their Moslem clerical or socialist competitors.[10] This apparent strength, however, did not accurately reflect the situation in Azerbaijan itself. Many of Musavat's supporters were Ottoman Turks from the Kars and Erivan provinces, or Moslemized

Georgians (the Ajars and Inghilois) from the Batum and Zakataly districts, all situated outside the boundaries of Azerbaijan. In the Baku and Ganja provinces of Azerbaijan, Moslem forces were much more splintered, while international Baku gave the majority of its votes to Armenian, Russian, or nonnational Communist and socialist tickets. This relative weakness of Musavat in Azerbaijan became evident in the fall of 1918, when Musavat was able to send to the Azerbaijani parliament only 38 deputies out of 120.[11] Hence, during the period of Azerbaijan's existence as an independent state, Musavat was much less solidly established than its Georgian and Armenian counterparts, and was permanently obliged to seek the support or collaboration of other parties, mainly of socialists and more conservative national democrats. Its nonexclusive position in Azerbaijan, however, did not prevent it from exercising considerable influence locally.

Compared with these popular Transcaucasian parties, the Bolsheviks were weak. Their tickets won only 85,960 of the total 1,996,263 votes cast in Transcaucasian elections to the Constituent Assembly.[12] Even in Baku they did not muster substantial support, and the city in 1917 continued to be dominated by a coalition of various socialist parties, including the Bolsheviks themselves.

After the October Revolution, the three main nationalities of Transcaucasia—Armenians, Georgians, and Azerbaijanis—refused to recognize the Soviet regime. Protected by the Caucasian Mountains and exploiting the initial weakness of the Bolsheviks, they succeeded in organizing a regional Transcaucasian government. Unwilling to secede from Russia,[13] this regional government was for a couple of months a local version of the defunct Provisional Government. It was built, however, not on the basis of Russian parties, but on local national-political organizations. After five months of existence, this Transcaucasian provisorium was compelled by the German and Ottoman Turkish high command to relinquish its theoretical ties with a nonexistent democratic Russia and to proclaim its independence. This triple-national republic existed for one month and a day; exposed to further external pressures and internal tensions, it disintegrated into Georgia, Azerbaijan, and Armenia. On May 26, 1918, there was announced the creation of the Georgian Republic, and, on May 28, of independent Azerbaijan. Some days later the Armenian Republic was born. The Azerbaijanis' proclamation of independence and the break with the Soviet government were due not only to the growth of national feeling and the simultaneous pressure of Ottoman generals, but also to sharp conflict with the Communists over the fate of the city of Baku. For many months after the Bolshevik revolution, Musavat leaders, a substantial number of whom still recollected the days of their cooperation with Stalin and other Bolshevik leaders in Hemmet, and who therefore remained to a considerable degree under the spell of the first Soviet manifestoes on the national program, hesitated to sever their relations with the Muscovite and Baku Communists. Only the Bolshevik upheaval in Baku which occurred on March 31, 1918, and the ensuing slaughter of the Moslem population by Armenian Dashnak military formations, finally put an end to Musavat's indecision. From April on, the Azerbaijani leaders looked entirely to Turkey.[14]

The Azerbaijanis succeeded in retaking Baku only with the assistance of Ottoman Turkish troops. The young republic lacked both arms and trained officers, and its own armed force did not come into being as a well-organized and disciplined body until the end of Azerbaijani independence. Therefore, the Moslem population enthusiastically greeted the Turkish army, in which it saw a protector against the Baku Soviet and an ally in the fight against the Armenians. Musavat's leaders, moreover, hoped that the day of their unification with Turkey had finally arrived. This hope found unequivocal expression in the speech of Khan Khoisky, Azerbaijani Prime Minister, with which he greeted the Ottoman forces:

Azerbaijan has finally attained its goal, and the century-old ideal of all Turkic peoples—unification under the banner of the Sultan—has been realized. The Tatars of the Volga, the Sarts of Transcaspia, the Uzbeks, Kirghiz, and the Khiva and Bukhara populations of Central Asia hopefully await the arrival of the Turkish army of liberation.

Khan Khoisky continued that "the total life of Azerbaijanis must be in full agreement with the broad world policy of the Ottoman Empire," and he promised that his government, as before, would continue "to carry out in life the idea of complete harmony of its plans and political actions with the political trends of the Ottoman Empire." [15] This speech was greeted by both Azerbaijanis and Turks with the cry, "Long live the Turkish army, long live the unification of all Turkic peoples!" No less categorical in his expression of Pan-Turkic sentiments was Topchibashev, President of the Azerbaijani Republic, in a statement to the Sultan:

With divine grace, I have managed to attain my goal: to see the Caliph of all Moslems and the Padishah of all Turks. Your Majesty! Some time ago you received the delegation of the small Turkic state, Azerbaijan, and you deigned to say, "The Azerbaijanis are my favorite children." We Azerbaijanis remember this honor . . . and shall live by the grace of the Caliph of all Moslems, the Padishah of Ottoman Turks, our great brother.[16]

Resul Zadeh and other members of the Azerbaijani delegation in Constantinople on September 6, 1918, also expressed in similar terms their conviction to prosper under the benevolent aegis of the Sultan-Caliph.[17]

These panegyrics, of course, were filled with the flowery formulas typical of Eastern stylistics, but nevertheless the character of Turkish-Azerbaijani relations bears witness to the fact that Musavat's leaders actually hoped to create, as the result of a German-Turkish victory, a state or federation directed by Turkey which would unify all the Turkic peoples. The Turkish-Azerbaijani military and political alliance was regarded as the first step toward attainment of this ultimate goal. This is further supported by the subsequent actions of the Turkish army, which, after occupying Baku, proceeded to enter Daghestan, revealing the intention to bring under its control other Russian territories populated by Moslems.

With the Allies' victory over the Central Powers, however, the situation in the Near East changed. The Turkish army halted its advance and on November 10, at the demand of the British staff, the Turks withdrew their troops from Baku and from all of Transcaucasia, after only two months of occupation. The short experience had indicated, however, that Turkish and Azerbaijani interests were not necessarily at one. While Musavat and the Azerbaijani government regarded the Turks as an "older brother," an ally and protector, they wanted to resolve their internal problems independently. But the Turks apparently regarded Azerbaijan merely as a new Ottoman province, which, although it had a provisional self-administration, was eventually to merge with Turkey. Khan Khoisky, who had welcomed the Turkish occupation in June and July 1918, complained to Nuri Pasha in the fall of the same year that "cases of meddling by military representatives of the Ottoman Empire in the internal affairs of Azerbaijan, and even of completely ignoring the Azerbaijani government, are becoming more and more frequent." [18] As a matter of fact, the Ottoman command forced Khan Khoisky to dismiss his socialist colleagues in the government, and disbanded the Azerbaijanis' trade unions and various socialist organizations. It is more than probable that if Turkey had emerged victorious from World War I, the independence of Azerbaijan would have ceased, and this young Turkic republic would have been absorbed by its more powerful neighbor as the first step in the initial phase of Turkish expansion outlined by Zia Gek Alp (see Chapter VIII). Perhaps E. H. Carr is too severe in calling the Musavat government of 1918 a "puppet of the Turkish military command," [19] but there is no doubt that Khan Khoisky's administration was significantly dominated by Ottoman generals.

On the same day that Turkish troops left Baku, the city was occupied by British detachments. The Azerbaijani government began to fear retaliatory measures from the Allies for its friendship with the Turks. In the speech of welcome delivered by Ziatkhanov, the new Minister of Foreign Affairs, to General Thompson, Ziatkhanov sought to convince the British of the Azerbaijanis' loyalty and called upon the magnanimity of the Allies, as Khoisky had done four months earlier in his welcome speech to Nuri Pasha: "A new and luminous era of solidarity, based upon common peaceful work, is opening for all disunited, bleeding, and martyred humanity. . . . Our people is full of . . . hope that its elder brothers, the peoples of Europe . . . will not refuse, in the name of the high and sacred ideal, to admit it into their family." [20] This time, oriental stylistics were skillfully replaced by Western democratic slogans in the speeches of Musavat's leaders.

TERRITORIAL CLAIMS AND INTERNAL POLICIES

Preoccupied with its foreign policy and day-by-day internal tensions, the Musavat government had little time to carry through any substantial reforms. Owing to the frequent changes in Baku's regime and to the occupations, it was unable to command sufficient authority to be regarded by the world at large, as well as by the Azerbaijani population itself, as more than just a provisional regime of expediency. Boundary quarrels led to steady hostilities with Armenia, Georgia, the White volunteer army, and even Persia. Despite its Pan-Turkic ideology, the government preached its own brand of Pan-Islamic expansionism and sought to annex various non-Turkic Moslems of bordering territories. As envisioned by Musavat's delegation to the peace conference in Paris, the boundaries of "Great Azerbaijan" were to include, besides the Baku and Ganja provinces, the Moslem population of Daghestan, the northern Caucasus, the Georgian-speaking Moslem Inghilois of Zakataly, the Turkish inhabitants of the Erivan and Kars provinces, and even the Georgian-speaking Moslem Ajars of the southeast shore of the Black Sea, who were isolated from Azerbaijani proper by Georgia and Armenia. Further, the Musavat government demanded the annexation of the Karabakh and Zangezur districts of Armenia, and even initiated their conquest.[21] These claims resulted inevitably in a sharpening of relations between Azerbaijan and its neighbors, and required so much attention from the inexperienced Azerbaijani rulers that they had no time for internal affairs.

Within the republic, relations remained critical with its two main minorities, the Armenians and the Russians, who formed a third of the population. Fundamental economic and agrarian problems also remained unsolved. In early 1918, before the dissolution of the Transcaucasian Republic, the Diet had passed a law expropriating the large-scale landholdings of the nobility. This enactment was of particular importance for western Azerbaijan, where the aghalar of the Ganja province owned over one quarter of all the land: 1,120,000 desiatins as against 2,800,000 held by the peasants. After the formation of the independent Azerbaijani government, this law was checked by a new decree put through by Musavat's right wing, the former Federalists, composed of Ganja's aristocratic landowners. The new government's conservative agrarian policies resulted in peasant disturbances, which in 1918 were frequently suppressed with the help of the Ottoman military.[22] In October 1919, half a year before the dawn of Azerbaijani independence, Musavat's left wing, supported by the socialists and some other leftist groups, made an attempt to restore the original agrarian legislation, but they could not overcome the opposition of the party's rightist faction.

Difficulties in the export of oil, Azerbaijan's main resource, led to an economic crisis. The wages of oil workers were low, and labor expressed its dissatisfaction in numerous strikes, which were widely exploited by Communist propaganda.

In one field, the short-lived Azerbaijani government was more successful. This was the Turkization of the educational network. Azerbaijani or Ottoman Turkish replaced Russian in all governmental schools, and several new Turkic secondary schools and a university were opened. The national press also flourished.

After the departure of Turkish troops in the winter of 1918–1919, and to appease British apprehension at Musavat's authoritarian method of government, an Azerbaijani parliament was convened. It played only a limited role, however, since power remained in the hands of Musavat politicians, oil men, and the Ganja landlords. Firuz Kazemzadeh accurately compares this ineffective coalition of conflicting heterogenous elements with the swan, the crayfish, and the pike of A. I. Krylov's fable.[23] Despite administrative pressure exercised during the elections, Musavat did not command a majority in the new parliament. Of one hundred twenty seats, Musavat won thirty-eight; the national democrats, led by Khan Khoisky, sent seven deputies; and the government's Moslem socialist allies, twelve. *Ehrar*, a progressive Sunnite group from the northwestern part of Azerbaijan, sent seven deputies. The parliament's extreme right wing was composed of thirteen delegates from Ittihad (conservative clerics), the sworn enemies of Musavat; the minorities were represented by twenty-one Armenian and ten Russian delegates. The remaining seats belonged to splinter groups.[24]

Unfortunately for the destiny of Azerbaijani independence, the main ruling party, Musavat, was not a homogenous political organization. Its left wing, led by Resul Zadeh, Gajinsky, and other Baku intellectuals, was liberally and often radically atuned. Its right wing, composed of the western Azerbaijani aristocracy, was supported by Khan Khoisky's national democrats, who remained at the head of the government from spring 1918 until winter 1919–20. Both wings were in a state of permanent feud. When a financial scandal compelled Khan Khoisky and his ministers to resign, they were supplanted by the cabinet of N. B. Usubbekov, who, despite his former Federalist and right-wing affiliations, came under the influence of Resul Zadeh and Gajinsky, the latter also a minister in the new cabinet. Resul Zadeh and Gajinsky secured the renewal of relations with the Soviet Union, and both were instrumental in initiating a more conciliatory policy regarding local Communists as well as in the legalization of the Communist party in Azerbaijan in early 1920.

The new policy of rapprochement toward the Soviet government unexpectedly won support not only in Musavat's left wing and among Moslem socialists, but also from the extreme rightist Ittihad. This group was less nationalistic than Musavat, and placed the religious principles of Islam at the basis of its party platform. The traditional animosity between Shiites and Sunnites, and the ancient ties of the Shiite clergy—which dominated Ittihad—with Persian religious life and culture, were certainly of vital importance for Ittihad's anti-Turkism. In their eyes, the nationalism of Pan-Turkists, who placed principles of linguistic or racial unity above religious ones, contradicted the teaching of the Prophet: "Islam has always been universal, and it is not concerned with national movements. Ittihad's members must think only in terms of the unity of Islam. . . . The very structure of our party, in which not only the Azerbaijani Turks but also Persians and Caucasian mountaineers participate, confirms the profundity of the internationalism preached by the Prophet." [25] Thus opposing the Sunnite Pan-Turkists, Ittihad involuntarily supported the internationalist doctrine and propaganda of Communism. The Bolsheviks, for their part, skillfully supported Ittihad in its struggle against Musavat, and the extreme right and extreme left were provisionally united under the principle of supranational unity.

THE END OF AZERBAIJANI INDEPENDENCE

Torn by internal division and weakened by conflict with its neighbors, Azerbaijan had no other choice in the early months of 1920 but to initiate a more amicable policy toward the Soviet government and the Communist Party, with which all relations had been broken after the Baku massacres of March–April 1918. With the departure of British forces from Transcaucasia and the collapse on March 27, 1920 of General Denikin's White Army—which, although it had occasioned the Azerbaijani government some alarm, had nevertheless protected it in the north from Soviet power for almost two years—Musavat found itself face to face with the Red Army. The Armenian Communist, Anastas Mikoyan, was delegated by the Moscow Central Committee in February 1920 to assume leadership of the Azerbaijani Bolshevik organization, replacing Shaumian who, together with twenty-five other Baku Communists, had been shot by the Mensheviks in Transcaspia after the Soviet evacuation of Baku in 1918. In Baku Mikoyan organized a separate Azerbaijani Communist Party, which was to play a role similar to that of the Turkic

national Communists under Vahitov, Sultangaliev, and Validov in
the Volga-Ural and other Turkic regions of Russia. This new party
concentrated its efforts on undermining Musavat's influence among
the Turkic population. At its first congress, held in February 1920,
party leaders frankly declared that their goal was establishment of
the Soviet system in Azerbaijan, ending their resolutions with the
words, "Long live an Azerbaijani Soviet state. . . . Long live the world
revolution." [26] Early in 1920 Moscow set up a special Caucasian
office (*Zakavkazskoe Buro*, or *Kavburo*), under the direction of
S. Ordzhonikidze, a Georgian, and S. M. Kirov, a Russian, both with
long revolutionary practice in Transcaucasia. It was Kavburo's task
to support Communists in Georgia, Armenia, and Azerbaijan, and
to prepare the transformation of these national republics into Soviet
satellites.

The work of Mikoyan and Kavburo in Azerbaijan was simplified
by the fact that Ottoman Turkey, led by Kemal Pasha (Ataturk),
did not impede, but even assisted, the transfer of this republic, as well
as of Armenia and Georgia, to Moscow's control. At war with Greece
and in conflict with the Allies and the Armenians, the Kemalists
looked to Moscow as an ally. The Soviets, in turn, were prepared to
supply Kemal Pasha with arms and ammunition. They hoped that,
like the Jadids in Central Asia and Vahitov's Moslem Communists
from Kazan, Kemal Pasha would become a convenient tool of their
revolutionary work in the East.

Azerbaijan could not withstand the combined efforts of the Com-
unists and the Kemalists, especially since, as Richard Pipes remarks,
Kemal Pasha, "who had beforehand renounced all interest in that
area, had every reason to welcome its conquest by the communists." [27]
Discord also reigned within the government; Khan Khoisky and the
conservative bourgeois wing refused to accept the policy of "peaceful cooperation" with the Communists and the Soviet government as
recommended by Resul Zadeh and Gajinsky. But the Red Eleventh
Army, consisting of some fifteen thousand men, was already stationed
in Daghestan on Azerbaijani's border, and Mikoyan's Communist cells
were growing stronger, directed by Kavburo. Coordinating their
activity with Kavburo, the Baku party organization reported to
S. M. Kirov, at the time in Astrakhan:

Our plan is the following: we will strengthen the work of combat
sections, organize our fighting forces underground, and wait. Our
action will be timed with the offensive from Astrakhan, without which

our action is inconceivable. In the city of Baku we command over 20,000 to 30,000 men, but they are not armed. In the Mungan steppe we have 8–10,000 armed men. The population of the Elizavetopol province [Ganja] is inclined toward revolution, and the same mood is felt in the Baku province. In the case of an upheaval, we will be stronger. We have 2,500 rifles, ammunition, bombs and revolvers. We await you with impatience.

On March 9, 1920, less than two months before the upheaval occurred, Kirov wrote to the Baku cells:

Organize regular liaison with your detachments, prepare your units for common action with the eleventh army, and inform me of your timing. Particular attention should be paid to the destruction of bridges, in order to prevent the evacuation of the enemy's armed trains. . . . Augment intelligence. We need to be informed regarding the location of military stores and the rear organization of the enemy. . . . Any major movement of your detachments in the rear of the enemy [Azerbaijani] army should be undertaken only with permission of our command.[28]

These elaborate preparations were to a great extent superfluous, for the Musavat government was weaker than the Soviets estimated. The republic's small and badly organized army was at war in Armenia, where, under the command of Ottoman Turkish officers, it was not likely to engage in defense of the country against the Communists— since the Turks were eagerly awaiting the establishment of land contact between the Kemalists and the Soviets, and were not opposed to Soviet penetration.

On April 27, 1920, Kavburo, in the name of the Soviet government and the Baku Communists, demanded that power be transferred to it within twelve hours. Backing up this ultimatum were the Eleventh Army regiments under Ordzhonikidze, stationed in Daghestan, only some thirty miles from Baku. The Azerbaijani parliament convened its last session, and, as it met, a Baku Communist detachment surrounded the building.[29] The ultimatum was accepted without opposition. The parliament voted its own and the national government's dissolution and transfer of power to the Bolsheviks.[30]

The next day a new Azerbaijani government was set up by the Baku Communist and former member of Hemmet, Nariman Narimanov. It included eight Azerbaijani Moslems (Communists, members of Hemmet, and one member of the Shiite-Persian Communist organization, *Adalet*) and three Russian Communists.[31] Many leaders of Musavat's bourgeois and aristocratic right wing, including Khan Khoisky and the former Minister of War, General Mehmendarov, were arrested. Resul Zadeh declined Stalin's personal invitation to join the Communist Party and fled abroad in 1921. Many other left-wing Musavatists did join the Communist ranks, forming the backbone of the Soviet regime in Azerbaijan in the early 1920's, but most of them were purged in the following years.

The legal existence of independent Azerbaijan came to an end two years later. On March 12, 1922, Azerbaijan, Georgia, and Armenia resurrected the defunct Transcaucasian federation, under Soviet control. On December 30 this federation, together with the RSFSR, Belorussia, and the Ukraine, formed the Soviet Union, and since that time Azerbaijan has belonged officially to the Soviet family of republics.

CHAPTER XVIII

Conclusion

The end of the Civil War in Russia in 1920 and the stabilization of the Soviet regime closed an important epoch in the history of Russia's Turks. This year saw the birth or final organization of five Turkic Soviet Republics, either as an "independent" Soviet state, as in the case of Azerbaijan, or as autonomous units, such as Tatary, Bashkiria, Kazakhstan, and Turkestan. To these should also be added the "people's democracies" of Bukhara and Khiva, where in 1920 the government was transferred from the hands of the khans to Communist groups and their Jadid fellow-travelers. The subsequent division in 1923 of autonomous Turkestan into four republics—each of which eventually received the status of a full-fledged member of the USSR—did not change the political situation in Central Asia because for all practical purposes its future had already been determined three years earlier. The Soviets apparently considered the national aspirations of the Turks of Russia satisfied by the creation of these autonomous republics, an attainment for which a whole generation of Turkic patriots had fought. Their national tongues were made the official languages of the republics, which were proclaimed the homes of the Turkic peoples and Turkic culture.

The final determination of the status of these Turkic Soviet Republics, however, could only frustrate Turkic national feelings. Simultaneously with their creation, these new Turkic autonomous territories came under the control of the Soviet state and the Communist Party. When Azerbaijan became a Soviet satellite in April 1920 and then, in 1922, a member of the Soviet Union, it lost its shaky, though still national, independence. Amendments to the constitution of Soviet Bashkiria promulgated in May 1920 deprived this little Ural territory of the last opportunity for genuine autonomous evolution. The formation in May 1920 of the Tatar Autonomous Republic, a mere shadow of the originally projected Idel-Ural state, was conditioned largely by Bolshevik propagandistic considerations, and this republic was under the strict supervision of the Soviet administration and Communist Party from its very inception. The same features characterized organization of the Kazakh ASSR, which in August 1920 replaced the Alash Orda autonomy of previous years. Finally, in Turkestan, the name "Turkic Soviet Republic," applied by the Jadids in 1919, was replaced in September 1920 by the name "Autonomous Soviet Republic," and the Jadids were eliminated from power.

ISLAM—SECULARIZATION AND NATIONALISM

Turkic national efforts certainly did not come to an end in 1920, however, and the last pages of the history of the Turkic national movement in Russia did not close with this date. But the period of relatively free expression of political opinion and of the opportunity to educate the younger generation in the national spirit, which had begun in 1905, quite clearly ended in 1920. A new era characterized by a previously inconceivable totalitarian control of the life and minds of Soviet subjects was initiated for the Turks of Russia.

Of perhaps still greater significance for the history of Russian Turks was the drastic decline of Islamic influence on their culture and life after 1920. Indeed, as we have seen, the process of secularization of Turkic civilization and thought started toward the middle of the last century in Turkey, when Shinasi, Namik Kemal, and Zia Pasha rejected the old literary and intellectual patterns. This cultural secularization became a characteristic of the life of Russian Turks after the introduction among them of the new-method school by Ismail bey Gasprinsky. Akchurin and Agaev carried this evolution a step further in placing the ideals of racial Turkism above those of Islam. This, however, remained no more than a movement of the intelligentsia, being neither extended to the entire population nor adopted by the state, and it barely affected the Moslem conservative mind in the Caucasus, in Central Asia, or even in the rural districts of the Volga-Ural region. After 1920, secularization became a compulsory and permanent feature of the government's program and ideology. Despite some temporary concessions, Islam ceased being taught in the schools attended by Turkic children; the muezzins were prohibited from announcing the hour of prayer from the minaret; mosques were partly closed; and students were discouraged from attending the few remaining madrasas.[1] Furthermore, the substitution for the Arabic alphabet in 1925–1927 of the Latin, and of the Cyrillic in 1937–1939, resulted in the cultural isolation of Russia's Turkic peoples from the rest of the Moslem world.

Indeed, the process of secularization of the Turkic Moslem population was not limited to the Soviet Union alone, which only aggravated the position of the Moslem religion in that country. Ottoman Turkey —which by the vigorous action of Kemal Ataturk in 1920 became the rejuvenated national Turkish republic—for at least three decades fought most violently the effects of long-standing Islamic influence on its people. In Turkey itself the Koran could not be printed, the study of liturgic Arabic was discontinued, and Latin letters replaced Arabic on the pages of Turkish books. Like the Soviet government, Kemal's regime dissolved the monastic dervish orders, closed all four hundred seventy-nine madrasas, and banned religion from the schools.[2] The situation of Islam in Turkey became very precarious, and Kemal's reformative activities offered many convenient patterns for the atheistic Communist policies. In 1920, therefore, an over-all spiritual crisis developed in all Turkic lands, putting an end to the hegemony of the Islamic religion, philosophy, social patterns, and legal system over the population. Although it is hard to forsee the final outcome of such policies in the Turkic areas of Russia, there can be little doubt that a new era began in 1920, an era in which Kazan, Baku, and Tashkent became more closely bound to the secularized patterns of contemporary Western culture than to the still religious ones of Karachi, Mecca, or Cairo.

The decrease of Islam's spiritual ascendance over the minds of Russian Turks has not necessarily implied their denationalization or even a weakening of their national feelings. On the contrary, it is possible to presume that this lessening of religious influence among the Soviet Turkic population may finally result in a more intensive crystallization of their national identity. The traditional Moslem political conceptions and the growth of Pan-Islamism doubtless contributed to the unification and effectiveness of the Moslems' political action in Russia in the years 1905–1917. At the same time, though, the feeling of affiliation with the Moslem community obscured that of national identity and created obstacles to the formulation and popularization of Turkic nationalism. Islam frequently overshadowed national thought among Russian Moslems; it was no mere coincidence that Akchurin's way to Pan-Turkism led through the rejection of

Pan-Islamism, or that such prominent exponents of Pan-Turkic or Pan-Turanian ideology as Agaev, Hussein Zadeh, and Zia Gek Alp insisted on a radical revision of the Turkic attitude toward religion. Similarly, Kemal's secularizing policies naturally arose out of this inevitable necessity to delimit the domains of spiritual and secular influence.

When in 1905–1906 the Turkic leaders in Russia organized their congresses and political parties, their persistent use of the terms "religion" and "Moslems" in place of "nation" and "Turks" might have been explained by a legitimate desire to disguise their actual aims in order to divert the suspicious attention of tsarist administrators. In 1917, however, when the democratic Provisional Government exhibited no signs of administrative intervention, the continued use of religious rather than national terminology only reflected the insufficient appeal of a purely nationalist plank for the still deeply traditionalist Moslem population of Russia. The decision of the First All-Russian Moslem Congress in May 1917 to call its executive organ a *Moslem* and not a *Turko-Tatar* Council was the most eloquent demonstration of the weakness of Turkic nationalist feelings among Russia's Turks. Even the Tatars, while elaborating their project for cultural autonomy in July–August 1917, persisted in identifying it as an autonomy of the *Moslems* of Inner Russia and Siberia.

In Central Asia and many areas of the Caucasus the situation was even more complicated, since the Moslem population there was not homogeneously Turkic and could never successfully be rallied around purely nationalist or racial banners. While the Musavat leaders themselves were preponderantly Turkic nationalists, their party catered to the local population on the strength of Moslem slogans. As a matter of fact, Musavat's success was due largely to support from the non-Turkic Moslem groups of Transcaucasia—such as the peoples of Daghestan, the Ajars, Inghilois, and the Iranian-speaking Talish and Tats. Resul Zadeh, as late as the 1950's, still had visions of an Azerbaijan federated with Daghestan and the mountaineers of the Northern Caucasus, primarily because the population of these areas professed Islam.[3]

The early writings of such Azerbaijani leaders as Resul Zadeh, Topchibashev, and Agaev bear witness to the fact that they were more influenced at the beginning of their political careers by the Pan-Islamic sermons of the Persian ideologist, Jemal al Din Afghani, than by any Turkic national considerations. In these writings they envisioned the revival and unification of the entire Moslem world, and it was the culture and religion of Islam, not the nation, which seemed to them the most suitable basis for further political action.

In Central Asia the term "Turkic" began to displace "Moslem" in political writings and speeches only as late as 1919, when the Jadids were allowed to infiltrate the Communist Party apparatus and Soviet administration, although even this terminological alteration to a great extent reflected the secularizing effect of Communist influence. The following of these Pan-Turkic Jadids was still extremely restricted; the majority of the native population resented these free-thinking nationalists almost as much as they did the Communists.

Such collisions between the religiously conditioned mentality and national ideology could only result in an undermining of the nationalist leaders' appeals. Pan-Turkism, or Turkic nationalism, remained little known to the bulk of Russia's Turkic population, and its effect on their political attitudes was consequently handicapped. In some cases religion not only limited but directly opposed any opportunity for the political growth of a national movement, and, from the very inception of Turkic nationalism, conservative clerics remained stubbornly hostile to it. Tatar mullahs denounced Jadid educators to the tsarist police, and in Turkestan Ulema disrelished its liberal competitors, fighting them first by sermon and press, then, in 1917, with stones, and finally, during the period of the Civil War and Basmachi movement, with more deadly weapons. The nationalist Jadids' early cooperation with the Communists served to increase the natives' dislike for the Jadids, whose persistence in clinging to the Soviet administration stemmed to a large extent from their isolation from and distrust of their traditionalist Moslem compatriots.

The only powerful anti-Communist movement among the Moslems of the Soviet Union born during the Civil War, the movement of the Basmachis, had little if anything in common with Turkic nationalist aims. The Basmachis were fighting rather for the mode of life of their forefathers, for the tribal social order and the Islamic faith, and were opposed to the "godless" Communists and the "godless" Jadids alike. Validov, himself a typical representative of the Jadid milieu, relates in his memoirs a story indicative of the Basmachis' attitude: a chieftain of the Lokai tribe in eastern Bukhara and the head of a Basmachi band, a certain Togai, once pointed to a pocketful of ears with the comment that these were the ears of Jadids killed by him and his men, and promised to cut off more of them.[4] A more convincing illustration of the Basmachis' aversion for Turkic nationalists could hardly be offered. After the Soviets took a more conciliatory attitude toward Islam, the Basmachi movement to a large extent abated, in accordance with the directives of a group of pro-Soviet mullahs who announced that, according to the Koran, every authority must be obeyed and that Communist teaching did not contradict the foundations of Islam. In the Volga-Ural region, where much of the clergy (led by Mufti Barudi) joined the Jadid movement, and in the Kazakh steppe, where the Moslem religion had never taken deep root, the traditionalist Ulema was not strong enough to oppose the liberal nationalists. But in the Caucasus during the two years of Azerbaijani independence, the conservative Shiah clergy of Ittihad caused great concern to Musavat. Ittihad's opposition was based on the Moslem political philosophy: "Islam is cosmopolitan; it is above national Pan-Turkism, and any nationalist contradicts this fundamental creed." This philosophy deeply undermined Musavat nationalism among the Shiah population and, as has been seen, was partially responsible for the weakening of Azerbaijani anti-Soviet resistance.

WEAKNESSES OF NATIONAL TRADITION

Another factor causing the Turkic national movement to be ineffective in the years of the Civil War was the absence of a clear-cut and realistic national program. The Pan-Turkic ideals developed by Akchurin and the émigrés were too vague, their historical foundation too remote, and the geographical setting too inadequate to inspire the Moslem population in Russia. Attila's, Genghis Khan's, and Tamerlane's glorious military deeds, so often extoled by Zia Gek Alp and other Pan-Turkists, were utterly forgotten by the vast majority of their people. A recollection of the deeds of these empire builders of the fifth, thirteenth, and fifteenth centuries could hardly form a satisfactory plank for political action in the twentieth century. The territory of these medieval empires had lost its geographical cohesion, and the Transcaucasian Azerbaijanis, the Volga Tatars, or the Tien Shan Kirghiz were now out of touch with each other. The Caspian Sea and the immense plains, now inhabited by Russians or other non-Turkic peoples, separated the Azerbaijani, Tatar, and Bash-

kir regions from each other and from their Turkic kinsmen of Central
Asia. The arid, sparsely populated steppes and deserts of Kazakhstan,
which lay at the center of the Turkic territories in Russia, divided
rather than united the Turks of Central Asia, the Kazakhs of the
northern steppes, and the Turkic population of European Russia.
Finally, centuries of Russian colonization had forced the Turkic
nationalities into territorially distinct groups. Even the languages of
these peoples had become so differentiated as to prohibit the adoption
of a common Turkic literary tongue. In view of the diversity of these
peoples' geographic, social, and economic conditions by the early
twentieth century, Pan-Turkic or common-Turkic solidarity meant
more than mere mutual sympathy only to a few intellectuals, and
these men were unable to overcome the many obstacles to a national
unification.

The recentness and often complete lack of local political tradition
likewise prevented the strengthening of nationalism on a regional
basis. As we have seen, in some parts of Russia's Turkic world the
native intelligentsia in the early twentieth century was still struggling
with the effects of Iranian cultural domination. In many of the Turkic
areas of Russia, regional national unity did not even exist before 1917.
Prior to Russian conquest, for instance, Azerbaijani territory never
formed a separate, united state, and even under Persian domination
eastern Transcaucasia was divided into a multitude of loosely connected feudal principalities. The very term "Azerbaijan" was rarely
applied before 1917 to the Elizavetopol and Baku provinces which
later formed the Azerbaijani Republic, this term being commonly
used only for the Persian provinces bordering Russian Transcaucasia.
Under such conditions, the growth of Azerbaijani national consciousness was little likely to flower in the short period of independence
which preceded the incorporation of Azerbaijan into the Soviet state.
Almost the same situation prevailed in Central Asia. As discussed
earlier, the Tatars for their part preferred an all-Russian cultural
autonomy for themselves and other Russian Moslems to the creation
of an autonomous territory, while the Bashkirs long hesitated in
determining the boundaries of their autonomy. In the face of these
uncertainties, the effectiveness of any national political action on a
regional basis was inevitably reduced, leading often to passivity and
resignation.

POLITICAL RADICALISM

The attitude of the Russian Turks in the revolutionary years 1917–1920 differed greatly from the position they took during the 1905 Revolution. The intervening years manifested definite signs of social radicalization. This change was particularly noticeable in European Russia, where the Turkic population experienced general social unrest in 1917, and it found its expression in the resolutions of the Second Moslem Congress in Kazan in July–August 1917, which was more radically inclined than the First Congress and where the socialist faction dominated the scene. The preponderance of the left was reflected in the very name of the Moslem ticket presented to voters at the Constituent Assembly: the All-Moslem Democratic Socialist Bloc.[5] A rival leftist ticket presented by a still more radical, purely socialist, group—to which Vahitov, Sultangaliev, Manatov, Validov, and other future collaborators with the Soviets belonged—won even more votes than the All-Moslem Bloc in the Volga region. In the Kazan province's elections to the Constituent Assembly, Moslem socialists polled 153,151 votes as against 100,000 votes for the nationalist All-Moslem Bloc;[6] in the October election to the Kazan municipal council the Moslem socialists won thirteen seats as against one obtained by the All-Moslem Bloc. In the Ufa province they won 75 per cent of the votes and five seats, while the All-Moslem Bloc received only some 25 per cent and one or two seats (data differ). In some districts in the southern Urals, for instance, the radical supporters of Validov won almost 90 per cent of the Moslem vote, and in Cheliabinsk the All-Moslem Bloc polled only 2,609 votes as against 20,978 for their radical competitors.[7]

In the Caucasus the leading party, Musavat, was forced by the circumstances of revolution and by the radical mood of its electors to adopt a very leftist, almost purely socialist, plank; among Musavat's opponents the Moslem socialists were the strongest and the conservatives the weakest party. The hesitation of Musavat, of the Jadids, of the Tatar Shuro, and of the Bashkir socialists in determining their positions regarding the Soviet regime was conditioned by the rapidity with which radical ideas spread throughout the Moslem population and by the latter's general passivity toward national and political problems. The Turkic intelligentsia, especially, experienced strong radicalization, and nationalist groups found themselves without any

effective young leadership. However, in Central Asia and Kazakhstan, radicalization affected only the few groups of Westernized and
secularized intellectuals and to some extent the urban proletariat;
the rest of the population remained impassive.

In Central Asia elections to the Constituent Assembly did not take
place, but the electoral alliance made in expectation of the vote
showed clearly the deep rift between the dominant Moslem right
wing and the vociferous, but still small, left Jadid front. The rightist
Ulema concluded a pact with the Russian monarchist group led by
N. Ostroumov. This alliance so disturbed the Tatars that they sent a
delegation of clerics to Tashkent in order to convince Ulema to be
"more nationalist and Moslem." [8] For their part, the Jadids came to
an agreement with Russian socialists, putting at the head of their
ticket A. Kerensky, who had been born in Central Asia, and M. Chokaev, the Jadid politician.

Similar alliances with Russian parties were concluded in the Orenburg province, where Moslems sided with the Cossacks; in Ufa, where
rightist Moslems formed an electoral coalition with the Union of
Russian Nobility; and in several other places.[9] In addition to these
alliances, which split and confused the Moslem voters, it should be
kept in mind that at the election to the Constituent Assembly an
apparently considerable number of Moslems voted for various all-
Russian, especially leftist—i.e., Socialist Revolutionary and Bolshevik—parties.

ISLAM AND COMMUNISM

One of the strangest phenomena in the early history of the Soviet
regime was the instance of alliance between conservative Moslem
clerics and the Communists. Moslem clerics were "rightist," not
necessarily politically and economically but intellectually, and the
internationalist and socialist slogans of Marxism and the Soviets did
not frighten them, even though the atheistic elements of Marxist
teaching were out of harmony with Islam. Such a case was the movement of Soviet Shariatists in the northern Caucasus and, to some
extent, among the Tatars. An Ulema–Soviet coalition proposed in
Tashkent in November 1917 by Sher-Ali Liapin, leader of the conservative Ulema,[10] was prevented only by the shortsightedness of the
Tashkent Communists. In 1922–1924 the Soviet government sought
to appease Ulema's hostility by temporarily reopening Moslem

schools and Moslem courts, and won their support in the struggle against the Basmachis. Quoting suras from the Koran which prescribe obedience to any authority, Central Asian mullahs helped the Soviets to appease the Basmachis. Some Moslem politicians joined the Communist Party and collaborated with the Soviets because they felt that Islam and Communism had many common elements. At one of the first Communist Party congresses in Tashkent, a Tatar Communist, M. Klevleev, announced that he became a Communist after attentively reading the Koran, whose teaching, in his opinion, was nearly as cosmopolitan and socialistic as that of Marxism. [11] In Baku, Ittihad's clerical leaders, seeking a rapprochement with the Soviets, pointed out that the Koran's cosmopolitanism and antinationalism reconciled Moslem conservatives with the Third International and caused them to reject racial or national Turkism. No doubt, propaganda which had insisted less blatantly on the immediate class struggle and on atheism could have won Communism even stronger support among Russian Moslems than that it succeeded in winning during the early revolutionary period.

A recent analysis of the Islamic social and political tradition made by the authoritative Lebanese thinker, Nabih Amin Faris, chairman of the Arab Studies program at the American University of Beirut, explains to a great extent Klevleev's and the Ittihadists' interpretation of the Koran's teaching:

The notion is widespread in the West that the Middle East is secure from the appeals of communism because of the religious deterrent of Islam. From a purely doctrinal point of view, this belief is sound. It is impossible to reconcile these two faiths—one spiritual, the other materialistic. The principal message of Islam is the existence of God; true communists must deny the existence of God as an article of their faith. The institution of private property, anathema to communists, is sanctioned in the Koran. Numerous other examples could be given, but this is not the point.

More important is the fact that many parallels exist between Islam and communism and these make a transition from Islam to communism possible and even natural, once the individual Moslem shifts his emphasis away from the spiritual sphere to the temporal. The apostate Moslem or even the backslider can find in communism familiar institutions and habits of mind which, when combined with all that communism offers or seems to offer, may make a potent appeal to him.[12]

Pointing out, further, that both the Islamic and Communist systems are essentially authoritarian in character, Professor Faris stresses the similarity in the supranational character of the two ideologies. As does Communism, "Islam claims universality and cuts clean across nationalities to bring them all within the faith." He recalls that many contemporary Moslem writers have re-emphasized this aspect of Mohammed's teaching and have called for a modern Islamic state which transcends linguistic and national boundaries, in order to unite all Moslems in one single fatherland. In their approach to social problems, also, Communism and Islam have considerable similarities, according to Faris, since both teachings encompass social justice. "All the social injustices and ills affecting this world would be rectified," he continues, "and a sort of Utopia would prevail when the external factors which have thrown society out of balance are done away with, and balance is restored by the establishment of a Moslem [universal] state. . . . The communists, too, believe that the proletarian Utopia is attainable once a set of external factors replace another set, once communism [on a universal level] replaces capitalism. . . . The only difference between Islam and communism in this respect are the means with which their respective Utopias are to be brought about." [13] This Utopian vision, common to Moslems and Communists alike, of a future world delivered from evil by the benefits of a victorious universal ideology was certainly instrumental in the success of Communist teaching among Russian Moslems after 1917 and, no doubt, among their brethren in faith of the Middle East in more recent years.

It may be added to Faris' comparative analysis of the two doctrines that Moslems and Communists also agree on and practice the enforced propagation of their ideas and systems. The Marxist-Leninist dogma of world revolution and the spread of universalist Communist teachings by means of power are not far removed from the universal Islamic expansion and conversion as practiced by successful Arabic and Turkic conquerors. For intellectuals reared in the Islamic pattern of political behavior, and especially for the more secularized ones, the Communists' method was hardly unusual or shocking and could readily be accepted as historically justifiable activity. From this point of view, the Communists' attitude was less alien to the Moslems than the Western belief in persuasion and gradual progress. Similarly, the concept of an administration of the people aimed at social justice was more understandable to Tatars or Uzbeks than the Western idea of a government by and for the people lacking any concrete social objectives.

In view of these parallels between Islamic and Communist political concepts, it is not hard to understand why so many Turkic Moslem intellectuals in Russia became deeply influenced by Communist propaganda, gave up resistance to Soviet authoritarianism, and in many instances joined the Communist Party, sacrificing their national cause. The revolt and ultimate victory of the non-Western—in this particular case, Islamic—world over European imperialism merged, in the eyes of Vahitov, Validov, Sultangaliev, and even Tsalikov, with the vision of social revolution, obscuring their initial national-religious goals.

THE PROBLEM OF SECESSION

These difficulties encountered by the nationalist movement of Russia's Turks certainly could not undermine either their particular cultural unity or their awareness of a distinct ethnic identity apart from the Russians. But just as their cultural unity did not result in political unification in time of revolution, their consciousness of being a distinct nationality did not necessarily evolve into political separatism. Before and during 1917, with the exception of a handful of émigrés residing in Turkey and Germany, no Turkic leaders in Russia included political independence in their national programs. Even Akchurin, the most radical nationalist among them, fluctuated in his demands between the achievement of national independence and the establishment of complete legal equality and cultural autonomy for Russian Turks. No Turkic nationalist party in Russia raised a voice for secession from the Russian state until late spring 1918.

The position taken by the Turks in Russia differed little at that time from that of other peoples of the empire. During the Provisional Government only the Poles and Finns demanded their political independence. The government met these demands sympathetically, and by its declaration of March 29, 1917, recognized the right of the Polish people to form an independent national state. Although appeals for autonomy were heard from other groups in Russia, there were no demands for secession. Lenin's attitude regarding political liberties, combined with his invitation to secede, finally resulted in the winter of 1917–1918 in a series of declarations of independence. These were regarded by most of the various peoples voicing them as attempts to sever relations with the Soviet regime, and not as the eruption of desires to break with the Russian state for the sake of an independent existence.

On December 6, 1917, Stalin personally hailed Finland's proclamation of independence, since the Bolshevik government hoped that proletarian forces would soon seize power in the new republic. The Soviet government became alarmed, however, when, under pressure from the German command, Lithuania and Latvia proclaimed their respective secessions from Russia on December 11 and January 12. Following suit in its turn, after the Bolshevik troops started their march on Kiev, the Ukrainian Central Rada proclaimed an independent Ukraine.

What is so often described as the disintegration of imperial ties in Russia in 1917 was, more accurately, the collapse of the central administration and the spread of anarchy throughout the entire country, in which all former officials were earmarked as reactionaries and enemies of liberty. The intention to preserve organizational ties with the Russian state in 1917 was confirmed in the case of the Turkic regions by their proclamations *only of autonomy*, rather than of secession—that is, Turkestan, the Bashkirs, Tatars, and Kazakhs. That these peoples wanted to maintain Russia's political unity is demonstrated by the speeches and writings of various leaders, such as, for instance, Tsalikov, chairman of All-Russian Moslem Council, Chokaev, head of the Turkestan autonomy in 1917–1918, Noah Jordania, president of the Georgian republic in 1918–1921, Dosmuhammedov, head of the Kazakh autonomy, and many others. Describing the situation in Turkestan at the time of the October upheaval, Chokaev relates:

We did not at that time have any definite, clear-cut national policy. We continued to regard Turkestan as a part of Russia, and its future fate we considered as tied to that of Russia. Even in regard to the new "Workers' and Peasants' government" formed in St. Petersburg, we adopted an attitude of waiting. If the conduct of the local Russian workers, soldiers, and peasants tended to alienate us from the local "Soviet power" [that is, the Tashkent government], the decrees and appeals of the Central Soviet Government to the right of each nation, irrespective of the degree of its development and backwardness, to separate and to form its own national independent state, and the right to demand "withdrawal of the armies of a stronger nation" seemed to us capable of reconciling Turkestanians to the new state regime in Russia. . . .

But the usurpation of power by the Bolsheviks, followed by the deprival of our people's political rights, compelled us hurriedly to take measures to oppose the will of our people to the decision of the usurpers.[14]

Noah Jordania, inviting the Transcaucasian conference on November 11, 1917, to organize a provisional government not dependent upon the Soviet regime, announced, "For a hundred years Transcaucasia has collaborated hand in hand with Russia, and considers itself indissolubly connected with her." [15] The new Trancaucasian government was formed by Jordania with the hope that the All-Russian Constituent Assembly would restore legal power throughout Russia and that Transcaucasia would maintain its ties with it. The resolution creating the Transcaucasian government limited its existence up to "the time of elections of deputies to an All-Russian Constituent Assembly and formation of a recognized central democratic power, and the opening of the authoritative All-Russian Constituent Assembly." [16] For his part, Dosmuhammedov, head of the Kazakh autonomy, stated, "We announced the autonomy in order to avoid the penetration of the Bolshevik contagion in the steppe." [17]

This nonsecessionist spirit dominated the political thought of most Turkic and other leaders in 1917. At the beginning of the Bolshevik regime they were still hopeful that after an initial period of anarchy and revolutionary violence, the Soviet government would become a legal Russian regime, recognizing Turkic cultural, religious, and political traditions and their aspirations for national autonomy. Only after Lenin's political methods became apparent did the psychological and political disintegration of the empire—or, more accurately, the "run" away from the Soviet regime—really begin.

Organization in summer 1918 of the socialist "all-Russian" government in Samara, which promised the Tatars, Bashkirs, Kazakhs, and other Turkic peoples recognition of national or cultural autonomy, was met, as has been seen, by the unanimous support of these nationalities' leaders, all of whom participated in this short-lived Komuch administration. However, the politically shortsighted White generals' rigid adherence to Russia's centralization was to a large extent responsible for many Turkic leaders' shifts to the side of the Soviets, who promised them autonomy. It must be added that the actions of the Cossacks, White Russian partisans, and the Czecho-Slovak legionnaires, especially in Siberia and eastern Russia, did not always differ greatly from the misdeeds of the Red Guardists, the

Latvian rifle regiments, Austrian and Hungarian "internationalists," Chinese "volunteers," and other voluntary or mercenary supporters of Soviet power in the time of the Civil War. Civil war is rarely attractive, and, disenchanted with Reds and Whites alike, Russia's Turks in most cases preferred to avoid fratricidal carnage by preserving neutrality. Whether such neutrality, however, reflected real political wisdom or simply oriental impassiveness remains a question; but, in view of these peoples' social and cultural conditions and the circumstances of civil war, their leaders could hardly have been expected to elaborate at that time a new political program that would be both realistic and achievable.

In any case, the revolution of 1917 caught the Russian Turkic world when it was in a state of transition. In many respects that period of Turkic history was similar to the time of Peter the Great, when Russia began to cast off the ancient Byzantine cultural heritage and replace it with new Western patterns. Such an era was dawning for the Turkic peoples, and at the moment of the Russian revolution their ideology was in flux and their leadership in the process of formation. Consequently, they were prevented from playing a more decisive role in the shaping of their own destinies.

NOTES

Notes

Abbreviations Used in Notes and Bibliography

AN	Akademiia Nauk
ARR	Arkhiv russkoi revoliutsii
ASaEER	American Slavic and East European Review
Az	Azerbaycan (Muenchen, 1952–)
AzVat	Azat Vatan (Muenchen, 1951–)
BA	Belyi arkhiv (Paris)
BEBE	Bolshaia entsiklopediia, publ. Brokkhaus a.Efron
BSEfe	Bolshaia Sovetskaia entsiklopediia, first edition
BSEse	Bolshaia Sovetskaia entsiklopediia, second edition
BSAGU	Biulleten Sredne-Aziatskogo gosudarstevennogo universiteta
ChIOIDR	Chteniia v imperatorskom obshchestve istorii i drevnostei rossiiskikh pri Moskovskom universitete
DiSIIa	Doklady i soobshcheniia instituta iazykoznaniia AN SSSR
DnO	Der neue Osten
GosDuma	Gosudarstvennaia Duma, Stenograficheskie otchety
InOb	Inorodcheskoe obozrenie, suppl. to Pravoslavnyi sobesednik
INU	Istoriia narodov Uzbekistana, publ. AN UzSSR
IOKU	Izvestiia obshchestva arkheologii, istorii i etnografii pri Kazanskom universitete
IstMar	Istorik marksist
IstZap	Istoricheskie zapiski
JRCAS	Journal of the Royal Central Asian Society
Kavkaz	Kavkaz (Muenchen, 1951–1954)
KomTad	Kommunist Tadzhikistana
KrAr	Krasnyi arkhiv
MI	Mir Islama (Petersburg, 1912–1913)
MG	Minuvshie gody
MpIT	Materialy po izucheniiu Tatarstana
MT	Millij Turkistan
NRS	Novoe russkoe slovo (New York)
NV	Novyi vostok
ObKav	Obiedinennyi Kavkaz (Muenchen, 1950–)
OE	Ost Europa
OLZ	Orientalische Literatur-Zeitung
Pril.k otch. GosDumy	Prilozhenie k otchetam Gosudarstvennoi Dumy
PrNat	Prosviashchenie natsionalnostei
PrRev	Proletarskaia revoliutsiia
PSZ	Polnyi svod zakonov Rossiiskoi imperii (1830)
RevVost	Revoliutsionnyi vostok
RiN	Revoliutsiia i natsionalnosti
RiNV	Revoliutsiia i natsionalyni vopros (ed. S. M. Dimanshtein)

RMM	Revue du Monde Musulman
SaEER	Slavonic and Eastern European Review (London)
SIO	Sbornik imperatorskogo russkogo istoricheskogo obshchestva
SobUz	Sobranie uzakonenii
SvKav	Svobodnyi Kavkaz (Muenchen, 1951–)
SV	Sovetskoe vostokovedenie
TDTK	Trudy doma tatarskoi kultury
TIIa	Trudy instituta iazykoznaniia AN SSSR
TOIKK	Trudy obshchestva izucheniia Kirgizskogo kraia
TV	Trudy po vostokovedeniiu, publ. Lazorevskii institut
Turkeli	Turkeli (Muenchen, 1950–)
UZIV	Uchenye zapiski instituta vostokovedeniia
Vestnik NKID	Vestnik narodnogo komissariata inostrannykh del
Vestnik NKVD	Vestnik narodnogo komissariata vnutrennikh del
VNOT	Vestnik nauchnogo obshchestva tatarovedeniia
VoenMysl	Voennaia mysl (Tashkent, 1920–)
Vostok	Vostok (Petrograd, 1922)
VS	Vostochnyi sbornik (Petrograd, 1915–1917)
WdI	Die Welt des Islams
YMY	Yana Milli Yul (Berlin)
ZhNat	Zhizn natsionalnostei
ZhMNP	Zhurnal ministerstva narodnogo prosviashcheniia
ZRIGO OE	Zhurnal Rossiiskogo imperatorskogo geograficheskogo obshchestva, Otdel Etnografii

Chapter I.   The Turks of Russia

1. G. E. Wheeler estimates the total number of Turkic-speaking peoples at forty six million. *Encyclopaedia Britannica* (1956), XXI, 623.

2. V. Bartold [W. Barthold], *Istoriia kulturnoi zhizni Turkestana* (Leningrad, 1929), p. 81. A good review of the theories on the Altaic origin of Turks may be found in A. Potapov, *Ocherki po istorii altaitsev* (Moskva, 1953), pp. 82–143.

3. H. Vambery, *Altosmanische Sprachstudien* (Leiden, 1901), pp. 31, 33; A. V. Gabain, *Oezbekische Grammatik* (Leipzig, 1945), pp. 3, 8, 15.

4. S. Wurm, *Turkic peoples of the USSR* (London, 1954), pp. 12–13; H. Vambery, *Cagataische Sprachstudien* (Leipzig, 1867), I, 12; c. Brockelmann, *Osttuerkische Grammatik der islamischen Literatur Mittelasiens* (Leiden, 1954), pp. 19–20.

5. Most contemporary turkologists classify the Turkic languages into these four basic groups and a separate Chuvash group. See G. E. Wheeler in *Encyclopaedia Britannica* (1956), XXI, 624; Wurm, pp. 23–27; J. Matthews, *The Languages of the USSR* (London, 1952), p. 64; M. Räsänen, *Materialien zur Lautlehre der tuerkischen Sprachen* (Helsinki, 1949); N. A. Baskakov, "Klassifikatsiia tiurkskikh iazykov," *TIIa*, X, (1952), 55–56 (Baskakov's classification, based on the historical development of Turkic languages, is more complicated). For a more complete bibliography, see Baskakov and Matthews.

6. This and further data on the statistics of the Turkic population in the USSR, when not otherwise stated, are taken from F. Lorimer, *The Population of the Soviet Union* (Geneva, 1946), pp. 136–138 (1939 census), and *Perepis 1926* (Moskva, 1927) for the 1926 census, pp. vii, x–xviii, and tables.

7. The estimates are based on the data of the 1959 census. The increase in population from 1926 to 1959 is calculated on the basis of the average rate of growth of the entire population of the USSR; see Lorimer, p. 138.

8. *Bolshaia Sovetskaia entsiklopedia* (new ed., Moskva, 1951), XXI, 102.

9. *Ibid.*, XLIV, 11; and P. G. Podiachikh, *Naselenie SSSR* (Moskva, 1961).

10. *Ibid.*, XLI, 471; and Podiachikh, *Naselenie SSSR*.

11. *Ibid.*, XXXVIII, 652; and Podiachikh, *Naselenie SSSR*.

12. Articles by the representative of the Tatar clergy were published in various Tatar newspapers in Kazan; see *Baian ul Hakk*, nos. 985, 909 (1912), and *Yulduz*, no. 776 (1912), as quoted in *InOb* (1912), 25, 27, 29.

13. A. Arsharuni and Kh. Gabidullin, *Ocherki panislamizma i pantiurkizma v Rossii* (Moskva, 1931), p. 138.

14. *Yulduz*, no. 776 (1912) and *Baian ul Hakk*, no. 985 (1912), as quoted in *InOb* (1912), 27, 29.

15. Gabain, p. 15; *Istoriia narodov Uzbekistana*, II (Tashkent, 1948), 59, 62; *Istoriia Uzbekskoi SSR*, I (Tashkent, 1956), 446–447.

16. *Shuro*, XXI (1914), 647, as quoted in *InOb* (1918), 640.

Chapter II.   Tatar Rebirth

1. The Huns crossed the Volga River about 360 A.D., when the Slavic Antes were members of the Gothic Kingdom (around 350–360 A.D.), which occupied the present south Russian steppes between the rivers Danube and Don; G. Vernadsky, *History of Russia*, I (New Haven, 1949), 103, 127, 155.

2. E. Schuyler, who visited Central Asia in 1870, still found slaves on the Bukhariote markets; E. Schuyler, *Turkistan* (New York, 1876), II, 101.

3. About the Kasimov princes see V. V. Veliaminov-Zernov's exhaustive work, *Issledovaniie o kasimovskikh tsariakh i tsarevichakh*, 4 vols. (Petersburg, 1863–1866).

4. In 1897 there were 2.5 million Tatars out of the 13.5 million Turks in Russia. After the annexation of the khanates of Khiva and Bukhara by the Soviet Union, the Uzbeks emerged as the most numerous and the most influential Turkic group in the USSR.

5. *Istoriia Tatarskoi ASSR* (Kazan, 1956), pp. 42–43; *Puteshestvie Ibn Fadlana na Volgu* (Moskva, 1939), p. 67; D. A. Khvolson, *Izvestiia o Khazarakh* (Petersburg, 1869), p. 5; Vernadsky, p. 222; C. A. Macartney, *The Magyars in the Ninth Century* (Cambridge, 1930), pp. 80, 97.

6. B. Spuler, *Die Goldene Horde* (Leipzig, 1943), p. 284; B. D. Grekov and A. Iakubovskii, *Zolotaia orda i ee padenie* (Moskva, 1937), pp. 65–66.

7. *Istoriia Tatarii v dokumentakh i materialakh* (Moskva, 1937), p. 149.

8. *Materialy po izucheniiu Tatarstana* (Kazan, 1925), pp. 109–110.

9. *ChIOIDR*, CXII (1880), 58.

10. *PSZ*, XI, nos. 8540, 8664, 8793.

11. *ChIOIDR*, CXII (1880), 62.

12. *ChIOIDR*, XXX (1859), part II, 62.

13. The text of the instructions of the Tatar murzas to their delegates in *SIO*, XIV, 135, 156–159, and in CXV, 306–307, 311.

14. *IOKU*, XIV, 493; *ChIOIDR*, CXII (1880), 101–102; N. Bazhenov, *Kazanskaia Istoriia* (Kazan, 1847).

15. A. Iskhaki [Iskhakov], *Idel Ural* (Paris, 1933), p. 35.

16. *PSZ*, XIX, nos. 13,996.

17. *PSZ*, XX, no. 14,540 and XXII, no. 15,936.

18. *PSZ*, XXII, no. 16,710.

19. *TDTK*, I, 205; *Istoriia Tatarii v dokumentakh*, pp. 311–312.

20. *PSZ*, XXXIV, nos. 28,535.

21. Part of the Finno-Ugric population and other natives of the Volga, the Urals, and Siberia were Tatarized after their annexation by Russia; *IOKU*, XIII, 254; Iskhaki, p. 22; M. A. Terentiev, *Rossiia i Angliia v borbe za rynki* (Petersburg, 1878), p. 287.

22. *Istoriia narodov Uzbekistana* (Tashkent, 1948), II, 212 [further abbr. *INU*].

23. *Istoriia Tatarii v dokumentakh*, p. 305.

24. A. Arsharuni and Kh. Gabidullin, *Ocherki panislamizma i pantiurkizma v Rossii;* J.[Dz.] Validov, *Ocherki istorii obrazovannosti i literatury volzhskikh Tatar* (Moskva, 1823), p. 19; *TDTK*, I, 207.

25. *INU*, p. 212; G. Ibragimov, *Tatary v revoliutsiiu 1905 goda* (Kazan, 1926, pp. 15–16.

26. M. Abdykalykov and I. A. Pankratova, eds., *Istoriia Kazakhskoi ASSR* (Alma-Ata, 1943) p. 143; V. M. Cheremshanskii, *Opisanie orenburgskago kraia* (Moskva, 1858), pp. 384–387.

27. Terentiev, p. 25.

28. Ibragimov, p. 15..

29. Arsharuni and Gabidullin, p. 27; *Istoriia Tatarskoi ASSR* (Kazan, 1956), p. 247.

30. *TDTK*, p. 209.

31. R. Mintslov, *Sekretnoe poruchenie* (Riga, 1930), pp. 170, 250–251; Cheremshanskii, p. 394.

32. *IOKU*, XIV, 495.

33. *Istoriia Tatarii v dokumentakh*, pp. 284–290.

34. *TDTK*, p. 205; *Istoriia Tatarii v dokumentakh*, pp. 311–312; Ibragimov, p. 15.

35. *Istoriia TatASSR*, pp. 243, 247; *INU*, II, 217–218, 222; A. G. Serebriannikov, *Sbornik materialov dlia istorii zavoevaniia Turkestanskago kraia* (Tashkent, 1914), IV, 77, 175.

36. *INU*, II, 273.

37. The first one was completed in 1899, the second one in 1906.

38. S. I. Asfendirov, *Istoriia Kazakstana* (Alma-Ata, 1934), p. 210.

39. Arsharuni and Gabidullin, pp. 8–9; Asfendirov, p. 210.

40. Arsharuni and Gabidullin, pp. 43–44.

Chapter III.   Pan-Islamism and Ismail bey Gasprinsky

1. Validov, *Ocherki istorii obrazovannosti i literatury volzhskikh tatar*, p. 32.

2. *Ibid.*, p. 33.

3. *Ibid.*, p. 34; Ibragimov, *Tatary v revoliutsiiu 1905 goda*, p. 29; Arsharuni and Gabidullin, *Ocherki panislamizma i pantiurkizma v Rossii*, pp. 10–11; *Istoriia TatASSR*, p. 389.

4. Until Nasyri introduced the popular Kazan dialect of Volga Tatars into Tatar literature, the Tatars used the archaic Chagatai (or Turki). Following the example of the Young Turks, who had replaced Iranian and Arabic words in Ottoman Turkish with words taken from colloquial Turkish, Nasyri, taking literary Chagatai as the basis for modern Tatar, purified it of archaisms

and replaced them with words and expressions derived from colloquial Tatar. His work was continued by Tatar writers of the twentieth century, and despite the competition with Ottoman Turkish the modernized language was definitively established by Tatar writers in 1926. G. Mende, *Der nationale Kampf der Russlandstuerken* (Berlin, 1936), pp. 41–43; Validov, pp. 25–30.

5. M. Ashtorin, "Ocherki literaturnoi deiatelnosti kazanskikh tatar," *TV*, LV (1901), 38; Arsharuni, pp. 11–12.

6. Ali-Rakhim, "Nasyri," *VNOT*, I–II, (1925), 5–9.

7. E. Voronets, "Uchitelskaia seminariia v Kazani," *Russkii vestnik* (July 1873); Iskhaki, p. 24.

8. G. Gubaidullin, "Iz proshlogo Tatarii," *Materialy po izucheniiu Tatarstana*, II (Kazan, 1925), 109–110.

9. *Agrarnye volneniia i krestianskoe dvizhenie v Tatarii* (Moskva, 1936), pp. 150, 158.

10. *ZhMNP*, CXXXIV (n.s., 1867), 76–96.

11. *Agrarnye volneniia*, pp. 213–220.

12. *Ibid.*, p. 480.

13. N. I. Ilminskii [Ilminsky], *Kazanskaia kreshcheno-tatarskaia shkola* (Kazan, 1887), p. 222.

14. *ZhMNP*, LV (n.s., 1915), 144.

15. The Koran and most of the theological and prayer books were published in Arabic. In the nineteenth-century Tatar school the entire curriculum was focused on the study of Arabic and the Koran. In the modern schools, even on the eve of 1917, about 53 per cent of the curriculum was devoted to the study of Arabic, the Koran, and Moslem law. See programs in *InOb* (1916), pp. 97–100.

16. Validov, p. 54.

17. Mende, p. 45.

18. E. J. W. Gibb, *A History of Ottoman Poetry* (Cambridge, London, 1907) V, 5, 7; V. Gordelevskii, "Ocherki po istorii novoi osmanskoi literatury," *TV*, XXXIX (1912), 94.

19. V. Gordelevskii, "K voprosu o panislamisme," *MI* (1913), p. 6; E. G. Browne, *The Persian Revolution* (Cambridge, 1910), pp. 3–10; H. A. R. Gibb, *Mohammedanism* (New York, 1957), p. 88.

20. E. Kirimal, *Der nationale Kampf der Krimtuerken mit besonderer Beruecksichtigung der Jahre 1917–1918* (Emsdetten, 1952), p. 10.

21. Arsharuni and Gabidullin, p. 27.

22. G. Burbiel, *Die Sprache Ismail Bey Gaspiralys* (Ph.D. dissertation, Hamburg, 1950), pp. 91–92.

23. *Tarjuman*, April 15, 1905.

24. I. Gasprinsky, *Russkoe musulmanstvo* (Bakhchisarai, 1881), p. 39.

25. I. Gasprinsky, *Russko-vostochnoe soglashenie* (Bakhchisarai, 1896), pp. 7, 12, 15ff.

26. *MI* (1913), pp. 95, 196, 316.

27. According to the statistics of the Ministry of Education, the number of Moslem parochial schools (maktabs) registered and controlled by the Ministry exceeded 10,000, while the number of registered madrasas (theological seminaries or combinations of high school and college) was 1,085. However, the majority of the madrasas were never registered, and their total number was over 25,000. *Vakyt* (1913), no. 1044, as quoted in *MI* (1913), p. 615. In

1926 there were 33.6 per 100 literate Tatars as against 45.1 among Russians.

28. "Medresse Povolzhia," *MI* (1913), pp. 431–461.

29. For example: I. Alkin, S. Maksudov, Agaev, Hussein Zadeh, A. M. Topchibashev, T. Enikeev, Sh. Syrtlanov, K. Tevkelev, Ziatkhanov, A. Iskhakov, Y. Akchurin, and many others.

30. The other main centers of Islam in the early twentieth century were Cairo, Constantinople, and Calcutta.

31. J. Dzhafarov, *Teatr imeni Azizbekova* (Moskva, 1951), p. 58. *Fiuzat* (Prosperity) was edited by the Russian educated Hussein Zadeh, and one of its main writers was the Russian- and French-educated Agaev; see Chapter VII.

32. Yusuf Akchurin had studied at the "Ecole des sciences politiques" in Paris and spoke French better than Russian.

33. *Istoriia TatASSR*, p. 399.

34. See, for example, the description of a Tatar village in such an overwhelmingly Russian province as Simbirsk in *InOb* (1915), p. 152ff.

Chapter IV.   The National Movement: Parties and Programs in 1905

1. K. F. Faseev, *Iz istorii tatarskoi peredovoi obshchestvennoi mysli* (Kazan, 1955), p. 168.

2. Ibragimov, *Tatary v revoliutsiu 1905 goda*, p. 35; J. [Dz.] Validov, *Ocherki istorii obrazovannosti i literatury volzhskikh Tatar*, pp. 64–65; Mende, *Der nationale Kampf der Russlandstuerken*, p. 82.

3. Ottomanism became an official part of the Young Turks' party program and was proclaimed as such at the congress of Turkish liberal leaders and of representatives from the Moslem and Christian minorities of the Ottoman Empire, in Paris, February 4–9, 1902. P. Fesh, *Constantinople aux derniers jours d'Abdul Hamid* (Paris, 1907), pp. 73, 368–370; Ch. R. Buxton, *Turkey in Revolution* (London, 1909), pp. 285, 142–143.

4. *La Revue du Monde Musulman*, XXI (1912), 174–175 and XXII (1913), 199–200; Zaverand, *Turtsiia i Panturanizm* (Paris, 1930), p. 22; Mende, pp. 82–83; G. Jaeschke, "Der Nazionalismus der Jungtuerken," *Die Welt des Islams*, I (1941), xxiii.

5. Zaverand, p. 42.

6. Arsharuni and Gabidullin, p. 23.

7. Ibragimov, p. 143.

8. Ibragimov, p. 143; Arsharuni and Gabidullin, p. 24.

9. Arsharuni and Gabidullin, p. 24.

10. Text in Arsharuni and Gabidullin, p. 25, and Ibragimov, p. 147.

11. There were more than a hundred participants at the Second Congress, but a large number of them were the delegates to the Kadet convention. Arsharuni and Gabidullin, p. 27; Ibragimov, pp. 57, 139, 172–176.

12. The newspaper *Kazan-Muhbire*, directed by Akchurin himself, also supported the common electoral campaign of Ittifak and the Kadets, indicating that the Moslems represented a faction of the Russian Kadets. Ibragimov, p. 172.

13. Ibragimov, p. 167.

14. Later on Ibragimov was persuaded by his political friends, who were upset by his opportunism, to repudiate this declaration. Arsharuni and Gabidullin, pp. 27–28.

15. The progressive faction of the Moslem clergy, led by Galimjan Barudi, a respected professor of the Muhammedieh madrasa in Kazan, decided to support Ittifak after the first Kazan consultations of 1904–1905. Ibragimov, p. 176.

16. Despite the same electoral regulations for the First and Second Duma the number of Moslem deputies in the First Duma was smaller because of the revolutionary events and transportation difficulties. The deputies from the Akmolinsk, Samarkand, Syr-Daria, Ferghana, and Transcaspian provinces arrived in Petersburg after the dissolution of the First Duma (in session from April 27 to July 8, 1906). Out of the 25 Moslem deputies, 8 were from the Caucasus, 4 from Kazakhstan, and 13 from the Volga and the Urals region. *Chleny Gosudarstvennoi Dumy* (Moskva, 1906).

17. *GosDuma*, I, 3.

18. *Krasnyi arkhiv*, LVII (1933), 92.

19. *Revoliutsiia 1905–1907 godov*, vol. A (Moskva, 1955), 562–611; vol. B, I, 124–139; vol. B, II, 262–310, 408–433; vol. C, II, 651–890; vol. C, III, 701–895; especially vol. C, II, 662. *Revoliutsiia 1905–1907 v natsionalnykh raionakh* (Moskva, 1955), pp. 455–801.

20. *Istoriia TatASSR*, pp. 474–475; *Revoliutsiia 1905–1907 g. v natsionalynkh raionakh*, p. 831; Faseev, p. 80.

21. Proceedings of the Congress, *1906 sano 16–21 Augustosda ictimag Rusya Musulmanlarynin nadvesi* [further abbr. *Proceedings*] (Kazan, 1906), p. 9; and *Vserossiiskii Musulmanskii Siezd* (Kazan, 1906). Some of the resolutions were reprinted by Arsharuni and Gabidullin, pp. 114–123.

22. *Proceedings*, p. 4.

23. *Ibid.*, p. 9.

24. *Ibid.*, pp. 9–10, 160.

25. Appendix to the *Proceedings*, pp. 1–18.

26. *Ibid.*, p. 8.

27. *Ibid.*, pp. 12–13.

28. *Ibid.*, p. 8.

29. Arsharuni and Gabidullin, p. 114.

30. *Ibid.*, pp. 115–116.

31. *Ibid.*, pp. 116–117; cf. *Proceedings*, p. 111.

32. *Proceedings*, p. 101, Arsharuni and Gabidullin, pp. 117–118.

33. *Proceedings*, pp. 157–158.

34. Despite the opposition of some conservative leaders, Ibragimov, the initiator of the Third Congress, received the largest number of votes: 219. He was closely followed by the real victor in the convention, Akchurin, who polled 216. They were followed by Alkin, Gasprinsky, Topchibashev, Apanaev, Barudi, and Maksudov, future leader of the Moslem faction in the Third Duma, who polled from 209 to 179 votes. Little-known Koshchegulov was the last, with only 81 votes. *Proceedings*, pp. 169–170.

35. *Istoriia TatASSR*, p. 458. In addition to its leader, Hasanov, the group consisted of four other Tatars—Kh. Atlasov, A. Najuminev, H. Maksudov, G. Badimsgin—and one Azerbaijani—M. Zeinalov, Duma member from the Baku electoral district. Ibragimov, p. 222.

36. *Istoriia TatASSR*, pp. 458, 485; Ibragimov, p. 222; Arsharuni and Gabidullin, p. 36.

37. *Istoriia TatASSR*, pp. 433, 450; Ibragimov, pp. 46, 56, 84; Faseev, pp. 61–67, 91–94, 167.

38. Chernyshev's article in *IOKU*, XXXIII (1925), 118; S. Rybakov, "Staro–i novometodnye shkoly v russkom islame," *MI* (1912), p. 866; Arsharuni and Gabidullin, pp. 18–21, 126–127.

39. *Yulduz*, no. 794 (February 16, 1912); *Koiash*, no. 366 (March 20, 1914), as quoted in *InOb* (1912), p. 30 and (1914), p. 580.

40. The text of the letter to the Russian police in Arsharuni and Gabidullin, p. 126.

41. The speeches of Sadri Maksudov and K. Hasanov in *Gos Duma II*, 2nd session, pp. 163, 165, 183, 185.

42. In the beginning of 1906 the Ministry of Education introduced certain new regulations which conditioned the opening of new Tatar schools and the use of foreign textbooks in them by the authorization of the Russian authorities. *MI* (1913), pp. 269–273; see Articles 32 and 36.

43. *GosDuma II*, 2nd session, p. 673.

Chapter V.   The Kazakh Problem

1. *Istoriia Kazakhskoi SSR*, ed. M. Auezov (Alma-Ata, 1951), p. 149.

2. N. G. Apollova, *Prisoedinenie Kazakhstana k Rossii* (Alma-Ata, 1948), p. 203.

3. Tevkelev's journal, as quoted in Appollova, p. 65.

4. *Istoriia Kazakhskoi SSR*, p. 264.

5. Khan Uzbek embraced Islam when he ascended the throne of the Golden Horde in 1313; B. Spuler, *Die Goldene Horde* (Leipzig, 1943), p. 217.

6. C. Valikhanov, *Sochineniia*, in *ZRIGO OE*, XXXIX (Petersburg, 1904), 171.

7. The governor, Baron Ingelstrom, pointed out in 1792 that only the upper ruling Kazakh society is interested in Islam. *Materialy po istorii Kazakhskoi SSR*, IV (Moskva, 1940), 124–125.

8. Valikhanov, *Sochineniia*, p. 172.

9. Radloff's report (1875) to the government, as quoted in K. Beisembiev, *Istoriia obshchestvennoi zhizni Kazakhstana vtoroi poloviny XIX veka* (Alma-Ata, 1957), p. 131.

10. G. Kasymov, *Ocherki po religioznomu i antireligioznomu dvizheniiu sredi Tatar* (Kazan, 1932), p. 12.

11. *PSZ*, XXII, nos. 16–170, 16171, 17099; *Materialy po istorii Kazakhskoi SSR*, p. 137.

12. *Materialy po istorii Kazakhskoi SSR*, p. 13; *Istoriia Kazakhskoi SSR*, p. 291.

13. *Tarjuman*, March 15, 1905.

14. V. Cherevanskii, *Zapiski po delam very musulman sunnitov* (Petersburg, 1906), p. 34.

15. Asfendirov, *Istoriia Kazakhstana*, pp. 209–210.

16. *ZhMNP* (July 1904), pp. 29–33.

17. Abdykalykov and Pankratova, p. 317; the preface to Valikhanov's *Sochineniia*, p. xv.

18. M. I. Fetisov, *Literaturnye sviazi Rossii i Kazakhstana* (Moskva, 1956), pp. 219, 248, 320.

19. *Minuvshie Gody*, I (1917), 226.

20. Valikhanov's biography by P. G. Potanin in the preface to Valikhanov's *Sochineniia*, pp. i–xxxi; Beisembiev, pp. 19–22; Fetisov, pp. 239–343.

21. C. Valikhanov, *Statii—Perepiska* (Alma-Ata, 1947), pp. 107–113.
22. F. M. Dostoevskii, *Pisma* (Moskva, 1938), pp. 200–202.
23. Valikhanov, *Statii—Perepiska*, pp. 110–111.
24. Valikhanov, *Sochineniia*, pp. 41–42.
25. *Ibid.*, p. 198.
26. *Ibid.*, pp. 63–64.
27. *Istoriia Kazakhskoi SSR*, p. 393.
28. *Letopis zhizni i deiatelnosti N. G. Chernyshevskogo* (Moskva, 1953), p. 232.
29. G. N. Potanin's preface to Valikhanov, *Sochineniia*, p. xxxi.
30. M. Auezov, *Velikii poet kazakhskogo naroda Abai Kunanbaev* (Moskva, 1954), p. 24; see also Auezov's novels, *Abai* (Moskva, 1949), p. 833, and *Put Abaia* (Moskva, 1952), p. 397.
31. Abai Kunanbaev, *Izbrannoe* (Moskva, 1945), p. 315.
32. *Ibid.*, p. 286.
33. *Ibid.*, p. 285.
34. Abdykalykov and Pankratova, p. 328.
35. N. I. Ilminski, *Vospominaniia o Altynsaryne* (Kazan, 1895); Beisembiev, p. 123ff.
36. *Istoriia Kazakhskoi SSR*, p. 547.
37. G. Folbrok and V. Chernousov, *Inorodcheskie i inovercheskie uchilishcha* (Petersburg, 1903), pp. 15–27.
38. *MI* (1913), p. 270, articles 3–4.
39. Kazakh literature, however, developed very slowly and in the period of 1906–1914 about 100 Kazakh books were published, most of them in Kazan; E. I. Chernyshev, "Vostochnaia pechat v epokhu reaktsii" *IOKU*, XXXIII (1925), part I, 120, 123, 127.
40. Abdykalykov and Pankratova, pp. 368–369; Asfendirov, p. 225; *Istoriia Kazakhskoi SSR*, pp. 440, 534, 556–557.
41. Mindlin, p. 220.
42. M. Dulatov, "Baitursunov," *TOIKK*, III (1922), 21–23.
43. *Ibid.*
44. *Revoliutsiia 1905–1907 g. v Kazakhstane* (Alma-Ata, 1955), pp. 63, 65, 69, 103, 141, 226; *Revoliutsiia 1905–1907 g. v natsionalnykh raionakh*, pp. 705–708.
45. Abdykalykov and Pankratova, p. 349.
46. Arsharuni and Gabidullin, p. 120.
47. *Chleny Gosudarstvennoi Dumy* (Moskva, 1906), pp. 491, 493, 496; *Revoliutsiia 1905–1907 g. v Kazakhstane*, p. 8.
48. For Semirechie see Abdykalykov and Pankratova, p. 288; S. N. Riazantsev, *Kirgiziia* (Moskva, 1951), p. 45.
49. *Istoriia Kazakhskoi SSR*, pp. 518–519.
50. *Ibid.*, pp. 416, 528.
51. The shortcomings of the village self-administration in the Kazakh provinces were well characterized in the depositions of witnesses after the revolt of 1916. See Tanyshbaev's deposition in L. V. Lesnaia, *Vosstanie 1916 g. v Kirgizstane* (Moskva, 1927), pp. 135–137, and the report of the Russian Governor General, A. N. Kuropatkin, "Dnevnik i doklad," *Krasnyi arkhiv*, XXXIV (1929).
52. Lesnaia, pp. 134, 159; Kuropatkin, p. 59.

Chapter VI. Uzbek Liberals and the Young Bukhariotes

1. Russian military operations started in 1865, when the city of Tashkent was stormed by Russian troops. In 1868 Russian detachments defeated the Bukhariote armies. Bukhara relinquished its northeastern provinces and accepted a Russian protectorate. In 1873 Khiva was forced to cede to Russia its possessions north of the Amu River, and recognized Russian suzerainty. In 1876 the khanate of Kokand was annexed. Subsequent operation in 1881–85 brought into Russia's possession the Turkomens of the Transcaspian regions (present Turkmenia).

2. V. Bartold, *Istoriia kulturnoi zhizni Turkestana* (Leningrad, 1929), p. 121.

3. Shiism was proclaimed the state religion of Persia by the founder of the Safavid dynasty, Shah Ismail (1486–1524).

4. Turks began their infiltration into Central Asia in the second half of the sixth century A.D., but the first migration *en masse* occurred around 1000 A.D. when the Seljuks and Karakhanids moved into the region of the Amu and Syr Daria rivers. During and after the Mongol invasion in the first half of the thirteenth century A.D., numerous Turkic tribes settled in Central Asia. The last Turkic migration into the region was that of the Uzbeks, toward 1500 A.D. Until the Russian revolution only the descendants of these last invaders, who preserved the tribal organization, were called Uzbeks. The Turkicized Iranians were called Sarts, while the other Turkic groups retained their original tribal names. Since 1920 all these groups, including the Sarts, have come to be called Uzbeks.

5. Bartold, pp. 67, 79, 96–97, 100, 103, 107, 110.

6. Fitrat's first books were written in Tajik, i.e., "Conversations of an Indian Guest with Europeans," "Stories of an Indian Traveller," and "Arguments of a Bukhariote Professor with a European." On Fitrat, see M. H. Erturk, "Abdul Rauf Fitrat," *Millij Turkistan*, nos. 80–81, pp. 9–10.

7. S. Aini, *Dokhunda* (Moskva, 1948), p. 14; *Kommunist Tadzhikistana*, April 4 and 26, 1953.

8. A. R. Borovkov, "Ocherk istorii uzbekskogo iazyka," *SV* (1949), VI, 24–52, and "Tadzhiksko-uzbekskoe dvuiazychie," *UZIV*, IV, 165; A. V. Gabain, *Oezbekische grammatik* (Leipzig, 1945), pp. 8, 15; *Voprosy uzbekskogo iazykoznaniia* (Tashkent, 1954), p. 144.

9. In 1897 the provinces of Semirechie and Transcaspia were also included in the General Governorship.

10. *Polozhenie ob upravlenii Turkestankogo kraia* (Petersburg, 1892), articles 73–115 on local government, 210–259 on the Moslem kazi; E. S. Schuyler, *Turkistan* (New York, 1876), II, 160–165.

11. Bartold, p. 336.

12. The power of the emir of Bukhara was strengthened by Russia when Russian troops entered the khanate of Bukhara in 1870 to support the emir against the local chieftains of Shahrisiab, Karshi, and Kitab. Later Russian detachments assisted the emir in suppressing revolts in Hissar, Kuliab, Baldjuan, and Darvaz. In 1910 Russian troops were sent to Bukhara at the request of the emir to put an end to riots in the capital. The khans of Khiva also preserved their throne with Russia's help when Russia assisted the khans in defending themselves against the Turkomens in 1873, 1877, 1912, and 1916.

13. On Moslem schools in Central Asia see S. Aini, *Bukhara* (Moskva, 1950), pp. 165–166; N. P. Ostroumov's articles in *ZhMNP* (1907), 1–59 and (1906), X, 122.

14. *Aziatskaia Rossiia* (Petersburg, 1911), I, 256. I. I. Gaier, *Turkestan* (Tashkent, 1909), p. 29, estimates that toward 1900 there were 67,000 students in 4,757 maktabs and 8,025 students in 267 madrasas in Central Asia.

15. In 1897 the total population of the Ferghana, Samarkand, and Syr Daria provinces was 3.9 million, of which 98 per cent were Moslems. About 2.5 million of them were sedentary Uzbeks and 500,000 Tajiks, and the rest were nomadic Kazakhs, Kirghiz, and Turkomens. At that time there were only 60,000 Russians in the area. *BEBE*, IV (suppl.), 571, 727, 810.

16. *Materialy po izucheniiu khoziaistva osedlogo naseleniia v Turkestanskom krae* (Petersburg, 1912), pp. 61–62; A. P. Rakhimbaev, *Tadzhikistan* (Moskva, 1926), p. 11; F. Iliutko, *Basmachestvo v Lokae* (Moskva, Leningrad, 1929), p. 36.

17. Bartold, p. 142.

18. N. V. Khanykov, *Bokhara: Its Amir and Its People* (London, 1845), pp. 271, 276–278; Aini, *Bukhara*, pp. 161–170; N. P. Ostroumov, *ZhMNP* (1906), X, 115–132; A. Polovtsoff, *The Land of Timur* (London, 1932), p. 97.

19. I. I. Umniakov, "K istorii novometodnoi shkoly v Bukhare," *BSAGU* (1927), XVI, p. 83. Comment on the inefficiency can be found throughout the entire literature on Central Asia from Khanykov (1840) to Aini (1950). See Khanykov, pp. 276–297; A. Vambery, *Travel in Central Asia* (New York, 1895) and *History of Bukhara* (London, 1873), p. 302; Schuyler, p. 176; Polovtsoff, pp. 97–98; Aini, pp. 163–165.

20. See the articles in *ZhMNP*, II (1906), by N. P. Ostroumov (p. 140), Baisamynov (p. 159), and Atabaev (p. 165).

21. The famous *Canon of Medicine* by Avicenna was considered, even in Western Europe, as the classic textbook in its field up to the end of the seventeenth century, and is still used in the Near East as a handbook on medical science.

22. Vambery, *History of Bukhara*, pp. 346–365; V. Bartold, "Bukhara," in *Encyclopedia of Islam*, I (Leiden, 1913), 782.

23. Bartold, pp. 124–125; K. P. Novitskii, "Politika tsarskogo pravitelstva . . . ," PrNat, VI (1924), 92.

24. Novitskii, pp. 19–23.

25. In 1892, for instance, the Governor General recommended that only natives with a knowledge of Russian, and particularly graduates of the Russian or "bilingual" schools, be appointed to positions of interpreter, local administrator, and judge. See *Okraina* (Samarkand), March 9, 1892, and N. O. Ostroumov, *Sarty*, 3rd ed., (Tashkent, 1909), p. 180; see also the March 2, 1907 instructions to the electors from the Syr-Daria oblast, and the Uzbeks' 1909 petition to Count Pahlen, in E. Fedorov, *Ocherki natsionalno-osvoboditelnogo dvizheniia v Srednei Azii* [further abbr. *Ocherki*] (Tashkent, 1925), p. 80.

26. N. Mallaev, *Uzbek adavieti tarihi* (Tashkent, 1955), pp. 195–247, *passim*.

27. *Vsia Sredniaia Aziia* (Tashkent, 1926), p. 73; Iskander, "Podgotovka Angliei Bukharskogo platsdarma dlia interventsii v Sovetskii Turkestan, 1918–1920," *IstZap*, XXXIV (1951), 32; *INU*, II, 243.

28. *Antologiia Tadzhikskoi poezii* (Moskva, 1951), pp. 18–19, 478–479; Gafurov, pp. 430–434; A. M. Donish, "History of the Mangit Khans," as quoted by B. Gafurov in *Istoriia Tadzhiksgogo naroda* (Moskva, 1949), p. 432; see also Aini, pp. 204–214; Mallaev, pp. 180–181.

29. *Antologiia Tadzhikskoi poezii*, p. 481; Gafurov, pp. 433–434.

30. Umniakov, p. 82.

31. Jarcek, "Munevver Kari, Patriot and Reformer," *Millij Turkistan,* no. 52 (1951), 7.

32. Strikes and disturbances in Central Asia in 1905 were entirely the work of Russian railway workers and soldiers. General Sakharov, Governor General of Central Asia, wrote in answer to Witte's telegram: "The natives are perfectly quiet and behave most correctly." E. Fedorov, *1905 god i korennoe naselenie Srednei Azii* (Moskva, 1926), p. 16 [further abbr. *1905 god*]. In 1906 the governor of Ferghana, Pokotillo, also reported that "peace and quiet reigned among the usually violent population of Ferghana." *Ocherki,* p. 22.

33. See reports of the chief of police in Tashkent, N. Karaulshchikov, from January 19, 1906, and of the imperial diplomatic agent in Bukhara, Mr. Ross, from July 27, 1906, in *Ocherki,* p. 22; see also *1905 god,* p. 15, and *INU,* II, 390.

34. There were, for example, over thirteen native bookstores catering to the liberal customers in the city of Kokand. *INU,* II, 390, 413.

35. Bartold, p. 372; *Ocherki,* p. 24.

36. *Ocherki,* pp. 44–45; N. Ostroumov, "Madrasy," *ZhMNP* (1907), I, 17.

37. Archives of the Tajik SSR, document no. 5, as quoted by K. P. Novitskii, p. 82.

38. Ostroumov, "Madrasy," p. 17.

39. *INU,* II, 314. For more details see S. Zenkovsky, "Kulturkampf in Prerevolutionary Central Asia," *ASaEER,* XIV (1955), 24–25.

40. The regime in Bukhara had not changed since the early nineteenth century when N. V. Khanykov wrote that "The administration is in the hands of the clergy and it cannot be otherwise as there exists no other law but the spiritual—namely, that which is founded on the Koran." Khanykov, p. 265.

41. Umniakov, p. 83.

42. *Ocherki,* p. 27. S. Aini wrote the first Tajik textbook for this school. See Aini, *Dokhunda* (Moskva, 1948), p. iv.

43. *INU,* II, 413; Gafurov, p. 455; *Ocherki,* pp. 28–29.

44. D. N. Logofet, *V strane bezpraviia* (Petersburg, 1909), pp. 178–183.

45. S. Aini, *Raby* (Moskva, 1951), pp. 129–172; Gafurov, p. 441. Cf. Schuyler, *Turkistan,* II, 100–109, 354. The state treasury was identical with the privy purse of the emir, and of the 30 million rubles comprising the state income, 27 million were spent for the monarch and his court.

46. *Tarjuman,* no. 27 (June 1909). Cf. *Ocherki,* pp. 27–29.

47. *Tarjuman,* no. 27 (June 1909), pp. 29–30.

48. As early as 1909 two special commissions were created to study Bukhara with a view to its annexation, and P. A. Stolypin, Russian Prime Minister, strongly supported abolishing the regime of the emir. See Gafurov, p. 445, and G. G. Georatskii, *Revoliutsiia pobezhdaet* (Tashkent, 1920), p. 4.

49. Aini, *Dokhunda,* p. iv; cf. *Kommunist Tadzhikistana* (April 4 and 26, 1953); F. Khodzhaev, "Dzhadidy," *Ocherki revoliutsionnogo dvisheniia v Srednei Azii* (Moskva, 1937), p. 11.

50. A. Fitrat, *Munizira,* translated into Russian by Col. Jagello under the title *Fitrat Bukharets, spor bukharskogo mudarrisa s evropeitsem v Indii o novometodnykh shkolakh* (Tashkent, 1911). See also M. H. Erturk, "Abdul Rauf Fitrat," *Millij Turkistan,* nos. 80–81 (1952), 9. A. Fitrat, *Rasskazy indiiskogo puteshestvennika* (Samarkand, 1913).

51. Fitrat, Munizira, pp. 50, 64.

52. *Ibid.,* pp. 53, 56, 72.

53. The society was founded in 1909 but became particularly active after 1910–1911. A. M. Samoilovich, "Pervo tainoe obshchestvo Mlado-Bukhartsev," *Vostok*, I (Leningrad, 1922), 98. The character and program of the society's educational activities are in Arsharuni and Gabidullin, pp. 133–135.

54. Arsharuni and Gabidullin, pp. 134–135.

55. Umniakov, p. 94.

56. "M.N.," "Pod znakom Islama," *Vovy vostok*, XVI (1924), 87; Samoilovich, p. 99.

57. Samoilovich, p. 98.

Chapter VII. Azerbaijani Awakening

1. *Ocherki po istorii SSSR* (Moskva, 1956), I, 443–447.

2. G. Vernadsky, *A History of Russia,* I (New Haven, 1946), 219–222; *Ocherki po istorii SSSR*, I, 484–485.

3. V. N. Sysoev, *Kratkii ocherk istorii Azerbaidzhana* (Baku, 1925), pp. 57, 143.

4. R. Grousset, *L'Empire des steppes* (Paris, 1948), p. 206; Sir Percy Sikes, *A History of Persia* (London, 1930), II, 182; B. Spuler, *Iran in fruehislamischer Zeit* (Wiesbaden, 1952), p. 253.

5. *Perepis 1926*, V (Moskva, 1927), 126; F. Lorrimer, *The Population of the Soviet Union* (Geneva, 1946), p. 138.

6. *Perepis 1926*, p. xx. The total population of Azerbaijan in 1939 was 3.2 million, of which 1,950,000 were Azerbaijan Turks, 513,000 Russians, 385,000 Armenians; *Bolshaia Sovetskaia Entsiklopedia* (new ed., Moskva, 1951), I, 440.

7. *Ocherki po istorii SSSR*, VI, 959–960; E. G. Browne, *A Literary History of Persia* (London, 1930), IV, 22; Sikes, *A History of Persia*, II, 159.

8. *Kavkazskii Kalendar na 1917 g.* (Tiflis, 1917), part II, 178–181.

9. *Kolonialnaia politika tsarisma v Azerbaidzhane v 20–60–kh gg. XIX veka* (Moskva, Leningrad, 1936), p. 9.

10. Akhond-Zadeh, while not the first Azerbaijani writer, was the most representative of the literature of the Turkic revival. Azerbaijani literature, especially poetry, written in Ottoman Turkish flourished already in the sixteenth century, when the poet Fuzali (died between 1556 and 1562) wrote his famous *Divan*. In the succeeding centuries the Iranian influence almost entirely displaced the Turkic in the works of Azerbaijani writers. J. H. Purgstall, *Geschichte der Osmanishschen Dichtung* (Pesth, 1837), II, 293–303; A. Karahan, *Fuzali*, (Istanbul, 1949); E. J. W. Gibb, *Ottoman Literature* (New York, London, 1901), pp. 85–99, 226; E. J. W. Gibb, *History of Ottoman Poetry* (1900–1909), VI, 70–107; and Mirza Bala, "Fatali", *ObKav*, XXIII (1953), 9–11 and XXVI (1953), 18–21.

11. Akhond-Zadeh's works were translated into English and French; see "The Magistrate" in *Turkish Literature* (London, 1901), pp. 25–66; A. Cillière, *Deux comédies turques* (Paris, 1888); C. Barbier de Meynard and S. Guyard, *Trois comédies* (Paris, 1886); C. Bouvat, *Monsieur Jourdan* (Paris, 1906). See also M. F. Akhundov [Akhond-Zadeh], *Sochineniia* (Tbilisi, 1938), p. 36; D. Dzhafarov, *Teatr imeni Ahundova* (Moskva, 1932), pp. 28–29.

12. Most of the subscribers to *Akinchi* were peasants, and the newspaper was published in colloquial Azerbaijani; *MI*, II (1913), pp. 884–885.

13. P. A. Khromov, *Ekonomicheskoe razvitie Rossii v 19 v.* (Moskva, 1950),

pp. 206, 318–319; P. I. Liashchenko, *Istoriia narodnogo khoziaistva SSSR* (Moskva, 1953), II, 147, 402–403, 563.

14. In 1908–1909 there were about 50,000 industrial workers in Baku—70 per cent of the total number of workers in Transcaucasia. In the 1890's 30 per cent of the workers were Armenian and only 12 per cent were Azerbaijanian, while the remainder consisted of Russians, Persians, etc. Most of the Baku oil fields and about 60 per cent of production were in the hands of foreigners (Nobel, Rothschild), and the rest belonged mostly to Armenians (Lianozov, Mantachev, Gukasov). By 1916 the population of Baku was about 400,000, of which a quarter was Russian, another quarter Armenian, and a half Azerbaijanian. The countryside was dominated by the Azerbaijanis: 81 per cent of them were peasants. Among Armenians only 47 per cent were peasants and 13 per cent tradesmen. *Kavkazskii Kalendar za 1917 god* (Tiflis, 1917), pp. 173–181; B. Ischchanian, *Nationaler Bestand, berufsmaessige Gruppierung und soziale Gliederung der kaukasischen Voelker* (Berlin, 1914), pp. 54–55; *MI*, II (1913), 608.

15. In Persian Azerbaijan the Iranian influence was still stronger, and even in the beginning of the twentieth century writers used Persian. *Türk Yurdu*, XXII (1912), 672, as quoted in *MI*, I (1912), p. 643.

16. E. Renan, *L'Allemagne* (New York, 1945), pp. 89, 173.

17. Ahmad Bey's [Agaev's] Series of Articles, "La Société Persane," in *Nouvelle Revue*, 1891–1893, especially 1891 (XC, 796–798); in *Kaspii*, no. 127 (1899); and in *Kavkaz*, no. 179, (1893).

18. Topchibashev, "Panislamism i ego kharakter," *Kaspii*, no. 87 (1900).

19. H. Munschi, *Die Republik Azerbaidschan* (Berlin, 1930), pp. 17–19; *MI*, I (1912), 281, 465, 615 and II (1913), 193–194; Zaverand, *Turtsiia i Panturanizm*, p. 43.

20. *MI*, II (1913), 294.

21. Munschi, p. 20. See also Agaev's articles in *Kavkaz*, no. 179 (1893) and *Kaspii*, no. 127 (1899).

22. M. D. Bagirov, *Iz Istorii bolshevistskikh organizatsii Baku i Azerbaidzhana* (Moskva, 1946), p. 51; I. Deutsch, *Stalin* (New York, London, 1949), p. 66; F. Kazemzadeh, *The Struggle for Transcaucasia*, (New York, 1951), pp. 19–20; *Stalin k shestidesiatiletiiu so dnia rozhdeniia* (Moskva, 1939), p. 105; see also the reports to the Minister of the Interior, Prince P. D. Sviatopolk Mirsky, in *Revoliutsiia 1905–1907 gg.*, vol. A (Moskva, 1955), 565–569, 572–576.

23. Report of the Viceroy of Caucasus, Count I. I. Vorontsov-Dashkov, in *Revoliutsiia 1905–1907 gg.*, vol. B, II (Moskva, 1955), 266–273.

24. In 1907, the first year of its existence, the society collected 15,778 roubles, while in 1911, only 1,700. *MI*, II (1913), 500–504.

25. Hussein Zadeh was even elected a member of the central committee of the Young Turks Party. Agaev became, in 1920, the editor of *Hakiemete Mille*, Kemal Pasha Ataturk's official newspaper, and was Hussein Zadeh's close adviser and a member of the Turkish National Assembly. Zaverand, pp. 42–44; *MI*, II (1913), 500.

26. Mirza Bala, "Resul Zadeh" in *ObKav*, XXX (1954), 25–26; Zaverand, pp. 71–72; *La Revue du Monde Musulman*, LI (1922), 245.

27. M. D. Guseinov, *Tiurkskaia demokraticheskaia partiia Musavat v proshlom i nastoiashchem* (Baku, 1927), p. 9.

28. *Ibid.*, pp. 10, 71, 73.

29. Kazemzadeh, p. 22.

30. A. Baikov, "Vospominaniia o revoliutsii v Zakavkazii," *Arkhiv russkoi revoliutsii* (Berlin, 1923), V, 108–109.

31. Zaverand, p. 102.

32. Guseinov, pp. 77–78.

Chapter VIII. Pan-Turkists and the Tatarists

1. Four deputies from Ufa, two from Kazan, one from Orenburg, one from the Baku and Elizavetpol provinces, and one from Daghestan.

2. Three from Ufa, one from Samara, one from Orenburg, one from Baku, and one from Daghestan. The deputy from Daghestan voted with the "progressists."

3. These 49,000 Tatars deserted from the ranks of some 165,000 Orthodox Tatars, *InOb* digest of Turkic press, I (1912), 3. It must be added that these Tatars never became devout Orthodox Christians; they had been converted to Orthodoxy in 1720–1740 under strong administrative and missionary pressure, and essentially remained faithful to their ancestral Islam. The remaining 115,000 Orthodox Tatars were the descendants of pagan Tatars who had been converted in the late sixteenth century by Bishop Gurius; they remained faithful to Orthodoxy.

4. Bishop Andrew's report to Prime Minister P. A. Stolypin in *Krasnyi arkhiv* [further abbr. *KrAr*], XXXV (1929), 130.

5. *MI* digest of Turkic press, II (1913), 269–273.

6. *KrAr*, XXXVI (1929), 79–83.

7. This general decrease in agitation and a more passive attitude toward political problems was characteristic for all of Russia in 1908–1914.

8. On the development of Turkish nationalism and Pan-Turkism see U. Heyd, *The Foundation of Turkish Nationalism* (London, 1950), pp. 108–109; on the Saloniki group and their activities see J. Deny, "Zia Gek Alp" in *La Revue du Monde Musulman* [further abbr. *RMM*], LXI (1925), part II, 6; R. Hartmann, "Zija Gek Alp" in *Orientalische Literatur-Zeitung* [further abbr. *OLZ*], 1925, p. 589ff.; E. F. Knight, *The Awakening of Turkey* (London, 1909), pp. 106, 111, 120; and C. R. Buxton, *Turkey in Revolution* (London, 1909), pp. 44–46.

9. As stated in Chapter I, the linguistic and racial relationship of the Altaic (Turko-Mongol) group to the Uralic (Finno-Ugric) is rather uncertain.

10. *L'Asie Française*, October-December 1917, pp. 174–175. An excellent presentation of the rise of the Pan-Turkic psychosis in Zaverand, *Turtsiia i Panturanizm*, pp. 65–66; see also the above-mentioned works of Denis and Hartmann.

11. Yusuf Akchurin came to Constantinople as a correspondent of the Tatar newspaper *Vakyt* (Orenburg).

12. Kirimal, *Der nationale Kampf der Krimtuerken*, p. 24.

13. Its aim was primarily to help the Central Asian students studying in Constantinople. For the text of the charter of the Society see Arsharuni and Gabidullin, pp. 133–135.

14. Kirimal, p. 26.

15. *RMM*, X (1910), 106.

16. *Türk Yurdu*, XXII (1912), as quoted in *MI*, I (1912), 64.

17. In *Türk Yurdu* Gasprinsky wrote mostly about educational problems. *Türk Yurdu*, VII–VIII (1912), as quoted in *MI*, I (1912), 487.

18. *Türk Yurdu*, I (1911), 14, as quoted in *MI*, I (1912), 490. Seventy to eighty million Turks is an absolutely fantastic total, since even in 1955–1956 their total number hardly exceeds forty five to fifty million. *Encyclopaedia Britannica* (1955), XXI, 623.

19. *Türk Yurdu*, II (1912), 39, as quoted in *MI*, (1912), 490.

20. *Türk Yurdu*, XVIII (1912), 547, as quoted in *MI*, I (1912), 635.

21. Zia Gek Alp's poems "The Turkish People" and "The Turan," *RMM*, LXVI, part II, 26 and *OLZ* (1925), p. 381.

22. *Türk Yurdu*, XV (1912), 1, as quoted in *MI*, I (1912), 635, 638.

23. R. Labonne, "La crise orientale et le nationalisme en Asie," *Le Correspondant* (1922), vols. 287–399.

24. Hartmann, p. 589.

25. *Türk Yurdu*, XVIII (1912), 559, as quoted in *MI*, I (1912), 641.

26. *Türk Yurdu* (1912), V, 137–138; I, 24; XIII, 559; XX, 612, 625—as quoted in *MI*, I (1912), 490, 491, 636, 641, 642.

27. *MI*, I (1912), 486.

28. *Shura*, no. 1 (1912), as quoted in *MI*, I (1913), 15.

29. *Shura*, nos. 2–3 (1912), as quoted in *MI*, I (1913), 22.

30. See the review of Gaty's work in *InOb*, I (1915), 224–225.

31. *Shura*, no. 8 (1912), as quoted in *MI*, I (1912), 28–29.

32. *InOb*, I (1915), 215–217.

33. *InOb*, I (1915), 222–223.

34. *Yulduz*, no. 786 (1912) and *Shura*, no. 1 (1914), as quoted in *InOb*, I (1915), 26, 642.

35. A. Tukaev, *Stikhi* (Moskva, 1946), pp. 27, 107. Since Tukaev was known for his negative attitude toward Turkic nationalism and émigrés, the Constantinople group was rather hostile toward him. *MI*, II (1913), 156–162; Faseev, p. 276.

36. *Koiash*, nos. 377, 382, 385–387, 394 (1914); *Yulduz*, no. 1170 (1914), as quoted in *InOb*, I (1915), 394–395; *Tarjuman*, no. 82 (1912).

37. *Türk Yurdu* (May 16, 1912), as quoted in *MI*, II (1913), 162, 169.

38. Kirimal, p. 25.

39. The total circulation of "Moslem" books published in Russia was about three million copies a year.

40. During 1908–1914 a clandestine nationalist organization, *Vatan* (Fatherland), was organized in Crimea; it developed considerable propaganda activities. Kirimal, pp. 27–28. The formation of Musavat (see Chapter VII) was a matter of local interest to Azerbaijani politicians and had little effect on the life of other Russian Moslems. An increase of interest for international Moslem affairs could be noticed only during the Turkish-Italian and the Balkan wars. See the review of the Moslem press in Russia in *InOb*, I (1912), 27–29, and Chernyshev's article in *IOKU*, XXXIII (1925), 126.

41. In a series of lectures Iskhakov stressed that the entire Tatar literature of 1908–1914 was characterized by "its spirit of democratism, fighting preparedness, and sacrifice for the people" (the word "people" was used in the sense it was used by Russian intelligentsia: the socially lower, "oppressed" groups of the population). In its examination of the evolution of Tatar letters and Tatar intelligentsia, *Türk Yurdu* also stressed that the "social spirit" was one of the most outstanding qualities of the Tatar intelligentsia and their writings. *MI*, II (1913), 165.

42. J. [Dz.] Validov, *Millet ve Milliet* (Nation and Nationalism) (Orenburg, 1914), quoted from a digest edited by A. Samoilovich in *Vostochnyi sbornik*, II, (Petrograd, 1916), 22, 27, 31.

43. Iskhaki, *Idel Ural*, p. 38.

44. In 1913 Sadri Maksudov became the head of the small Moslem caucus in the Duma and represented Ittifak there.

45. According to the statistics of the Moslem Ecclesiastic Administration in Ufa, by January 1, 1912 there were only 16,220,000 Moslems in Russia. This total included about 2,000,000 Caucasian mountaineers and about 100,000 Tajiks, who speak other than Turkic languages. *MI*, II (1913), p. 761.

46. See Maksudov's speeches in *GosDuma III* (stenographic reports), II, 1273, 1275, 1651, 2575, 2643, 2645, and III, 472–476.

47. Kh. Khasatov's interview with M. I. Jafarov in *Ikbal*, no. 340 (1913), as quoted in *MI*, II (1913), 102.

48. *MI*, II (1913), p. 109.

49. *MI*, II (1913), p. 102.

50. *Sibir*, no. 996 (1912), as quoted in *MI*, II (1913), p. 625.

51. *KrAr*, LXXIX (1936), 19–21; and *Pril.k otch. GosDumy*, 2nd session, II, 1–7.

52. *Vakyt*, nos. 917, 918, 932, 947, 985, 990, 991, 1010, 1024 (1912), as quoted in *MI*, I (1912), 265, 464, 610, 611.

53. *Vakyt*, nos. 1567, 1576 (1914); *Yulduz*, nos. 778, 798 (1912); *Baian ul Hakk*, no. 969 (1912), as quoted in *InOb*, I (1912–1914), 25–26, 31, 555.

54. After his trip to Central Asia, Maksudov recommended a reduction of Russian classes in Moslem schools. Arsharuni and Gabidullin, p. 41.

55. *Ikbal* (1912), as quoted in *MI*, I (1912), 627; cf. *DiSIIa* (1955), VIII, 102.

56. See, for instance, *1906 sano 16–21 aug. ictimag itmek Rusia musulmanlarinin nadvasi* (Kazan, 1906), pp. 107, 111, 116, 121, 140–145ff; and *Butun Rusia musulmanlarinin 1917nci yilda 1–11 maida Meskevde bulgan umumi isiezdinin protocollari* (Petrograd, 1917), pp. 59, 66, 71, 79, 160ff.

57. *MI*, II (1913), 57.

58. 361 in Tatar, 40 in Uzbek, 36 in Kazakh, 24 in Azerbaijani. Azerbaijanis read primarily the Ottoman Turkish books. Chernyshev, p. 114; *MI*, II (1913), 57.

59. For example, read the information in the digest of the Moslem press in *MI*, I (1912), 261, 263, 264, 268, 277, 465, 472, 763.

60. The Fourth Congress of the Moslems of Russia was devoted to the problem of religious organization of Islam in Russia. The congress took place in Petersburg in June 1914. A. M. Topchibashev complained about governmental policies of educational Russification. Arsharuni and Gabidullin, pp. 47–49.

61. Since the beginning of the twentieth century, Russian clergy tried to re-establish the elective Patriarchate and to free the church from the control of the governmental *Ober-Prokuror* (governmental supervisor of the church). G. Florovskii, *Puti russkago bogosloviia* (Paris, 1937), p. 777.

Chapter IX. World War I and the Central Asian Revolt of 1916

1. *Kazanskii Telegraf*, August 28, 1914, as quoted in *InOb* digest of the Turkic press, I (1914), 558.

2. *Turmush*, October 2, 1914, as quoted in *InOb*, I (1914), 625.

3. *Istoriia Tatarskoi ASSR* (Kazan, 1955), p. 505; Arsharuni and Gabidullin, pp. 49–50.

4. *Turmush*, October 31, 1914, as quoted in *InOb*, I (1914), 618.

5. *KrAr*, XXXIV (1929), 80.

6. *Kaspii*, January 1, 1915.

7. *Kazanskii Telegraf*, August 26, 1914, as quoted in *InOb*, I (1914), 637.

8. *Koiash*, November 23, 1914, as quoted in *InOb*, I (1914), 609.

9. *Kazanskii Telegraf*, October 22, 1914, as quoted in *InOb*, vol. I (1914), p. 612.

10. *Turmush*, October 26, 1914, as quoted in *InOb*, I (1914), 622–623.

11. See Chapter VII.

12. M. D. Guseinov, *Tiurkskaia demokraticheskaia partiia federalistov, Musavat v proshlom i nastoiashchem* (Baku, 1924), pp. 36–37.

13. B. Elagin, "Natsionalisticheskie illiuzii krymskikh Tatar v revoliutsionnye gody," *Novyi Vostok*, V (1925), 192.

14. Arsharuni and Gabidullin, p. 54.

15. *Byloe*, XXVII–XXVIII (1924), 243–245.

16. *Istoriia narodov Uzbekistana* (Tashkent, 1947), II, 450–451.

17. Zaverand, *Turtsiia i Panturanism*, pp. 107–108.

18. Arsharuni and Gabidullin, p. 57.

19. Memorandum of the Committee for Defense of Moslem Rights, *Die Welt des Islams* [further abbr. *WdI*] (1916), IV, 33–43.

20. *Le Temps*, December 14, 1915; *Das groessere Deutschland* (1916), pp. 542–543, 555–556; *WdI*, IV, 39, 43.

21. *RRM*, LIV (1923), 146–147; B. Spuler, *Idel Ural* (Berlin, 1942), pp. 88–89.

22. *RRM*, LVI (1922), 81; IV (1916), 207.

23. E. Insolato, *L'Islam et la politique des Alliés* (Paris, 1920), p. 200.

24. P. Liashchenko, *Istoriia narodnogo khoziaistva SSSR* (Moskva, 1952), II, 615.

25. *Kazakh*, January 24, 1915, as quoted in *InOb* (1915), pp. 252–257; cf. Tanyshbaev's opinion of the Kazakh mobilization, L. V. Lesnaia, *Vosstanie 1916 g. v Kirgizstane* (Moskva, 1927), pp. 142, 168, 177, 179, 184.

26. Lesnaia, p. 143.

27. M. Sokolovskii's (governor of Astrakhan) telegram in *KrAr*, XVI (1926), 55.

28. General A. N. Kuropatkin's diary in *KrAr*, XXXIV (1929), 46.

29. *Istoriia narodov Uzbekistana*, II, 433. E. D. Sokol offers in his book, *The Revolt of 1916 in Russian Central Asia* (Baltimore, 1953), a very detailed and accurate account of the happenings in Jizak and other cities of Central Asia.

30. For detailed reports on the revolt and Russian military operations in Kirghizia, see Lesnaia, p. 167, and *Istoriia Kirgizii* (Frunze, 1956), pp. 397–404.

31. P. Galuzo's introduction to Kuropatkin's diary and report in *KrAr*, XXXIV (1929) 43. In his report to Nicholas II, Kuropatkin reported 2,325 men killed and 1,384 missing—probably also killed. *Ibid.*, p. 85.

32. *Istoriia Kirgizii*, pp. 403–404.

33. G. Stepniak, "Kirgizskoe vosstanie," *Sibirskie Ogni*, I (1928), 133–135, 140, 145.

34. Abdykalykov and Pankratova, *Istoriia Kazakhskoi ASSR*, p. 391.

35. *Ibid.*, pp. 385, 393; Kuropatkin, pp. 61–65; Asfendirov, *Istoriia Kazakhstana*, p. 230.

36. *KrAr*, XVI (1926), 55; *Kazakh*, July 8, 1916, as quoted in *Kazakhstan*, ed. S. Nurpesov (Moskva, 1926), p. 7.

37. Abdykalykov and Pankratova, pp. 394–395; Asfendirov, p. 241.

38. M. Dulatov, "Baitursunov," *TOIKK*, III (1922), p. 22.

39. Sokol, p. 90. Very important new material on participation of Jadids in the revolt of 1916 can be found in *Materialy nauchnoi sessii posviashchennoi istorii Srednei Azii i Kazakhstana v dooktiabrskii period* (Tashkent, 1955), pp. 295, 332, 359, 400.

Chapter X.   Russia's Moslems in the Revolution of 1917

1. *Revoliutsiia i natsionalnyi vopros*, ed. S. Dimanshtein [further abbr. *RiNV*] (Moskva, 1930), III, 287; Arsharuni and Gabidullin, pp. 58–59.

2. *Istoriia Tatarskoi ASSR* (Kazan, 1956), pp. 552–553. The order for General Sandetsky's arrest was not carried through, and he remained at the head of the Kazan military district until May 1917. N. F. Kalinin, *Kazan* (Kazan, 1936), p. 184.

3. *Istoriia Tatarskoi ASSR*, pp. 553–554; *RiNV*, p. 280; E. Grachev, *Kazanskii Oktiabr* (Kazan, 1926), p. 28.

4. *RiNV*, p. 287.

5. By 1897 there were 675,000 Tatars in the Kazan province out of the total population of 2,170,665; in Orenburg, 92,000 out of 1,600,145; in Ufa, 184,817 out of 2,196,642; in Samara, 165,191 out of 2,751,330, etc. *Perepis 1897*, VII, 4.

6. Grachev, pp. 34–35.

7. R. M. Raimov, *Obrazovanie Bashkirskoi ASSR* (Moskva, 1952), p. 80.

8. B. Hajit, *Die nationale Regierung von Kokand und Alasch-Orda* (Muenster, 1950, mimeographed), p. 22.

9. Kirimal, *Der nationale Kampf der Krimtuerken*, pp. 39, 41–42. At that time the Crimean Tatars constituted about a quarter of the total population of the peninsula.

10. *Bütün Rusya müsülmanlarinin 1917nci yilda 1–11 mayda Meskevde bulgan umumi isyezdinin protokollari* (Petrograd, 1917) [Proceedings of the All-Russian Moslem Congress in Moscow, May 1–11, 1917], pp. 4–6.

11. *Ibid.*, pp. 8–12.

12. *Ibid.*, pp. 19–20.

13. *Ibid.*, p. 22.

14. *Ibid.*, pp. 44–45.

15. *Ibid.*, pp. 87–88.

16. *Ibid.*, pp. 116–118.

17. *Ibid.*, p. 184.

18. *Ibid.*, p. 196.

19. *Ibid.*, pp. 212–217.

20. *Ibid.*, p. 208.

21. *Ibid.*, pp. 154–157.

22. *Ibid.*, p. 211.

23. *Ibid.*, p. 223.

24. *Ibid.*, p. 243.

25. *Ibid.*, p. 201.

26. *Ibid.*, p. 250.

27. *Ibid.*, p. 325.

28. *Ibid.*, p. 373.

29. *Ibid.*, p. 451.

30. *Ibid.*, pp. 246, 298.

31. *Ibid.*, p. 152.

32. *Ibid.*, p. 152.

33. *Ibid.*, p. 154.

34. *Ibid.*, p. 416.

35. *Ibid.*, p. 420.

36. *Ibid.*, pp. 391, 426, 449.

37. *Ibid.*, p. 117.

38. At this particular meeting the breakup of the council was still successfully evaded. Iskhakov's speech in *RiNV*, p. 307.

39. *Ibid.*, pp. 307–308. Maksudov predicted that the "tribal dissensions of Russian Moslems will lead to their ruin."

40. A. Popov, "Iz istorii revoliutsii v Vostochnom Zakavkazii," *Revoliutsionnyi vostok*, VII (1924), 113.

41. A. Iskhakov's memoirs in *YMY*, no. 114 (1937), 3–6 *passim*.

42. *DnO* (1917), II, 858–859, and Tsalikov's comment to the author.

43. M. L. Murtazin, *Bashkiriia i bashkirskie voiska v grazhdanskuiu voinu* (Leningrad, 1927), pp. 52–53.

44. *RiNV*, p. 315.

45. Grachev, p. 132, indicates August 1, 1917 as the date of the proclamation of autonomy, while Mende, pp. 126–127, records July 22, 1917.

46. Mende's (p. 127) translation of the official Tatar text published in *Muhtariet*, January 16, 1918; cf. *RiNV*, pp. 319–324, and Grachev, pp. 129–131.

47. Zaverand, p. 111.

48. *KPSS v rezoliutsiiakh i resheniiakh siezdov* (Moskva, 1953), II, 315–316.

49. *Ibid.*, p. 346.

50. *Ibid.*, p. 361.

51. *Bolshaia Sovetskaia entsiklopediia* (new ed., Moskva, 1951), VII, 62.

52. I. Deutscher, *Stalin* (London, 1949), p. 182.

53. *Dekrety oktiabrskoi revoliutsii* (Moskva, 1933), I, 28–30; *Istoriia sovetskoi konstitutsii* (Moskva, 1957), p. 57.

54. *Politika sovetskoi vlasti po natsionalnomu voprosu za tri goda, 1917–1920* (Moskva, 1920), pp. 4–5; *Istoriia sovetskoi konstitutsii*, pp. 66–68.

55. *Sobranie Uzakonenii, 1917–1918* (Petrograd, 1919), no. 6 Art. 107, no. 17 Art. 243.

56. *Ibid.*, no. 17 Art. 243.

57. *DnO* (1917), II, 344, 857, 858, and A. Tsalikov's comment to the author.

58. Iskhakov's memoirs in *YMY*, no. 114 (1937), 10.

59. J. Stalin, *Sochineniia* (Moskva, 1947), IV, 6–7.

60. See N. Jordania's (first president of Georgia) declarations of December 24, 1917. G. Urtadze, *Obrazovanie i konsolidatsiia Gruzinskoi Demokraticheskoi Respubliki*, Institute for the Study of the USSR, series no. 29 (Muenchen, 1956), pp. 27–28.

61. Text of the Bolshevik faction's resolution in *KPSS v resoliutsiakh i resheniakh siezdov*, II, 316.

Chapter XI. Idel-Ural Dreams

1. M. Sultangaliev, "Tatarskaia ASSR," *Zhizn natsionalnostei*, no. 1 (1923), 30.

2. A. Bochkov, *Tri goda sovetskoi vlasti v Kazani 1917–1920* (Kazan, 1921), p. 14.

3. *Vpered* (Ufa, October 27, 1917), as quoted in R. M. Raimov, *Obrazovanie Bashkirskoi ASSR* (Moskva, 1952), p. 103.

4. *Beznen Yul* [Our Path] (Ufa, November 5, 1917), as quoted in Raimov, pp. 103–105.

5. *Gazeta vremennogo raboche-krestianskogo pravitelstva* (December 10, 1917), as quoted in *Politika sovetskoi vlasti za tri goda, 1917–1920* (Moskva, 1920), p. 80.

6. *Pravda*, no. 2 (January 17, 1918), as quoted in V. Lenin, *Sochineniia*, XXVI (Moskva, 1946), 385–387.

7. In Russian, *Zabulachnaia respublika*.

8. The period of time when the Milli Mejilis was in session is uncertain. G. von Mende, *Der nationale Kampf der Russlandtuerken* (Berlin, 1936), p. 130, dates it from November 20, 1917 to January 11, 1918; whereas A. Battal, *Kazan Turkleri* (Istanbul, 1925), p. 225, dates it from October 17, 1917 to January 9, 1918.

9. The committee consisted of Russian anti-Communist parties, Kazakhs and Bashkirs (Validov's supporters), the Kazakhs (Kirgiz), and the Orenburg cossacks.

10. *DnO* (1917), III, 344.

11. The Russian word *shtat*, used by the Tatars for the qualification of their autonomy, designates a self-governed, autonomous territory and not a sovereign nation.

12. S. Atnagulov, *Bashkiriia* (Moskva, 1925), pp. 61–63; Mende, p. 130; and Iskhakov in *YMY*, no. 117 (1937), 11–12.

13. *DnO* (1917), II, 403.

14. *Atnagulov*, p. 61.

15. Atnagulov, p. 63; Validov's comment to the author.

16. N. Kalinin, *Kazan* (Kazan, 1956), p. 202.

17. *Bolshaia Sovetskaia entsiklopedia* (old ed., 1917–1948), LIII (1946), 637, indicates that the Tatars had 14,000 men; M. Sultangaliev, p. 29, estimates the number of Moslem soldiers in the area at 50,000. Iskhakov, in *Idel Ural*, p. 41, writes that the Nazarats and the Harbi Shuro were in control of the situation over the entire Idel-Ural. This is surely an exaggeration, although in the Tatar districts where military units (consisting of Moslems) were stationed the Harbi Shuro undoubtedly had great influence. The cities, however, including Kazan and Ufa, were securely in the hands of the Bolsheviks.

18. Kirimal, *Der nationale Kampf der Krimtuerken*, pp. 141–142.

19. Grachev, p. 147. In addition, the Bolsheviks won 22 seats; the left and right socialists, 33; the Kadets, 30; others, 6 seats. Atnagulov, p. 57; Bochkov, p. 18; Sultangaliev, p. 30.

20. Kalinin, pp. 101–102.

21. Sultangaliev, p. 28.

22. *20 Let Tatarskoi ASSR* (Kazan, 1940), p. 42; Atnagulov, p. 64.

23. Bochkov, pp. 19–20.

24. The head of the Tatar military revolutionary headquarters was Col. Beglov. Atnagulov, p. 64; Bochkov, p. 20; Sultangaliev, p. 30.
25. Sultangaliev, pp. 28–29.
26. Bochkov, p. 21.
27. *Pravda*, no. 32 (February 27, 1918), as quoted in Lenin, *Sochineniia*, XXVII, 13–14.
28. *Izvestiia Ufimskogo gub. SNK*, no. 56 (March 28, 1918), as quoted in Raimov, pp. 172–173.
29. *Vpered*, no. 48 (Ufa, March 11, 1918), as quoted in Raimov, p. 173.
30. *Izvestiia*, March 24 (11), 1918; cf. *Vestnik nauchnogo obshchestva tatarovedeniia* (Kazan, 1925), III, 33–34 [further abbr. *VNOT*].
31. *VNOT*, III, 33–35; *Sobranie Uzakonenii* (Petrograd, 1920), nos. 285–288 for 1919.
32. E. H. Carr, *The Bolshevik Revolution*, I (London, 1950), 321.
33. *Izvestiia*, February 26, 1918.
34. Text in *VNOT*, III, 31.
35. Bochkov, pp. 21–22; Atnagulov, p. 64; Kalinin, pp. 209–210.
36. *VNOT*, III, 30–31; Mende, p. 138; Iskhaki, *Idel Ural*, p. 41; *Zhizn natsionalnostei* (1924), I, 30.

Chapter XII. The Road to Red Tatary

1. Stalin, *Sochineniia*, IV (Moskva, 1951), 49–50.
2. *Pravda*, March 3, 1918.
3. R. M. Raimov, *Obrazovanie Bashkirskoi ASSR*, pp. 152, 164.
4. Raimov, p. 164.
5. *Izvestiia Uralskogo Oblastnogo Soveta* (June 5, 1918), as quoted by Raimov, p. 188.
6. F. Samoilov, *Malaia Bashkiriia* (Moscow, 1933), p. 43ff; M. L. Murtazin, *Bashkiriia i bashkirskie voiska v grazhdanskuiu voinu* (Leningrad, 1927), p. 185.
7. Sh. Siungelei, "Ordenonosnaia Tatariia," *RevVost*, XXXI (1935), 158–159.
8. *Nasha gazeta* (Tashkent, January 25, 1918), as quoted in G. Safarov, *Kolonialnaia revoliutsiia* (Moskva, 1921), p. 78.
9. K. Kasymov, "M. N. Vakhitov," as quoted in Kh. Khasanov, "Protiv burzhuaznogo natsionalizma v tatarskoi istoricheskoi literature," *RevVost*, XI–XII (1931), 212.
10. G. Ibragimov, "O sudbakh natsionalnoi kultury v usloviiakh diktatury proletariata" (1924), as quoted in Khasanov, p. 212.
11. See also articles on G. Ibragimov in *VNOT*, VIII (1925), 5–50; *Zhizn natsionalnostei* (October 5, October 12, November 2, 1919).
12. Stalin's comment on Galiev is mentioned in S. Dimanshtein's article in *RiN* (Moskva, 1931).
13. *20 let Tatarskoi ASSR* (Kazan, 1940), p. 52.
14. Stalin, *Sochineniia*, IV, 87, 92.
15. The commission was composed of four Tatar-Bashkirs, one Russian, one Chuvash, and one Mari. *Pravda*, May 24, 1918.
16. *Pravda*, May 24, 1918; *Puti revoliutsii*, III (1923), 35–36; *BSEfe*, LIII, 637; Atnagulov, p. 64.
17. The Czecho-Slovak Legions were organized in 1915–1917 in Russia from the Czechs and Slovaks, former soldiers of the Austrian army, who had voluntarily surrendered to the Russians. The total number of legionnaires

reached 100,000—an impressive force in these months of anarchy. After the peace of Brest-Litovsk, the Czecho-Slovak Legions left the Austro-German front and began to retreat eastwards. They sought to reach Vladivostok, whence they were to be shipped to France. During their retreat they became involved with the anti-Communist Russian movement.

18. Raimov, p. 207.

19. Raimov p. 192.

20. I. Rakhmatullin, "Mulla Nur Vakhitov," *Puti revoliutsii*, III (1923), 34.

21. The central committee of this TSDWP later transferred to Orenburg. Raimov, pp. 93, 212.

22. *Izvestiia*, June 30, 1918; cf. *VNOT*, III (1925), 32. In favor of the organization of a special Moslem party were, besides Vahitov, M. Sultangaliev and Fedavsi. Against it were the left Communists among the Tatars and Bashkirs —for instance, Atnagulov and Shamigulov; *RevVost*, III (1935), 157–158. R. Pipes, *The Formation of the Soviet Union* (Cambridge, 1954), p. 160, was not certain whether the Moslem Communist Party of Bolsheviks was created with or without the permission of Moscow. The appeal of the All-Russian Council of the People's Commissars in *Izvestiia* (June 30) for the creation of Moslem Socialist Committees, Vahitov's main weapon in the development of the Moslem Communist Party, indicates that Stalin and the Soviet government continued to support Vahitov's initiative as they did during the conference in May 1918, and that the Moslem Communist Party was created with the permission of Moscow.

23. *RevVost*, VII (1929), 179.

24. Bochkov, p. 14, Rakhmatullin, p. 40. Tatar detachments formed an insignificant part of the forces of the eastern front, which was under the command of Vatsetis. The bulk of the Fifth Army fighting around Kazan was composed of Latvian regiments. L. Trotsky, *Sochineniia*, XVII, part I (Moscow, 1926), 726–727.

25. Rakhmatullin, p. 40.

26. Iskhaki, *Idel Ural*, p. 43; M. Vishniak, *Vserossiiskoe Uchreditelnoe Sobranie* (Paris, 1935), p. 161.

27. Iskhaki, p. 43; G. K. Ginns, *Sibir, Soiuzniki i Kolchak* (Peking, 1941) p. 208; I. I. Serebrennikov, *Moi Vospominaniia* (Tientsin, after 1930), p. 141; Vishniak, p. 178; Rakhmatullin, p. 40.

28. Text in V. Maksudov and A. Turunov, *Khronika Grazhdanskoi Voiny* (Moskva, 1926), pp. 233–238.

29. Among the signatories of the declarations were: M. Chokaev, chairman of the Turkestan autonomous government and S. A. Mufti Zadeh and A. Urazov, his colleagues; A. Bukeikhanov, chairman of the eastern Kazakh government, and his colleague, A. Alimbekov; for the Tatar autonomy were M. Janturin, A. Iskhakov, S. B. Memliaev; among other Turkic signatories were the Tatars F. Tuktarov, V. Tanashev, and G. Teregulov, and the Kazakhs A. Baitursunov, A. Beremjanov, and G. Alibekov. Maksudov and Turunov, pp. 237–238.

30. Vahitov and Sultangaliev joined the Moslem Socialist Committee in March 1917. Rakhmatullin, p. 34.

31. Sultangaliev, pp. 30–32. The total strength of the Turkestan Army was about 12,000–14,000 men. N. V. Ogorodnikov, *Udar po Kolchaku* (Moskva, 1938), p. 85.

32. Trotsky, pp. 516–532.
33. Bochkov, p. 32. This congress was officially regarded as the First Congress of Moslem Communists (Bolshevik).
34. *Zhizn natsionalnostei*, no. 3 (November 3, 1918); no. 7 (December 22, 1918); and no. 10 (March 9, 1919).
35. *Pravda*, November 19, 1918; Stalin, *Sochineniia*, IV, 164.
36. *Zhizn natsionalnostei*, no. 3 (November 24, 1918), 1; Stalin, p. 171.
37. Sultangaliev, p. 32.
38. *20 let Tatarskoi ASSR*, pp. 57–58; Stalin, IV, 32.
39. *Izvestiia*, March 18, 1919.
40. *Sotsialnyi i natsionalnyi sostav VKPb* (Moskva, 1927), pp. 14–18. Kh. Gabidullin, *Tatarstan za 7 let* (Kazan, 1927), pp. 19–20.
41. Gabidullin, p. 14.
42. The other members of the collegium were G. K. Klinger and M. N. Pavlovich; G. I. Broido was Stalin's deputy from Narkomnats. *Zhizn natsionalnostei*, no. 1 (1923), 32.
43. The SNK already during the session of May 4, 1920 selected a commission for drafting a new statute for the Tatar ASSR; the commission was composed of Stalin, Kamenev, Vladimirskii, Sultangaliev, and Said Galiev. The decree concerning the formation of the Tatar ASSR was published in *Izvestiia*, May 29, 1920.

Chapter XIII. Validov's Little Bashkiria

1. For a more detailed treatment of the revolutionary events in Bashkiria, see R. Pipes, *The Formation of the Soviet Union*, pp. 161–168; Pipes, "The First Experiment in Soviet National Policies—The Bashkir Republic," *Russian Review*, IX (1950); and S. Zenkovsky, "The Tataro-Bashkir Feud of 1917–1920," *Indiana Slavic Studies*, II (1958). For statistics, see *Materialy po istorii Bashkirskoi ASSR* (Moskva, 1956), IV/I, 11; *Perepis 1926*, IV (Moskva, 1928), x, 64–65.
2. Raimov, pp. 47, 49.
3. Raimov, p. 80.
4. M. L. Murtazin, *Bashkiriia i bashkirskie voiska v grazhdanskuiu voinu* (Leningrad, 1927), p. 51–52, 53; S. Tipeev, *K istorii natsionalnogo dvizheniia v Bashkirii* (Ufa, 1929), p. 15–16.
5. Murtazin, p. 53.
6. See H. Jansky's article in *Zeki Velidi Togan'a Armagan* (Istanbul, 1955), pp. 17–18.
7. Sh. Tipeev, *Bashkorstan tarihi* (Ufa, 1930), p. 144, mentions several cases of clashes between nomadic Bashkirs and Tatar peasants.
8. Raimov, pp. 91–93, Sh. Manatov, "Bashkirskaia AR," *Zhurnal natsionalnostei* (1923), I, 41; S. Atnagulov, *Bashkiriia* (Moskva, 1925), p. 56.
9. Raimov, p. 104; Abdykalykov and Pankratova, eds., *Istoriia Kazakhskoi ASSR*, p. 427; Murtazin, p. 56. Manatov, p. 42, gives November 17 (30) as the date of the declaration of Bashkir autonomy.
10. All these lands were in the sixteenth to seventeenth centuries populated by the Bashkirs, but in the early twentieth century the Bashkirs lived primarily in the eastern parts of the Ufa and Orenburg provinces.
11. As mentioned earlier, many Tatars of Bashkiria still called themselves Bashkirs. Their number was about twice as large as that of the Bashkirs. These

Tatars of Bashkiria spoke the eastern (or Bashkiria) dialect of Tatar. J. Validov, "O dialektakh kazanskogo tatarskogo iazyka," *VNOT*, VI (1927), 52.

12. Murtazin, p. 57, 63.

13. F. Samoilov, *Malaia Bashkiriia v 1918 i 1920 g.* (Moskva, 1933), p. 6.

14. Sh. Manatov became a Narkomnats' collaborator during the session of the All-Russian Constituent Assembly in Petrograd in January 1918. He was its member from the Ufa province as the deputy of Bashkir nationalists (six other Moslem deputies of this province—five socialists and one liberal—represented an all-Moslem ticket). *VNOT*, III (1925) 29.

15. Murtazin, p. 64.

16. Raimov, p. 152.

17. Raimov p. 154.

18. This Cheliabinsk consultation started on August 23, 1919, with the participation of Bashkirs, Tatars, and Kazakhs. I. I. Serebrennikov, *Moi vospominaniia* (Tientsin, 1930), pp. 141–166. The Bashkir representative, M. Agdamov, also participated in the Ufa "state conference" of Russian anti-Communist parties. Ginns, *Sibir, Soiuzniki i Kolchak*, p. 208; Vishniak, *Vserossiiskoe Uchreditelnoe Sobranie*, p. 171.

19. S. P. Melgunov, *Tragediia admirala Kolchaka* (Belgrade, 1930), p. 204.

20. Samoilov, p. 7.

21. V. I. Lenin, *Sochineniia, XXVIII* (Moskva, 1952), 423.

22. Murtazin, p. 71. According to Pipes, *Formation of the Soviet Union*, p. 162, there were only 2,000 Bashkir soldiers to join the Red Army. Ogorodnikov, *Udar po Kolchaku*, p. 85, indicates that there were less than 1,300 Bashkir soldiers on the front. It is possible that some of them were kept as reserves. A Bashkir detachment under Kurbangaliev remained faithful to the anti-Communist movement. Atnagulov, p. 67.

23. Ogorodnikov, pp. 85–86. General Geppner, "Nachalo i konets Kolchaka," *Revoliutsiia i grazhdanskaia voina v opisaniiakh belogvardeitsev* (Moskva, 1927), IV, 51.

24. Text of the agreement in *Sbornik Dekretov 1919* (Petrograd, 1920), pp. 293–298.

25. Samoilov, pp. 14, 15.

26. Samoilov, p. 15.

27. *Sotsialnyi i natsionalnyi sostav VKPb* (Moskva, 1928), p. 118.

28. *Zhurnal natsionalnostei*, September 21, 1919.

29. A considerable number of the local soviets in the Ufa province, dominated by the peasantry, adopted motions condemning the activities of the Bashrevkom. Kh. Iumagulov, "Ob odnom neudachnom opyte," *PrRev*, III (1928), 173. On the other hand, the Bashrevkom strove to restrict the work of local Communist cells and organizations. Samoilov, p. 30. In some places, for instance in the village of Dmitrovka, armed clashes occurred between the peasants and Bashkir nationalist troops. Raimov, p. 306.

30. *Sotsialnyi i natsionalnyi sostav VKPb*, p. 90.

31. *20 let Tatarskoi ASSR*, p. 58.

32. Some documents seized by the Red Army in the Alash Orda headquarters indicated that before joining the Soviet regime in January 1919, Validov had warned the Kazakhs not to trust the Bolsheviks. Tipeev, p. 209; see also Raimov, p. 301.

33. Raimov, p. 301.

34. Samoilov, pp. 43, 45; Murtazin, p. 168. After the transfer of Bash-revkom to Sterlitamak, its chairman became Kh. Yumagulov—a Bashkir Com-munist appointed by Moscow—who under Validov's influence supported the aims of the Bashkir autonomists.

35. While taking these steps to ensure the security in Bashkiria, Frunze an-nounced, however, that the "central government will not tolerate any attempts to curtail the Bashkir autonomy and will give it its full support," *M. V. Frunze na frontakh grazhdanskoi voiny* (Moskva, 1941), p. 268.

36. In his speech against M. Sultangaliev on June 10, 1924, Stalin announced: "I have heard already a similar reproach from Shamigulov [Bashkir Communist antiautonomist] that despite his advice to finish with Validov with one stroke, I protected him, trying to preserve him for the Party. I really did, hoping that Validov would improve." Stalin, *Sochineniia* (Moskva, 1952), V, 304.

37. *Izvestiia*, May 22, 1920.

38. Samoilov, p. 59.

39. A. Z. Velidi Togan [Validov], *Bügünkü Turkili* (Istanbul, 1942–1947), pp. 371, 398, 402.

40. Validov's letter to Bashrevkom. Samoilov, pp. 88–89.

41. In November of the same year G. Shamigulov was relieved of the power and was banished from Bashkiria. P. Mostovenko, "Bolshie oshibki maloi Bashkirii," *PrRev*, LXXVI (1929), 124; Raimov, p. 304.

42. Pipes, p. 168.

43. During this year of famine the mortality among the Russian population of Bashkiria was 16.2 per cent; among the Tatars, 19.2 per cent; while among the nomadic Bashkirs it reached 29.1 per cent. Raimov, p. 373; Tipeev, p. 94.

44. *Sobranie Uzakonenii* (Moskva, 1922), No. 41, p. 485.

45. The famine resulted in the following changes of the Bashkir population:

	1920	1926
Total population	3,134,000	2,666,000
Bashkirs	36.4%	23%
Tatars	15%	19%
Russians	37%	40%

F. Lorimer, *The Population of the Soviet Union* (Geneva, 1948), pp. 55–63; Raimov, p. 373.

Chapter XIV.   The Civil War and the Kazakhs

1. According to the data of the 1926 census, which rather closely reflected the demographic situation of 1917, the total population of the Kazakh SSR amounted to 6,503,006, out of which 3,713,394 were Kazakhs; 1,279,979, Rus-sians; and 860,822, Ukrainians. *Perepis 1926*, IV (Moskva, 1928), 82.

2. These conferences and congresses took place in March–April 1917. *Turkestanskii Golos*, May 6, 1917, and *Golos Tatarii*, September 23, 1917, as quoted in *RiNV* (Moskva, 1930), pp. 360–363; Abdykalykov and Pankratova, eds., *Istoriia Kazakhskoi SSR*, p. 408; P. Alekseenkov, "Natsionalnaia politika Vremennogo Pravitelstva v Turkestane," *PrRev*, VII (1928), 122–126.

3. Alash is the name of a mythical ancestral father of the Kazakhs, while "Orda" is the Kazakh form of "horde." Hence, Alash Orda means the Horde of Alash.

4. *RiNV*, pp. 361–363.

5. *RiNV*, p. 307.

6. *RiNV*, pp. 363–365.

7. Z. Mindlin, "Kirgizy i revoliutsiia," *NV*, V (1924), 223; Sapargaliev 57.

8. Sapargaliev, p. 57.

9. Alekseenkov, pp. 120–121; T. Ryskulov, *Kirgizstan* (Moscow, 1935), p. 61.

10. Alekseenkov, p. 121.

11. *Ibid.*, p. 123.

12. Abdykalykov and Pankratova, p. 427.

13. *RMM*, LI (1922), 173.

14. *Zhizn natsionalnostei*, August 3, 1919.

15. *Uchreditelnyi siezd Sovetov Kirgizskoi (Kazakhskoi) ASSR* (Alma-Ata, 1936), p. xi [further abbr. *Uchreditelnyi*].

16. *Obrazovanie Kazakhskoi ASSR* (Alma-Ata, 1957), p. 55, 69, 81.

17. Abdykalykov and Pankratova, pp. 450–452; Mindlin, p. 224.

18. The Kipchak and Adai tribes were in a feud because of a "baranta"— a semilegal robbery of cattle. Abdykalykov and Pankratova, p. 420; *RMM*, LI (1922), 176.

19. *Uchreditelnyi*, p. xvi; Sapargaliev, p. 81; *Obrazovanie KazASSR*, pp. 93, 94, 179.

20. S. Zenkovsky, "Ideological Deviation in Central Asia," *SaEER*, LXXIX (1955), p. 436.

21. *Izvestiia VTsIK'a*, no. 98 (May 12, 1918).

22. O. Caroe, *The Soviet Empire—The Turks of Central Asia and Stalinism* (London, 1953), p. 104.

23. Velidi Togan, *Bügünkü Türkili*, pp. 370–371.

24. Mindlin, p. 228.

25. Baitursunov, a convinced Kazakh nationalist, was neither for the Reds nor the Whites. He hoped that an agreement with the Soviets would bring peace into the Kazakh steppe.

26. Abdykalykov and Pankratova, p. 476.

27. *Sovetskaia Step*, no. 220 (1927).

28. *Sbornik dekretov 1919 g.* (Petrograd, 1920), p. 216.

29. *Sotsialnyi i natsionalny sostav VKPb* (Moskva, 1927), p. 147.

30. *Iz istorii partiinogo stroitelstva v Kazakhstane* (Alma-Ata, 1936), p. 81 [further abbr. *Iz istorii*].

31. See Velidi Togan, p. 402.

32. The Southeastern Federation was also supposed to include Kazakhstan and Central Asia.

33. *Iz istorii*, p. 220.

34. *Iz istorii*, p. 150.

35. *Uchreditelnyi*, p. xxvi.

36. *Iz istorii*, p. 151.

37. *Ibid.*, p. 154.

38. Report on the Kazakh OrgBiuro [Organizational Bureau of the party] to the Central Committee of RKP(b), *Iz istorii*, p. 155.

39. *Izvestiia*, September 1, 1920 and *Sobranie Uzakonenii*, LXXVI (September 5, 1920), 359; *Obrazovanie KazASSR*, p. 251.

40. *Uchreditelnyi*, p. xxix.

41. *Izvestiia*, October 27, 1920; G. T. Taimanov, *Razvitie sovetskoi gosudarstvennosti v Kazakhstane* (Moscow, 1956), p. 33.

42. *Uchreditelnyi*, p. xxx.

43. *RiNV*, p. 94.
44. *Uchreditelnyi*, pp. 39, 51, 60, 98.
45. *Ibid.*, pp. xxxi, 13.
46. *Obrazovanie KazASSR*, p. 264.
47. *Izvestiia*, May 22, 1921, and *Pravda*, November 7, 1921.
48. *Pravda*, February 12, 1921.
49. *Pravda*, February 22, 1921.
50. *Izvestiia*, June 7, 1921, announced the organization of the Kazakh administration in Akmolinsk province. Cf. Abdykalykov and Pankratova, p. 491.
51. *Izvestiia*, May 17, 1921.
52. The Soviet government decreed the "national delimitation" on October
14, 1924, and it was carried out in early 1925.
53. Resolution of the Fifth All-Kazakh Congress of Soviets, April 19, 1925.
Abdykalykov and Pankratova, p. 503.
54. The Kazakh language became the official language of Kazakhstan in
March 1920. *Izvestiia*, March 24, 1920.
55. A. Sadakvasov's words quoted in *RiN*, VII (1920), 95.

Chapter XV. The Revolution in the Central Asian Oases

1. R. Olzscha and G. Cleinow, *Turkestan* (Leipzig, 1942), p. 375.
2. *RiNV*, III (1930), 345. *Türk Yurdu*, I–II (n.s., 1924), 69, indicates 440
delegates; as quoted in B. Hajit, *Die nationalen Regierungen von Kokand und
der Alasch Orda* (Muenster, 1950), p. 22.
3. Hajit, p. 46; S. Muraveiskii, *Ocherki po istorii revoliutsionnogo dvizheniia
v Srednei Azii* (Tashkent, 1926), pp. 13–14; P. Alekseenkov, "Natsionalnaia
politika Vremennogo Pravitelstva v Turkestane v 1917 g.," *PrRev*, LXXIX, 120.
4. *Nasha gazeta* (Tashkent), September 5, 1917, as quoted in *RiNV*, p. 345;
Hajit, p. 46.
5. Hajit, p. 24.
6. The future leader of the "Kokand government" and well known as a
writer and journalist.
7. Hajit, p. 24.
8. From Samarkand Behbudi actively participated in Young Bukhariote
work.
9. Alekseenkov, p. 121.
10. *Ibid.*, p. 111, M. A. Kushbegiev's (Shuro-i-Islam) report to the National
Center.
11. *Ibid.*, p. 111, reports by I. V. Chertov and B. A. Varaksin.
12. *Ibid.*, pp. 109–110.
13. Chokaev wrote later: "All of us in 1917 suffered from the ailment of
federation and unitarianism, because we had faith in Russian democracy and
were *afraid to lose our influence on the people.*" Hajit, p. 27.
14. The former governor of Ferghana, Lukoshkin, was elected mayor; a
former high official of the imperial administration, Markov, became his assistant. *RiNV*, p. 351.
15. In Kokand five members of the Moslem Labor Union were killed by
the mob, directed by Ulema. Alkseenkov, p. 122.
16. In the Tashkent Soviet the Moslems formed only 5 per cent of the
deputies. Hajit, p. 19. Mufti Zadeh became the leader of the only active group
of Moslem socialists in Tashkent; among these socialists the most numerous

were the construction workers, most of whom became Communists. To this group belonged Ikramov, secretary of the RKP(b) in Uzbekistan from 1924–1937. *Voina v peskakh* (Moskva, 1935), pp. 51, 176; Muraveiskii, p. 14; Alekseenkov, p. 14.

17. In November 1917 the regional Moslem Bureau of the labor unions was organized, the members of which were Rakhimov, Narbutabekov, Sultan Hojaev, et al. *Voina v peskakh*, p. 185.

18. Hajit, pp. 33–34.

19. G. Safarov, *Kolonialnaia revoliutsiia—Opyt Turkestana* (Moskva, 1921), p. 64.

20. *Ibid.*

21. *Alekseenkov*, p. 123.

22. M. Chokaev, *Turkestan pod vlastiu sovetov* (Paris, 1935), p. 13.

23. Safarov, p. 68.

24. *Ibid.*, p. 70; *Vestnik otdeleniia mestnogo samoupravleniia NKVD*, December 27, 1917, p. 8.

25. From the declaration of the united caucus of Bolsheviks and Maximalists. *Nasha gazeta* (Tashkent), November 23, 1918, as quoted in Safarov, p. 70.

26. The theses of all non-Moslem Communists who protested against the creation of the Tatar Republic were almost identical. Karl Grassis was against autonomous Tatary because there were not enough Communists among the Tatars. *Zhizn natsionalnostei*, January 20, 1920.

27. This Tashkent Soviet government was not purely Communist: until January 1919, the Socialist Revolutionaries participated in it. The First Congress of RKP(b) in Tashkent took place on June 17–23, 1918. *Uzbekistanskaia Pravda*, July 10, 1933.

28. The authority of the Tashkent government was recognized in the main cities of Central Asia only in December 1917; in Semirechie, in February–March 1918.

29. J. Castagné, "Turkestan depuis la Revolution russe," *RMM*, L (1922), 46.

30. In these negotiations Tashkent was represented by Kolesov, Uspensky, and Poltoratsky; Kokand by Munevver Kari. M. Chokaev, "Turkestanskoe Vosstanie," *DNI*, August 25, 1936.

31. Safarov, p. 71; Castagné, p. 52.

32. *Politika sovetskoi vlasti po natsionalnomu voprosu, 1917–1920* (Moskva, 1920), pp. 77–78.

33. Castagné, p. 47; Safarov, p. 72.

34. *Volia naroda*, December 18, 1917.

35. The number and the names of the government's members differ in various sources. Hajit, p. 79; Velidi Togan, *Bügünkü Türkli*, p. 365; *Revoliutsiia v Srednei Azii*, I (1930), 5.

36. Hajit, p. 77; F. Wilfort, *Turkestanisches Tagebuch* (Wien, 1930), p. 322.

37. *Lenin i Stalin o Srednei Azii* (Moskva, 1941), p. 163, as quoted in Hajit, p. 69.

38. On December 13, the birthday of Mohammed, Russian underground officers' groups organized a demonstration of the Moslems, consisting of 30–40,000 demonstrators. The Moslems, led by Russian officers, liberated from the jail Russian anti-Communist leaders arrested by the Bolsheviks, but the Tashkent Soviet finally mastered the situation. *Vestnik NKVD*, February 14,

1918; Captain A. Brun, *Troublous Times—Experience in Bolshevik Russia and Turkestan* (London, 1931), p. 60; F. Gnesin, "Turkestan v dni revoliutsii," *Belyi arkhiv,* I (Paris, 1926), 91.

39. *Voina v peskakh,* pp. 400–414.

40. The victory at Orenburg caused an outburst of enthusiasm among the Bolsheviks. *Pravda* and *Izvestiia,* January 24, 1918; *Voina v peskakh,* p. 509.

41. These Hungarian and Austrian soldiers were paid mercenaries; they received 200 rubles a month. *Pravda,* March 22, 1918; Willfort, p. 93.

42. The date of Kokand's capitulation differs in various sources: Safarov, p. 80, gives February 19 (6); Muraveiskii, p. 19, and Chokaev (in *Dni,* August 25, 1936), give February 13.

43. *Voina v peskakh,* p. 527.

44. Captain Brun, who visited Kokand in 1918, found the city half-empty; thousand of skeletons were still in the streets. Brun writes that the German, Austrian, and Hungarian mercenaries who participated in the occupation of the city plundered up to 100,000 rubles each. Brun, pp. 79–80.

45. S. Ginsburg, "Basmachestvo v Ferghane," *NV,* X–XI (1925), 176; Brun, pp. 80–81.

46. Description of the events on the Aktiubinsk front in D. Salikov, "Borba za Orenburg" and K. Vlasov, "Petrovsky otriad," in *Voina v peskakh,* pp. 504–519, 525–528.

47. The operations in the Transcaspia were described in many Russian and British works, the best of which are S. T. Filippov, *Boevye deistviia na Zakaspiiskom fronte* (Ashkhabad, 1928); L. V. Blacker, *On Secret Patrols in High Asia* (London, 1922); and W. Mallesson, "The British Mission to Turkestan," *JRCAS,* IX (1922), 96–110.

48. The population of Semirechie consisted of Kirghiz, Kazakhs, Chinese-speaking Moslem Dungans, Russians, and Ukrainians. In the war operations only Russian Cossacks participated, on the side of the Whites, and new settlers, on the side of the Reds.

49. At the beginning, the Turkomens supplied 1,000–1,500 mounted militia; their numbers fell to 130 in June 1919. Filippov, pp. 62–63.

50. Internationalists—mostly Hungarian, but also Austrian and German mercenaries—were the main strength of the Tashkent regime. Filippov, pp. 3, 35; Brun, pp. 78, 136.

Chapter XVI.   The Jadids and the Communist Party

1. A. M. Samoilovich, "Pervoe tainoe obshchestvo mladobukhartsev," *Vostok,* I (Leningrad, 1922), 99: D. Soloveichik, "Revoliutsionnaia Bukhara," *NV,* II (1922), 12.

2. J. Benzing, *Turkestan* (Berlin, 1943), p. 23.

3. O. Glovatskii, *Revoliutsiia pobezhdaet* (Tashkent, 1930), p. 23.

4. S. Aini, *Dokhunda* (Moskva, 1933), pp. 15, 133–140; I. Kolychevskii, "Bukhara," *VoenMysl,* I (Tashkent, 1920), 302.

5. F. Kolesov, "Vosstanie v Bukhare," *Voina v peskakh* (Moskva, 1935), p. 238.

6. His detachment, consisting of Austrians and Tashkent reserve soldiers, counted less than 1,000 men. From the very start, this campaign, like the Kokand operation, turned into a pillage operation. Brun, *Troublous Times,* p. 104.

7. J. Castagné, "Le Bolchevisme et l'Islam," *RMM*, LI (1922), 218.

8. See *Istoriia sovetskoi konstitutsii* (Moskva, 1957), p. 126. Moscow's alarm at the activities of the Tashkent Soviet of People's Commissars resulted in a telegram of April 22, 1918, sent by Lenin and Stalin to the Fifth Congress of the Soviets of the Turkestan Region. The telegram greeted the congress very cautiously and expressed the hope that the Tashkent Sovnarkom "will support the autonomy of the region on Soviet principles" and that there would be "full contact" with the existing Soviets, and asked for the clarification of the "relations of the territorial plenipotentiary organ to the Soviet of People's Commissars." Apparently, Lenin and Stalin were not sure at all about the loyalty of the Tashkent group. Stalin, *Sochineniia*, IV, 81.

9. The government also included two Moslems: the Kirghiz Ibragimov and the Uzbek Jadid, Tursun Hojaev. Muraveiskii, p. 20.

10. K. K. Troitskii, "1–i siezd KP(b) Turkestana," *Uzbekistanskaia Pravda*, June 10, 1933. Safarov, in *Kolonialnaia revoliutsiia—Opyt Turkestana*, p. 86, indicates that, at this time, there were also 125 Moslem "sympathizers" in Tashkent.

11. Muraveiskii, p. 21; Safarov, p. 86.

12. Stalin, *Sochineniia*, IV, 231–232.

13. F. M. Bailey, in *Mission to Tashkent* (London, 1946), p. 143, thinks that Lenin and the Central Committee were forced to give moral support to the Tashkent Socialist Revolutionaries and Bolsheviks, since they had no men close at hand for the government of Turkestan.

14. Osipov instigated an open revolt against the Tashkent Soviet government during which a number of Communist leaders were executed. The revolt was suppressed by the re-established coalition of Bolsheviks and left Socialist Revolutionaries, who soon merged with the Communists into one party. See *Turkestanskaia Pravda*, January 19, 1923; S. Bolotov, "Iz istorii Osipovskogo miatezha," *PrRev*, no. 6/53/ (1926), 114–137; *Voina v peskakh*, pp. 393–399; Brun, p. 181; Bailey, p. 121.

15. Muraveiskii, p. 26.

16. *Izvestiia Turkestanskogo TsIK'a*, June 7, 1919, as quoted in Safarov, p. 97.

17. Muraveiskii, p. 26.

18. Muraveiskii, pp. 27–28.

19. Tursun Hojaev was one of the first Jadids to join the Communist Party and since April 1918 was People's Commissar in Tashkent.

20. Lenin, *Sochineniia*, XXIX, 138.

21. V. Melikov, "Krasnyi Vostok," *Izvestiia*, November 11, 1919, pointed out that "Soviet Turkestan has become the revolutionary school of the East," and that it would be necessary to "develop broad agitation activities, which would reach, over Afghanistan, a fertile ground in India." Stalin himself, at the opening of the Second All-Russian Congress of the Communist Organizations of Oriental Peoples on November 22, 1919, stressed that "only a tight union of Moslem Communist organizations of Oriental peoples—first of all that of Tatars, Bashkirs, Kirghiz, the peoples of Turkestan—only by their close union can one explain the rapid development of events, which we observe in the East," and he hoped that the work "in the awakening of the peoples of the East" would continue. Stalin, *Sochineniia*, IV, 280.

22. *Izvestiia Turkestanskogo TsIK'a*, February 5, 1920; Safarov, p. 110.

23. Safarov, p. 110.

24. Safarov, p. 109.

25. TurkCommission was created by the resolution of the Central Committee of October 3, 1919; the commission was accompanied by the new head of the Cheka, Bokii. *RMM*, L (1922), 61; T. Ryskulov, *Revoliutsiia i korennoie naselenie Srednei Azii* (Tashkent, 1925), p. 199. See also *M. V. Frunze na frontakh grazhdanskoi voiny* [further abbr. *Frunze*] (Moskva, 1941), p. 119.

26. Safarov, p. 111, asserts that he was the one who discovered "Pan-Turkism" in the tactics and ideology of Jadid Communists.

27. Frunze's report to the commander-in-chief of the armed forces of RSFSR, May 1920. *Frunze*, p. 131.

28. From the archives of Frunze. *Frunze*, pp. 119–120.

29. Lenin, *Sochineniia*, XXXI, 231.

30. Peters' article in *Istorik marksist*, V (1937), 151.

31. In Khiva the revolution resulting in the establishment of a government which was friendly to and controlled by the Soviet authorities took place in November 1919. See G. Skalov, "Khivinskaia revoliutsiia," *NV*, III (1920), 251; N. Genalin, "Sobytiia v Khorezmskoi respublike," *VoenMysl*, I (Tashkent, 1921), 228; S. Mikhailov, "Khivinskii front," *VoenMysl*, I (1921), 251.

32. The Young Bukhariotes and Bukharian Communists—feuding in 1918–1920—merged under the pressure of the Tashkent Communists on the very eve of the operations in Bukhara. Glovatskii, pp. 24–27; "Materialy po istorii Bukharskoi revoliutsii," *Vestnik NKID*, nos. 4–5 (1922), 125; N. Kolychevskii, "Bukhara," *VoenMysl*, I (1920), 306. Frunze massed against Bukhara about one half of all the Red forces in Central Asia—1,000 infantry and about 2,500 cavalry; the emir assembled an army of about 9,000 infantry and 7,500 cavalry for the defense of the capital. *Frunze*, pp. 139–140.

33. The chief leader of behind-the-scenes machinations of the Young Bukhariote government was the head of the Maksumov's family—Mirza Mukhiddin; his son, Mirza Abdul Kadyr, became the Prime Minister; Mirza Amin Mukhid was the Ambassador in Moscow; F. Hojaev became Minister of Foreign Affairs. *Vestnik NKID*, nos. 3–6 (1921), 75; Velidi Togan, pp. 405–406. About the beginnings of the liberal and Young Bukhariote movement see S. Zenkovsky, "Kulturkampf in Prerevolutionary Central Asia," *ASaEER*, XIII (February 1955), 36, 38–41.

34. Glovatskii, p. 27.

35. *Ibid.*, pp. 27–28, and *Sredniaia Aziia* [Spravochnaia Kniga na 1916 g.] (Tashkent, 1926), p. 15. From the original group of Bukharian Communists only Akchurin entered the government. *Vestnik NKID*, nos. 5–6 (1921), 75.

36. For the support of the new regime—detested by conservative circles—Soviet troops were left in Bukhara, while the government had special advisers, Liubimov (Russian) and Khakimov (Tatar), appointed by TurkCommission. Velidi Togan, p. 406.

37. Iskander, "Podgotovka Angliei Bukharskogo platsdarma dlia interventsii v Sovetskii Turkestan, 1918–1920," *Istoricheskie Zapiski*, XXXVI (Moscow, 1951), 34ff.

38. Narbutabekov's speech at the First Congress of the Peoples of the East, *Pervyi siezd narodov Vostoka* (Moscow, 1921), p. 89.

39. *Ibid.*, pp. 84, 89, 90.

40. Resolution of the Central Committee in Moscow, Safarov, pp. 120–121.

41. *Ibid.*, p. 121.

42. "5–i siezd RKP(b) Turkestana," *Izvestiia TsIKa TurkRespubliki*, Sep-

tember 17, 1920, as quoted in *Zhizn natsionalnostei*, no. 38 (1920); Muraveiskii, p. 32.

43. *Pravda*, December 11, 1921.

44. *Pravda*, January 18, 1921; *Turkestanskaia Pravda*, January 21, 1923.

45. *Sobranie Uzakonenii*, XXXII, no. 172 (1921); *Istoriia Sovetskoi Konstitutsii* (Moskva, 1957) pp. 282–283. Some authors regard this decree as a declaration of the autonomy of Soviet Turkestan. It is, however, an essential error, since the autonomy had been already formally proclaimed on April 20, 1918.

46. *Pravda*, April 14, 1921 and *Sobranie uzakonenii*, XXXII, no. 173 (1921).

47. Texts of the decrees on the formation of the Central Asian republics, in *Istoriia sovetskoi konstitutsii*, pp. 482, 484, 485, 487–489, 493, 610.

Chapter XVII.   Two Years of National Azerbaijan

1. An excellent study of the efforts of the Crimean Tatars to create their own national state is E. Kirimal's *Der nationale Kampf der Krimtuerken*. Pipes in his *Formation of the Soviet Union* offers the best report on the happenings in the Crimea in English; see pp. 79ff, 184ff. It is hard to determine the composition of the Crimean population in 1917–1920 because of the considerable fluctuations in the demography of the peninsula in these years. In 1926, 179,094 Tatars inhabited the peninsula, comprising 25 per cent of the total population. *Perepis 1926* (Moskva, 1927), p. 71.

2. B. Hajit, *Die nationale Regierungen von Kokand und der Alasch Orda* (Muenster, 1950, mimeographed), p. 49.

3. *RiNV* (1936), pp. 341–345.

4. S. Belenkii and A. Manvelov, *Revoliutsiia 1917 g. v Azerbaidzhane* (Baku, 1927), p. 35.

5. *RiNV*, p. 336.

6. *Kaspii*, April 2, 1917.

7. Belenkii and Manvelov, p. 51.

8. A. Raevskii, *Partiia Musavat i ee Kontrrevoliutsionnaia Rabota* (Baku, 1929), p. 10.

9. W. A. Woytinski, *La Democratie Georgienne* (Paris, 1921), p. 113.

10. *Ibid.*

11. Kazemzadeh, *The Struggle for Transcaucasia* (New York, 1951), p. 222.

12. M. Kuliev, *Vragi oktiabria v Azerbaidzhane* (Baku, 1927), p. 13ff; Woytinski, p. 113.

13. G. I. Urtadze, *Obrazovanie i Konsolidatsiia Gruzinskoi Demokraticheskoi Respubliki* (Muenchen, 1956), pp. 27–28.

14. More details on the situation in Baku can be found in Pipes' and Kazemzadeh's books.

15. R. Ratgauzer, *Borba za Sovetskii Azerbaidzhan* (Baku, 1938), p. 37.

16. Kuliev, pp. 32–33; Zaverand, p. 114.

17. A. L. Popov, "Iz istorii angliiskoi interventsii v Zakavkazii," *PrRev*, VI–VII (1923), 225.

18. Ratgauzer, p. 31.

19. E. H. Carr, *The History of the Bolshevik Revolution*, I, 343.

20. Ratgauzer, p. 28; Kazemzadeh, p. 165.

21. *The Claims of the Peace Delegation of Caucasian Azerbaijanis presented to the Peace Conference in Paris* (Paris, 1919), pp. 28–31.

22. R. Guseinov, *Oktiabr v Azerbaidzhane* (Baku, 1927), p. 8.

23. Kazemzadeh, p. 222.

24. The data on the repartition of the seats in Azerbaijani parliament differs in various sources, Kazemzadeh, p. 222; cf. Kuliev, p. 13.

25. Kuliev, p. 35; cf. A. G. Karaev, *Iz nedavnogo proshlogo* (Baku, 1926), p. 193.

26. D. E. Enukidze, *Krakh imperialisticheskoi interventsii v Zakavkazii* (Tbilisi, 1954), p. 196; cf. M. Bagirov: *Iz istorii bolshevitskoi organizatsii v Zakavkazii* (Moskva, 1946), p. 193.

27. Pipes, p. 223.

28. Letters of Baku committee to Kirov and Kirov's letter to Mikoyan, as quoted in Enukidze, pp. 196–197.

29. Azerbaijani government's reports, Archives of Georgian SSR, No. F2.d. 362, p. 198, as quoted in Enukidze, p. 198.

30. A. Raevskii, *Angliiskie druziia i musavatskie patrioty* (Baku, 1927), p. 190.

31. The list of the commissars in *RMM*, LI (1922), 112.

Chapter XVIII. Conclusion

1. Moslem maktabs and Moslem judges (Kazis) survived, however, till the late 1920's. See *NV*, XXIII–XXIV (1928), 213, and P. Gidulanov, *Otdelenie tserkvi ot gosudarstva v S.S.S.R.* (Moskva, 1925), pp. 516–517.

2. A detailed report on Kemal Ataturk's antireligious policies can be found in N. Berke's, D. Rustow's, and H. Reed's articles in *Islam and the West*, ed. R. Frye ('S.-Gravenhage, 1957), pp. 41, 77–83, 109–111. See also Mirza Bala, "Mirza Fatali," *ObKav*, XXIII (1953), 9–11.

3. Mirza Bala, "Resul Zadeh," *ObKav*, XXIV (1953), 24–25, and Resul Zadeh's articles in *ObKav*, IX–XII (1952), and *Az*, I (1952), 41–48.

4. Velidi Togan, *Bükünkü Türkili*, p. 467.

5. Pipes, p. 78.

6. O. Radkey, *The Election to the Russian Constituent Assembly* (Cambridge, 1950), p. 27.

7. *Borba za sovetskuiu vlast na iuzhnom Urale* (Cheliabinsk, 1957), pp. 307–308, and E. Grachev, *Kazanskii Oktiabr* (Kazan, 1926), p. 147.

8. *YMY*, no. 114 (1937), 8.

9. *DnO* (1917–1918), II, 858–859.

10. *Nasha gazeta* (Tashkent), November 23, 1917, as quoted in Safarov, *Kolonalnaia revoliutsiia*, p. 68.

11. Safarov, p. 85.

12. N. A. Faris' articles in *The Islamic Review* (June 1956), pp. 28–31 and *Near Eastern Forum* (Summer 1956), pp. 8–9.

13. Faris' article in *The Islamic Review*, p. 31.

14. M. Chokaev, "Turkestan and the Soviet Regime, *JRCAS*, XVIII (1931), 406.

15. G. Urtadze, *Obrazovanie i konsolidatsiia Gruzinskoi demokraticheskoi respubliki* (Muenchen, 1956), p. 27.

16. *Ibid.*, p. 13.

17. *Uchreditelnyi siezd Sovetov Kirgizskoi (Kazakhskoi) ASSR* (Alma-Ata, 1936), p. xi.

BIBLIOGRAPHY

See the list at the beginning of the Notes
for abbreviations used in the Bibliography.

Bibliography

I. General

A. EARLY HISTORY

Barthold, W., *Histoire des Turks d'Asie Centrale* (Paris, 1945). One of the best works on the earliest history of Turks.

Encyclopedia of Islam, ed. M. T. Houtsma, A. J. Wensinck, and H. A. R. Gibb, I–IV (Leiden, 1913–1938).

Gibb, H. A. R., *Mohamedanism* (New York, 1957).

Gibb, H. A. R., and Harold Bowen, *Islamic Society and the West*, I–II (London, 1950–1957).

Grekov, B., and A. Iakubovskii, *Zolotaia orda i ee padenie* (Moskva, 1937).

Grousset, R., *Empires des Steppes* (Paris, 1948).

Ocherki po istorii SSSR, publ. AN of the USSR, I–VIII (Moskva, 1953–). Very important for the early history of Russia's Turks.

Polnoe Sobranie Zakonov Rossiiskoi Imperii (Petersburg, 1830).

Spuler, B., *Die Goldene Horde* (Leipzig, 1943).

Velidi Togan, A. Z., *Bügünkü Türkili (Turkistan) ve yakin Tarihi* (Istambul, 1942–1947). Important.

Vambery, H., *Das Tuerkenvolk in seinen ethnologischen und ethnographischen Beziehungen* (Leipzig, 1855).

Vernadsky, G., *History of Russia*, I–III (New Haven, 1949–1954). Important for the early history of Russia's Turks.

B. 1800–1916

Abbot, A. F., *Turkey in Transition* (London, 1909).

Akcoraoglu, Yu., *Uc Tarz i Siyaset* (Istanbul, 1938).

Alektorov, N., "Novye techeniia v zhizni musulmanskikh shkol," *ZhMNP*, I (April 1909).

Alp, Tekin, *Turkismus und Panturkismus* (Weimar, 1915).

Arsharuni, A., and Kh. Gabidullin, *Ocherki panislamizma i pantiurkizma v Rossii* (Moskva, 1930). Very important.

Birge, J. K., *A Guide to Turkish Area Studies* (Washington, 1949).

Browne, E. G., *A Literary History of Persia*, I–IV (London–Cambridge, 1902–1930).

Browne, E. G., *The Persian Revolution* (Cambridge, 1910).

Buxton, Ch. R., *Turkey in Revolution* (London, 1909).

Cherevanskii, V., *Zapiski po delam very musulman sunitov* (Petersburg, 1906).

Cherevanskii, V. L., *Mir islama i ego probuzhdenie*, I–II (Petersburg, 1901).

Chernousov, V., and G. Folbrok, *Inorodcheskie i inovercheskie uchilishcha* (Petersburg, 1903).

Chernyshev, E. I., "Vostochnaia pechat v epokhu reaktsii," *IOKU*, XXXIII, part I (1925).

Chleny gosudarstvennoi dumy (Petersburg–Moscow, 1906).

Dennais, J., *La Turquie nouvelle et l'ancien regime* (Paris, 1909).

Fesh, P., *Constantinople aux derniers jours d'Abdul Hamid* (Paris, 1907).

Gibb, E. J. W., *A History of Ottoman Poetry*, V (Cambridge–London, 1907).

Gibb, H. A. R., *Whither Islam* (London, 1932).

Gordelevskii, "K voprosu o Pan-Islamizme," *MI*, II (1913).

—— "Ocherki po istorii novoi osmanskoi literatury," *TV*, XXXIX (1912).

Gosudarstvennaia Duma–Stenograficheskie otchety (official publications of stenographic reports; Petersburg, 1906–1917).

Hammer Purgstall, J., *Geschichte der Osmanischen Dichtung*, V (Pesth, 1837).

Hostler, C., *Turkism and the Soviets* (New York, 1957). Useful handbook on the Turkic peoples in Russia and the inception of Turkic nationalism.

Inorodcheskoe Obozrenie (Kazan, 1912–1917), suppl. to the *Pravoslavnyi Sobesednik*. Contains most valuable digest of the Turkic press and books published in Russia.

Insolatto, E., *L'Islam et la politique des Allies* (Paris, 1920).

Jaeschke, G., "Der Weg zur russisch-tuerkischen Freundschaft," *WdI*, XVI (1934).

—— "Der Nazionalismus der Yungtuerken," *WdI*, XXIII (1941).

Klimovich, L., *Islam v tsarskoi Rossii* (Moskva, 1936).

Knight, E. F., *The Awakening of Turkey* (London, 1909).

Kohn, H., *Geschichte der nationalen Bewegungen im Orient* (Berlin, 1928).

1906 sano 16–21 aug. ictimag itmek Rusya müsülmanlarinin nadvasi (Proceedings of the Moslems of Russia Congress, August 16–21, 1906; Kazan, 1906). Most important material for the study of nationalist movement among Moslems of Russia in 1905–1906.

Labonne, R., "La crise orientale et le nationalisme en Asie," *Le Correspondant*, vol. 287 (1922).

Literaturnaia entsiklopediia, I–XI (Moskva, 1929). Articles on Turkic literatures: Tatar, Azerbaijani, Uzbek, etc.

Mende, G. von., *Der nationale Kampf der Russlandstuerken* (Berlin, 1936). Important.

—— "Ismail Bey Gasprinsky" *OE*, X (1934).

—— "Yusuf Akchura," *OE*, X (1934).

Mir Islama (Petersburg, 1912–1913). Important. Contains valuable digests of Turkic publications in Russia.

Miropiev, M. A., *O polozhenii russkikh inorodtsev* (Petersburg, 1901), p. 515.

"Panislamizm i pantiurkizm," *MI*, II (1931).

Ukhtomskii, Bishop Andrei, "Doklad P. Stolypinu," *KrAr*, XXXIV (1929).

"Pantiurkizm v Rossii," *MI*, II (1913).

Revoliutsiia 1905–1907 godov v natsionalnykh raionakh Rossii (Moskva, 1957).

Vestnik nauchnogo obshchestva tatarovedeniia (Kazan, 1926–). Contains important material on the history of Tatary.

Vserossiiskii musulmanskii siezd: Postanovleniia i resoliutsii (Kazan, 1906).

"Zasedanie mezhduvedomstvennogo soveshchanniia," *KrAr*, XXXVI (1929).

Zaverand, *Turtsiia i Panturanizm* (Paris, 1930). Important.

Zenkovsky, S., "Rossiia i Tiurki," *Novyi zhurnal*, XLIV (1956).

C. REVOLUTION AND CIVIL WAR

Benzing, J., "Bolshevismus, Tuerkvoelker und Islam," *OE*, XIII (1937).

Bütün Rusya müsülmanlarinin 1917nci yilda 1–11 mayda Meskevde bulgan umumi isyezdinin protokollari (Proceedings of the All-Russian Moslem Congress in Moscow, May 1–11, 1917; Petrograd 1917). Most important source on Moslem policies in 1917.

Carr, E. H. *The Bolshevik Revolution*, I (London, 1950).

Castagné, J., "Le Bolschevisme et l'Islam," *RMM, LI* (1922).

Dekrety oktiabrskoi revoliutsii, I (Moskva, 1933).

Dekrety Sovetskoi vlasti, I [1917–1918] (Moskva, 1957).

Deutscher, I., *Stalin* (London, 1949).

Geppner, General, "Nachalo i konets Kolchaka," *Revoliutsiia i Grazhdanskaia Voina v opisaniakh belogvardeitsev*, IV (Moskva, 1927).

Gins, G. K., *Sibir, Soiuzniki i Kolchak* (Peking, 1921).

Heyd, U., *Formation of Turkish Nationalism* (London, 1950).

Istoriia sovetskoi konstitutsii (Moskva, 1956). Collection of documents.

Jaeschke, G., "Kommunismus und Islam im tuerkischen Befreiungskriege," *WdI*, XX (1938).

―――― "Der Islam in der neuen Turkei," *WdI*, I (n.s., 1951).

Jansky, H., "Die tuerkische Revolution und der Russische Islam," *Der Islam*, XVIII (1929).

Khronika grazhdanskoi voiny v Sibiri, ed. N. Maksakov and A. Turunov (Moskva, 1926). Collection of documents.

Kliuchnikov, Yu. V. and A. Sabanin, *Mezhdunarodnaia politika noveishego vremeni v dogovorakh, notakh i deklaratsiakh*, I–II (Moskva, 1926–1928).

Kolarz, W., *Russia and Her Colonies* (London, 1953).

KPSS v rezoliutsiakh i resheniakh siezdov, I–II (Moskva, 1953).

Melgunov, S., *Tragediia admirala Kolchaka*, I–II (Belgrade, 1930). Important for the study of the Civil War in eastern Turkic regions of Russia.

Ogorodnikov, N. V., *Udar po Kolchaku* (Moskva, 1938).

Pipes, R., *Formation of the Soviet Union* (Cambridge, 1954). Very important. Contains very good chapters on the Turkic peoples in the time of the Revolution and Civil War. Bibliography.

Politika sovetskoi vlasti po natsionalnomu voprosu za tri goda 1917–1920 (Moskva, 1920). Important.

Pervyi siezd narodov Vostoka (Moskva, 1921).

Revoliutsiia 1905–1907 g. v Rossii (Moskva, 1955).
 Vol. A: *Nachalo pervoi revololitusii.*
 Vol. B: *Vserossiiskie politicheskie stachki, okt. 1905* (2 vols).
 Vol. C: *Vyschii podiem revoliutsii* (3 vols).

Revoliutsiia i natsionalnyi vopros, ed. S. M. Dimanshtein, III (the only published volume; Moskva, 1930). The best collection of materials and documents on the national problems in Russia in 1917.

La Revue du Monde Musulman. Numerous articles and documents on the history of Turkic movement in Russia, especially in the years 1920–1925.

Rybakov, C., "Staro i novometodnye shkoly v russkom islame," *MI*, I (1912).

Sbornik dekretov 1917–1918 godov (Moskva, 1920).

Sbornik dekretov 1919 goda (Petrograd, 1919).

Serebrennikov, I. I., *Moi vospominaniia* (Tientsin, 1930). Interesting details on the Turks in the Civil War.

Sobranie Uzakonenii (Petrograd-Moskva, 1917–1924).

Sotsialnyi i natsionalnyi sostav VKP(b) (Moskva, 1927), publ. by Central Executive Committee of VKP(b).

Sovetskaia politika za desiat let po natsionalnomu voprosu, ed. I. Lazovskii, (Moskva, 1928). A systematic collection of decrees, 1917–1927.

Vishniak, M., *Vserossiiskoe uchreditelnoe sobranie* (Paris, 1935).

D. LINGUISTICS

Baskakov, N. A., "*Klassifikatsiia tiurkskikh iazykov,*" *TIIa*, I (1952). Bibliography.

Borovkov, A. R., "Ocherk istorii uzbekskogo iazyka," *SV*, VI (1949).
—— "Tadzhiksko-uzbekskoe dvuiazychie," *UZIV*, IV (1951).

Brockelmann, C., *Osttuerkische Grammatik der islamischen Literatur Mittelasiens* (Leiden, 1954).

Gabain, A. von., *Oezbekische Grammatik* (Leipzig-Wien, 1945).

Räsänen, M., *Materialien zur Lautlehre der tuerkischen Sprachen* (Helsinki, 1949). Bibliography.

Ulkutasir, S., *Kasgarli Mahmut* (Istanbul, 1948).

Vambery, H., *Altosmanische Sprachstudien* (Leiden, 1901).
—— *Cagataische Sprachstudien* (Leipzig, 1867).

Voprosy uzbekskogo iazykoznaniia (Tashkent, 1954).

Wurm, S., *Turkic Peoples of the USSR* (London, 1954). Bibliography.

E. STATISTICS

Lorrimer, F., *The Population of the Soviet Union—History and Prospects* (League of Nations, Geneva, 1946).

Perepis 1926: Vsesoiuznaia perepis naseleniia 17 dek., 1926 g., publ. Central Statistical Administration of USSR, IV [Narodnost i rodnoi iazyk naseleniia SSSR] (Moskva, 1928).
*Perepis 1897: Pervaia vseobshchaia perepis naseleniia Rossiiskoi imperii 189*7, publ. Central Statistical Committee, I–VIII (Moskva, 1897–1905).

II. Tatary

A. EARLY HISTORY

Bazhenov, N., *Kazanskaia Istoriia* (Kazan, 1847).
Battal, A., *Kazan Turkleri: Tarihi vesiasi gorushler* (Istanbul, 1925).
Firsov, N., "Nekotorye cherty iz istorii . . . Povolzhiia," *IOKU*, XIV (1897).
Firsov, N. N., *Proshloe Tatarii* (Kazan, 1926).
Gubaidullin, G., *Tatar Tarihi* (Kazan, 1925).
Iskhaki, A., *Idel Ural* (Paris, 1933).
Istoriia Tatarskoi ASSR, I (Kazan 1955).
Istoricheskie svedeniia o Ekaterinenskoi komissii (speeches of Tatar Murzas), *SIO*, XIV (1875) and CXV (1903).
Kalinin, N., *Kazan* (Kazan, 1955). Important. Bibliography.
Kazanskaiia Istoriia (Moscow, 1954). One of the most important chronicles on Kazan history written in late sixteenth century.
Materialy po izucheniiu Tatarstana, II, ed. G. Ibragimov and N. I. Vorobiev (Kazan, 1926).
Mozharovskii, A., "Izlozhenie khoda missionerskogo dela po prosviashcheniiu Kazanskikh inorodtsev, 1552–1867," *ChIOIDR*, CXII (1890). Important.
Puteshestvie Ibn Faldana na Volgu, ed. V. Krachkovskii (Moskva, 1939).
Spuler, B., *Idel Ural* (Berlin, 1942).
————— "Die Wolga Tataren und Baschkiren unter russischer Herrschaft," *WdI*, XXIX (1949).
Veliaminov-Zernov, V. V., *Izsledovanie o kasimovskikh tsariakh i tsarevichakh*, I–IV (Petersburg, 1863–1866).

B. 1800–1916

Adres-Kalendar i Spravochnaia kniga goroda Kazani i Kazanskoi gubernii (Kazan, 1916).
Ali Rakhim, "Nasyri," *VNOT*, I (1925).
Ashmarin, M., "Neskolko slov o sovremennoi literature kazanskikh tatar," *ZhMNP* (1905).
————— "Ocherki literaturnoi deiatelnosti kazanskikh tatar," *TV*, LV (1901).
Faseev, K. F., *Iz istorii tatarskoi obshchestvennoi mysli* (Kazan, 1955).
Firsov, N. N., "Nekotorye cherty iz torgovopromyshlennoi zhizni Povolzhiia," *IOKU*, XV (1897).
Fukhs, K., *Kazanskie tatary v statisticheskom i etnograficheskom otnasheniiakh* (Kazan, 1844).

Gasprinskii, I., *Russkoe musulmanstvo* (Bakhchisarai, 1883).
—— *Russko-vostochnoe soglashenie* (Bakhchisarai, 1896).
Gubaidullin, Kh., "Iz proshlogo Tatar" *MplT*, I (Kazan, 1925).
—— "Iz Istorii torgovogo klassa privolzhskikh tatar," *Vostokovedenie*, I (Baku, 1926).
Ibragimov, G., *Tatary v revoliutsiiu 1905 goda*. (Kazan, 1926). Very important.
Istoriia Tatarii v dokumentakh i materialakh, ed. N. L. Rubinshtein, (Moskva, 1937).
Ilminskii, N. N., *Kazanskaia kreshcheno-tatarskaia shkola* (Kazan, 1887).
Istoriia Tatarskoi ASSR, ed. N. Vorobiev, I (Kazan, 1956).
Kaium Nasyri [1825–1945] materialy k 100–letiu rozhdeniia (Kazan, 1948).
Kasymov, G., *Ocherki po Istorii religioznogo i anti-religioznogo dvizheniia sredi Tatar* (Kazan, 1932).
Katanov, N. and Ia. Koblov, "Obzor . . . tatarskikh uchebnikov po istorii," *InOb*, II (1916).
Katanov, N., "Novye trudy po tatarskoi istorii" (survey of Tatar historians), *InOb*, I (1912–1915).
Materialy po istorii Tatarii vtoroi poloviny XIX veka. Part I: *Agrarnyi vopros*, pub. AN USSR (Moskva, 1936).
"*Medresse povolzhiia*," *MI*, II (1913).
Muhammediarov, "Tatary Musulmane o panislamizme," *InOb*, I (1912–1915).
Saifi, F., "Tatary do revoliutsii," *TDTK*, I (1930).
Sputnik po Kazani, ed. N. Zagoskin (Kazan, 1895). Important.
"Tatary-Musulmane-Shkola i verovaniia," *InOb*, I (1912–1915).
Tukaev, A., *Stikhi* (Moskva, 1946).
Tukai, G., *Stikhi i poemy* (Kazan, 1951).
Validov, J. [Dzhemaleddin], *Millet ve Milliet* (Orenburg, 1914). Russian condensation in *Vostochnyi Sbornik*, II (1916).
—— *Ocherki isitorii, obrazovannosti i literatury volzhskikh tatar* (Moskva, 1913).
Vejsi, "Iskhaki," *Wschód-Orient*, XXV–XXVI (1937).
—— "A. Tukai," *Wschód-Orient*, XXVIII (1938).
Vorobiev, N., *Kazanskie tatary* (Kazan, 1953). Important.
Voronets, A., "Uchitelskaia seminariia v Kazani," *Russkii Vestnik* (July 1873).
Zenkovsky, S., "A Century of Tatar Revival," *ASaEER*, XII (1953).

C. REVOLUTION AND CIVIL WAR

Bochkov, A., *Tri goda sovetskoi vlasti v Kazani 1917–1920* (Kazan, 1921).
Borozdin, N., "Sovremennyi Tatarstan," *NV*, X–XI (1925).
"Dokumenty o sozdanii Tatarskoi ASSR," *VNOT*, III (1925) .
Dvadtsat let Tatarskoi ASSR (Kazan, 1940). Collection of articles.
Firsov, N., "G. Ibragimov kak istorik-politik," *VNOT*, VIII (1928).

Galiev, S., "Tatrespublika i Lenin," *PrRev*, IX (1925).

Grachev, E., *Kazanskii oktiabr* (Kazan, 1926).

Gabidullin, Kh., *Tatarstan za sem let, 1920–1927* (Kazan, 1927).

"Materialy i dokumenty po natsionalnomu voprosu i organizatsii Tat-respubliki," *VNOT*, VIII (1928). Important.

Otchet TsIK i SNK Tatarskoi SSR [Fifth congress of the Soviets] (Kazan, 1925).

Puti Revoliutsii (periodical; Kazan, 1922–). Contains important material on the revolutionary period in Tatar regions.

Rakhmatullin, I., "Mullanur Vakhitov," *Puti Revoliutsii*, III (Kazan, 1923).

Saadi, A., "G. Ibragimov i ego literaturnoe tvorchestvo," *VNOT*, VIII (1928).

Samoilovich, A., "G. Ibragimov kak tataroved," *VNOT*, VIII (1928).

Siungeli, Sh., Ordenonosnaia Tatariia," *RevVost*, XXXI (1935).

Stenograficheskii otchet IX oblastnoi konferentsii Tatarskoi organizatsii VKP (b) (Kazan, 1924).

Sultangaliev, M., "Tatarskaia AR," *ZhNat*, I (1923).

―――― "Sotsialnaia revoliutsiia i vostok," *ZhNat*, nos. 38, 39, 42 (1919).

―――― *Metody antireligioznoi propagandy sredi Musulman* (Moskva, 1922).

Syromolotv, F., "Lenin i Stalin v sozdanii Tataro-Bashkirskoi respubliki," *RiN*, LXVI (1935).

Tarasov, A., "Kontrrevoliutsionnaia avantiura tatarskoi burzhuazii," *IstMar*, VII (1940).

Tretiaia sessiia TsIK Tatarskoi SSR (Kazan, 1923).

Trotskii, V., *Revoliutsionnoe dvizhenie v srednevolzhskom krae* (Samara, 1930).

Zhizn zamechatelnykh liudei Kazani, I–II (Kazan, 1940–1941). Biographies of M. Vahitov, Sheinkman, etc.

III. Bashkiria

A. EARLY HISTORY

Materialy po istorii Bashkirskoi ASSR, I–IV, publ. AN SSSR (Moskva-Leningrad, 1936–1956).

Rudenko, S., *Bashkiry* (Moskva, 1955). Historical-ethnographic articles.

Tikhaev, Kh., *Bashkiriia* (Moskva, 1950).

Tipeev, S., *Bashkorstan tarihi* (Ufa, 1930).

―――― *Ocherki po istorii Bashkirii* (Ufa, 1930).

B. 1800–1917

Cheremshanskii, V. M., *Opisanie orenburgskogo kraia* (Moskva, 1858).

Polozhenie o bashkirakh 1902–1906 (Ufa, 1909).

Remezov, N. V., *Ocherki iz zhizni dikoi Bashkirii* (Moskva, 1889).

C. REVOLUTION AND CIVIL WAR

Atnagulov, S., *Bashkiriia* (Moskva-Leningrad, 1925).

Borba za sovetskuiu vlast na iuzhnom Urale (Cheliabinsk, 1957). Important collection of documents and materials.

Desiat let sovetskoi Bashkirii 1919–1929 (Ufa, 1929).

Dimanshtein, S., "Bashkiriia v 1918–1919 g.," *PrRev*, LXXVI (1928).

Jansky, H., "Ahmet Zeki Velidi Togan," *Zeki Velidi Togan'a Armagan* (Istanbul, 1955).

Kuznetsov, P. A., *Grazhdanskaia voina v Bashkirii* (Ufa, 1932).

Manatov, Sh., "Bashkirskaia Avtonomnaia Respublika," *ZhNat* I (1923).

Mostovenko, P., "Bolshie oshibki maloi Bashkirii," *PrRev*, LXX (1929).

Murtazin (Murteza), M. L., *Bashkiriia i bashkirskie voiska v grazhdanskuiu voinu* (Leningrad, 1927).

Otchet TsIK i SNK Tatarskoi SSR [Third and Fourth Congresses of Soviets] (Kazan, 1923).

Pipes, R., "The First Experiment in Soviet National Policies—the Bashkir Republic," *Russian Review* (1950).

Raimov, R. M., *Obrazovanie Bashkirskoi ASSR* (Moscow, 1952). Important. Bibliography.

Samoilov, F., *Malaia Bashkiriia v 1918 i 1920 gg.* (Moskva, 1933).

Sovetskaia Bashkiriia, ed. R. Kuzeev (Ufa, 1957). Collection of articles.

Tipeev, S., *K istorii natsionalnogo dvizheniia v Bashkirii* (Ufa, 1929).

Zenkovsky, S., "The Tataro-Bashkir Feud of 1917–1920," *Indiana Slavic Studies*, II (1958), 37–62.

IV. Kazakhstan

A. EARLY HISTORY

Abdykalykov M., and A. Pankratova, *Istoriia Kazakhskoi SSR* (Alma-Ata, 1943).

Apollova, N., *Prisoedinenie Kazakhstana k Rossii* (Alma-Ata, 1943).

Asfendirov, S., *Istoriia Kazakhstana s drevneishikh vremen* (Alma-Ata, 1934). Bibliography.

Istoriia Kazakhskoi SSR, ed. M. Auezov, I (Alma-Ata, 1957).

Materialy po istorii kasakhskoi SSR (1735–1828), IV, publ. AN USSR (Moskva-Leningrad, 1940).

B. 1800–1917

Abai [Kunanbaev], *Izbrannoe* (Moskva, 1945).

Alektorov, A. E., "Ocherki iz razvitiia inorodcheskogo obrazovaniia v Rossii," *ZhMNP* (June 1904).

Auezov, M., *Abai* (Moskva, 1949).

—— *Put Abaia* (Moskva, 1952).

—— *Velikii poet kazakhskogo naroda Abai Kunanbaev* (Moskva, 1954).

Baisamynov, "Maktaby u Kirgiz," *ZhMNP* (February 1906).

Beisembiev, K., *Iz istorii obshchestvennoi mysli Kazakhstana vtoroi poloviny XIX veka* (Alma-Ata, 1957). A study of Valikhanov's and and Altynsaryn's roles in the growth of the Kazakh national consciousness.

Fetisov, M. I., *Literaturnye sviazi Kazakhstana s Rossiei* (Moskva, 1956).

Ilminskii, N. I., *Vospominaniia ob Altynsaryne* (Kazan, 1895).

"Kirgizy-musulmane i voina," *InOb*, II (1916).

Mironov, N., "Ocherk o russko-kirgizskikh shkolakh Uralskoi oblasti," *ZhMNP* (August 1910).

Revoliutsiia 1905–1907 godov v Kazakhstane (Alma-Ata, 1949). Documents and materials.

Valikhanov, Ch., *Statii-Perepiska* (Alma-Ata, 1947).

────── *Sochineniia*, *ZRIGO OE*, XXXIX (1904).

The bibliography on the revolt of 1916 is included in the section on Central Asia.

C. REVOLUTION AND CIVIL WAR

Akulinin, I. G., *Orenburgskoe kazachee voisko v borbe s bolshevikami* (Shanghai, 1937).

Dulatov, M., "Baitursunov," *TOIKK*, III (1929).

Iz istorii partiinogo stroitelstva v Kazakhstane (Alma-Ata, 1936).

Melnikov, G., *Oktiabr v Kazakhstane* (Alma-Ata, 1930).

Mindlin, Z., "Kirgizy i revoliutsiia," *NV* (1924).

"Nationalismus in Kazakhstan," *OE*, XII (1937).

Obrazovanie Kazakhskoi SSR, ed. S. N. Pokrovskii (Alma-Ata, 1957). Collection of documents.

Popov, F., *Dutovshchina* (Moskva-Samara, 1934).

Sapargaliev, M., *Vozniknovenie kazakhskoi sovetskoi gosudarstvennosti* (Alma-Ata, 1948).

Taimanov, G. T., *Razvitie sovetskoi gosudarstvennosti v Kazakhstane* (Moskva, 1956).

Uchreditelnyi Siezd Sovetov Kirgizkoi ASSR [Kazakh ASSR] 7–20 Oct. *1920 g.*, ed. E. G. Fedorov (Alma-Ata, 1936).

V. Central Asia

A. EARLY HISTORY

Antologiia Tadzhikskoi Poezi (Moskva, 1951).

Antropov, P., *Chto i kak chitat po istorii revoliutsionnogo dvizheniia v Srednei Azii* (Samarkand, 1929). Bibliographical guide.

Bartold, V. V. [W. Barthold], *Four studies on the history of Central Asia* (Leiden, 1956).

────── *Istoriia kulturnoi zhizni Turkestana* (Leningrad, 1927). The best work on cultural life in prerevolutionary Central Asia.

Istoriia Kirgizii, I–II, pub. AN Kirgiz SSR (Frunze, 1956).

Istoriia Narodov Uzbekistana, I–II (Tashkent 1947–1951). Very important.

Istoriia Uzbekskoi SSR, I, parts I–II (Tashkent, 1956). Important work on prerevolutionary Central Asian history. Excellent bibliography.

Schuyler, E., *Turkistan*, I–II (New York, 1876).

Vambery, A., *A History of Bukhara* (London, 1873).

B. 1800–1916

Aini, S., *Bukhara* (memoirs), I–II (Moskva 1950), III (Moskva, 1957).

—— *Dokhunda* (Moskva, 1948).

—— *Raby* (Moskva, 1951).

Atabaev, M., "Maktaby u Turkmen Zakaspiiskoi oblasti," *ZhMNP*, (February 1906).

Aziatskaia Rossiia, I–III (Petersburg, 1911–1914). Very important.

Baisamynov, "Maktaby v Syr Dariinskoi oblasti," *ZhMNP* (February 1906).

Benzing, J., "Das turkestanische Volk im Kampf fuer seine Selbstaendigkeit," *Wdl*, XIX (1937).

—— *Turkestan* (Berlin, 1943).

Dzhidzhihia, A., "O poslednikh sobytiakh v Bukhare" *Voennyi sbornik*, V (1910).

Ezturk, M. H., "Abdul Fitrat," *Millij Turkistan*, no. 80–81 (1952).

Fedorov, E., *Ocherki natsionalno-osvoboditelnogo dvizheniia v Srednei Azii* (Tashkent, 1925).

—— *1905 god i korennoe naselenie Srednei Azii* (Moskva, 1926).

Fitrat, A., *Rasskazy indiiskogo puteshestvennika* (Samarkand, 1913).

Fitrat Bukharets, spor bukharskogo mudarissa s evropeitsem v Indii o novometodnykh shkolakh (Tashkent, 1911). Russian translation of Fitrat's *Munizira.*

Gaier, I. I., *Turkestan* (Tashkent 1909).

Hakim-Bey, "Zeitungsgeschichte Turkestans," *OE*, VIII (1932).

"Instruktsia starshim mudarissam tuzemnykh shkol Turkestanskogo kraia," *Turkestanskaia Tuzemnaia Gazeta*, no. 15 (1894).

Khanykov, N. V., *Bokhara—Its Amir and its people* (London, 1945).

Khodzhaev [Hojaev], "Dzhadidy," *Ocherki revoliutsionnogo dvizheniia v Srednei Azii* (Moskva, 1937).

Logofet, D. N., *V strane bezpraviia* (Petersburg, 1909).

Mallaev, N. M., *Uzbek adabieti tarikhi* (Tashkent, 1955).

Masalskii, N. M., *Turkestanskii Krai* (Moskva, 1910), publ. in geographical series "Rossiia," ed. A. Semenov-Tianshanskii.

Materialy nauchnoi sessii posviashchennoi istorii do okt. perioda Srednei Azii i Kazakhstana (Tashkent, 1955).

Materialy po izucheniiu khoziaistva osedlogo naseleniia v Turkestanskom krae (Petersburg, 1912).

Mironov, N., "Ocherk o russko-kirgizskikh shkolakh," *ZhMNP* (August 1910).

Nalivkin, V., *Svedeniia o sostoianii tuzemnykh madras v Syr Dariinskoi oblasti* (Tashkent, 1916).

Nalivkine, V., *Histoire du Khanat de Khokand* (Paris, 1889).

Novitskii, K. P., "Politika tsarskogo pravitelstva v oblasti narodnogo prosviashcheniia v Tsentralnoi Azii," *PrNat* (November 1924).

Ostroumov, N., "Madrasy v Turkestanskom Krae," *ZhMNP* (January 1907).

—— "Musulmanskaia vysshaia shkola," *ZhMNP* (October 1906).

—— "Musulmanskie maktaby . . . v Turkestanskom krae," *ZhMNP* (February 1906).

—— *Sarty* (3rd ed., Tashkent, 1909).

Polovtseff, A., *The Land of Timur* (London, 1932).

Polozhenie ob upravlenii Turkestanskogo kraia (Petersburg, 1892).

Ryskulov, T., *Kazakhstan* (Moskva, 1927).

—— *Kirgizstan* (Moskva, 1935.)

Samoilovich, A. M., "Pervoe tainoe obshchestvo mladobukhartsev," *Vostok*, I (1922).

Serebriannikov, A. G., *Sbornik materiialov dlia istorii zavoevaniia Turkestanskogo kraia*, I (Tashkent, 1914).

Terentiev, M. A., *Rossiia i Angliia v borbe za rynki* (Petersburg, 1878).

Vambery, A., *Travel in Central Asia* (New York, 1895).

Zenkovsky, S., Kulturkampf in Prerevolutionary Central Asia," *ASaEER*, XIV (1955).

C. THE REVOLT OF 1916

Broido, G., "Materialy k istorii vosstaniia kirgiz," *NV*, VI (1924).

Chokaev, M., "Turkestanskoe vosstanie," *Dni* (August 1925).

"Dzhizakskoe vosstanie 1916 goda," *KrAr*, LVI (1933). Documents.

"K istorii vosstaniia kirgiz," *KrAr*, XVI (1926). Documents.

Kuropatkin, A., "Dnevnik," *KrAr*, XXXIV (1929).

—— "Iz dnevnika," *KrAr*, XX (1927).

Ryskulov, T., "Vosstanie tuzemtsev Turkestana v 1916 godu," *Ocherki revoliutskionnogo dvizheniia v Srednei Azii* (Moskva, 1937).

Sokol, E. D., *The Revolt of 1916 in Russian Central Asia* (Baltimore, 1953). Bibliography.

Stepniak, G., "Kirgizskoe Vosstanie," *Sibirskie Ogni*, I (1928).

Vosstanie 1916 goda, ed. L. V. Lesnaia (Moskva, 1927). Collection of documents. Very important.

D. REVOLUTION AND CIVIL WAR

Alekseenkov, P., "Kokandskaia avtonomiia," *Revoliutsiia v Srednei Azii.*

—— "Natsionalnaia politika Vremennogo Pravistelstva v Turkestane v 1917 g," *PrRev*, LXXIX (1928).

Antropov, P., "Pervyi siezd KP Turkestana," *Revoliutsia v Srednei Azii.*

Bailey, F. M., *Mission to Tashkent* (London, 1946).

Blacker, L. V., *On Secret Patrols in High Asia* (London, 1922).

Bolotov, S., "Iz istorii Osipovskogo miatezha v Turkestane," *PrRev*, LIII (1926).

Brun, A., *Troublous Times—Experiences in Bolshevik Russia and Turkestan* (London, 1931).

Caroe, O., *Soviet Empire—The Turks of Central Asia and Stalinism* (London, 1953).

Castagné, J., *Le Turkestan depuis la revolution russe, 1917–1921* (Paris, 1922).

Chokaev, M., "Fifteen Years of Bolshevik Rule in Turkestan," *JRCAS*, XX (1933).

—— "Turkestan and the Soviet Regime," *JRCAS*, XVIII (1931).

—— *Turkestan pod vlastiiu sovetov* (Paris, 1937).

Dunsterville, L. C., *The Adventure of the Dunsterforce*, (London, 1932).

Filipov, S. T., *Boevye deistviia na Zakaspiiskom fronte* (Ashkhabad, 1928).

M. V. Frunze na frontakh grazhdanskoi voiny (Moskva, 1941). M. V. Frunze's writings and correspondence. Important.

Glovatskii, O., *Revoliutsiia pobezhdaet* (Tashkent, 1930).

Gnesin, F., "Turkestan v dni revoliutsii i bolshevizma," *BA*, I (1926).

—— "Memoirs" (in Russian), manuscript, private.

Golubev, R., "Sentiabrskie sobytiia v Tashkente," *IstMar*, IV (1941).

Hayit, B., *Die nationale Regierungen von Kokand und Alash Orda* (Muenster, 1950). Mimeographed edition.

—— *Turkestan in XX Jahrhundert* (Darmstadt, 1956). Bibliography.

Iskander, "Podgotovka Angliei bukharskogo platsdarma dlia interventsii v Sovetskii Turkestan," *IstZap*, XXXVI (Moskva, 1951).

Istoriia Kirgizii, I–II, ed. M. P. Viatkin (Frunze, 1956).

Kary-Niiazov, T. N., *Ocherki kultury sovetskogo Uzbekistana* (Moskva, 1955).

Kulturnoe stroitelstvo v Kirgizii 1917–1928 (Frunze, 1957).

Malleson, W., "The British Military Mission to Turkestan, 1918–1920," *JRCAS*, IX, (1922).

"M.N.," "Pod znakom islama," *NV*, IV (1924).

Muraveiskii, S., *Ocherki po istorii revoliutsionnogo dvizheniia v Srednei Azii* (Tashkent, 1926). Important.

—— "Sentiabrskie sobytiia v Tashkente," *PrRev*, X (1924).

Olbeg, P., "Russian Policy in Turkestan," *Contemporary Review* (London), CXXII (1922).

Olzscha, R. and G. Cleinow, *Turkestan* (Leipzig, 1942).

Parks, A. G., *Bolshevism in Turkestan, 1917–1927* (New York, 1957). Important. Bibliography.

Rakhimbaev, A., *Tadzhikistan* (Moskva, 1926).

Revoliutsiia v Srednei Azii, I (Tashkent, 1929). Important collection of articles and documents on the early years of Soviet rule in Central Asia.

Riazantsev, S. N., *Kirgiziia* (Moskva, 1951).

Ryskulov, T., *Revoliutsiia i korennoe naselenie Srednei Azii* (Tashkent, 1925).

Ryskulov, T., et al., *Ocherki revoliutsionnogo dvizheniia v Srednei Azii* (Moskva, 1936).

Safarov, G., *Kolonialnaia Revoliutsiia* (Moskva, 1921). Very important.

Salikov, D., "Borba za Orenburg," *Voina v peskakh* (Moskva, 1935). Important memoirs.

Salikov, P., "Osipovskii miatezh," *IstMar*, IV (1941).

Sredniaia Aziia-Spravochnaia Kniga na 1926 god (Tashkent, 1926).

Tchokay, M., *Yash Turkestan*, Paris, 1949–1950. Remained inaccessible to the author.

Todd, J. K., "The Mallesson Mission to Transcaspia in 1918," *JRCAS*, XXVII (1940).

Vlasov, K., "Petrovskii Otriad," *Voina v peskakh* (Moskva, 1935).

Voina v peskakh [Materialy po istorii grazhdanskoi voiny] (Moskva, 1935). Important.

Vsia Sredniaia Aziia (Tashkent, 1926).

Wilfort, F., *Turkestanisches Tagebuch* (Wien, 1930).

Zenkovsky, S., "Ideological Deviation in Soviet Central Asia," *SaEER*, XXXII (1954).

E. BUKHARA AND KHIVA (KHOREZM)

Bogomolova, K., "K istorii revoliutsionnogo dvizheniia v Bukhare," *Soobshcheniia Tadzh. Filiala AN SSSR*, XXV (1951).

Genalin, N., "Sobytiia v Khorezmskoi respublike," *VoenMysl*, I (1921).

Ishanov, A. I., *Sozdanie bukharskoi narodnoi sovetskoi respubliki* (Tashkent, 1955).

Khodzhaev (Hojaev), F., "O mladobukhartsakh," *IstMar*, I (1926).

Kolesov, F., "Vosstanie v Bukhare," in *Voina v peskakh* (Moskva, 1935).

Kolychevskii, I., "Bukhara," *VoenMysl*, I (1920).

"Materialy po istorii Bukharskoi revoliutsii," *Vestnik NKID* nos. 4–5 (1922).

Mikhailov, S., "Khivinskii Front," *VoenMysl*, I (1921).

Said Alim Khan, *La voix de la Bukharie opprimée* (Paris, 1929).

Skalov, G., "Khivisnskaia revoliutsiia," *NV*, III (1923).

Soloveichik, D., "Revoliutsionnaia Bukhara," *NV*, II (1922).

Velikaia oktiabrskaia revoliutsiia i grazhdanskaia voina v Kirgizii (Frunze, 1957).

F. THE BASMACHI MOVEMENT

Castagné, J., *Les Basmachis* (Paris, 1925).

Chokaev, M., "The Basmaji Movement in Turkestan," *The Asiatic Review* (London), XXIV (1928).

Ginsburg, S., "Basmachestvo v Fergane," *Ocherki revoliutsionnogo dvizheniia v Srednei Azii* and in *NV*, X–XI (1925).

Iliutko, F., *Basmachestvo v Lokae* (Moskva-Leningrad, 1929).

Kuibyshev, V., "Basmacheskii front," *ZhNat*, no. 16 [73] (1920).

Maier, A., *Boevye epizody—Basmachestvo v Bukhare* (Moskva-Tashkent, 1934).

Skalov, G., "Sotsialnaia priroda basmachestva v Turkestane," *ZhNat*, nos. 3–4 (1923).

Vasilevskii, "Fazy basmacheskogo dvizheniia v Srednei Azii," *NV*, XXIX (1929).

VI. Azerbaijan

A. EARLY HISTORY

Karahan, A., *Fuzali* (Istanbul, 1949).
Spuler, B., *Iran in fruehislamischer Zeit* (Wiesbaden, 1952).
Sykes, P., *A History of Persia*, I–II (London, 1930).
Sysoev, V. M., *Kratkii ocherk istorii Azerbaidzhana* (Baku, 1925).

B. 1800–1917

Ahmad Bey [A. Agaev], "La Société Persane," *La Nouvelle Revue* (1891–1893).
Akhundov, M. F. [Akhond-Zadeh], *Sochineniia* (Tbilisi, 1936).
Dzhafarov, Zh., *Teatr imeni Azizbekova* (Moskva, 1951).
Ischchanian, B., *Nationaler Bestand, berufsmaessige Gruppierung und soziale Gliederung der kaukasischen Voelker*, (Berlin, 1914).
Ishkanian [Ischchanian], B., *Narodnosti Kavkaza* (Petrograd, 1916).
Kavkazskii Kalendar na 1917 god (Tiflis, 1917).
Kolonialnaia politika tsarizma v Azerbaidzhane v 20–kh i 40–ykh godakh XIX veka., publ. AN USSR, (Moskva-Leningrad, 1936).
Lvov, A., "1905 g.v Baku," *NV*, XIII–XIV (1926).
Topchibashev, A., "Panislamizm i ego kharakter," *Kaspii*, no. 87 (1900).

C. REVOLUTION AND CIVIL WAR

Bagirov, M. D., *Iz Iztorii bolshevistskoi organizatsii Baku i Azerbaidzhana* (Moskva, 1946).
Baikov, B., "Vospominaniia o revoliutsii v Zakavkazii," *ARR*, V (1923).
Belenskii, S., and A. Manvelov, *Revoliutsiia 1917 goda v Azerbaidzhane*, publ. IstPart (Baku, 1917). Very important collection of information.
Claims of the Peace Delegation of the Republic of Caucasian Azerbaijan presented to the Peace Conference in Paris (Paris, 1919).
Denikin, A., *Ocherki Russkoi smuty*, I–V (Berlin, 1924–1926).
Enukidze, D., *Krakh imperialisticheskoi interventsii v Zakavkazie* (Tbilisi, 1954).
Gasanov, G., and N. Sarkisov, "Sovetskaia vlast v Baku v 1918 g," *IstMar*, LXIX (1938).
Guseinov, T., *Oktiabr v Azerbaidzhane* (Baku, 1927).
Guseinov, M. D., *Tiurkskaia demokraticheskaia partiia federalistov Musavat v proshlom i nastoiashchem* (Tiflis, 1927). Important. Contains program and manifestos of Musavat.
Ishkanian, B., *Kontrrevoliutsiia v Zakavkazie* (Baku, 1919).
——— *Velikie chasy v gorode Baku* (Tiflis, 1920).
Jaeschke, G., "Die Republik Azerbaidschan," *WDI*, XXIII (1941).
——— "Transkaukasus," *OE*, XI (1935).

Karaev, A. G., *Iz nedavnego proshlogo* (Baku, 1926).

Kachapuridze, G. V., *Bolsheviki Gruzii v boiakh za pobedu sovetskoi vlasti* (Moskva, 1947).

Kazemzadeh, F., *The Struggle for Transcaucasia, 1917–1921* (New York, 1951). Best study of Transcaucasia in revolutionary period. Bibliography.

Kazu, B., "Gandzhinskoe vosstanie protiv bolshevikov," *Az*, nos. 11–12 (1953).

Khudadov, V. N., "Sovremennyi Azerbaizhan" *NV*, III (1923).

Kryczynski, O, "A. Sulkiewicz," *Wschód-Orient*, XX–XXI (1935).

Kuliev, M., *Vragi oktiabria v Azerbaidzhane* (Baku, 1927).

Mirza Bala, *Milli Azerbaycan Hareketi* (Berlin, 1938). Remained inaccessible to the author.

Munschi, H., *Die Republik Azerbaidschan* (Berlin, 1930).

"Pamiati N. Narrimanova," *NV*, VII (1925).

Popov, A. L., "Iz istorii angliiskoi interventsii v Zakavkazii," *PrRev*, VI–VII (1923).

Raevskii, A., *Angliiskie druziia i musavatskie patroity* (Baku, 1927).

—— *Partiia musavat i ee kontr-revoliutsionnaia rabota* (Baku, 1929).

Rasul Zade [Resul Zadeh], M. E., *O Panturanizme v sviazi s kavkazskoi problemoi* (Paris, 1930).

—— *L'Azerbaidjan en lutte pour l'independence* (Paris, 1930). Remained inaccessible to the author.

Ratgauzer, Ia., *Borba za sovetskii Azerbaidzhan* (Baku, 1928).

—— *Revoliutsiia i grazhdanskaia voina v Baku* (Baku, 1927).

Sef, S. E., *Kak Bolsheviki prishli k vlasti v 1917–1918 godakh v Bakinskom raione* (Baku, 1927).

Semenov, Yu., "Zakavkazskaia respublika," *Vozrozhdenie*, I (1949).

Urtadze, G. I., *Obrazovanie i konsolidatsiia Gruzinskoi demokraticheskoi respubliki* (Muenchen, 1956).

Woytinsky, W., *La Democratie Georgienne* (Paris, 1921). Contains valuable material on the elections to the Constituent Assembly in Transcaucasia.

Ziatkhanov, A., *Aperçu sur l'histoire, la litterature et la politique de l'Azerbaidjan* (Baku, 1919).

VII. The Crimea

Bochagov, A. K., *Milli Firka* (Simferopol, 1933).

Bunegin, M. F., *Revoliutsiia i grazhdanskaia voina v Krymu* (Simferopol, 1927). Important.

Elagin, V., "Natsionalisticheskie illiuzii krymskikh tatar v revoliutsionnye gody," *NV*, V, VI (1924–1925).

Kirimal, E., *Der nationale Kampf der Krimtuerken, mit besonderer Beruecksichtigung der Jahre 1917–1918* (Emsdetten, 1952). Excellent, though strongly nationalistic, survey of the years 1917–1918 in the Crimea. Exhaustive bibliography.

Pasmanik, D. S., *Revoliutsionnye gody v Krymu* (Paris, 1926).

Pipes, R., *The Formation of the Soviet Union* (Cambridge, 1954). The only comprehensive treatment of the Crimean problem in English. Bibliography.

Seydamet, D., *La Crimée* (Lausanne, 1921).

Zenkovsky, S., "Tragediia krymskikh tatar," *NRS*, October 19, 1952.

Index

Abai, 66
Abai. *See* Kunanbaev, Abai
Abdul Ahad, A. (Emir of Bukhara, 1885–1910), 81, 87
Achyg Soz, 126
Adais, 215, 222
Adat, 42, 58, 73
Afghani, Jemal al Din (Moslem ideologist, 1839–1897), 31, 38, 271–272
Agaev (Aga-Oglu), Ahmed bey (Azerbaijani journalist and politician), 39, 40, 97, 100, 103, 104, 107–108, 111, 112, 114, 117, 127, 129, 269, 270, 271
"Aid, The," 84
Aikap, 66, 67
Aina (The Mirror), 83
Aini, Sadreddin (Tajik Jadid and writer, 1879–1954), 74, 88
Akchurin (Akchura-Oglu), Yusuf (Tatar politician, creator of Pan-Turkism, 1876–1935), 21, 36, 38–39, 41, 42, 46, 47, 50, 104, 107, 112, 116, 127, 129, 269, 270, 279
Akinchi, 94, 99
Akmola, 66
Akmolinsk, 223, 224
Akhond-Zadeh (Ahond-Zade), Fath Ali (Azerbaijani playwright, 1812–1878), 94, 95
Akhtiamov, Ibrahim (Tatar Social Democrat), 52, 124, 144, 165, 188
Aktiubinsk, 214, 215
Alash, 66
Alash Orda, 68, 199, 205, 210, 212, 213–220, 222, 224, 243, 247, 269
Al Biruni (Moslem scholar), 72
Al Farabi (Moslem scholar), 72
Al Khwarizmi (Moslem scholar), 72
Alkin, Ilias (Tatar left socialist), 150, 158, 171, 173, 187
Alkin, Seid Girey (Tatar Duma member), 40, 45, 50, 51, 123–125
All-Moslem Democratic Socialist Bloc, 158, 274
All-Russian Moslem congresses. *See* Congresses and conferences
All-Russian Moslem Council. *See* Shuro
All-Russian Provisional Moslem National Council (*milli merkezi shuro*). *See* Shuro
Alp, Zia Gek (Turkish writer and ideologist), 107, 109–111, 112, 117, 261, 270, 273

Altynsaryn, Ibrai (Kazakh educator, 1841–1889), 61, 63–64, 67
Amangeldy. *See* Imanov, Amangeldy
Apanaev, Abdulla (Tatar leader), 21, 40, 46, 49, 50, 187
Armenia, 50, 98–99, 111, 183, 257–267
Asia, 83
Astrakhan, 13, 19, 21, 33, 185, 189, 265
Atnagulov, S. (Bashkir left Communist), 169, 170, 173, 181, 186
Atlasov, Hadi (Tatar leader), 151, 169
Avicenna (Ibn Sina), 72, 77
Avksentiev, N. D., 188
Azerbaijan, 44, 50, 51, 116, 156; émigrés, 37–39; early history, 92–94; Iranian influence on, 94; Turkic revival in, 94–97; and 1905 Revolution, 98–99; press, 97–98; national independence, 97, 254–267, 273, 274; territorial claims and internal policies, 261–264; Azerbaijan Social Democrats, 98, 100, 256; Azerbaijan Communist Party, 264–267
Azerbaijan Soviet Republic, 268, 274
Azizbekov, Meshadi (Azerbaijani Communist), 98

Baiazet conference, 103
Baikov, A., 102
Baitursunov, A. B. (Kazakh leader, 1872–1928), 65, 66–68, 132, 136, 205, 211, 217, 220, 221–222
Bakhchisarai, 34, 49, 50, 107, 121
Baku, 11, 93, 94–100, 121, 124, 125, 150, 250–251, 257, 258–261, 270; Baku Communists, 264–267
Barudi, Galimjan (1857–1921; Mufti, 1911–1921), 46, 48, 49, 50, 151, 273
Bashkir ASSR, 6, 192, 201, 204, 208, 268
Bashkiria, 6, 181, 248; autonomy, 163, 168, 188–189, 195–208, 268, 274; Little Bashkiria, 195–208; Great Bashkiria, 197, 208; Communists in, 200–201; coup of January 1916, 203–204, 247
Bashkirs, 6, 13, 54, 55, 59, 117, 124, 143, 156, 179, 180, 196, 197, 211, 216, 219, 254, 273–274, 275; and problems with Tatars, 162–163, 168–170, 179–180, 192–194, 195–197; and union with Kazakhs, 204–206, 219–221, 234. *See also* Tataro-Bashkiria
Bashkir Voisko, 195n
Bashkurstan, 180; PRCB (Provisional

Revolutionary Council of Bashkurstan), 180, 198
Bashrevkom (Provisional Bashkir Revolutionary Committee), 200–208
Basmachi movement, 189, 206, 226, 236,
237, 247, 248, 250, 272–273, 277
Bayazidov, A., 40
Behbudi, Mahmud Hoja (Uzbek Jadid,
d. 1919), 44, 82, 84, 88–89, 227
Bigeev, Musa (Tatar theologian and
writer, 1875–192?), 50, 143, 151
Bobinski, Abdulla and Gainulla, 40, 50,
53
Bolshevik nationalities program, 159–164
Bolsheviks, 53, 66, 97, 104, 156, 159–164,
165, 171, 174–176, 181, 182, 190, 199,
200, 202, 214, 216, 218, 221, 226–237,
256, 264, 268, 276, 280, 281
Bukeev Horde (Horde of Bukei), 56,
67–68, 217
Bukeikhanov, A. (Kazakh leader and
Duma member), 65, 67, 68, 132, 136,
205, 211, 213, 217
Bukhara, 10, 12, 19, 20, 24, 56, 57, 59, 62,
72–91, 225, 226, 239, 248, 249, 251, 253,
257, 268; educational reform in, 85–88;
liberalism in, 84–91; Bukhara People's
Republic, 88, 249; Communist Party in,
248–249; Soviet conquest of, 248–249.
See also Young Bukhariotes
Bukhara-i-Sherif, 90

Catherine II, and tolerance toward Moslems, 17–19, 26, 28, 58
Caucasian mountaineers, 9, 93, 105, 122,
124, 142, 155, 161, 162, 271
Central Asia, Moslems in, 156–157, 179,
194, 207, 253, 269, 271, 272, 276; trade,
19–20; composition of population, 73–
74; Russian administration and education, 74–79; Moslem schools, 76–77;
1916 revolt, 123–139; and 1917 Revolution, 225–237; autonomy, 228; and Civil
War, 236–237; Communist Party in,
240–242
Central Bureau of Communist Organizations of Peoples of the East (March
1919), 190
Centralists vs. territorial autonomists,
141–153, 168–169, 181
Chagatai (literary language), 2, 25, 31,
32, 59, 74, 115, 147
Chanyshev, Yakub (Tatar Communist),
165, 173
Cheliabinsk, 198, 208, 275

Cheremiss (Maris), 9, 29, 176, 180, 184,
186
Chernov, V. M., 155
Chicherin, Georgi, 175
Chodorowski, Joseph (Communist leader
in Kazan), 181, 193, 194
Chokaev, Mustafa (Turkestani political
leader, 1890–1941), 187, 227, 232, 235,
276, 280
Chulpan Ildizi (Northern Star), 37
Chuvash, 3, 8, 9, 14, 27, 29, 177, 180, 184,
186
Civil War (Russian): and Tatars, 170–
174, 184–190; and Bashkirs, 198–208;
and Kazakhs, 209–224; and Central
Asia, 236–237; and Turkic movement
(summary), 272–273
Commissariat for the Affairs of the Na-
tionalities (Narkomnats). See Narkom-
nats
Committee for Defense of the Rights of
Moslem Turko-Tatar Peoples of Rus-
sia, 127, 129
Committee for Moslem Affairs, 162, 176
Congresses and conferences
    All-Russian Moslem congresses: First
    (August 1905), 40–41, 67, 85, 99; Sec-
    ond (January 1906), 41–43, 67, 85, 99;
    Third (August 1906), 45–51, 67, 85,
    99, 105, 115, 116, 126; Special All-
    Russian Moslem Congress (December
    1914), 124; Congress of the Peoples of
    Russia (1916), 129; First (postrevolu-
    tionary) All-Russian Moslem Congress
    (May 1917), 9, 140, 142–153, 158–159
    (and military congress), 178, 196, 211,
    228, 255, 271, 275; Second (July 1917),
    154, 156–159, 169, 196, 211, 275
    Moslem Communist congresses: First
    All-Russian Party of Moslem Com-
    munists (Bolshevik) Congress (No-
    vember 1918), 190; Second (November
    1919), 191–192, 203; First Conference
    of Moslem Communists in Central
    Asia (May 1919), 241–242; Third Re-
    gional Conference of Moslem Com-
    munists, 244–245, 247
    Moslem Central Asian conferences:
    First (April 1917), 229–230; Second
    (September 1917), 229–230; Third
    (November 1917), 232; Fourth (No-
    vember 1917), 233–234
    Other national congresses: First All-
    Bashkir National Conference, 196–197;
    First, Second, and Third All-Kirghiz

(Kazakh) Congresses (1917), 210–211, 213; First All-Azerbaijani Congress (Federalist Party), 256

Soviet congresses: Third All-Russian Congress of Soviets, 167; Seventh Party Congress, RKP(b), 175; Third Congress of Soviets (January 1918), 179; Fifth All-Russian Congress of Soviets, 200; First Turgai Congress of Soviets, 218; First Constituent Congress of Kazakh Soviets, 222; Twelfth Party Congress, RKP(b), 224; Third Regional Congress of Soviets (November 1917), 232; Fourth Regional Congress of Soviets, 236; Fifth Congress of Central Asian Soviets, 239; First Regional Party Congress, RKP (b), 239–240; Second Regional Party Conference, RKP(b), 241; Seventh Congress of Central Asian Soviets, 241; Eighth All-Russian Party Congress, RKP(b), 243; Fifth Regional Party Congress, 243, 244; First Congress of the Peoples of the East (Baku, September 1920), 250; Third International, 243, 248, 277

Constituent Assembly (All-Russian), 137, 154, 155, 158, 171, 172, 184, 187, 188, 257, 275, 276, 281

Constitutional Commission (of Mejilis), 169, 170, 173, 176, 177

Cossacks, 11, 168, 213, 214, 216, 223, 234, 235, 237, 281

Council of People's Commissars: and Kazan Republic, 165; and Bashkir agreement, 199. *See also* Sovnarkom

Council of Russian Social Organizations, 228

Crimean Tatar Republic, 254

Cultural-National Autonomy of the Moslems of Inner Russia, 166, 170, 271

Czecho-Slovak Legions, 184–187, 198, 214, 281

Daghestan, 147, 163, 262, 267, 271

Dala Valaiaty, 65

Dashnaktsutiun (Armenian socialist party), 98, 257, 259

Davidovich, Mustafa (Crimean leader), 40, 50

Davletchin, A. (Tatar leader), 41, 52, 124

Declaration of the Rights of the Peoples of Russia (1917), 161–163

Declaration of the Rights of the Toiling and Exploited People (1918), 167–168

Democratic Convention (of socialist parties), 155

Dimanstein (Dimanshtein), S. M. (member of Narkomnats), 182, 217, 272

Donish, Ahmad Mahdum Kalla (Bukhariote writer, 1827–1897), 80–81, 249

Dosuhammedov, Kh. (Kazakh leader), 144, 147–148, 150, 187–188, 211, 213, 214, 217, 280, 281

Dostoevsky, Feodor, 60, 61, 122

Dulatov M. (Kazakh writer), 65, 136–137, 211

Duma, 45, 52

Dumachelar, 52–53

Dungan (Chinese Moslems), 134

Dutov, General A. I., 168, 170, 171, 173, 197, 213, 214, 216, 231, 233, 234, 235

Effendiev, M. (Turkish officer), 242, 245

Ehrar, 263

Eliava, S. Z., 93

Emigrés in Constantinople, 127–130

Engalychev, Sagid (Tatar leader), 162, 169

Faris, Nabin Amin, 277–278

Federalists, 256–257, 262–263

Federalist Turkic Party–Musavat, 256–257

Feitskhani, Hussein (Tatar educator, 1826–1866), 25

Ferghana district, 7, 62, 74, 75, 83, 84, 127, 133, 206, 226, 229, 230, 233, 247

Firdousi (Persian writer, author of *Shah Nameh*), 110

Fitrat, Abdul Rauf (Uzbek writer), 74, 79, 88–89

Fiuzat, 36, 96

Frunze, M. V., 189, 204, 246, 248, 251

Gajinsky, M. H. (Azerbaijani politician), 256, 263, 265

Galiev, Said (Tatar Communist), 165, 173, 179, 186, 194, 203

Ganja province, 257, 258, 262

Gasprinsky, Ismail bey (Crimean Tatar educator, father of Moslem movement, 1851–1914), 30–34, 37, 45, 46, 50, 59, 67, 81–82, 86, 87, 95, 107–108, 114, 121, 245, 269; and Ottoman revival, 30–31; three principles of Moslem unity, 30–33; attitude toward Russia, 33–34; influence on Jadids, 34–35

Genç-Kalemar, 107
Georgia, 183, 257–267, 280
Godunov, Boris, 13, 114
Goldberg, 181, 194
Goremykin, G. I., 118
Grassis, Karl, 165, 181, 193
Great Horde, 56–57
Gulistan treaty of 1813, 93–94
Gurius, 15, 16

Haiat, 44
Halidé Edib (Turkish authoress), 98, 107
Hamid, Sultan Abdul, 31, 106
Harbi Shuro (All-Moslem Central Military Council), 158–159, 166–167, 169, 170, 172–174, 175, 177–178
Hemmet, 98, 100, 104, 256, 259, 266
Hoja, Asadulla (Uzbek Jadid), 227
Hoja, Islam (statesman in Khiva), 91
Hoja, Nizametdin (adviser to Emir of Bukhara), 238
Hoja, Ubaidulla (Uzbek Jadid, d. 1938), 227
Hojaev, Abdullah (Turkestani conservative politician), 83, 144, 148, 151
Hojaev, Faizulla (Uzbek Communist), 239
Hojaev family, 88, 239, 249
Hojaev, Nizametdin (Uzbek Jadid), 219, 241, 242
Hojaev, Sultan (Uzbek Communist), 252
Hojaev, Tursun (Uzbek leader), 220, 241, 243
Hurshid, 44
Husseinov, Ahmed bey (Tatar industrialist), 40
Husseinovs, 21, 122
Hussein Zadeh, Ali bey (Azerbaijani journalist and politician, 1864–19??), 39, 40, 95, 96, 97, 100, 107, 121, 127, 128, 271

Ibragimov, Galimjan (Tatar novelist and politician), 113, 115, 117, 162–163, 169, 177, 179, 182, 186
Ibragimov, Reshid (Tatar leader and kazi), 37–38, 39, 41, 45–46, 50, 127, 129
Idel-Ural, 157, 165–178, 268; definition, 157n
Idel-Ural Constitutional Commission, 175
Ikbal, 97, 120
Ilminsky, N. I. (Russian educator), 28, 29, 30, 36, 64, 78; educational program enacted, 28–30

Imanov, Amangeldy (Kazakh Communist, 1873–1918), 135–136, 215, 218, 222
Inghilois, 262, 271
Iron Squads, 172, 173
Ishik, 98
Iskhakov (Iskhaki-Idilli), Ayaz (Tatar writer and leftist-nationalist, 1878–1954), 41, 46, 47, 52, 117–118, 121, 144, 149, 154, 163, 168–169, 174, 187, 194
Islam: early predominance of, 8–10; in Central Asia, 72–91 *passim*, 226; and secularization and nationalization (summary), 268–274; and Communism, 276–279
Ishtiraki Yun, 240
Ismailov, 179, 194, 202, 204
Ittifak (Union of Russian Moslems), 40, 41–43, 46–48, 51, 53, 67, 85, 97, 99, 117, 125, 126, 137, 140
Ittifak-ul-Misilmin, 233
Ittihad (Unity) Party, 141, 257, 263, 264, 272, 277
Ittihad-ve-Tarakki (Unity and Progress), 220, 248
Izvestiia: Ufa, 202; Uzbek, 240

Jadids, 34–35, 53, 82–91, 138, 205, 218–219, 220, 227, 228, 229, 237, 238–253, 265, 268–269, 272–273, 275, 276; origin, 34; among Uzbeks, 82–85; press, 83; schools, 85–88; cultural influence on Central Asia, 84–85; and Communist Party, 237, 238–253; beliefs, 244–245
Jangeldin, A. N. (Kazakh Communist, 1884–1953), 215, 216, 217, 218, 222
Jihan, Mulla M. Ch., 127, 143
Jizak, 133, 138
Jordania, Noah, 280, 281

Kabardinians, 9
Kadets (Constitutional Democratic Party), 36, 40, 42, 43, 47, 48, 49, 51, 52, 54, 67, 68, 98, 99, 102, 105, 117, 118, 122, 136, 154, 210
Kadimists, 35, 53; opposition to Jadids, 85
Kaganovich, L., 248, 250
Karakalpaks, 7
Kara Kitais, 226
Kari, Munevver (Uzbek Jadid, d. 1933), 82, 83, 88
Karimov, Fatyh (Tatar leader and writer), 21, 40, 86
Kaspii, 96, 97, 125
Kaufman, K. P., 75, 84

Kavburo (Caucasian office), 265–266
Kavkaz, 96
Kazakh, 65, 66, 67, 68, 130, 131, 136, 210
Kazakhs, 6, 9, 11, 53, 54, 55–71, 155, 188, 210, 211, 212, 223, 224, 246, 254, 274; political divisions of, 55–56; early history, 55–59; hostility toward Tatars, 58–60; and Islam, 57–61; influence of Russian thought on, 60–64; educational system, 64–66; rise of intelligentsia, 64–67; press, 65–66; coolness toward Pan-Turkism, 66–68; and 1905 Revolution, 66–68; language, 67, 147; 1916 military service, 130–132; land problems, 131–132, 209–210, 223–224; uprising, 133–135; autonomy, 163–164, 188, 213, 221, 280, 281; and Civil War, 209–224; Communists, 218–219
Kazakh-Bashkir federation, 203, 247
Kazakh-Kirghiz, 209–224 *passim*; distinction between, 55, 55n, 209n; land policy of government, 131–133
Kazakh Soviet Republic (ASSR), 6, 209n, 217, 221, 222, 223, 224, 269
Kazakhstan, 2, 3, 6, 7, 11, 20, 22, 55, 56, 57, 60, 61, 63, 71, 181, 194, 203, 205, 207, 209, 211, 217, 248, 268, 276; effects of Russian colonization, 68–71
Kazan, 5, 6, 10, 16, 17, 21, 25, 26, 28, 29, 33, 35, 36, 40, 44, 52, 106, 112, 113, 120, 121, 123, 125, 126, 140, 141, 142, 148, 153, 154, 157, 162, 172, 173, 174, 175, 176, 181, 182, 184, 185, 189, 190, 207, 211, 235, 265, 270, 275; Bolsheviks seize, 165–171; during Civil War, 186–187; Communist Party in, 192–194
Kazan Muhbiré, 44, 45
Kazan Soviet Republic, 165
Kazemzadeh, Firuz, 101, 263
Kemal Pasha (Ataturk), 245, 265, 270, 271
Kemal Pasha (Namik), 30
Kerensky, A., 137, 155, 159, 165, 213, 228, 230, 276
Khiva, 12, 20, 56, 59, 62, 73, 74, 80, 85, 91, 127, 225, 226, 227, 253, 259, 268; liberalism in, 91
Khoisky, Fatali Khan (Azerbaijani prime minister, 1876–1920), 259, 260–261, 263, 265, 267
Kipchaks: Ferghana, 226, 226n, 236; Kazakh, 215, 216, 222, 226n
Kirghiz, 2, 6–7, 11, 55, 58, 59, 73, 155, 209n, 209–224 *passim*, 259, 273; rebellion, 133–137. *See also* Kazakhs
Kirghizia Soviet Republic, 253

Kirghiz (Kazakh) Bureau, 216
Kirrevkom (Kirghiz Revolutionary Committee), 217, 219–220, 221–222
Kirov, S. M., 265–266
Kobozev, 239–243
Kokand, 11, 57, 73, 83, 84, 135, 171, 230, 242
"Kokand autonomy," 163, 232, 233–236, 238
Kolchak, Admiral A. V., 188, 199, 201, 203, 206, 216, 217
Kolesov, F. (Russian Communist leader, Tashkent), 231, 232, 234, 236, 239
Komuch (Committee of the Constituent Assembly), 184, 187, 198, 199, 214, 216, 254, 281
Koran, 10, 26, 29, 34, 36, 77, 121, 162, 166, 270, 277
Kornilov, General L., 155, 170, 230
Korovnichenko, General, 230–231
Koschi, Union of, 252
Koshchegulov, Shah Mardan (Kazakh politician), 46, 50, 67–68
Kunanbaev, Abai (Kazakh poet, 1845–1904), 61, 63–64, 67
Kuropatkin, General A. N., 132, 137
Kursavi, Abdul Nazir (Moslem reformer, 1775–1813), 24
Kurultai (Bashkir Pre-Parliament), 168, 170, 197, 198
Kzyl Bairak (The Red Banner), 161, 165

Language, Turkic, 2–8, 48, 50–51, 151–152, 240, 249; literary, 2, 74, 255; Ottoman Turkish, 2, 31–34, 49–51; 66, 67, 105, 107, 109, 111, 114–116, 120, 249, 255, 263; Kazakh, 2, 67; Tatar, 59, 114–116, 254; of Soviet Republics, 253, 268. *See also* Chagatai
Lenin, V. I., 159, 160, 161, 167, 168, 169, 170, 175, 178, 183, 184, 186, 192, 193, 199, 205, 206, 217, 221, 241, 245, 247–248, 249, 250, 251; and self-determination policy, 163–164
Liapin, Sher-Ali (Uzbek conservative), 227, 232, 276
Little Bashkiria. *See* Bashkiria
Little Horde, 56–57, 59
Lokais, 226

Maksudov, Hadi (Tatar journalist), 50, 113
Maksudov (Maksudi-Arsal), Sadri (Tatar lawyer, leader of Moslem caucus in Duma, 1879–1957), 50, 87, 118, 141,

145, 147, 155, 157–158, 159, 168, 169, 170, 171
Maksumov family, 81, 88, 249
Manasyrov, A., 159, 174
Manatov, Sharaf (Tatar leader), 162–163, 180, 197
Ma'arifat and *Barakat*, 90
Mehmendarov, General G., 124, 267
Mejilis (Milli Mejilis; Tatar National Parliament), 157, 158, 167, 168–170, 171, 173, 176, 177, 187. *See also* Constitutional Commission
Melikov-Zarbadi, Hassan (editor of *Akinchi*), 94, 99
Mensheviks, 104, 141, 250, 257
Merjani, Shihabeddin (Tatar scholar, 1818–1889), 24–25, 113
Mikoyan, A., and Azerbaijan, 264–267
Mindeshev, 217, 218, 223
Mir Islama, 44
Moslem Communist Party, 179, 181–182, 185, 186, 189–190, 192–193, 207, 219, 240, 241, 247, 248
Moslem congresses. *See* Congresses and conferences
Moslem Council (of 1917 First Congress). *See* Shuro
Moslem Corps, 172
Moslem Ecclesiastic Administration, 18, 24, 26, 37, 40, 42, 49, 53, 59, 62, 83, 122, 143, 157, 168, 211–212
Moslem Military Council. *See* Harbi Shuro
Moslem Peoples' Party, 50, 67–68
Moslem Revolutionary Headquarters (Kazan), 162
Moslem Socialist Committee, 141, 161, 165, 173, 180, 183, 185, 186, 189
Muhammedieh madrasa, 34, 35, 49
Mullah Nasreddin, 95, 98
Munizira, 88
Musavat (Equality) Party, 100–104, 126, 129, 255–267, 271, 272, 275; opposition to, 103–104

Nakhichevan, Khan of, 122, 124
Narimanov, Nariman (Azerbaijani Communist, 1872–1925), 98, 266
Narkomnats (Commissariat for the Affairs of the Nationalities), 161–162, 166, 173, 175–178, 180, 182, 185, 186, 189, 194, 198, 204, 216, 217, 222, 241
Nasyri, Abdul Kaium (Tatar writer, 1824–1907), 25, 31, 51, 115
Nasyr Khan Tiuria, 83, 88, 227, 238

National Center. *See* Turkestan Moslem Central Soviet
Navoi, 72, 83
Nazarats (Tatar), 157, 168, 167, 169, 170, 178
Neshir-i-Sherif, 99
New method (*Usul jadid*): slogan, 34; schools, 34–35, 53, 86
Nicholas II, 67, 105, 122, 124, 140, 206
Nizhni Novgorod, 3, 40, 41, 45, 99
Nurimanov, Bagau, 166, 185

October Revolution. *See* Revolution of 1917
Olkenicki, Gersh, 165, 181
Ordzhonikidze, S., 265, 266
Orenburg, 18, 19, 20, 21, 35, 36, 44, 49, 50, 52, 57, 59, 60, 64, 112, 125, 162, 168, 169, 170, 176, 180, 195, 196, 197, 198, 210, 211, 213, 214, 216, 222, 235, 236, 276
Ossets, 9
Ostroumov, N., 78–79, 276
Ottoman Turkey, 1, 2, 8, 27, 30, 31, 38, 39, 49–51, 129, 259, 265, 270. *See also* Turkey
Ozakom (Special Transcaucasian Committee), 255

People's Democracy, 249, 268
Persia, influence on Turks, 10–11, 30–31
Pestkowski, S., 217, 220
Peter the Great, 15–16, 21, 282
Peters, Ya., 248, 250
Petrograd Soviet of Soldiers' and Workers' Deputies, 143, 152, 153, 155
Pishpek, 134
Pobedonostsev, K., 29, 238
PRCB. *See* Bashkurstan
Provisional Central Bureau of Russian Moslems, 140, 143, 145, 178
Provisional Government (Russian), 136, 143, 150, 158, 159, 161, 165, 188, 211, 212, 230, 231, 255, 258, 271, 279
Provisional Moslem Military Council, 159
Provisional National Council, 153
Pugachev rebellion, 16, 17
Pushkin, A., 115, 122

Radek, Karl, 250
Rameev, Zakir (publisher and Duma member, 1857–1912), 66, 112
Regional Bureau of Moslem Organizations, 241, 242, 243, 244, 251–252
Renan, Ernest, 38, 96, 108

Resul Zadeh, Mehmed Emin bey (Azerbaijani leader, 1884–1955), 98, 100, 103, 104, 107, 126, 129, 146–147, 149, 150, 153, 255, 256, 257, 260, 263, 265, 267, 271
Revkom (Revolutionary Committee): Ufa, 166, 199; Kazan, 189–190; Tatar, 194; Tashkent, 231, 232. *See also* Bashrevkom; Kirrevkom
Revolution of 1905: Turkic reaction to, general, 43–44, 275; and Kazakhs, 66–68; and Uzbeks, 82–83; and Azerbaijanis, 98–100
Revolution of 1917, 11, 22, 52, 91, 129, 195, 258, 275, 280; effect on Moslems, 139–164; Stalin's speech on the revolution and the peoples of the East, 190–191; and Central Asia, 225–237
Revolutionary Military Council (May 1918), 185
RSFSR, 176, 186, 244, 253, 267
Ryskulov, Turar (Uzbek Communist), 219, 220, 241, 242, 246, 251, 252

Sada-i-Turkestan, 83
Safarov, G., 248, 250, 251
Samara, 27, 28, 184, 185, 187, 197, 198, 214
Samarkand, 62, 72, 75, 81, 82, 84, 133, 227, 229, 233
Samarkand, 83
Sarts, 73, 212, 259
Savage Division, 124, 155
Secession, Turkic reluctance toward, 279–282
Sedelnikov, 205, 220, 221, 222
Seitovsky Posad, 19
Semipalatinsk, 19, 21, 60, 66, 63, 135, 213, 214, 218, 223, 224
Semirechie, 55, 57, 68, 133, 134, 212, 213, 214, 215, 223, 227, 233, 234, 236, 237, 247
Seydamet, Jafer (Crimean leader, 1889–?), 154–155, 254
Shamigulov, Galim (Bashkir Communist), 181, 186, 202, 204, 207
Sharaf, Galimjan (Tatar leader), 157n, 169, 170, 171
Shariat, 42, 58, 68, 73, 86, 163, 249
Shariatists, Soviet, 163, 276
Sheinkman, Jacob, 165, 181, 186
Shiites, 49, 72, 74, 86, 87, 89, 90, 93, 95, 103, 264
Shinasi, 30, 31, 269
Shura, 66, 112, 113
Shuro (All-Russian Provisional Moslem National Council), 147, 153–156, 162, 173, 178, 211, 228, 271, 275, 280; activity in 1917, 153–156
Shuro-i-Islam, 227–229, 232, 233
Social Democrats, 45, 52, 98, 100, 117, 228, 229, 256
Socialist Revolutionaries, 45, 46, 47, 52, 117, 141, 184, 187, 196, 200, 229–234, 239, 257, 276
Sokolnikov (Brilliant), G., 248, 250
Southeastern Turkic federation, 205–206, 219–221, 234
Sovnarkom (Council of People's Commissars), 165–166, 176, 186, 194, 199
Stalin, J. V., 98, 100, 161, 162, 163, 165, 166, 173, 176, 177, 179, 181, 183, 184, 189, 190–192, 193, 194, 198, 199, 204, 217, 222, 235, 241, 248, 259, 267
Statute on Soviet Tatary, 183
Sterlitamak, 201, 202, 203, 204, 206, 207
Stolypin, P. A., 23, 68, 105, 196, 201, 206
Sulkiewicz, General Suleyman, 122, 159, 172, 254
Sultangaliev, M. (Tatar Communist, 1895–1930), 154, 179, 182, 184, 186, 189, 194, 203, 242, 265, 275, 279
Sultanov, Mufti Muhammed Yar, 40, 53, 125
Sunnites, 49, 72, 73, 86, 87, 89, 90, 93, 95, 103, 264
Syrtlanov, Shahaidar (Tatar Duma member, 1847–19??), 40, 43, 46, 50, 124

Tagiev, Zeinulla Abdin (Azerbaijani industrialist), 40, 97, 124, 125
Tagiev family, 122
Tajiks, 7, 9, 19, 73, 74, 82, 85, 105, 142, 226
Tajikistan Soviet Republic, 7, 76, 253
Talish, 271
Tanachev, V., 211, 213
Tan (Dawn), 45, 52
Tangchelar (Tangists), 52, 117
Tanyshbaev, M. (Kazakh politician), 65, 67, 68, 154, 212, 227, 235
Tanzimat era, 11, 30
Tarakki (Progress), 83, 84, 85
Tarjuman (The Interpreter), 30–32, 34, 67, 82, 87, 95, 114, 115, 118
Tashkent, 19, 62, 75, 82–83, 84, 85, 87, 91, 107, 120, 133, 143, 205, 209, 212, 213, 215, 223, 224, 228, 229, 231, 235, 241, 243, 246, 251, 270, 276
Tashkent Soviet, 227, 230, 231, 233–236, 238, 242–243, 253
Tashkent and Kokand governments, 233–236

Tatar Communists, ideology, 181–184

Tatar Social Democratic Workers' Party, 185

Tatar Socialist Committee, 185

Tatar Socialist Revolutionaries, 45, 47, 117, 127

Tatar Soviet Republic (ASSR), 6, 187, 194, 204, 268

Tataro-Bashkiria, 179–194, 202, 204; Tatar-Bashkir controversies, 156–158, 162–163, 179–194, 195–197; Tatar-Bashkir Soviet Republic, 176–177, 178–181

Tatars, 2, 3, 10, 12–23, 52, 55, 75, 79, 82, 83, 86, 91, 105, 126, 128, 129, 142, 143, 153, 199, 227, 254, 259, 273, 276; leadership of Turkic peoples, 8–9, 140–141, 211–212; ethnic background, 14; Russian colonization, 14–17; trade and economic expansion, 18–23; cultural revival, 25–28, 35–36, growth of nationalism, 26–28, 30–34; early twentieth-century culture, 35–36; press, 44–45; in Second Duma, 51–54; influence on Central Asia, 84–85; and Pan-Turkism, 112–122; and Russian influences, 116–125; at First Moslem Congress, 147–149; autonomy, 156–159, 167–168, 173–177, 188–190, 191–194, 247, 274; pro- vs. anti-Soviet, 173–174; and Civil War, 184–190

Tats, 93, 271

Territorialists. See Centralists vs. territorial autonomists

Teregulov, Omer (Tartar leader), 151, 168–169, 187, 188

Tevkelev, K. M. B. (Tatar Duma member, 1850–192?), 40, 124, 129, 137

TMMS. See Turkestan Moslem Central Soviet

Togan. See Validov, Ahmed Zeki

Tokumbetov, H., 158, 166–167, 174

Tolstoy, Leo, 112, 122

Topchibashev, Ali Mardan bey (journalist and president of Azerbaijani Republic, 1862–193?), 40, 41, 45, 46, 50, 51, 97, 99, 103, 125, 144, 149, 155, 256, 259–260, 271

Trans-Bulak Republic, 167, 174, 175, 177

Transcaspia, 229, 233, 236, 247

Transcaucasia, 44, 49, 93, 130, 164, 254, 256, 257, 258, 260, 262, 267, 271, 281

Transcaucasian federation, 258, 267, 281

Trotsky, L., 174, 175, 190, 194, 250

Tsalikov, Ahmed (Daghestani politician,

president of Shuro, 1882–?), 9, 140, 143–144, 145–146, 147–148, 150, 152–156, 162–163, 169, 178, 279, 280

Tukaev, Abdulla (Tatar poet, 1886–1913), 115–116, 117

Tuktarov, Fuad (Tatar socialist), 41, 52, 141, 148, 187

Turan, 90

"Turan, The" (Alp), 110

Turanism (Turan), 1, 96, 107, 108–112, 113

Turgai, 135, 212, 214, 218

Turgaiskaia gazeta, 66

Türk, 38

Turkestan, 20, 22, 23, 57, 72, 87, 239, 240, 244, 246, 251, 272; autonomy, 234–235, 236, 280; Communist Party, 244–245, 252

Turkestan ASSR, 224, 239–240, 244, 253, 268–269

Turkestan Central Executive Committee (TurkTsIK), 239–240, 242, 244, 246, 247, 251

Turkestan Commission (TurkCommission), 246–248, 250–252; and Jadids, 246–250

Turkestan Federated Republic, 229

Turkestan General Governorship, 75, 76, 84, 85, 272

Turkestan Moslem Central Soviet (TMMS or National Center), 227–229

Turkey, 8, 11, 26, 34, 50, 59, 67, 83, 90, 92, 96, 100, 101, 103, 104, 105, 110, 125, 255, 260; and relation to Pan-Turkists, 106–108. See also Ottoman Turkey

Turkic Communist Party, 200, 205, 244, 247

Turkic Federalist Party, 256

Turkic languages. See Language, Turkic

Turkic peoples: linguistic groups and distribution, 1–8; early general history, 1–11

Turkic Soviet Republics in 1920, 268–269

Turkic-Turkish distinction, 1

Turkist-Tatarist controversy, 112–121

Turkmenistan Soviet Republic, 253

Türk Ojak, 107

Turkomens, 2, 8, 11, 58, 73, 91, 124, 236, 237

Turko-Tatars, 113, 117, 128; Council, 153

Türk Yurdu (Turkic Fatherland), 100, 108, 110–112, 115, 127

Tuva (Tuvas), 8, 21

Ufa, 18, 35, 36, 37, 40, 43, 59, 112, 120,

129, 143, 156, 157, 158, 165, 166, 167,
168, 169, 170, 176, 178, 180, 181, 184,
185, 189, 195, 196, 197, 207, 212, 275,
276
Ulema (Ulema Jemyeti; Board of
Learned Men), 227, 228, 229–231, 250,
272–273, 276
Ural, 45, 52
Uralchelar, 52–53, 117
Ush Zhuz (Three Hordes), 215–216. *See
also* Zhuz
Ush zhuz, 66, 212
Usubbekov (Yusuf-Beyli), Nassip bey
(Azerbaijani leader), 98, 256, 263
Uzbek Communists, 205–206, 241–242,
244–245, 249, 251
Uzbeks, 2, 7, 11, 12, 19, 55, 57, 127, 157,
212, 216, 259; liberalism among, 72–91;
press, 83. *See also* Jadids
Uzbek Soviet Republic (Uzbekistan), 6,
7, 55, 74n, 253

Vahitov, Mullanur (Tatar Communist,
1885–1918), 141, 161, 162–163, 165, 173,
176, 177, 180, 182, 183, 184–187, 242,
264, 265, 275, 279
Vakyt (The Time), 44, 112, 118, 119, 131
Validov (Velidi-Togan), Ahmed Zeki
(Bashkir leader, 1890–   ), 113, 114, 148,
149, 168, 169, 170, 180, 196–208, 218,
220, 242, 243, 247, 248, 265, 272, 275,
279; and Little Bashkiria, 195–208
Validov, Jemaleddin (Tatar historian),
112, 113, 114, 115, 117

Vatan, 143

Valikhanov, Chokan (Kazakh geographer
and anthropologist, 1835–1865), 58, 60,
61–63, 64, 65, 67
Velihazret, M., 53
Volia, 200, 205
Volia naroda, 234
Votiaks, 9, 29

Wolves' Detachments, 172, 173
World War I, 121–122; and the Central
Asian revolt, 123–139
Wrangel, General P. N., 206, 221

Yakuts, 8, 11, 244
Yakubov, Kamil (Tatar Communist),
165, 173
Yanyshev, Nushirvam, 21, 114–115
Yeni Lisan (New Word), 107
Young Bukhariotes, 72–91 *passim*, 227,
236, 238, 248–250; formation of, 90;
publications, 90; opposition to, 90–91
Young Turks, 30, 32, 38, 88, 90, 96, 99,
102–103, 106–107, 111, 127–128
Yulduz, 50, 118, 120
Yumagulov, Kh. (Bashkir Communist),
200, 204
Yunusov, Ibragim (Tatar industrialist),
21, 25

Zabulachie, 167, 173, 178
Zhuz (Kazakh Hordes), 56–59, 215
Ziia Gökalp, 107, 109–112, 117
Zinoviev, G., 250
Zwilling, S. M., 198, 216, 231

RUSSIAN RESEARCH CENTER STUDIES

The Russian Research Center of Harvard University is supported by a grant from the Carnegie Corporation. The Center carries out interdisciplinary study of Russian institutions and behavior and related subjects.

1. *Public Opinion in Soviet Russia: A Study in Mass Persuasion,* by Alex Inkeles

2. *Soviet Politics — The Dilemma of Power: The Role of Ideas in Social Change,* by Barrington Moore, Jr.*

3. *Justice in the U.S.S.R.: An Interpretation of Soviet Law,* by Harold J. Berman. Revised edition

4. *Chinese Communism and the Rise of Mao,* by Benjamin I. Schwartz

5. *Titoism and the Cominform,* by Adam B. Ulam*

6. *A Documentary History of Chinese Communism,* by Conrad Brandt, Benjamin Schwartz, and John K. Fairbank*

7. *The New Man in Soviet Psychology,* by Raymond A. Bauer

8. *Soviet Opposition to Stalin: A Case Study in World War II,* by George Fischer*

9. *Minerals: A Key to Soviet Power,* by Demitri B. Shimkin*

10. *Soviet Law in Action: The Recollected Cases of a Soviet Lawyer,* by Harold J. Berman and Boris A. Konstantinovsky

11. *How Russia Is Ruled,* by Merle Fainsod. Revised edition

12. *Terror and Progress USSR: Some Sources of Change and Stability in the Soviet Dictatorship,* by Barrington Moore, Jr.*

13. *The Formation of the Soviet Union: Communism and Nationalism, 1917–1923,* by Richard Pipes. Revised edition

14. *Marxism: The Unity of Theory and Practice,* by Alfred G. Meyer

15. *Soviet Industrial Production, 1928–1951,* by Donald R. Hodgman

16. *Soviet Taxation: The Fiscal and Monetary Problems of a Planned Economy,* by Franklin D. Holzman

17. *Soviet Military Law and Administration,* by Harold J. Berman and Miroslav Kerner

18. *Documents on Soviet Military Law and Administration,* edited and translated by Harold J. Berman and Miroslav Kerner

19. *The Russian Marxists and the Origins of Bolshevism,* by Leopold H. Haimson

20. *The Permanent Purge: Politics in Soviet Totalitarianism,* by Zbigniew K. Brzezinski*

21. *Belorussia: The Making of a Nation,* by Nicholas P. Vakar

22. *A Bibliographical Guide to Belorussia,* by Nicholas P. Vakar*

23. *The Balkans in Our Time,* by Robert Lee Wolff

24. *How the Soviet System Works: Cultural, Psychological, and Social Themes,* by Raymond A. Bauer, Alex Inkeles, and Clyde Kluckhohn†

25. *The Economics of Soviet Steel,* by M. Gardner Clark

26. *Leninism*, by Alfred G. Meyer*

27. *Factory and Manager in the USSR*, by Joseph S. Berliner†

28. *Soviet Transportation Policy*, by Holland Hunter

29. *Doctor and Patient in Soviet Russia*, by Mark G. Field†

30. *Russian Liberalism*, by George Fischer

31. *Stalin's Failure in China, 1924–1927*, by Conrad Brandt

32. *The Communist Party of Poland*, by M. K. Dziewanowski

33. *Karamzin's Memoir on Ancient and Modern Russia. A Translation and Analysis*, by Richard Pipes

34. *A Memoir on Ancient and Modern Russia*, by N. M. Karamzin, the Russian text edited by Richard Pipes*

35. *The Soviet Citizen: Daily Life in a Totalitarian Society*, by Alex Inkeles and Raymond A. Bauer†

36. *Pan-Turkism and Islam in Russia*, by Serge A. Zenkovsky

37. *The Soviet Bloc: Unity and Conflict*, by Zbigniew K. Brzezinski.‡ Revised edition

38. *National Consciousness in Eighteenth-Century Russia*, by Hans Rogger

39. *Alexander Herzen and the Birth of Russian Socialism, 1812–1855*, by Martin Malia

40. *The Conscience of the Revolution: Communist Opposition in Soviet Russia*, by Robert V. Daniels

41. *The Soviet Industrialization Debate, 1924–1928*, by Alexander Erlich

42. *The Third Section: Police and Society in Russia under Nicholas I*, by Sidney Monas

43. *Dilemmas of Progress in Tsarist Russia: Legal Marxism and Legal Populism*, by Arthur P. Mendel

44. *Political Control of Literature in the USSR, 1946–1959*, by Harold Swayze

45. *Accounting in Soviet Planning and Management*, by Robert W. Campbell

46. *Social Democracy and the St. Petersburg Labor Movement, 1885–1897*, by Richard Pipes

47. *The New Face of Soviet Totalitarianism*, by Adam B. Ulam

48. *Stalin's Foreign Policy Reappraised*, by Marshall D. Shulman

49. *The Soviet Youth Program: Regimentation and Rebellion*, by Allen Kassof

50. *Soviet Criminal Law and Procedure: The RSFSR Codes*, translated by Harold J. Berman and James W. Spindler; introduction and analysis by Harold J. Berman

51. *Poland's Politics: Political Idealism vs. Political Realism*, by Adam Bromke

52. *Managerial Power and Soviet Politics*, by Jeremy R. Azrael

53. *Danilevsky: A Russian Totalitarian Philosopher*, by Robert E. MacMaster

* Out of print.

† Publications of the Harvard Project on the Soviet Social System.

‡ Published jointly with the Center for International Affairs, Harvard University.